The Cambridge Companion to Nineteenth-Century American Women's Writing

The Cambridge Companion to Nineteenth-Century American Women's Writing is a specially commissioned collection designed for use by students. Providing an overview of the history of writing by women in the period, it establishes the context in which this writing emerged, and traces the origin of the terms which have traditionally defined the debate. It includes chapters on topics of recent concern, such as women and war, erotic violence, the liberating and disciplinary effects of religion, and examines the work a variety of women writers, including Harriet Beecher Stowe, Rebecca Harding Davis, and Louisa May Alcott. The volume plots new directions for the study of American literary history, and provides several valuable tools for students, including a chronology of works and suggestions for further reading.

THE CAMBRIDGE
COMPANION TO
NINETEENTH-CENTURY AMERICAN WOMEN'S WRITING

CAMBRIDGE COMPANIONS TO LITERATURE

The Cambridge Companion to Shakespeare
on Film
edited by Russell Jackson

The Cambridge Companion to Spenser
edited by Andrew Hadfield

The Cambridge Companion to Ben Jonson
edited by Richard Harp and Stanley Stewart

The Cambridge Companion to Milton
edited by Dennis Danielson

The Cambridge Companion to Samuel
Johnson
edited by Greg Clingham

The Cambridge Companion to Keats
edited by Susan J. Wolfson

The Cambridge Companion to Jane Austen
edited by Edward Copeland and
Juliet McMaster

The Cambridge Companion to Charles
Dickens
edited by John O. Jordan

The Cambridge Companion to George Eliot
edited by George Levine

The Cambridge Companion to Thomas
Hardy
edited by Dale Kramer

The Cambridge Companion to Oscar Wilde
edited by Peter Raby

The Cambridge Companion to George
Bernard Shaw
edited by Christopher Innes

The Cambridge Companion to Joseph
Conrad
edited by J. H. Stape

The Cambridge Companion to D. H.
Lawrence
edited by Anne Fernihough

The Cambridge Companion to Virginia
Woolf
edited by Sue Roe and Susan Sellers

The Cambridge Companion to James Joyce
edited by Derek Attridge

The Cambridge Companion to T. S. Eliot
edited by A. David Moody

The Cambridge Companion to Ezra Pound
edited by Ira B. Nadel

The Cambridge Companion to Beckett
edited by John Pilling

The Cambridge Companion to Harold Pinter
edited by Peter Raby

The Cambridge Companion to Tom Stoppard
edited by Katherine E. Kelly

The Cambridge Companion to Herman
Melville
edited by Robert S. Levine

The Cambridge Companion to Edith
Wharton
edited by Millicent Bell

The Cambridge Companion to Henry James
edited by Jonathan Freedman

The Cambridge Companion to Walt
Whitman
edited by Ezra Greenspan

The Cambridge Companion to Henry David
Thoreau
edited by Joel Myerson

The Cambridge Companion to Mark Twain
edited by Forrest G. Robinson

The Cambridge Companion to William
Faulkner
edited by Philip M. Weinstein

The Cambridge Companion to Ernest
Hemingway
edited by Scott Donaldson

The Cambridge Companion to Robert Frost
edited by Robert Faggen

The Cambridge Companion to Eugene
O'Neill
edited by Michael Manheim

The Cambridge Companion to Tennessee
Williams
edited by Matthew C. Roudané

The Cambridge Companion to Arthur Miller
edited by Christopher Bigsby

CAMBRIDGE COMPANIONS TO CULTURE

The Cambridge Companion to Modern
German Culture
edited by Eva Kolinsky and
Wilfried van der Will

The Cambridge Companion to Modern
Russian Culture
edited by Nicholas Rzhevsky

The Cambridge Companion to Modern
Spanish Culture
edited by David T. Gies

The Cambridge Companion to Modern
Italian Culture
edited by Zygmunt G. Baranski and
Rebecca J. West

THE CAMBRIDGE
COMPANION TO
NINETEENTH-CENTURY
AMERICAN WOMEN'S
WRITING

EDITED BY
DALE M. BAUER AND PHILIP GOULD

CAMBRIDGE
UNIVERSITY PRESS

PUBLISHED BY THE PRESS SYNDICATE OF THE UNIVERSITY OF CAMBRIDGE
The Pitt Building, Trumpington Street, Cambridge, United Kingdom

CAMBRIDGE UNIVERSITY PRESS
The Edinburgh Building, Cambridge CB2 2RU, UK
40 West 20th Street, New York, NY 10011-4211, USA
477 Williamstown Road, Port Melbourne, VIC 3207, Australia
Ruiz de Alarcón 13, 28014 Madrid, Spain
Dock House, The Waterfront, Cape Town 8001, South Africa

http://www.cambridge.org

First published 2001

Printed in the United Kingdom at the University Press, Cambridge

Typeface Sabon 10/13 pt.   *System* LATEX 2ε [TB]

A catalogue record for this book is available from the British Library.

Library of Congress Cataloguing in Publication Data
The Cambridge companion to nineteenth-century American women's writing / edited by
Dale M. Bauer and Philip Gould.
p.   cm. – (Cambridge companions to literature)
Includes bibliographical references and index.
ISBN 0 521 66003 3 (hardback) – ISBN 0 521 66975 8 (paperback)
1. American literature – Women authors – History and criticism. 2. Women and
literature – United States – History – nineteenth century. 3. American literature – nineteenth
century – History and criticism. 1. Bauer, Dale M., 1956– 11. Gould, Philip, 1960–
111. Series.
PS147.C36 2001
810.9′9287′09034 – dc21   2001025736

ISBN 0 521 66003 3 hardback
ISBN 0 521 66975 8 paperback

CONTENTS

Contents

ILLUSTRATIONS

CONTRIBUTORS

DALE M. BAUER is Professor of English and Women's Studies at the University of Kentucky. She is the author of *Feminist Dialogics* (1988) and *Edith Wharton's Brave New Politics* (1994), and a Bedford cultural edition of "The Yellow Wallpaper" (1998). Her book in progress, "Sex Expression and American Women," is a study of women's writing on sexuality from 1860 to 1940.

PHILIP GOULD is Associate Professor of English at Brown University. He is the author of *Covenant and Republic: Historical Romance and the Politics of Puritanism* (1996) and the coeditor, along with Leonard Tennenhouse, of the special issue of the journal *differences*, entitled "America the Feminine?" (2000). He is currently working on a book on eighteenth-century antislavery literature and commercial culture.

FARAH JASMINE GRIFFIN is Associate Professor of English at the University of Pennsylvania. She is the author of *"Who Set You Flowin'?": the African American Migration Narrative* (1995).

SUSAN M. GRIFFIN is Professor of English at the University of Louisville, editor of *Henry James Review*, and author and editor of a number of works on James. She is completing a study of Anglo-American anti-Catholicism during the nineteenth century, parts of which have been published in *PMLA* and *Legacy*.

MARY KELLEY is Professor of History at Dartmouth College. She is the author of *Private Woman, Public Stage: Literary Domesticity in Nineteenth-Century America* (1984) and *The Power of Her Sympathy: the Autobiography and Journal of Catharine Maria Sedgwick* (1993). With Jeanne Boydston and Anne Margolis, she is the coauthor of *The Limits of Sisterhood: the Beecher Sisters and Women's Rights and Woman's Sphere* (1998).

LISA A. LONG is Assistant Professor of English and Chair of the Gender and Women's Studies Program at North Central College. She is the editor of Paul Laurence Dunbar's *The Fanatics* (2001) and has published on American women writers, African-American literature, and the American Civil War. She is finishing a book on representations of the American Civil War, health, and history.

DANA D. NELSON is Professor of English and Social Theory at the University of Kentucky. She is the author of *The Word in Black and White* (1992) and *National Manhood* (1998). She has edited reprints of Rebecca Rush's *Kelroy*, Lydia Maria Child's *A Romance of the Republic*, and a dual edition of Frances A. Kemble and Frances A. Leigh's *Principles & Privilege: Two Women's Lives on a Georgia Plantation*. She is writing a series of essays on masculinity and sentimentality, and coediting *Materializing Democracy* with Russ Castronovo.

ELIZABETH A. PETRINO is an Assistant Professor of English at Fairfield University. She wrote *Emily Dickinson and Her Contemporaries: Women's Verse in America, 1820–1885* (1998). She has also written articles on popular nineteenth-century genres written primarily by women, such as the child elegy and the language of flowers. She is working on a book that examines how theories of perception illuminate the culturally mediated observation of nature in authors from Franklin to Dickinson.

YOLANDA PIERCE is Assistant Professor of English and African-American Studies at the University of Kentucky. She has published essays on African-American participation in nineteenth-century camp meetings and on African-American conversion narratives. She is currently working on the African-American performance tradition in the twentieth century.

SHIRLEY SAMUELS is Professor of English and Women's Studies at Cornell University. She edited *The Culture of Sentiment* (1992) and wrote *Romances of the Republic: Women, the Family, and Violence in the Literature of the Early American Nation* (1996). Her current project is entitled "Facing America: National Iconography and the Civil War."

GAIL K. SMITH is Associate Professor of English at the Mississippi University for Women, and has published on Harriet Beecher Stowe, Louisa May Alcott, and Elizabeth Stuart Phelps. She is currently completing a book project on Stowe and the politics of reading in nineteenth-century America.

STEPHANIE A. SMITH is Associate Professor of English at the University of Florida. She is the author of *Conceived by Liberty: Maternal Figures and Nineteenth-Century American Literature* (1995), along with three novels:

Other Nature (1995), *The Boy Who Was Thrown Away* (1987), and *Snow-Eyes* (1985). She is working on a new novel and a new scholarly study, "Household Words: Composing Common Sense in a Democratic Culture."

KATHRYN ZABELLE DEROUNIAN-STODOLA is Professor of English at the University of Arkansas at Little Rock and has published widely on captivity narratives and on early American women's writing. Most recently, she has edited *Women's Indian Captivity Narratives* (1998).

FREDRIKA J. TEUTE is editor of publications at the Omohundro Institute for Early America History and Culture. As a documentary editor, she has contributed to the publication of volumes of *The Papers of James Madison* and *The Papers of John Marshall*. She has published several articles about Margaret Bayard Smith and is currently working on a book about Smith and early American political culture.

PRISCILLA WALD is Associate Professor of English at Duke University. She is the author of *Constituting Americans: Cultural Anxiety and Narrative Form* (1995) and coeditor, with Christine diStefano and Judith Wiesenfeld, of the *Signs* special issue, "Institutions, Regulations, and Social Control." She is writing a book about contagion and Americanism.

SANDRA ZAGARELL teaches at Oberlin College. She has published widely on nineteenth-century American literature. She has coedited (along with Lawrence Buell) Elizabeth Stoddard's *The Morgesons and Other Writings*, and has edited *"A New England Nun" and Other Stories*.

ROSEMARIE ZAGARRI is Professor of History at George Mason University. She is the author of *The Politics of Size: Representation in the United States, 1776–1850* (1988) and *A Woman's Dilemma: Mercy Otis Warren and the American Revolution* (1995). Her articles on early America have appeared widely in numerous scholarly journals.

ACKNOWLEDGMENTS

With great advice from no less than six anonymous readers for Cambridge University Press, we contacted scholars at various stages of their academic careers: from the newly graduated assistant professors to the senior scholars in the field. We are proud of this effort to chart the constellation of new work in nineteenth-century American women's writing. Yet we are still daunted by how much we had to leave out and how many people – through their distinction, passion, and scholarly dedication to the topic – *should* have contributed to this volume.

We want to thank the indefatigable efforts of Ann Beebe and Jennifer Workman Pitcock, both of whom shaped the project from the beginning (Ann) to the end (Jenny). Lloyd Pratt compiled – expertly and efficiently – both the chronology and the index. Our editors at Cambridge – starting with Ann Sanow, who conceived of the project, to Ray Ryan, who saw it through – have been enthusiastic and encouraging all along. Rachel DeWachter saved us from panic at other stages. Most of all, we are grateful, as ever, to Gordon Hutner, friend to Phil and partner to Dale – and consummate editor for us both. And even more grateful to our families, especially Sophia Alexandra Gould, and Dan and Jake Hutner, who kept us sane.

1773   Phillis Wheatley. *Poems on Various Subjects, Religious and Moral.*
        London.
1776   Declaration of Independence.
        Abigail Adams writes to her husband, John Adams, asking him to
        "Remember the ladies. . . . " At the time, he was serving in
        the Continental Congress, a group of delegates from the
        revolutionary colonies that would later form the United States.
        Ann Lee establishes the first American Shaker settlement at
        Niskeyuna, New York.
1777   British occupation of Philadelphia.
        Congress adopts the Articles of Confederation, the first US
        Constitution. In 1787 a new US Constitution was adopted,
        replacing the relatively weak Articles.
1779   Margaret Corbin receives a lifetime pension from the Continental
        Congress after taking her fallen husband's place in the
        Revolutionary War.
1781   States ratify the Articles of Confederation.
1782   Deborah Sampson disguises herself as a man and enlists in the
        4th Massachusetts Regiment.
1783   Treaty of Paris ends the American Revolution.
1786   Daniel Shays leads western Massachusetts attacks on foreclosure
        courts and a US arsenal. Although Shays was eventually defeated,
        these protests against high taxes and harsh economic times
        led to changes that lightened the debt burden of Massachusetts
        citizens.
1787   Philadelphia hosts the Constitutional Convention of the United
        States.
1789   US Congress holds its first meeting in New York City.
        George Washington is elected first president of the United States.
        The first ten amendments to the US Constitution collectively

known as the Bill of Rights proposed in Congress. These amendments outline individual rights and the limits placed on goverment intervention.

1790   American religious revival known as the Second Great Awakening begins; women's participation far exceeds that of men.
United States passes its first copyright law.
Washington, DC founded.
First meeting of the US Supreme Court.

1791   Female academies begin training women in the tenets of "republican motherhood."
Congress ratifies the first ten amendments to the Constitution collectively known as the Bill of Rights.

1793   First Fugitive Slave Law passes Congress.
Eli Whitney applies to patent the cotton gin.

1795   Naturalization Act establishes guidelines for US citizenship.

1800   At 7.04 per woman, US birthrate is the highest in recorded history.
Congress passes a bill establishing the Library of Congress.
Thomas Jefferson elected president.
Gabriel Prosser leads an unsuccessful slave rebellion in Richmond, Virginia.
District of Columbia becomes capital of the United States.
Margaret Bayard Smith. "The Evils of Reserve in Marriage," *Monthly Magazine, and American Review* and "Lines by a Young Lady. Written at The Falls at Passaick, July 1800," *Monthly Magazine, and American Review.*

1801   Tabitha Tenney. *Female Quixotism.*

1802   Richmond, Virginia *Recorder* publishes a story about Thomas Jefferson's relationship with one of his slaves, Sally Hemmings.

1803   France sells the Louisiana Territory to the US for a cost of 60 million francs.

1804   Congress orders Indians east of the Mississippi River removed to Louisiana.
Lewis and Clark expedition officially departs from St. Louis with a young Shoshoni woman, Sacajawea, accompanying them as an interpreter.
After more than a decade of struggle against the French that begins with a slave revolt in 1791, black leaders declare Haiti an independent republic.
New Jersey is the final northern state to abolish slavery.

1805   Lewis and Clark's guide, Sacajawea, gives birth to a son in February; the expedition reaches the Pacific Ocean in November.

Virginia law requires that all freed slaves leave the state or face either deportation or imprisonment.

Margaret Bayard Smith. *The Diversions of Sidney.*

Mercy Otis Warren. *The History of the Rise, Progress, and Termination of the American Revolution.*

1807   Robert Fulton's "North River Steam Boat" successfully navigates the Hudson River from New York to Albany and back. Congress passes the Embargo Act and cuts off all export trade.

1808   Joseph Charles publishes the first newspaper west of the Mississippi in St. Louis.

US and Britain officially ban the international slave trade; a widespread "internal" slave trade continues in the US.

1809   President James Madison annexes western Florida for the US. Congress repeals the Embargo Act.

1812   US declares war against Britain and begins the War of 1812. Rebecca Rush. *Kelroy, A Novel.*

1813   The British blockade Long Island Sound.

1814   Dolley Madison rescues Gilbert Stuart's portrait of George Washington and other important documents from president's house as British troops burn Washington, DC.

1815   General Andrew Jackson and his troops defeat the British at the Battle of New Orleans two weeks after the official end of the War of 1812.

1817   Construction begins on the Erie Canal.

American Colonization Society advocates returning people of African descent to Africa.

First Seminole War begins in Florida. The Seminoles were a North American Indian tribe of Creek origin who in the late eighteenth century moved south from Georgia into northern Florida.

1820   Congress passes the controversial Missouri Compromise banning slavery in Louisiana territories north of latitude 36° 30'.

James Eastburn and Robert Sands. *Yamoyden: A Tale of the Wars of King Philip.*

1821   First US public high school opens in Boston.

1822   American colony of Liberia is established in Africa.

Denmark Vesey and thirty other slaves are executed after whites discover their plan for a slave revolt in Charleston, South Carolina.

Stephen F. Austin is the first Anglo-American to colonize Texas.

1823   Margaret Bayard Smith. *American Mother; or, The Seymour Family.*

1824   Anna and Sarah Peale are elected to the Pennsylvania Academy of Fine Arts.
Lydia Maria Child. *Hobomok*.
James E. Seaver. *A Narrative of the Life of Mrs. Mary Jemison*.
Margaret Bayard Smith. *A Winter in Washington, or Memoirs of the Seymour Family*.

1825   Completion of Erie Canal expands trade to the Great Lakes region and the west.

1827   Catharine Maria Sedgwick. *Hope Leslie, or, Early Times in Massachusetts*.
Sarah Josepha Hale. *Northwood: a Tale of New England*.

1828   Women make up 90 percent of the workforce in the New England textile industry.
Andrew Jackson wins the presidency for the newly established Democratic Party.
"Jim Crow" minstrel character first introduced in Louisville, Kentucky.

1831   Nat Turner leads a slave rebellion in Southampton County, Virginia.

1832   The Boston Female Anti-Slavery Society founded.
Jackson reelected president.

1833   Founding of Oberlin College, first US institution of higher education to admit women and men on equal standing.
Lydia Maria Child. *An Appeal in Favor of that Class of Americans Called Africans*.
Harriet Beecher Stowe. "Modern Uses of Language." *Western Monthly Magazine*.

1834   Women workers at a Lowell, Massachusetts mill successfully strike to protest pay cuts.
Founding of the New York Female Moral Reform Society.
Antiabolition riots break out in New York and Philadelphia.
Forced removal of Seminole Indians from Florida.
Sarah Josepha Hale. "The Ursuline Convent." *American Ladies' Magazine*.
Sarah Josepha Hale. "How to Prevent the Increase of Convents." *American Ladies' Magazine*.
Sarah Josepha Hale. "Convents are Increasing." *American Ladies' Magazine*.
Lydia Huntley Sigourney. *Poems*.

1835   Sarah Josepha Hale. *Traits of American Life*.
Rebecca Theresa Reed. *Six Months in a Convent; or, The*

Narrative of Rebecca Theresa Reed, Who was Under the Influence of the Roman Catholics about Two Years, and an Inmate of the Ursuline Convent on Mount Benedict, Charlestown, Mass., Nearly Six Months, in the Years 1831–1832 With Some Preliminary Suggestions by the Committee of Publication.

1836   Grimké sisters lecture against slavery to crowds of women and men.
Mexican troops lay siege to the Alamo.
Angelina Grimké. *An Appeal to Christian Women of the South.*
Sarah Moore Grimké. *An Epistle to the Clergy of the Southern States.*
Lucinda Martin Larned. *The American Nun; or, The Effects of Romance.*
Maria Monk. *Awful Disclosures of the Hotel Dieu Nunnery of Montreal, Revised, with an Appendix.*

1837   Mount Holyoke Female Seminary, forerunner of Mount Holyoke College, opens.
New York City hosts the first national women's antislavery convention.
Margaret Fuller. "Governor Everett Receiving the Indian Chiefs."
Financial depression brings widespread bank closures and business failures.

1838   Underground railroad helps southern slaves gain freedom.
Morse code is introduced.

1839   First Married Women's Property Act passes in Mississippi giving women limited rights to property ownership and other legal actions formerly denied them under the auspices of "coverture." Under coverture, married woman's legal personhood was transferred to her husband.

1840   World's antislavery convention in London refuses to recognize women delegates, leading Lucretia Mott and Elizabeth Cady Stanton to convene the first women's rights convention.
National Anti-Slavery Standard begins publication.

1843   Phoebe Palmer. *The Way of Holiness.*

1845   US annexes Texas.
John L. O'Sullivan describes North American colonization as the "manifest destiny" of the United States.

1846   US declares war on Mexico.
Zilpha Elaw. *Memoirs of the Life, Religious Experience, Ministerial Travels and Labours of Mrs. Zilpha Elaw, An American Female of Colour Together with Some Account of the Great Religious Revivals in America. Written by Herself.*

1847   Frederick Douglass begins publishing the antislavery newspaper the *North Star.*

1848   Seneca Falls, New York is the site of the first women's rights convention.

Astronomer and former librarian Maria Mitchell becomes the first woman elected to the American Academy of Arts and Sciences.

US pays Mexico $15 million to cede the territories that will make up California, New Mexico, and portions of Arizona and Nevada.

Martin Van Buren runs for President as the Free-Soil Party candidate.

Elizabeth Ellet. *The Women of the American Revolution.*

1849   Elizabeth Blackwell becomes the first woman doctor to graduate from a US medical school.

Beginning of the California gold rush.

Harriet Tubman escapes from slavery. She returned to the South repeatedly and led nearly 300 slaves through the Underground Railroad.

1850   Over 1,000 attend the first national women's rights convention in Worcester, Massachusetts.

Women begin training as physicians at Philadelphia's Female Medical College of Pennsylvania.

Congress passes the second Fugitive Slave Act, a federal mandate demanding the return of fugitive slaves to their owners, even when those slaves had escaped to and been found in states where slavery no longer existed.

Susan Warner. *The Wide, Wide World.*

1851   Sojourner Truth gives her famous "A'n't I a Woman?" speech while touring in Ohio. In the speech, Truth highlights the failure of traditional ideas of womanhood.

First training school for black women teachers opens in Washington, DC.

1852   Harriet Beecher Stowe. *Uncle Tom's Cabin; or, Life Among the Lowly.*

1853   First ordained woman minister of a Protestant congregation, Antoinette Brown, ministers to two First Congregational churches in New York.

Amelia Jenks Bloomer. "Mothers of the Revolution." *Hear Me Patiently: the Reform Speeches of Amelia Jenks Bloomer.*

Fanny Fern [Sara Payson Willis Parton]. *Fern Leaves From Fanny's Portfolio.*

Harriet Beecher Stowe. *The Key to Uncle Tom's Cabin.*

1854   Orvilla S. Belisle. *The Archbishop; or, Romanism in the United States.*

Maria Cummins. *The Lamplighter.*

Frances Ellen Watkins Harper. *Forest Leaves and Poems on Miscellaneous Subjects.*

Julia Ward Howe. *Passion-Flowers.*

Ann Sophia Stephens. *Fashion and Famine.*

Harriet Beecher Stowe. *Sunny Memories of Foreign Lands.*

1855   University of Iowa admits women, the first state college or university to do so.

Decision in *Missouri v. Celia, a slave*, declares black women "property" and prohibits them from defending themselves against rape by their masters.

Orvilla S. Belisle. *The Prophets.*

Josephine Bunkley. *The Testimony of an Escaped Novice: From the Sisterhood of St. Joseph, Emmettsburg, Maryland, the Mother-House of the Sisters of Charity in the United States.*

Helen Dhu [pseudo. Charles Edwards Lester]. *Stanhope Burleigh: the Jesuits in Our Homes.*

Fanny Fern [Sara Payson Willis Parton]. *Ruth Hall.*

Mary Anne Sadlier. *The Blakes and the Flanagans: a Tale Illustrative of the Irish Life in the United States.*

Harriet Beecher Stowe. *First Geography for My Children.*

Harriet Beecher Stowe. "The Old Oak of Andover – A Reverie."

Augusta Jane Evans (Wilson). *Inez; a Tale of the Alamo.*

1856   Harriet Beecher Stowe. *Dred: a Tale of the Great Dismal Swamp.*

1858   Lydia Sigourney. *Lucy Howard's Journal.*

1859   American Medical Association opposes abortion.

E. D. E. N. Southworth. *The Hidden Hand.*

Harriet Beecher Stowe. *The Minister's Wooing.*

Harriet Wilson. *Our Nig.*

1860   First English-language kindergarten opens in the US with Elizabeth Palmer Peabody at the helm.

Mary Bryant. "How Should Women Write?"

Ann Sophia Stephens. *Malaeska: the Indian Wife of the White Hunter.*

1861   Civil War begins with the bombing of Fort Sumter in South
Carolina.
Rebecca Harding Davis. "Life in the Iron Mills." *Atlantic
Monthly*. *Life in the Iron Mills and Other Stories*.
Harriet Jacobs. *Incidents in the Life of a Slave Girl*.
Henry Mayhew. *London Labour and the London
Poor*.

1862   Oberlin College becomes the first US institution to award a
baccalaureate to an African American woman, Mary Jane
Patterson.
Single women begin claiming land under the Homestead Act.
Rebecca Harding Davis. *Margaret Howth: a Story of To-Day*.
Elizabeth Drew Stoddard. *The Morgesons*.
Harriet Beecher Stowe. *Agnes of Sorrento* and *The Pearl of Orr's
Island: a Story of the Coast of Maine*.

1863   Louisa May Alcott. *Hospital Sketches*.
Gail Hamilton. "A Call to My Country-Women." *Atlantic
Monthly*.
Mary Anne Sadlier. *Bessy Conway; or, The Irish Girl in
America*.
E. D. E. N. Southworth. *Ishmael*.
Elizabeth Drew Stoddard. "Lemorne *versus* Huell."

1864   Mary Anne Sadlier. *Confessions of an Apostate* and *Con
O'Regan; or, Emigrant Life in the New World*.
Augusta Jane Evans (Wilson). *Macaria; or, Altars of Sacrifice*.

1865   The more than 1.9 million slave women living in the US are
freed with the close of the Civil War.
Astronomer Maria Mitchell becomes the first female professor
at Vassar College.
Abraham Lincoln assassinated.

1866   Congress passes the 14th Amendment to the Constitution,
extending male voting rights but for the first time defining
"citizens" and "voters" as male.
Louisa May Alcott. *A Long Fatal Love Chase*.
Augusta Jane Evans (Wilson). *St. Elmo*.
Marion Harland. *Sunnybank*.

1867   Cigar makers union becomes the first national union to accept
African Americans and women.
Frances Ellen Watkins Harper. "Affairs in South Carolina."

Elizabeth Stuart Phelps (Ward). "At Bay." *Harper's New Monthly*.
Elizabeth Stuart Phelps (Ward). *Gypsy Breynton*.

1868   Rebecca Harding Davis. *Dallas Galbraith*.
Elizabeth Stuart Phelps (Ward). *The Gates Ajar*.
E. D. E. N. Southworth. *Fair Play*.

1869   Women's suffrage movement splits into the National Woman's
Suffrage Association and the American Woman Suffrage
Association.
First transcontinental railroad is completed.
Arabella Mansfield of Iowa becomes the first woman attorney in
the United States.
Women in the Wyoming territory win suffrage.
Frances Ellen Watkins Harper. *Minnie's Sacrifice* and *Moses:
a Story of the Nile*.
E. D. E. N. Southworth. *How He Won Her*.
Harriet Beecher Stowe. *Oldtown Folks*.
Harriet Beecher Stowe. "The True Story of Lady Byron's
Life." *Atlantic Monthly*.

1870   Women in Utah territory win suffrage.
Pamela Cowan. *The American Convent as a School for
Protestant Children*.
Rebecca Harding Davis. *Put Out of the Way*.
Helen Hunt Jackson. *Verses by H. H.*
Elizabeth Stuart Phelps (Ward). "The Woman's Pulpit."
Atlantic Monthly.
Harriet Beecher Stowe. *Lady Byron Vindicated. A History of the
Byron Controversy*.

1871   Smith College established; opens in 1875.
Frances Ellen Watkins Harper. *Poems*.
Elizabeth Stuart Phelps (Ward). *The Silent Partner*.
Elizabeth Stuart Phelps (Ward). "Unhappy Girls." *The
Independent*.
Harriet Beecher Stowe. *My Wife and I* and *Pink and White
Tyranny*.

1872   Charlotte E. Ray admitted to the bar in the District of Columbia
as the first African American woman lawyer in the US.
Maria Amparo Ruiz de Burton. *Who Would Have Thought It?*
Frances Ellen Watkins Harper. *Sketches of Southern Life*.
Marion Harland. *True as Steel*.

1873   Comstock Act defines contraceptive information as "obscene."
        The Act's effects are felt far into the twentieth century.
        Formation of the Association for the Advancement of Women.
        Edward H. Clarke. *Sex in Education; or, A Fair Chance for
        the Girls.*
        Harriet Beecher Stowe. *Woman in Sacred History.*
1874   Founding of the Woman's Christian Temperance Union.
        US Supreme Court refuses to extend 14th Amendment protections
        to women.
        Abba Goold Woolson, ed. *Dress Reform: a Series of Lectures
        Delivered in Boston, On Dress as it Affects the Health
        of Women.*
1875   Partial suffrage for women in Michigan and Minnesota.
        Mary Baker Eddy. *Science and Health.*
        Harriet Beecher Stowe. *We and Our Neighbors.*
1876   Partial suffrage for women in Colorado.
        Rebecca Harding Davis. "How the Widow Crossed the Lines."
1877   Helen Magill earns her doctorate in Greek from Boston
        University and becomes the first woman to receive a Ph.D.
        from an institution in the US.
        Elizabeth Stuart Phelps (Ward). *The Story of Avis.*
        Susan B. Warner. *Diana.*
1878   Partial suffrage for women in New Hampshire and Oregon.
        Harriet Beecher Stowe. *Poganuc People: Their Loves and Lives.*
1879   Mary Baker Eddy founds the Mother Church of Christian
        Science, later renamed the Church of Christ, Scientist.
        Partial suffrage for Massachusetts women.
1880   Sarah Winnemucca, granddaughter of two Northern Paiute
        chiefs, leads protests against the state of Indian reservations.
        Partial suffrage for women in Mississippi, New York, and
        Vermont.
1881   Clara Barton organizes the American Association of the Red Cross.
        The school for black women that later becomes Spelman College
        opens in an Atlanta, Georgia church basement.
        The Association of Collegiate Alumnae, later the American
        Association of University Women, begins promoting
        "educational equity for all women and girls."
        Helen Hunt Jackson. "Tidal Waves." *Atlantic Monthly.*
        Elizabeth Cady Stanton and Susan B. Anthony. *History
        of Woman Suffrage*, vol. 1.
1882   Emma Lazarus. "The New Colossus."

1883   Emma Lazarus. "The Jewish Problem." *Century.*
        Ella Wheeler Wilcox. *Poems of Passion.*
        Sarah Winnemucca Hopkins. *Life Among the Piutes: Their Wrongs
        and Claims.*
1885   Joseph Taylor founds Bryn Mawr College.
        Ada S. Ballin. *The Science of Dress in Theory and Practice.*
1887   Partial suffrage for women in Arizona, Montana, New Jersey,
        North Dakota, and South Dakota.
        Utah women lose the right to vote.
        Lizette Woodworth Reese. *A Branch of May.*
1889   Barnard College opens.
        Rebecca Harding Davis. "Anne."
1890   Partial suffrage for women in Oklahoma and Washington.
        Wyoming becomes a state and has full suffrage for women,
        allowing women to vote in local, state, and national elections.
        Daughters of the American Revolution established.
1891   Liliuokalani becomes queen of Hawaii.
        Sophia Alice Callahan. *Wynema: a Child of the Forest.*
        Lucy Delaney. *From the Darkness Cometh the Light;
        or, Struggles for Freedom.*
        Elizabeth Cady Stanton. "The Degradation of Disfranchisement."
        Woman's Tribune.
1892   Sociology department at the University of Kansas offers a course
        in the "Status of Women in the United States."
        Rebecca Harding Davis. *Kent Hampden* and *Silhouettes of
        American Life.*
        Frances Ellen Watkins Harper. *Iola Leroy; or, Shadows
        Uplifted.*
1893   Woman's Building at the World's Columbian Exposition in
        Chicago showcases the accomplishments of American women.
        National Council of Jewish Women founded.
        Full suffrage for women in Colorado.
        Partial suffrage for women in Connecticut.
        Amanda Berry Smith. *Autobiography: the Story of the
        Lord's Dealings with Mrs. Amanda Smith, the Colored Evangelist.*
1894   Chartering of Radcliffe College.
        Woman's Era begins publishing news of the national black
        women's club movement.
        Partial suffrage for Iowa and Ohio women.
        Loss of partial suffrage for New Jersey women.
1895   Elizabeth Cady Stanton. *The Woman's Bible.*

1896   First women's intercollegiate basketball game between Berkeley
        and Stanford.
        National Federation of Afro-American Women and the National
        League of Colored Women merge to form the National
        Association of Colored Women.
        Full suffrage for women in Idaho and Utah.
        Homer Plessy sues when a train company denies him a seat in
        a rail car with white passengers. The case is appealed all the way
        to the US Supreme Court. The court's decision in *Plessy
        v. Ferguson* sanctions the segregation of African Americans
        in public accommodations, setting the standard that would be
        followed for decades to come.
        Sarah Orne Jewett. *The Country of the Pointed Firs.*
        Elizabeth Stuart Phelps. *Chapters from a Life.*
1897   Evangelina Cisneros. *The Story of Evangelina Cisneros
        (Evangelina Betancourt Cosio Y Cisneros), told by Herself* [and]
        Her Rescue by Karl Decker.
1898   Partial suffrage for women in Delaware and Louisiana.
        Elizabeth Cady Stanton. *Eighty Years and More –
        Reminiscences 1815–1897.*
1899   Carry Nation publicly hatchets bottles and bars to protest
        alcohol.
        Lillian Galbreth is the first female commencement speaker at the
        University of California at Berkeley.
        Rebecca Harding Davis. "The Curse of Education."
1900   Some women in Wisconsin gain partial suffrage.
        Zitkala-Sa. "Impressions of an Indian Childhood." *Atlantic
        Monthly.*
        Zitkala-Sa. "The School Days of an Indian Girl." *Atlantic
        Monthly.*
        Zitkala-Sa. "An Indian Teacher Among Indians." *Atlantic
        Monthly.*
1902   Myra Kelley. *Little Citizens: the Humours of School Life.*
1903   Founding of the Women's Trade Union League.
1904   Helen Keller graduates cum laude from Radcliffe College.
        The National Child Labor Committee lobbies to eliminate
        child labor.
        Rebecca Harding Davis. *Bits of Gossip.*
1909   International Ladies' Garment Workers' Union and the Women's
        Trade Union League support striking shirtwaist workers in
        New York.

Founding of the National Association for the Advancement of Colored People.

Edith Maud Eaton (Sui Sin Far). "Leaves from the Mental Portfolio of an Eurasian." *The Independent.*

1910　Partial suffrage for women in New Mexico.

Full suffrage for women in Washington State.

1911　Women in California win full suffrage.

La Liga Femenil Mexicanista organized in Laredo, Texas.

1912　Juliette Gordon Low organizes the first American Girl Guide troop, predecessor of the Girl Scouts. 500,000 turn out to watch a parade of over 20,000 suffrage supporters in New York.

Women in Arizona, Kansas, and Oregon win full suffrage.

National American Woman Suffrage Association stages a march on the Capitol the day before Woodrow Wilson's inauguration as president.

Mary Antin. *The Promised Land.*

1913　Partial suffrage for Illinois women.

Women in the Alaska territory win full suffrage.

1914　Reproductive health activist Margaret Sanger indicted for distributing the birth control pamphlet *Family Limitation.*

Full suffrage for women in Nevada and Montana.

1915　Creation of the Woman's Peace Party.

1916　Jeannette Rankin is elected a US Representative from Montana and becomes the first female member of Congress.

Margaret Sanger is tried and imprisoned after opening the first US birth control clinic.

1918　Over one million women working for industry connected to World War One.

1920　The 19th Amendment to the US Constitution guarantees women the right to vote.

Anzia Yezierska. "How I Found America." *Hungry Hearts and Other Stories.*

1922　Equal Rights Amendment to the US Constitution first proposed.

Scammon Lockwood. "She Didn't Have Any Sense." *McClure's* (June).

1925　Anzia Yezierska. *Bread Givers: a Struggle Between a Father of the Old World and a Daughter of the New.*

DALE BAUER AND PHILIP GOULD

Introduction

Writing in response to the question "How Should Women Write?" (1860), Mary Bryant prescribed a literature that would be at once intellectual and intense, written "honestly and without fear" to suit the seriousness of the era. This volume is our effort to meet Bryant's challenge, to bring her charge to bear on the history of American women's writing and the legacy of and prospects for its criticism to date.

Once dismissed as simply sentimental and thus undeniably inferior, nineteenth-century American women's writing, for at least the last twenty years, has been newly "recovered" or "rediscovered." The critical occasion for the *Cambridge Companion to Nineteenth-Century American Women's Writing* derives of course from the extensive revitalization of this scholarly discipline. Yet this volume also provides an account of the changing critical assumptions that govern the contemporary study of American women's writing itself.

Contemporary reappraisals of nineteenth-century American women's writing have changed both the shape of the American literary canon and the discipline of American literary history. Influential studies abound, from Ann Douglas's *The Feminization of American Culture* (1977) and Nina Baym's *Woman's Fiction: a Guide to the Novels by and about Women in America, 1820–1870* (1978, 1993) to Jane Tompkins's *Sensational Designs: The Cultural Work of American Fiction, 1790–1860* (1985) and Cathy N. Davidson's *Revolution and the Word: the Rise of the Novel in America* (1986). Important anthologies of women's writing have also contributed to the critical recovery of American women's literary history, including Judith Fetterley's *Provisions: a Reader from Nineteenth-Century American Women* (1985), Lucy Freibert and Barbara White's *Hidden Hands: an Anthology of American Women Writers, 1790–1870* (1985), Karen Kilcup's *Nineteenth-Century American Women Writers: an Anthology* (1997), and Paula Bennett's *Nineteenth-Century American Women Poets* (1997). These works have introduced a generation of scholars and students to previously unavailable or unrecognized texts. Indeed, the great success of Rutgers University Press's

American Women Writers Series; the Early Women Writers Project offered by Brown University and Oxford University Press; the Schomburg Library of Nineteenth-Century Black Women Writers; the genesis of the journal *Legacy* devoted to American women's writing: all of these publications print a growing body of work suggesting the catalyst for the current Companion volume.

Traditionally characterized as "domestic" or "sentimental," the discipline's genres include, in fact, history-writing, letters and diaries, reform journalism and religious tracts, as well as gothic, domestic and sentimental fiction, poetry, and drama. Like the anthropological work of Clifford Geertz, scholars have given us "thick description" of the cultural contexts and functions of individual texts. This Companion volume, however, challenges the "seamlessness" of cultural contexts by reexamining such crucial premises for critical study as the nature of "domesticity," the function of sentimentalism, and the relations between "private" and "public" domains. In this way, it suggests the germane questions over the meanings of such key terms as the "sentimental," "separate spheres," and the "public," as well as newly important ones like "assimilation" and "sanctification," that shape the field's future. It contains individual case studies that collectively model directions for future criticism. We cannot claim comprehensiveness, given the expansiveness of this field; yet the chapters assembled here provide new models of envisioning both the literary and critical canon to date.

The project of "recovery" devoted to nineteenth-century American women's writing derives immediately from the changes in the academy and the canon that the rise of Women's Studies and Ethnic Studies Programs inaugurated in the 1970s. Yet the politics undergirding the recovery project can be traced to the 1940s and 1950s – the era in which American Studies developed. As Dana Nelson's chapter in this volume argues, women's writing suffered during this era under the ideological assumptions wielded by the most influential or the most banal critics. How and why, one might ask, did this occur? In "Melodramas of Beset Manhood" (1981), Nina Baym outlined the features of much of this literature that so offended the critical status quo: its popularity, its affinity for social and domestic realities, and its pervasive use of sentiment in narrative and characterization. Alternatively, the "American" literary tradition – articulated in part through efforts to define a national culture – privileged male writing that supposedly exemplified cultural "essence" in its romantic recoil from both popular culture and surface realism: Baym calls it a form of "consensus literature of the consensus," which reaffirms cultural norms as it enacts its own melodramatic fantasy of isolation ("Melodramas," 129).

Rather than see American critics as simply misguided, or at worst misogynistic, we might instead seek to explain why cultural politics devalued sentimentality in American women's writing. During the 1930s and 1940s, American liberalism self-consciously redefined itself against the "Left": the loose association of utopian socialists and Soviet-inspired Marxist communists whose political influence was waning in America, a result largely of such political events as Stalin's purge trials and the Nazi–Soviet alliance of 1939. Centrist (or "new") liberals now viewed the traditional Left as morally bankrupt and defined themselves against the viability of "ideology" itself. In its place, they substituted the principles (or one might say ideology) of irony, ambiguity, and isolation – exactly the values that Baym has so astutely demystified for us. They also saw communal and utopian ideals as yet another form of cultural totalitarianism; interpreted popular, or mass, culture as the chief expression of this danger; and, perhaps most important, espoused a Calvinistic view of human nature that favored a hard-edged "realism" as opposed to sentimentality. These were principles of literary taste as well. Liberal tenets that privileged "artistic" consciousness (in the face of a mass audience), the use of irony (as opposed to "ideology"), and romantic technique meant to capture psychological (as opposed to sociological) reality all served to undermine the canonical status of much of women's writing – with the exception of an Emily Dickinson or Edith Wharton, who could wield irony in all the right ways.

Most egregious of all to this cultural movement was the sentimentality perceived or apprehended in much of American women's writing. For postwar liberals, sentiment took on overtly political meanings. Consider, for example, the foundational text of postwar politics, Arthur Schlesinger, Jr.'s *The Vital Center* (1949), which proclaimed at the outset that "American liberalism . . . has stood for responsibility and achievement, not for frustration and sentimentalism" (xix). Schlesinger even went so far as to lampoon the "sentimental abstractions of [Leftist] fantasy" and to accuse American radicals of a "somewhat feminine fascination with the rude and muscular power of the proletariat" (46). Schlesinger's rejection of sentimentalism must be understood in the context of his rudimentary construction of class politics and sexuality, as well as his vexed preference for "realism" to which sentimental women's writing was subjected and compared. Critics like Schlesinger faulted the sentimental novel's investment in social realism and affective relations, its fidelity to the facts of the daily lives of bourgeois white women, and its simultaneous failure, as Baym argues, to depict "the pure American self divorced from specific social circumstances" ("Melodramas," 131).

Much of the work devoted to American women's writing in the 1970s and 1980s represents the revision of this postwar critical tradition. Such revisionism has facilitated both the recovery of forgotten texts and the discovery of new ones. In turn, the critical assumptions animating this recuperation have over time been continually – and productively – revised. One salient issue that many of our contributors address is the debate over the critical languages that have structured subjects such as sentiment, sensation, and emotion. In the historical and critical context for sentimentalism, Ann Douglas's *The Feminization of American Culture* appears to be an extension of a liberal narrative, for she argues that nineteenth-century American women's writing actively participated in the creation of a debased form of American mass culture predicated on particularly sentimental forms of consumerism. Not unlike Schlesinger, Douglas proclaims: "Sentimentalism . . . might be defined as the political sense obfuscated or gone rancid. Sentimentalism, unlike the modes of genuine sensibility, never exists except in tandem with failed political consciousness" (254). During the 1980s, however, Jane Tompkins, in *Sensational Designs*, led the revisionary rebuttal to such a view. Taking novels like Harriet Beecher Stowe's *Uncle Tom's Cabin* (1852) and Susan Warner's *The Wide, Wide World* (1850) as literary exemplars, Tompkins recontextualized these texts within a rich array of religious, evangelical and moral reform discourses (e.g., sermons, conversion narratives, missionary tracts) to argue for their feminized – and feminist – reorganization of culture. These novels, she argued, served a functional purpose of "doing cultural work," a phrase that has been celebrated as the *raison d'être* of women's writing in general, as though women's writing had to justify itself purely by the work it can – or should – do. Assumptions about women's work and its invisibility certainly die hard.

Valuable as such a revision has been to the field, critics have even begun to question the dichotomies upon which our critical understanding of sentiment was founded and what such affect reproduces. For example, in her introduction to *The Culture of Sentiment: Race, Gender and Sentimentality in Nineteenth-Century America* (1992), Shirley Samuels represents a view that is now more willing to recognize ideological inconsistencies, and even shortcomings, in women's sentimental writing. The limits of sympathy, moreover, often reveal the possible tensions existing on the "margins" of nineteenth-century America. As many critics have shown, African-American women put sentiment to different uses from their white, bourgeois counterparts. These writers challenge the category of the sentimental, specifically its capacity to fulfill the aspirations of women on the social margins; in fact, many see the sentimental as replicating social distinctions and oppressive categories. Ann Sophia Stephens's *Fashion and Famine* (1854) or *Malaeska* (1860), for example, illustrate the failure of white women to embrace their ethnic or working-class "sisters." Harriet Wilson's autobiographical novel *Our Nig* (1859) particularly deflates domestic ideology's egalitarian claims by exposing its racial limitations. Indeed, the male characters in this novel – set in New

England – demonstrate greater sympathy for the protagonist Frado than do the noxiously racist Mrs. Bellmont and her daughter. Critics such as Carla Kaplan and Ann duCille argue that in *Incidents in the Life of a Slave Girl* (1861) Harriet Jacobs shows how African-American women are excluded from the domestic institution of marriage and, thereby, from the privileges of ownership. Moreover, Priscilla Wald's chapter on immigrant women in this volume shows how the prescriptions for the "American woman" limited the possibilities of assimilation for different races and classes.

Critics now view the sentimental as something necessarily didactic: it not only teaches but needs to be taught. As Elizabeth Barnes has argued, the "pedagogy" of sympathy inculcating the virtue of sentimental benevolence was not inherent in the individual, and was certainly not women's sole birthright. Domesticity and intimacy become the center of the social controversies over women's place in culture and politics. Antebellum novels thus are premised upon important questions about gender and authority. What was women's relation to national culture? Could they participate in the abstract cause of nation-building, or were they "naturally" limited by their domestic sensibilities?

Thus, sentimentalism is not so much a feminine possession or "essence," but is a widely circulating cultural discourse. Again, the terms of criticism have shifted: where we had once imagined emotions as women's sphere, critics posit emotional life as a cultural construct; where we had once imagined women in the private sphere, social historians have more recently identified the intersubjectivity of citizens and the interpenetrating realms of home and work.

Such a conflation of spheres introduces a second important area of critical revision: the social and ideological relations between the "public" and the "private." The ostensibly "separate" arenas of men's and women's activities emerged as the ideological counterpart to the economic shift in the 1830s and 1840s, a shift predicated on a basis of commerce outside the home and the attendant rise of the middle class; hence, the "domestic" or bourgeois woman was invented. As Linda K. Kerber argued in 1988, however, historians are now willing "to show how women's allegedly 'separate sphere' was affected by what men did, and how activities defined by women in their own sphere, influenced and even set constraints and limitations on what men chose to do – how, in short, that sphere was socially constructed both for and by women" ("Separate Spheres," 18). Yet we are not ready to throw out the baby with the bathwater; even as the concept of separate spheres is being phased out, the "baby" is still with us in the stylistic and political differences among women writers, especially in relation to their male counterparts. This work is still too new to be dismissed out of hand as finished.

Like the suspect model of "separate spheres," the cultural geography of the "center" and "margins" also raises troubling questions. What, for example, happens when we incorporate race and ethnicity into this model of center and margins? Do women, such as Sarah Winnemucca, a Native American autobiographer whose *Life Among the Piutes* appeared in 1883, share the same cultural and political vision as their white "sisters"? Winnemucca and the Native American novelist Alice Callahan (whose *Wynema* appeared in 1891) both employ sentimental conventions to stage moments of cross-cultural exchange, but does this mean that their works endorse the model of "sisterhood" one finds, for example, in Margaret Fuller's political "conversations" of the late 1830s? The limitations of this model, moreover, have concerned critics such as Robyn Warhol and Karen Sánchez-Eppler, who have argued for the sentimental hegemony in white women's antislavery writing over both white readers and black bodies. The ending to *Uncle Tom's Cabin*, where Stowe expatriates her African American characters to evangelize Africa, makes these limitations clear. How, then, does one conceptualize the literary dynamic of sentimental identification? How can we feel with someone of different race or class, when the liberal individual is defined by his or her difference (see Ammons, *Conflicting Stories*)?

Directly related to the politics of sentimentalism is the question of the presumed "radicalism" of American women's writing. During the 1970s and 1980s, critics recuperated the canonical importance of this writing (especially the sentimental novel) by arguing for its cultural significance, particularly its antipatriarchalism. But as June Howard has argued, sentimental politics may be suspect at times because the emotions are associated "with tears, with humanitarian reform, with convention and commodification" ("What is Sentimentality?," 74). The interior life of emotions shows the fascination with middle-class individuality that is simultaneously the cornerstone of nineteenth-century liberalism. Traditionally, critics juxtaposed sentiment and liberal capitalism as the gendered opposition of "female" and "male" values. But is this opposition historically tenable? There is ample evidence to question it. As Nina Baym has argued, much of nineteenth-century women's historical writing situates the female "voice" within the ideological confines of Protestant bourgeois culture.

So, too, with the political ambiguities of women's writing about antislavery. The issue of women's rights significantly divided American abolitionists during the late 1830s. But does this mean we read Lydia Child's *An Appeal in Favor of that Class of Americans Called Africans* (1833), or Angelina Grimké's "Appeal to Christian Women of the South" (1836), as necessarily "radical" writings? Certainly, these works' progressive ideas infuriated conservative readers (Child, for example, lost her library privileges), but to our eyes they may at moments perpetuate racial and social stereotypes. How do we avoid "presentism" – imposing our contemporary assumptions and mores on historical subjects – while still acknowledging the historical limitations of women's perspectives? What do we bring to their writing, and what do we expect from it?

Indeed, the current turn in work on women's literature has clarified the earlier focus on women's particular networks, especially about such issues as temperance, poverty, and prostitution; politics (where women sent petitions to political leaders); or ladies' societies. Scholars now chronicle women's constant and multivocal public dialogues throughout the nineteenth century. Influential studies by Lori Ginzberg, Christine Stansell, and Mary Ryan have challenged the traditional wisdom of separate spheres by examining such diverse groups as women's associations and the urban poor. As Ryan notes, there is a lot at stake in this historiography, for "the public [is] a richly evocative term, a linguistic marker of highly privileged meaning, both moral and political" (*Women in Public*, 10). In this regard, then, "feminist political theorists push at the boundaries of the public by holding that sphere to the highest standards of openness, accessibility, [and] tolerance of diversity" (12).

Hence the feminist critique of the influential work of Jürgen Habermas, who historically conceptualized the rise of the "public" as a masculine site of sociability and intellectual exchange. "By omitting any mention of the childrearer role," Nancy Fraser has argued, "and by failing to thematize the gender subtext underlying the roles of worker and consumer, Habermas fails to understand precisely how the capitalist workplace is linked to the modern, restricted, male-headed, nuclear family" ("What's Critical About Critical Theory?," 45). How much was (and is) childrearing really a public role, and not merely domesticated "influence"?

These theoretical alterations made upon the "public" simultaneously suggest ways to rethink the "home." Critics now argue that, instead of being a haven, the home that nineteenth-century women's writing constitutes was never an uncontested site: either as a reflection of the market economy (as Gillian Brown argues) or as a place of violence and aggression (as Shirley Samuels suggests in this volume). For Lora Romero, this may involve the mingling of the gothic with the familiar, while for Amy Kaplan domesticity provides the ideological site of legitimating nineteenth-century American imperialism. One genre that certainly illustrates this spatial complexity is women's historical writing. For example, Elizabeth Ellet's *The Women of the American Revolution* (1848–50) dramatizes the British (and perhaps her reader's) inability to interpret creatively American women and their homes. This occurs when Nancy Hart (a woman "ignorant of all the conventional civilities of life, but a zealous lover of liberty") hides a fugitive patriot in her home and sends him out the back door when the British arrive: "Presently some tories rode up to the bars, calling vociferously for her. She muffled up her head and face, and opening the door, inquired why they disturbed a sick, lone woman. They said they had traced a man they wanted to catch near to her house" (227, 229). In this case Ellet demonstrates the linkage between the stereotypes of passive "womanhood" and the "home." The scene depends upon the necessity of interpretive conventions: the line is imperfectly "traced" because its patriarchal readers refuse to acknowledge the merging of public and private spaces.

Ellet's history-writing also touches on a third area of critical reappraisal involving the meanings of gender in the nineteenth century. Between the American Revolution and the antebellum era, as Ruth Bloch has argued, the meaning of "virtue" gradually underwent a process of cultural feminization which associated this key word with the sentimental affections. Throughout the eighteenth century, both men and women could be hailed as "virtuous citizens," although there was often a good deal of rhetorical ambiguity about just what the epithet actually meant. This process certainly helped to produce what Jeanne Boydston calls the "plasticity" of gender in early American literature. Such gender fluidity occurs in Lydia Maria Child's characterization of the heroic Native American in *Hobomok* (1824), Margaret Fuller's theory of "Muse" and "Minerva" for female identity, Rebecca Harding Davis's symbol of the korl woman in "Life in the Iron Mills" (1861), *The Lamplighter*'s depiction of Willie Sullivan, Louisa May Alcott's complex personae, and Sarah Orne Jewett's *The Country of the Pointed Firs* (1896). The list goes on, but the point is that gender was always more flexible than fixed.

This volume not only demonstrates contemporary critical trends, but also articulates theoretical and methodological concerns that continue to challenge the scholarly field. One recurring critical issue concerns the category of "cultural work" itself. Why do we read women's writing primarily for its advocacy of social change? The very paradigm of "cultural work" might be read as a legacy of one strain of Enlightenment thinking that privileges reason, order, and utilitarian function. On its surface, the new significance of sentimentality in critical discourse appears to be a move *away* from the traditionally masculine norm of reason (a norm associated in recent theoretical movements with the fallacy of "logocentric" thinking). Perhaps the new interest in the suprarational corrects the long-standing fixation on male voices in American literary studies; perhaps the move beyond rationality into the cultural life of emotions can be linked to the examination of a political ideology which has been too long repressed. But if many American women writers offer a vision of emotions every bit as culturally efficacious as that of rationality and individuality, the explanatory power of "cultural work" answers to the *rational* need to describe literature's "function." The traditional question "Is it any good?" has been translated into "What good does it do?"

The critical move away from formalism in the name of ideology still leaves us with the larger issue of the nature – and role – of aesthetics in women's writing. As Joanne Dobson has argued, we need to understand sentimentalism as an aesthetic language, or collection of languages, that enables us to read, for example, Ellen Montgomery's incessant tears in Susan Warner's *The Wide, Wide World* in ways that do not immediately resort to arguments about its mawkishness or gender politics. The issue of aesthetics is connected to the crucial question of audience. Who were the contemporaneous readers of American women's writing? Cathy Davidson, Janice Radway, and Nina Baym have all offered sociologies of reading, specifically the reconstruction of the world of "female readers." Whereas Davidson posits the feminist identification of female readers and the early American novel, Baym suggests that these readers intuited a critical difference between fictional heroines and their own lives – the difference that the protagonist of Tabitha Tenney's *Female Quixotism* (1801) *cannot* discern. But the larger questions about literacy – who had access to education, who achieved "community" by virtue of reading – are crucial. Who, where, and what one could read provide key historical contexts for the formal and thematic features of texts themselves. Indeed, one might consider the structural changes in bourgeois homes, which facilitated the possibility of greater privacy, as part of the historical and interpretive matrix for the female "self" (see Fliegelman, *Prodigals and Pilgrims*).

Two related questions also appear in this volume: first, the history of reception in particular and print culture in general and, second, the integration of studying women's writing in relation to other disciplines such as anthropology, psychology, and sociology. What did women read, and what was easily or freely available to them? The growth of newspapers and syndicated columns in the 1880s and 1890s (after the popularity of Jennie June's fashion columns and Fanny Fern's humor pieces in antebellum America) brought an important site of women's advancement as writers into greater focus. Moreover, syndicated fictions brought regionalist writers to the fore and interested more women readers than ever before. How did the varying markets for women authors change the production of texts?

Scholarly work on American women's writing is striving constantly to keep up with the calls for interdisciplinary work in American studies and cultural studies. This raises important disciplinary – or rather interdisciplinary – questions about critical methods. Should our methodologies broaden, even as our fields of interest seem to become more focused? Or should we widen our scope of inquiry at the same time that we utilize the methods and bodies of knowledge in other, related scholarly disciplines? The latter possibility raises the specter of trying to tackle too much, especially in light of the fact that the field continually tries to recover and discover new writers and texts. And this of course involves the question of national borders. Nineteenth-century American women's writing might be read most productively from a comparatist perspective – that is, transatlantically, bringing Stowe, for example, into dialogue with the Brontës or continental European writers. Can we extend such a methodology to Latin American women's work, or third world cultural contacts? As Carolyn Porter argues, "what we know that we don't know" is how common, cross-culturally, the patterns of US women's writing appear in South American fiction or in Canadian literature.

The first part of this *Companion* accordingly provides historical and theoretical backgrounds to nineteenth-century American women's writing. In "The Postcolonial Culture of Early American Women's Writing," Rosemarie Zagarri discusses the gradual professionalization of women's writing in the context of the social and cultural changes informing women's lives between the 1790s and 1840s. As Zagarri notes, the cultural emergence of "republican womanhood," whereby middle-class women were partly responsible for the moral character of the American republic, invested greater importance in women's education and literacy. If such change was rooted partly in Scottish Enlightenment philosophy about human moral growth, it also helped to shape changes in the meanings of "virtue" in American culture. Dana D. Nelson's "Women in Public" analyzes the cultural legacy of republican womanhood, specifically the enabling tensions it produces between women's private and public responsibilities. By tracing the history of the concept of "separate spheres" in modern criticism, Nelson gives it the literary–critical attention that Kerber had initiated in the field of women's history.

Nowhere better are these tensions captured than in the "texts" of women's dress, a subject that Stephanie A. Smith takes up in "Antebellum Politics and Women's Writing." Smith offers an expansive account of the cultural politics of women's fashion through the specific history of "bloomers" (named after the innovation by the temperance advocate Amelia Jenks Bloomer in the 1850s), which symbolically questioned contemporary gendered assumptions about the "nature" of "woman." Like the changing meanings of "virtue," there was the semantic change from "Bloomers" to "bloomers," revealing the depoliticization of the term over the course of the nineteenth century.

The second section, "Genre, Tradition, and Innovation," shows how theories of American women's writing emerge as much *from* these texts as they circumscribe their readings. The tropes of captivity and liberation in this poetry are the subject of Kathryn Zabelle Derounian-Stodola's "Captivity and the Literary Imagination." Her chapter invokes the critical paradigms by Toni Morrison and Sandra Gilbert and Susan Gubar to trace the discourses of oppression and emancipation in both autobiography and the novel. Those discourses, she argues, themselves historically derive from (and later accompany) the slave narrative and the Indian captivity narrative. Elizabeth Petrino's "Nineteenth-Century American Women's Poetry" examines the critical premises devaluing women's poetry – with the exception, of course, of Emily Dickinson. Petrino not only argues for the literary significance of women poets such as Lydia Sigourney and Frances Osgood, but also situates their work comparatively with canonical figures such as Philip Freneau and Edgar Allan Poe. In the same way, Susan Griffin's examination of anti-Catholic fiction constellates the issues of generic continuity and change in this section. Arguing that these fictions destabilized Protestant American culture, Griffin demonstrates how antipapist works dramatized the dangers of patriarchal religious control and meanwhile offered veiled critiques of Protestant theology.

Such ambivalence about women's assumed emotional or spiritual "nature" highlights Shirley Samuels's "Women at War," which sketches the appearance of women's rage in the home (between mothers and daughters) and on the Civil War battlefield (as cross-dressing soldiers). Samuels explores what critics have long ignored because of assumptions of women's assumed peaceful sentiments and natural sympathy: the repressed rage that leads to misdirected hostility or outright aggression, not to mention the refusal to submit to male authority. And such violence need not be explicit. As Priscilla Wald demonstrates, immigrant women's narratives and fictions are filled with fears of violence and aggression. Anxiety permeates the rhetoric of "assimilation" in their works, and it also represents their struggle with dominant paradigms of socialization, stemming from the early responses to New World womanhood that are embedded in narratives such as Lydia Maria Child's *Hobomok* (1824) or Catharine Maria Sedgwick's *Hope Leslie* (1827). All of these chapters evince the methodological and theoretical shifts – from recovery to complicity – in the study of nineteenth-century American women's writing.

The specific case studies in this volume read individual writers whose work exhibits particular aesthetic and cultural issues in nineteenth-century US women's writing. Fredrika J. Teute's "The Uses of Writing in Margaret Bayard Smith's New Nation" illustrates many of the literary and historical issues in Zagarri's chapter. Reading the social and political life informing

Bayard Smith's observations, Teute shows how they constitute a revisionist history of women's contribution to the emerging national community. In "The Sentimental Novel: the Example of Harriet Beecher Stowe," Gail K. Smith discusses Stowe's well-known novels alongside works like *Lady Byron Vindicated* (1870) to depict the linguistic self-consciousness of sentimental writing. Situating Stowe biographically and culturally in the context of contemporary biblical scholarship known as "higher criticism," Smith goes on to explore Stowe's theories of textuality, sacred and secular language, and the gendered ramifications of reading itself. Throughout her prolific career Stowe dramatized in her many novels and prose works scenes of interpretation that often exposed the instability – and multivalence – of language.

As Yolanda Pierce's analysis of spiritual narrative demonstrates, however, that Protestant religion was still one of the best claims to power for black women in antebellum America. By examining in particular the career of Zilpha Elaw, Pierce argues for the many levels of meaning upon which the languages of conversion signified. These texts form an ideological counterpart to slave narratives focused more on resistance than on "sanctification."

That the discourse of reform permeates American women's writing is well established; the assumption of women's sympathetic nature undergirds much of the century's claims for women's writing. However, as Lisa A. Long argues in "The Postbellum Reform Writings of Rebecca Harding Davis and Elizabeth Stuart Phelps," the reform novel inevitably challenges the categories of both genre and gender. After the Civil War, these writers did not simply indict patriarchal power structures but more profoundly connected such power to notions of "womanhood" that circulated freely in the antebellum era (and that have shaped so much modern criticism of Davis and Phelps). The very premise of such a distinction raises the issue of the exclusion of women from republican citizenship, a subject that Farah Griffin's "*Minnie's Sacrifice*: Francis Ellen Watkins Harper's Narrative of Citizenship" places in racial contexts particularly during the Reconstruction era. By reading Harper's post-Civil War writings (including letters and poetry as well as her serialized novel), Griffin charts Harper's movement from an integrationist vision to "an emergent black nationalism" that would become more apparent in later works such as *Iola Leroy* (1892).

Sandra A. Zagarell's close reading of the formal structure and gendered politics of Elizabeth Stoddard's highly complex novel, *The Morgesons* (1862), makes a case for the modern quality of its antisentimental self-consciousness. As a female *Bildungsroman*, Stoddard's work anticipates the formal complexity, ambiguous characterization, and ironic detachment of later modernist writers of the early twentieth century such as Virginia Woolf and Gertrude Stein. "Strenuous Artistry" illustrates Stoddard's resistance to the claims of sentimentalism and reform in the dominant tradition of women's writing.

Once seen as too realistic for romance, and too idealistic for American "reality," women's writing was entrapped within a modern critical narrative that called paradoxically for both the recoil from and confrontation with the "facts" of American life. If revisionist scholarship of the 1970s and 1980s reformulated both the realism and politics of women's writing, the chapters in this volume further explore the critical stakes of those texts. Reading Zabelle Stodola's chapter in tandem with Priscilla Wald's shows, for example, how "captivity narratives" also provided a paradigm for later assimilation stories. Considering Shirley Samuels's charting of aggression on the "erotic battlefield" alongside Susan Griffin's claims about anti-Catholic violence gives another picture of the competing discourses about the primacy of what Nancy Cott called "the bonds of womanhood." Such reconsiderations characterize this Companion volume as a whole. While acknowledging the importance of traditional paradigms and perspectives, the contributors have built on them to suggest how much more work there is to do in the genres of American women's writing.

WORKS CITED

Ammons, Elizabeth. *Conflicting Stories: American Women Writers at the Turn of the Century*. New York and Oxford: Oxford University Press, 1991.
Barnes, Elizabeth. *States of Sympathy: Seduction and Democracy in the American Novel*. New York: Columbia University Press, 1997.
Baym, Nina. *Woman's Fiction: a Guide to Novels by and about Women in America, 1820–1870*. Ithaca: Cornell University Press, 1978, 1993.
"Melodramas of Beset Manhood: How Theories of American Fiction Exclude Women Authors." *American Quarterly* 33 (1981): 123–39.
Bennett, Paula. *Nineteenth-Century American Women Poets: an Anthology*. Malden, MA: Blackwell, 1998.
Bloch, Ruth. "The Gendered Meanings of Virtue in Revolutionary America." *Signs: Journal of Women in Culture and Society* 13.1 (1987): 37–58.
Boydston, Jeanne. "The Woman Who Wasn't There: Women's Market Labor and the Transition to Capitalism in the United States." *Wages of Independence: Capitalism in the Early Republic*. Ed. Paul A. Gilje. Madison: Madison House, 1997.
Brown, Gillian. *Domestic Individualism: Imagining Self in Nineteenth-Century America*. Berkeley: University of California Press, 1990.
Cott, Nancy. *The Bonds of Womanhood: "Woman's Sphere" in New England, 1780–1835*. New Haven: Yale University Press, 1977.
Davidson, Cathy N. *Revolution and the Word: the Rise of the Novel in America*. New York and Oxford: Oxford University Press, 1986.

Dobson, Joanne. "Reclaiming Sentimental Literature." *American Literature* 69.2 (1997): 263–88.

Douglas, Ann. *The Feminization of American Culture.* New York: Knopf, 1977.

DuCille, Ann. *The Coupling Convention: Sex, Text, and Tradition in Black Women's Fiction.* New York and Oxford: Oxford University Press, 1993.

Ellet, Elizabeth, *The Women of the American Revolution,* 3 vols. 1848–50. New York: Haskell House, 1969.

Fetterley, Judith, ed. *Provisions: a Reader from Nineteenth-Century American Women.* Bloomington: Indiana University Press, 1985.

Fliegelman, Jay. *Prodigals and Pilgrims: the American Revolution Against Patriarchal Authority, 1750–1800.* New York and Cambridge: Cambridge University Press, 1982.

Fraser, Nancy. "What's Critical About Critical Theory?" *Feminism as Critique: on the Politics of Gender.* Ed. Seyla Benhabib and Drucilla Cornell. Minneapolis: University of Minnesota Press, 1987.

Freibert, Lucy and Barbara White, eds. *Hidden Hands: an Anthology of American Women Writers, 1790–1870.* New Brunswick: Rutgers University Press, 1985.

Ginzburg, Lori. *Women and the Work of Benevolence: Morality, Politics, and Class in the Nineteenth-Century United States.* New Haven: Yale University Press, 1990.

Howard, June. "What is Sentimentality?" *American Literary History* 11.1 (spring 1999): 63–81.

Johanningsmeier, Charles A. *Fiction and the American Literary Marketplace: the Role of Newspaper Syndicates in America, 1860–1900.* New York and Cambridge: Cambridge University Press, 1997.

Kaplan, Amy. "Manifest Domesticity." *American Literature* 70.3 (September 1998): 581–606.

Kaplan, Carla. *The Erotics of Talk.* New York and Oxford: Oxford University Press, 1996.

Kerber, Linda K. "Separate Spheres, Female Worlds, Woman's Place: the Rhetoric of Women's History." *Journal of American History* 75 (June 1988): 9–39.

Kilcup, Karen L., ed. *Nineteenth-Century American Women Writers: an Anthology.* Oxford: Basil Blackwell, 1997.

Porter, Carolyn. "What We Know That We Don't Know: Remapping American Literary Studies." *American Literary History* 6.3 (fall 1994): 467–526.

Radway, Janice. *Reading the Romance: Women, Patriarchy, and Popular Literature.* Chapel Hill: University of North Carolina Press, 1984, 1991.

Romero, Lora. *Home Fronts: Domesticity and its Critics in the Antebellum United States.* Durham: Duke University Press, 1997.

Ryan, Mary. *Women in Public: Between Banners and Ballots, 1825–1880.* Baltimore: Johns Hopkins University Press, 1981.

Samuels, Shirley, ed. *The Culture of Sentiment: Race, Gender and Sentimentality in Nineteenth-Century America.* New York and Oxford: Oxford University Press, 1992.

Sánchez-Eppler, Karen. *Touching Liberty: Abolition, Feminism, and the Politics of the Body.* Berkeley: University of California Press, 1993.

Schlesinger, Arthur, Jr. *The Vital Center: the Politics of Freedom.* Boston: Houghton Mifflin, 1949.

Stansell, Christine. *City of Women: Sex and Class in New York, 1789–1860.* New York: Knopf, 1982; Urbana: University of Illinois Press, 1987.

Tompkins, Jane. *Sensational Designs: the Cultural Work of American Fiction, 1790–1860.* New York and Oxford: Oxford University Press, 1985.

Warhol, Robyn. *Gendered Interventions: Narrative Discourse in the Victorian Novel.* New Brunswick: Rutgers University Press, 1989.

I

HISTORICAL AND
THEORETICAL BACKGROUND

I

ROSEMARIE ZAGARRI

The postcolonial culture of early American women's writing

The decades after the American Revolution witnessed the first great out-pouring of women's published writing in American history. That women expressed themselves through their writing was not a new development. From the earliest days of settlement, as Sharon M. Harris's recent anthology, *American Women Writers to 1800* demonstrates, women composed a vast number of works in a variety of genres. Yet colonial women usually wrote only for a limited audience – for their own satisfaction, for the edification of family members, or for the entertainment of friends in a private social circle. Rarely, and only through exceptional circumstances, did the works of an Anne Bradstreet or a Phillis Wheatley make it into print. What most distinguished the postcolonial culture of women's writing, then, was that substantial numbers of women began to write with the explicit intention of seeking publication for their work.

What effected this change? This chapter explores the transitional period between 1780 and 1830, a time during which women shifted from writing primarily for private audiences to writing for a broader public. One part of the answer lies in the expansion of print culture. While electoral politics continued to exclude women, publication did not. Whereas the "public sphere," as Jürgen Habermas has called it, consisted of males, the "literary public sphere" easily assimilated women.[1] The enormous increase in the number of books, newspapers, and magazines being published created new audiences, including women. The demand for more material called forth the entry of new writers into the field, especially women. Women's perceptions of themselves changed, too: rather than consumers of literature, they began to conceive of themselves as producers, as active agents who had something important to say to a public audience. Women found writing a particularly congenial endeavor, representing an extension of their domestic role rather than a separate and distinct enterprise. Writing for publication greatly expanded the scope of woman's influence. An author who published her works could affect strangers as well as friends, people in all parts of the country, men as well as women. Social strictures forbidding women to speak in public did not apply to print. Women could freely – even anonymously – express their opinions as well as inculcate virtue, reform social evils, and cultivate society's manners. Women could change the world with their words.

American female authorship developed within the larger context of the Anglo-American world. By the early eighteenth century, thinkers on both sides of the Atlantic had begun to challenge the notion of women's inherent intellectual inferiority and to propose that both sexes shared an equal capacity for reason. John Locke, Mary Astell, and others suggested that women's apparent inadequacies resulted more from their failure to receive an adequate education than from any innate deficiency of mind. "Instead of inquiring why all Women are not wise and good," wrote Astell in 1694, "we have reason to wonder that there are any so. Were the Men as much neglected, and as little care taken to cultivate and improve them, perhaps they wou'd be so far from surpassing those whom they now dispise, that they themselseves wou'd sink into the greatest stupidity and brutality." The "Incapacity" of the female mind, "if there be any," she concluded, "is acquired, not natural."[2] A greater appreciation for the female intellect led to calls for improvements in female education. Not only should girls be taught to read, they should be exposed to serious intellectual subjects, such as philosophy and history. While some thinkers doubted feminine abilities, or feared that educated females might become masculine women, others saw the advantages of having educated wives and mothers.

The Anglo-American intellectual climate put a new emphasis on the contributions of women to society. In the late seventeenth and eighteenth centuries, authors began to produce a new genre of works – the earliest histories of women – that celebrated the accomplishments of eminent female historical figures. By the nineteenth century, women such as Mary Hays, Lydia Maria Child, Anna Maria, and Sarah Josepha Hale would dominate the genre; but male writers authored the first women's histories. These volumes recounted a wide range of female accomplishments, including the literary achievements of the ancient poetess Sappho, the political genius of Queen Elizabeth of England, and the intellectual prowess of Laura Bassi, an Italian woman who received a doctorate in philosophy from the University of Bologna. These works raised interesting questions about the relative influence of nature and nurture. One of the most popular of the histories, William Alexander's *History of Women*, first published in Britain in 1779 and reprinted several times in the United States, observed that women continually overcame the disabilities society imposed on them, "often fully compensat[ing] ... for all the disadvantages they are laid under by the law, and by custom."[3] After perusing the works, some readers raised more general questions about women's status and the relations between the sexes. "Why, notwithstanding these [historical examples]," said one New Yorker, "are the ladies condemned to remain in ignorance? It is because the majority of men have an interest in concealing knowledge from them" (*New-York Magazine*, 90). Others drew even more radical conclusions. "The history of women," asserted the "Female Advocate" of Connecticut in 1800, "is forever intruding on our unwilling eyes, bold and ardent spirits, who no tyrant could tame, no prejudice enslave ... FEMALE CITIZENS, follow examples so glorious; accept the station nature intended for you, and double the knowledge and happiness of mankind" (*Female Advocate*, 12). The implication was clear: custom, not nature, limited the scope of women's achievements.

Philosophers of the eighteenth-century Scottish Enlightenment also engaged in a reevaluation of women's role. Devising a four-stage theory of history that took into account the position of women in society, Lord Kames, John Millar, Adam Ferguson, and others traced humanity's development through four eras beginning with the savage phase, which yielded to the pastoral age, which gave way to chivalry, which ultimately led to the modern, commercial era, the pinnacle of civilization and progress. At each stage, women both benefited from change, by receiving better treatment, and contributed to it, by stimulating social development. While men ventured out into the larger world of politics, commerce, and war, women acted to soften men's brutish manners, encourage virtuous behavior, and provide a realm of leisure and refinement, removed from the cares of the world. "The gentle and insinuating manners of the female sex," noted Kames, "tend to soften the roughness of the other sex; and where-ever women are indulged with any degree of freedom, they polish sooner than men."[4] Whereas in previous eras, women had been men's slaves or concubines, in the modern, mercantile stage, women shaped men's morals and manners. They stood as men's social (though not political) equals – their friends and companions. As American readers assimilated this theory, they injected their own republican spin, concluding that society as well as individuals benefited if women were well educated. "Cultivation of the female mind," reflected one commentator, "is of great importance, not only with respect to private happiness only, but with respect to society at large. The ladies have it in their power to form the manners of the gentlemen, and they can render them virtuous and happy, or vicious and miserable" (*Christian, Scholar's*, 497). Ordinary as well as exceptional women thus helped to mold society and make its history.

In America, the coming of the Revolution heightened the public dimension of women's role. The war for independence represented not just a conflict between Britain and America, but a civil war, a contest that split towns, counties, and communities into antagonistic factions. Victory in such a war involved winning the hearts and minds of the people. Patriot leaders were quick to realize that success depended, at least in part, on persuading women to support their side. Utilizing print media in a new way, they appealed to women through poems, essays, and orations, urging them to boycott imported luxury goods, produce homemade fabric and clothing, and, if necessary, sacrifice their husbands, sons, and brothers on the field of battle. Women responded to men's pleas. Women were as heroic in their own sphere as men were in more public arenas. As writers and speakers reflected on women's contributions to the Revolution, they articulated a new understanding of women's role, a concept that historian Linda Kerber has called "republican motherhood." It was now understood that women, though creatures of the domestic realm, had a political role to play. In their capacity as wives and mothers, women influenced the men who would fight the wars, vote for the legislators, and sit in the assemblies; thus, women indirectly helped govern the polity. As a rhetorical construct, the genius of republican motherhood was its "Janus-faced" quality: it looked forward in time by anticipating women's political influence; it also looked backward by affirming the gender status quo. Those who voiced the notion could accentuate women's political contributions and at the same time confirm traditional gender roles.[5]

Republican motherhood linked the private and public realms. In a self-governing republic even more than a monarchy, government depended on the existence of a virtuous, educated, participatory citizenry. Women, it was now understood, shaped the behavior of their husbands and children. They would inculcate patriotism, teach virtue, and encourage self-sacrifice for the public good. Their actions shaped the future of the republic. "Female education," noted an article in a ladies' literary magazine, "is all important to the public welfare. The sons of Columbia who are to command her armies and direct her counsels, receive most of their impressions for the first twelve years of their lives, from the example and instructions of their mothers! What an important bias may be given to the character during that interesting period!"[6]

Recognition of women's political contributions accelerated the expansion of women's educational opportunities, which in turn spurred tremendous increases in female literacy. In the colonial era, the Puritan emphasis on the Bible meant that northern mothers taught their children to read. While over half of all New England females could read, they did not necessarily know how to write. Writing was regarded as a vocational skill, necessary to conduct business or engage in a trade, but not essential for those who would grow up to be wives and mothers. In the South, educational opportunities were extremely limited for both boys and girls. Only the elite received any formal education. These patterns changed after the Revolution. Between 1790 and 1830, almost 400 hundred new "female academies" were founded. In addition to teaching feminine skills such as dancing, embroidery, and musicianship, they also instructed their pupils in history, geography, mathematics, and the natural sciences. Writing – both penmanship and composition – was now taught along with reading. By 1800, 80 to 90 per cent of all New England women could read; nearly half of all southern white women could do so. The percentages grew steadily thereafter. By 1850, women's literacy rate throughout the United States approached that of men.[7]

Literacy transformed women's relationship to print culture. More widespread literacy meant that more women had access to a vast world of ideas. In addition to the Bible and other spiritual readings, women began to devour histories, biographies, travel literature, conduct books, periodicals, newspapers, and novels. Extensive reading had enormous consequences for women's perceptions of themselves and their relation to society. Through reading, as historian Mary Kelley notes, women could find "alternative models of womanhood ... that enabled [them] to resist constraints and to pursue more independent courses of self-definition" ("Reading Women," 404, 406). Their minds need not be bound by domestic life or the ideology that confined them there.

Broader intellectual trends also raised the moral standing of women in society. Older representations of woman as Eve, the temptress and corrupter, were being replaced by the image of a woman on a pedestal, the symbol of purity, piety, and selflessness. In fact, as historian Ruth Bloch has noted, the gendered connotations of the term "virtue" shifted, increasingly referring to women rather than men. Throughout much of the eighteenth century, virtue had been considered a predominantly masculine trait, associated with martial ardor and patriotic vigor. Virtue meant civic virtue, a man's willingness to take up arms to defend the polity, or his sacrifice of his own interests for the common good. By the early nineteenth century, however, various social and intellectual forces, including American Protestantism, Scottish moral philosophy, and literary sentimentalism, transformed virtue into a feminine characteristic – indeed, perhaps the preeminent feminine attribute. Virtue shifted from being primarily a male, political trait to being a nonpolitical feature associated with women. The feminization of virtue accompanied the rise of democracy and capitalism in the United States. Men came to be regarded as profit maximizers and seekers of their own self-interest. Women, on the other hand, came to represent generosity and the ability to sacrifice for the larger public good; they embodied a higher, more pure moral standard – the repositories of virtue in a corrupt world (Bloch, "Gendered Meanings," 52–3).

The feminization of virtue led to a discourse that explained women's relationship to society in terms of their "influence." Because of their ability to shape the morals, manners, and ideas of men, women, it was claimed, should direct their abilities toward reforming society, enlightening its culture, and strengthening its values. Unlike men, women would not use brute force or logical syllogisms to overcome their opponents; they would employ the feminine arts of modesty, emotion, charm, and at times, seduction. Their strategy would be persuasion, not coercion. "The influence of the fair sex gives a bias to the moral conduct of our sex," noted a male writer, "is an axiom that has stood the test of ages. Women, conscious of their natural imbecility to govern men by dint of force, found out a more gentle way of subduing them" (*New-York Weekly*, 22). The stakes were high, not just for individuals, but for the whole country. "Republics," insisted one female founder of a female academy, "have failed when [women] calmly suffered that influence, to become enlisted in favour of luxuries and follies wholly incompatible with the existence of freedom."[8] As the Grimké sisters later proved in their campaign against slavery, moral suasion constituted a powerful weapon for influencing society.

Literature represented a particularly effective way for women to use their influence. An obscure poem, called "Literary Talents of Females," published in 1819 in a minor periodical, summarizes the cultural expectations for women at the time. Written by the pseudonymous "Ella" (perhaps Margaretta Van Wyck Bleecker Faugères), the poem recounts the sad tale of women's intellectual bondage throughout history and expresses the hope that America will offer different possibilities. Women's minds, the author said, had been constricted throughout the past. Even in feudal times, women, while protected or praised, were not able to express their own talents or abilities. Yet women, she claimed, deserved far better; they had "An equal right to culture and to fame,/To share the praise of every mental grace,/That raises and adorns the human race." Ella asked whether her American readers would respond to the challenge and raise women to a new level.

> Are there not some noble spirits still,
> That with the power, possess the generous will
> To advocate the cause of woman's mind,
> And raise it to the height by Heaven design'd –
> A height from which her virtues may dispense
> The most auspicious and diffusive influence?

The answer reflected a growing nationalist pride. In the United States, she believed, "mental gloom, expel'd Columbia's shore,/Shall darken female intellect no more." In this country, "female genius may display its powers" and

> No more imprison'd like fair Chinese feet,
> To keep them down, diminutively neat,

The female mind, its fetters shall escape,
And beauteous rise into the natural shape.

The result would benefit husbands, children, and families by "promoting public, social, [and] private happiness." In the home,

Enlighten'd taste with fond parental care
Shall then illustrate the domestic sphere,
Maternal love shall wake man's infant powers,
As genial spring awakes the nascent flowers.

The cultivation of women's intellect and encouragement of literary pursuits among females would, Ella concluded, bring the entire society to a higher level of social development.[9]

Just as the post-Revolutionary intellectual climate cultivated the ambitions of educated women who might choose to write, so changes in print culture provided women with new opportunities for publication. The number of newspapers in the country doubled during the Revolution, then tripled during the 1790s. Newspapers were cheap and widely available. Print media increasingly sought to appeal to a female audience. Newspapers published articles and poetry addressed to women. Sensing the emergence of a new market, publishers issued books that they believed women would buy, especially novels, women's histories, conduct books, and household companions.[10] Most importantly, the growth of periodicals as a separate genre provided a whole new outlet for women's reading and writing.

Before the Revolution, most colonists imported their magazines from England. Afterward, the number, kind, and quality of periodicals printed in the United States increased exponentially, to serve a public interested in affirming its patriotism, expanding its knowledge, and becoming polite ladies and gentlemen. The ladies' magazine formed a distinct subset of this genre. With Addison and Steele's *Spectator* as a model, American printers began publishing their own periodicals aimed at attracting a female audience. The first magazine to put "lady" in the title was Job Weedon and William Barret's *The Gentleman and Lady's Town and Country Magazine*, published in 1784. In 1792, a Philadelphia printer issued the *Ladies' Magazine and Repository of Entertaining Knowledge*, which was designed to enhance "the province of female excellence alone, with the beams of intellectual light, which illuminates the paths of literature." Even before the appearance of *Godey's Lady's Book* in 1830, more than 100 periodicals specifically geared toward women appeared in the United States. Women actually edited a handful of these publications, including Mary Clarke Carr's *International Regale or Ladies Tea Table* or *The Western Ladies Casket*, printed by "A Lady."

Whoever published them, most women's magazines disappeared after only a few issues. A few, like *The Weekly Visitor or Ladies' Miscellany*, published in New York, survived from 1804 until 1811. The very existence of these periodicals, however, reflected both the growth in the number of female readers and the potential for the growth of female authorship.[11]

Magazines gave American women unparalleled opportunities to become published writers. General interest periodicals as well as ladies' magazines were often desperate for material. Working on a shoestring budget, printers usually could not pay their authors. They filled their pages by borrowing from other publications and asking for voluntary contributions from their readers. Appeals for submissions were often directed to women. In 1827, for example, the editor of *The Ariel and Ladies' Literary Gazette* announced in his inaugural issue that he intended to be "more than commonly attentive ... to the Ladies ... The pages of the *Ariel* will be graced with the literary productions of able writers, and of either sex" (1). As magazines became dependent on women's contributions, women sensed increasing opportunities – and more power. An 1803 piece in a Boston magazine, the *Port Folio*, satirized the pretensions of "literary ladies." In a subsequent issue, an outraged female correspondent rebuked the editor, reminding him of the importance of his female audience. "In a periodical paper," she said, "you must so much depend on women for support both in the reading and writing way, that I am surprised you should there introduce such a satire." Expressing disgust at the article, she asked him, "How could you for a moment lose sight of your own interest, and of the duty you owe to your female correspondents?" Ending with a demand for an apology, she urged the editor to "rejoice at having given an opportunity of literary exertion to the American women" (n.p.). Women knew that without their support, most magazines could not exist. Margaret Beetham's observation about English magazines applies equally well to the American periodicals. "The early magazines ... positioned [women] as members of a reading/writing community rather than simply as consumers ... The magazine was a communal space in which the fair sex felt welcome. It extended the reader's community beyond the domestic circle to which she was increasingly confined" (*Magazine of Her Own?*, 20). Periodicals enhanced women's sense of their own power both as consumers and producers of literature.

Ironically, most women who wrote for magazines did not publish under their own names. Journalistic conventions of this time dictated that most pieces, whether by men or women, be published anonymously or under a pseudonym. It is thus impossible to tell what proportion of the articles women actually wrote. It seems clear, however, that women were frequent contributors. Even when they did not sign their given names, many authors published under a female pseudonym or identified themselves as "A Lady." Anonymity may have actually encouraged women to write for publication. As Amy Beth Aronson points out, "Anonymity protected all contributors from post-publication ridicule, and shielded women particularly from gendered accusations of un-'feminine' expression. The American magazine formally and conventionally suited to both subvert and redress women's silence in the public sphere" ("Understanding Equals," 101). The early periodicals, then, represented an easily accessible and socially sanctioned outlet for women authors.

As significant as new publication opportunities were, most women in the early national period did not regard writing as a career. While it is true that only a few men made a living from their writing, women faced even more obstacles to becoming published authors. The demands on a woman's time were prodigious. Most women had to take care of their children, minister to their husbands, and manage their numerous household duties before they could even consider setting pen to paper. Writing, then, was an avocation, a hobby that women pursued in their spare time. In the 1790s, Mercy Otis Warren realistically assessed women's situation. "Whatever delight we may have in the use of the pen, or however eager we may be in the pursuit of knowledge . . . yet heaven has so ordained the lot of female life that every literary attention, must give place to family avocations, and every page, except the sacred one, must be unfolded, till all matters of oeconomy which belong to her department are promptly adjusted." By the late eighteenth century, however, more women did have time for writing. A growing number lived in towns and cities and did not face the demands imposed by agricultural life. The increasing availability of consumer goods lessened the need for women to make everything from scratch. Middle-class as well as elite women could afford to hire domestic servants to help around the house. Thus a "methodical arrangement of time," as Warren put it, could give a woman the leisure she needed to engage in literary pursuits.[12]

By the early nineteenth century, the convergence of means and opportunity allowed a whole generation of women to begin to write for publication. As they sought their public voices, women experimented with a variety of literary genres. A small number, including Mercy Otis Warren and Judith Sargent Murray, wrote about topical political events of the day. Murray, a staunch Federalist, advocated the ratification of the US Constitution in the 1780s and supported the Federalist Party in the 1790s. Warren had a different political viewpoint. After having written poems and plays in support of the American Revolution, she became disaffected with the course of American politics. Writing under the pseudonym, the "Columbian Patriot," she rejected the proposed US Constitution, pointing out defects

that ranged from an overreliance on central authority, to a tendency to promote aristocracy, to the lack of a bill of rights. Her subsequent work criticized
major political figures such as George Washington and John Adams. In 1805
she published, under her own name, a *History of the American Revolution* that gave a highly politicized account of independence and the early
years of the republic. Rather than a detached rendering of events, she argued that Federalist policies violated the spirit of the Revolution, producing
a pervasive moral decline throughout the country marked by elitism, greed-
iness, and the spread of antidemocratic tendencies. Offended by her perspective, John Adams dismissed Warren's effort, saying, "History is not the
Province of the Ladies."[13] Despite such resistance, Warren was not the only
woman to venture into the masculine realm of politics through her writing.
Hannah Adams (no relation to John) successfully published several histories
of New England. In addition, as Nina Baym has shown in *American Women
Writers and the Work of History*, many other women published works of
fiction, poetry, and drama that contained significant historical content.

As highly politicized as Warren and Murray were, even they did not demand that women receive the same political rights as men. Instead, they
focused their attention on women's intellectual potential and viewed education as the best route to equality. Beginning in 1790 with "On the Equality
of the Sexes," published in the *Massachusetts Magazine*, and then in 1798
in the *Gleaner*, Murray insisted that women's minds "are naturally as susceptible to every improvement, as those of men" (710). Education would
allow women to realize the full capabilities of their intellect; they would be
able to think, write, and converse with the most educated of men. "Such is
my confidence in THE SEX," she proclaimed, "that I expect to see our young
women forming a new era in female history" (703). If women were widowed or economically bereft, education would enable them to find a means
to support their families – and hence gain a measure of independence. Yet
her dreams for women had limits. Denying any desire to "unsex" her colleagues, she admitted that most women would continue to be wives and
mothers. More learning, however, would allow women to "fill with honour
the parts allotted to them" (731; 704). Women would perform their traditional roles to the best of their ability; they would be a credit to their sex.
This universalistic understanding of women's intellectual equality with men
would soon be superseded. As Nina Baym points out, "Whereas early literary
women and their male supporters attributed all differences between male and
female minds to differences in education, Victorian women were attracted
to an idea of innate mental and sexual differences. But these differences,
they believed, made women intellectually, morally, and spiritually superior
to men, and thus better suited than the other sex to conduct the nation's

important cultural work" (*American Women Writers*, 30). As the idea of sameness gave way to difference, women would use this notion to carve out a place for themselves. But difference would also be the means of containing women in a subordinate status.

Whatever the legal constraints they faced, women continued to experiment with other literary genres. In the post-Revolutionary era, the theatre came into vogue in many American cities, including Boston, where it had previously been banned. Theatre companies needed new material. Women helped provide it. Warren and Murray, for example, both wrote plays in addition to nonfiction and poetry. Warren's *The Ladies of Castile* and *The Sack of Rome*, written in the 1780s, featured strong female characters. Although her plays were never performed, they were published as part of Warren's collected works in 1790.[14] Murray's dramatic efforts, such as *The Medium*, *The African*, and *The Traveller Returned*, were performed in Boston and Philadelphia – though none met with great success (Skemp, Murray, 101–3). Susanna Rowson, the novelist, on the other hand, composed one of the most popular – and controversial – plays of the period, a historical drama with satirical bite called *Slaves in Algiers* (Rowson, *Charlotte Temple*, xxv). Her work, performed in Philadelphia, sparked a vituperative exchange with William Cobbett, a reactionary newspaper editor who maligned her feminist sympathies and democratic tendencies. Whether or not women's plays succeeded, their performance sent an important signal about the penetration of women into the literary public sphere.

Women also made inroads in another genre. Poetry, which had long been viewed as an appropriate vehicle for feminine expression, now became specifically identified with women. The explosion of newspapers and periodicals in the post-Revolutionary era gave women many new opportunities to publish their work. Sarah Wentworth Apthorp Morton, who wrote under the pseudonymn "Philenia," published poems in *The Massachusetts Magazine* as well as the *Universal Asylum & Columbian Magazine*. "Ouabi" was an especially haunting tale about nature told through a Native American's perspective. Anna Eliza Schuyler Bleecker recounted her daughter's tragic death while in flight from the British in "Written in the Retreat from BURGOYNE," which appeared in the *New-York Magazine* of March 1790. Some women eventually sought to cement their reputations by publishing books. After years of writing poetry in the *New-York Magazine* under the pen name "Ella," Margaretta Van Wyck Bleecker Faugères, daughter of a wealthy New York family, found a publisher for her and her mother's poetry, which appeared in 1793. Lydia Sigourney, Maria Gowen Brooks, and Sarah Josepha Hale all published significant collections of poetry under their own names before 1830. Yet even when women did not get credit for authorship, they determined the tone, voice, and subject matter of much of the poetry published in periodicals of the day.[15]

The emergence of the novel as a distinct literary genre offered unparalleled possibilities for women. By the mid-eighteenth century, the appearance of English works such as *Pamela* and *Clarissa* signaled the dawn of a new era in fiction-writing. The sentimental novel emphasized individual experience, realistic characters, and personal emotion. Passion and romance – failed, tragic, or grand – figured largely in the plots. Depicting a world inhabited by men and women who lived in recognizable (if extreme) conditions, novels appealed to a wide, popular readership. The genre became, as Cathy Davidson notes, "the single most prevalent cultural form in the nation."[16] In addition to British imports, more than 100 American novels were published before 1820. Women, in particular, read novels with an insatiable zest.

Despite the genre's popularity, many social commentators of both sexes disapproved of novel-reading, especially for women. Novels, it was said, were a waste of time, a useless indulgence that implanted unrealistic ideas about life and about the relation between the sexes. An advice book for women, *The American Lady's Preceptor*, warned against novels for a variety of reasons. "Love," the author noted, is the "superstructure of most novels. But what kind of love is there taught? Not that tender sympathy of two mutual hearts, whose love is founded on reason, prudence, and virtue; but a blind, violent and impetuous passion which hurries its readers unhappy victims into endless woes, teaches children disobedience to parents, [and] inspires them with notions of self-sufficiency" (19). In addition, women's delicate senses might be offended or their morals tainted by the references to illicit sexual matters. Hannah Webster Foster insisted, "Novels are the favourite, and most dangerous kind of reading, now adopted by the generality of young ladies. I say dangerous ... [because they] fill the imagination with ideas which lead to impure desires ... and a fondness for show and dissipation ... They often pervert the judgment, mislead the affections, and blind the understanding" (quoted in Kerber, *Women*, 239). Foster's solution was to take up novel-writing herself, so as to insure that the contents would be morally sound.

American women soon made their mark in the field of novel-writing. As early as 1801, female novelist Tabitha Gilman Tenney claimed that women had taken to fiction-writing with such zeal that "the ladies of late seem to have almost appropriated this department of writing."[17] Susanna Haswell Rowson was the most successful. Her best-selling *Charlotte Temple* (1791) sold nearly 40,000 copies within ten years of its publication. Many female writers began their careers by publishing short fiction in literary periodicals and then, after having gained some experience, went on to write larger works published under their own name. In addition to her plays and political writings, Judith Sargent Murray produced a series of stories about a young woman named Margaretta, collected as part of her *Gleaner* volume (1798). Hannah Webster Foster published two successful novels, *The Coquette; or, The History of Eliza Wharton* (1797) and *The Boarding School* (1798). Although most women wrote in a sentimental vein, some authors, such as Ann Eliza Schuyler Bleecker, wrote historical novels. What began as a trickle in the eighteenth century became a torrent by the nineteenth century, when female authors such as Catharine Maria Sedgwick, Lydia Maria Child, and Harriet Beecher Stowe appeared on the scene.[18]

Strongly didactic in tone, early American novels often spoke explicitly to a female audience. Courtship, in particular, came under scrutiny. Choosing between suitors thrust women into a liminal space, creating a time of maximum freedom and independence, but also the time of peril and hidden danger. Seduction and betrayal threatened at every turn. If a woman should compromise her virtue – meaning her chastity and good reputation – then a bleak future of disgrace and/or spinsterhood awaited her. If she should make a foolish choice of mates, based on appearances rather than character, her married life would be a torment. Many novels urged women to make a judicious choice and avoid the fate of their impetuous heroines. Parents' advice should be heeded. A wise woman, says *Charlotte Temple*, will "listen not to the voice of love, unless sanctioned by paternal approbation ... Resist the impulse of inclination when it runs counter to the precepts of religion and virtue" (29). This message reflected larger social changes in American society. In earlier generations, parents played a key role in selecting a mate, guiding their children to the appropriate choice. By the late eighteenth century, parents exercised less economic control over their children. Children often made up their own minds about whom to marry, without much guidance from parents. Novels stepped into the breech, providing women with savvy advice about the ways of the world and the temptations of would-be seducers. In an unfamiliar world increasingly inhabited by strangers rather than family and friends, novels provided a template for romantic encounters.

As a genre, the novel offered women a new-found sense of agency and control over their lives. While the seduction scenario seemed to portray women as powerless victims, the act of reading was itself empowering. According to Cathy Davidson, "by reading about a female character's good or bad decisions in sexual and marital matters, the early American woman could vicariously enact her own courtship and marriage fantasies. She could, at least in those fantasies, view her life as largely the consequence of her own choices and not merely as the product of the power of others in her life" (*Revolution and the Word*, 123). Novels, then, provided an alternate vision of women's lives. They also sanctioned the idea of women's education and promoted a positive notion of female learning. Most authors explicitly or implicitly condoned the need for greater educational opportunities for women – if for no other reason than to better arm females against threats to their much-vaunted virtue. Novels provided women with the intellectual self-confidence they needed to function in a changed social and political environment.

This changed environment included a host of disturbing and unresolved questions about gender issues. The concept of republican motherhood contained many internal contradictions. Did independence mean greater equality between the sexes and a more egalitarian marriage relationship? If women raised the virtuous male citizens of the republic, why were they denied full citizenship? What were the implications of the American rejection of patriarchy for other patriarchs, especially the father and husband of each family?[19] While the Revolution might be seen as an enhancement of women's political potential, it also could be considered an affirmation of women's traditional domestic roles. Philip Gould points out that republican motherhood should be understood as a fluid discourse rather than a static concept. As a discourse, republican motherhood "was highly contextual, contingent upon immediate purpose, audience, and genre. It could both add radical undertones to naturally conservative voices and constrain naturally radical voices within the limits of republican propriety" (*Covenant and Republic*, 99). Thus, the message was mixed. Depending on the context, republican motherhood could be used to alter or affirm women's traditional role.

Nineteenth-century women used fiction as a means of exploring the internal tensions within the concept of republican motherhood. Fictional characters could say things that real women or men might hesitate to express. In *The Coquette*, for example, Mrs. Richman bluntly asserted her political opinions and defended her right to do so, saying, "We think ourselves interested in the welfare and prosperity of our country, and, consequently, claim the right of inquiring into those [political] affairs, which may conduce to, or interfere with the common weal. We shall not be called to the senate or the field to assert its privileges, and defend its rights, but we shall feel for the honor and safety of our friends and connections, who are thus employed" (44). Novels provided a glimpse of both the restrictions and potentialities of women's role: of women who struggled against their own lack of education and economic opportunity as well as of politicized women who spoke their minds publicly. By imaginatively playing with gender issues, female fiction writers opened the door for future discussions when the larger society was more receptive to change.

The entry of women into the literary public sphere challenged the hegemony of separate spheres ideology. A normative ideal rather than a description of reality, the notion of separate spheres postulated that men inhabited the public world of work, wages, and politics while women inhabited an entirely distinct realm bounded by home and family. Although limited by class and region, the ideology was pervasive in early nineteenth-century literature and had a powerful impact on perceptions of gender roles.[20] Women's reading and writing, however, eroded the rigid distinctions between the sexes and made women fuller participants in public life. Reading women participated in an imagined community that discussed a wide variety of social, political, and moral issues. Women reformers made their views known to a large audience and helped frame the scope of public discourse. Women's fiction and poetry helped elevate the moral and cultural tone of society, providing a more refined and virtuous vision of social interaction. Participation in the literary public sphere made women both the subjects and objects of debate, thus forever altering men's perceptions of women and women's perceptions of themselves.

NOTES

1. Jürgen Habermas, "Further Reflections on the Public Sphere," 421–61; see also Nancy Isenberg, *Sex and Citizenship in Antebellum America*, 55; Nina Baym, *American Women Writers and the Work of History, 1790–1860*, 5–6.
2. Mary Astell, *A Serious Proposal to the Ladies, for the Advancement of their True and Greatest Interest* (1694), 198–9; Melissa Butler, "Early Liberal Roots of Feminism," 148–59; Hilda L. Smith, *Reason's Disciples*, 56–8.
3. William Alexander, *History of Women, from the Earliest Antiquity, to the Present Time*, vol. II, 336; Jacqueline Pearson, *Women's Reading in Britain, 1750–1835*, 49–55.
4. Lord Kames, *Six Sketches on the History of Man* (abridged version), 195; Rosemarie Zagarri, "Morals, Manners, and the Republican Mother," 192–215; Sylvana Tomaselli, "The Enlightenment Debate on Women," 101–24.
5. Linda K. Kerber, *Women of the Republic*, 73–113, 269–88; Linda K. Kerber, "Republican Ideology of the Revolutionary Generation," 484; Mary Beth Norton, *Liberty's Daughters*, 155–94; Betsy Erkkila, "Revolutionary Women," 189–223.
6. *Masonic Miscellany and Ladies' Literary Magazine*, 328; Mary Kelley, " 'Vindicating the Equality of Female Intellect,' " 1–27.
7. E. Jennifer Monaghan, "Literacy Instruction and Gender in Colonial New England," 53–80; David A. Copeland, *Colonial American Newspapers*, 169–71; Richard D. Brown, *Knowledge is Power*, 160–96; William J. Gilmore, *Reading Becomes a Necessity of Life*, 116–21; Catherine Hobbs, ed., *Nineteenth-Century Women Learn to Write*, 101–2; Joel Perlmann and Dennis Shirley, "When Did New England Women Acquire Literacy?," 64; Robert E. Gallman, "Changes in the Level of Literacy in a New Community of Early America,"

574; Julia Cherry Spruill, *Women's Life and Work in the Southern Colonies*, 185–207.

8. Emma Willard, *An Address to the Public Particularly to Members of the Legislature of New York, Proposing a Plan for Improving Female Education*, 29. For a critic's view that depicts women's influence as "a means of devious social control," see Ann Douglas, *Feminization of American Culture*, 8–10, 68–76.

9. *Literary and Musical Magazine*, July 12, 1819 (Philadelphia): 90. For a fascinating example of nineteenth-century women's poetry that subverted conventional expectations about women's role, see Susan S. Lanser, "Toward a Feminist Narratology," 610–29.

10. Donald H. Steward, *Opposition Press of the Federalist Period*, 12–22, 630; Copeland, *Colonial American Newspapers*, 279; Brown, *Knowledge is Power*, 218, 247 n. 1.

11. Mary Clarke Carr, "Preface," *International Regale or Ladies Tea Table*, 1815 (Philadelphia), II: 1, 3; "By a Lady," *Western Ladies Casket* (Connersville, Indiana, 1823); Bertha Monica Stearns, "Before *Godey's*" and "Early Philadelphia Magazines for Ladies," 479–91.

12. Mercy Otis Warren to a very young lady, n.d. and Mercy Otis Warren to Mrs. M. Warren, November 1791, Letterbook, Mercy Otis Warren Papers, Massachusetts Historical Society, 114–15, 486.

13. John Adams to Elbridge Gerry, April 17, 1813, *Warren-Adams Letters*, vol. II, 380; Sheila L. Skemp, *Judith Sargent Murray*, 108–11; Rosemarie Zagarri, *A Woman's Dilemma*, 120–3, 140–8.

14. Baym, *American Women Writers*, 192–6; Zagarri, *Woman's Dilemma*, 134–8.

15. Baym, *American Women Writers*, 67–91; Harris, *American Women Writers*, 325–7, 337–40, 386–7. I would like to thank Paula Bennett for information on Sigourney, Brooks, and Hale as well as other insights into early American women's poetry.

16. Cathy N. Davidson, "Novel as Subversive Activity," 287; Davidson, *Revolution and the Word*, 17, 37.

17. Tabitha Gilman Tenney, "From *Female Quixotism*," 408.

18. Davidson, *Revolution and the Word*, 17, 27; Baym, *American Women Writers*, 186.

19. For exploration of such issues, see Jay Fliegelman, *Prodigals and Pilgrims*; Jan Lewis, "The Republican Wife," 689–721; Rosemarie Zagarri, "The Rights of Man and Woman in Post-Revolutionary America," 203–30.

20. For a summary of the debate on separate spheres ideology, see Linda K. Kerber, "Separate Spheres, Female Worlds, Woman's Place," 9–39.

WORKS CITED

Alexander, William. *History of Women, from the Earliest Antiquity, to the Present Time*. 2 vols. Philadelphia: J. H. Dobelbower, 1796.

The American Lady's Preceptor, 9th edn. Baltimore: Edward J. Coale, 1821.

Ariel & Ladies' Literary Gazette [Philadelphia] (April 14, 1827): 1.

Aronson, Amy Beth. "Understanding Equals: Audience and Articulation in the Early American Woman's Magazine." Ph.D. dissertation, Columbia University, 1996.

Astell, Mary. *A Serious Proposal to the Ladies, for the Advancement of their True and Greatest Interest. 1694. Women in the Eighteenth Century.* Ed. Vivien Jones. London: Routledge, 1990. 198–9.

Baym, Nina. *American Women Writers and the Work of History, 1790–1860.* New Brunswick: Rutgers University Press, 1995.

Beetham, Margaret. *A Magazine of Her Own? Domesticity and Desire in the Woman's Magazine, 1800–1914.* London: Routledge, 1996.

Bloch, Ruth H. "The Gendered Meanings of Virtue in Revolutionary America." *Signs: Journal of Women in Culture and Society* 13.1 (1987): 52–3.

Brown, Richard D. *Knowledge is Power: the Diffusion of Information in Early America, 1700–1865.* New York and Oxford: Oxford University Press, 1989.

Butler, Melissa. "Early Liberal Roots of Feminism: John Locke and the Attack on Patriarchy." *American Political Science Review* 72 (March 1978): 148–59.

"By a Lady." *Western Ladies Casket.* Connersville, Indiana. 1823.

Carr, Mary Clarke. "Preface." *International Regale or Ladies Tea Table.* II. Philadelphia, 1815.

Christian, Scholar's, and Farmer's Magazine [Elizabethtown, NJ] June and July 1789: 497.

Copeland, David A. *Colonial American Newspapers: Character and Content.* Newark: University of Delaware Press, 1997.

Davidson, Cathy N. *Revolution and the Word: the Rise of the Novel in America.* New York and Oxford: Oxford University Press, 1986.

"The Novel as Subversive Activity: Women Reading, Women Writing." *Beyond the American Revolution: Explorations in the History of American Radicalism.* Ed. Alfred F. Young. DeKalb: Northern Illinois University Press, 1993.

Douglas, Ann. *The Feminization of American Culture.* New York: Farrar, Straus, and Giroux, 1977.

Erkkila, Betsy. "Revolutionary Women." *Tulsa Studies in Women's Literature* 6 (fall 1987): 189–223.

Fliegelman, Jay. *Prodigals and Pilgrims: the American Revolution Against Patriarchal Authority, 1750–1800.* New York and Oxford: Oxford University Press, 1982.

Gallman, Robert E. "Changes in the Level of Literacy in a New Community of Early America." *Journal of Economic History* 48 (September 1988): 567–83.

Gilmore, William J. *Reading Becomes a Necessity of Life: Material and Cultural Life in Rural New England, 1780–1835.* Knoxville: University of Tennessee Press, 1989.

Gould, Philip. *Covenant and Republic: Historical Romance and the Politics of Puritanism.* New York and Cambridge: Cambridge University Press, 1996.

Habermas, Jürgen. "Further Reflections on the Public Sphere." *Habermas and the Public Sphere.* Ed. Craig Calhoun. Cambridge, MA: MIT Press, 1994. 421–61.

Harris, Sharon M. ed. *American Women Writers to 1800.* New York and Oxford: Oxford University Press, 1996.

Hobbs, Catherine, ed. *Nineteenth-Century Women Learn to Write.* Charlottesville: University Press of Virginia, 1995.

Isenberg, Nancy. *Sex and Citizenship in Antebellum America.* Chapel Hill: University of North Carolina Press, 1998.

Kames, Lord [Henry Home]. *Six Sketches on the History of Man.* Abridged version. Philadelphia, 1776.

Kelley, Mary. "Reading Women/Women Reading: the Making of Learned Women in Antebellum America." *Journal of American History* 83 (September 1996): 401–24.

"'Vindicating the Equality of Female Intellect': Women and Authority in the Early Republic." *Prospects: An Annual of American Cultural Studies* 17 (1992): 1–27.

Kerber, Linda K. *Women of the Republic: Intellect and Ideology in Revolutionary America.* New York: W. W. Norton, 1980.

"The Republican Ideology of the Revolutionary Generation." *American Quarterly* 37 (fall 1985): 474–96.

"Separate Spheres, Female Worlds, Woman's Place: the Rhetoric of Women's History." *Journal of American History* 75 (June 1988): 9–39.

[A Lady.] *The Female Advocate.* New Haven: Thomas Green and Son, 1801.

Lanser, Susan S. "Toward a Feminist Narratology." *Feminisms.* Ed. Robyn R. Warhol and Diane Price Herndl. New Brunswick: Rutgers University Press, 1997. 610–29.

Lewis, Jan. "The Republican Wife: Virtue and Seduction in the Early Republic." *William and Mary Quarterly* 44 (October 1987): 689–721.

Literary and Musical Magazine [Philadelphia] (July 12, 1819): 90.

Masonic Miscellany and Ladies' Literary Magazine [Lexington, KY] (December 1822): 328.

Monaghan, E. Jennifer. "Literacy Instruction and Gender in Colonial New England." *Reading in America: Literature and Social History.* Ed. Cathy N. Davidson. Baltimore: Johns Hopkins University Press, 1989. 53–80.

Murray, Judith Sargent. *The Gleaner.* 1798. Ed. Nina Baym. Schenectady: Union College Press, 1992.

New-York Magazine; or, Literary Repository (February 1790): 90.

New-York Weekly Magazine (July 15, 1795): 22.

Norton, Mary Beth. *Liberty's Daughters: the Revolutionary Experience of American Women, 1750–1800.* Ithaca: Cornell University Press, 1980.

Pearson, Jacqueline. *Women's Reading in Britain, 1750–1835.* Cambridge: Cambridge University Press, 1999.

Perlmann, Joel and Dennis Shirley. "When Did New England Women Acquire Literacy?" *William and Mary Quarterly* 48 (January 1991): 50–67.

Port Folio [Philadelphia] (March 5 and April 16, 1803).

Rowson, Susanna. *Charlotte Temple.* 1791. Ed. Cathy N. Davidson. New York and Oxford: Oxford University Press, 1986.

Skemp, Sheila L. *Judith Sargent Murray: a Brief Biography with Documents.* Boston: Bedford Books, 1998.

Smith, Hilda L. *Reason's Disciples: Seventeenth-Century English Feminists.* Urbana: University of Illinois Press, 1982.

Spruill, Julia Cherry. *Women's Life and Work in the Southern Colonies.* New York: W. W. Norton, 1938.

Stearns, Bertha Monica. "Before *Godey's.*" *American Literature* 2 (1930): 248–55.

"Early Philadelphia Magazines for Ladies." *Pennsylvania Magazine of History and Biography* 64 (1940): 479–91.

Steward, Donald H. *The Opposition Press of the Federalist Period.* Albany: State University of New York Press, 1969.

Tenney, Tabitha Gilman. "From *Female Quixotism.*" *American Women Writers to 1800.* Ed. Sharon M. Harris. New York and Oxford: Oxford University Press, 1996.

Tomaselli, Sylvana. "The Enlightenment Debate on Women." *History Workshop* 20 (autumn 1985): 101–24.

Warren, Mercy Otis. Letterbook, Mercy Otis Warren Papers, Massachusetts Historical Society (reel 1, microfilm edition): 114–15, 486.

Warren-Adams Letters, Being chiefly a correspondence among John Adams, Samuel Adams, and James Warren. vol. II. Boston: Massachusetts Historical Society, 1917.

Willard, Emma. *An Address to the Public Particularly to Members of the Legislature of New York, Proposing a Plan for Improving Female Education.* Albany: I. W. Clark, 1819.

Zagarri, Rosemarie. *A Woman's Dilemma: Mercy Otis Warren and the American Revolution.* Wheeling: Harlan Davidson, Inc., 1995.

"Morals, Manners, and the Republican Mother." *American Quarterly* 44 (June 1992): 192–215.

"The Rights of Man and Woman in Post-Revolutionary America." *William and Mary Quarterly* 55 (April 1998): 203–30.

2

DANA D. NELSON

Women in public

Introduction: separate spheres

The notion of "the separate spheres" has been used for over a century to endow emerging cultural hierarchies with the obviousness of gender (male/female) opposition: elite literature v. popular literature; high culture v. mass culture; professional and market culture v. domestic culture; business-place competition v. sentimental equality; public sphere rationality v. domestic feeling. These multiple, seemingly rigid definitions for various complementary and/or oppositional practices have long informed our study of nineteenth-century women's literature and the historical contexts that shaped its concerns in the United States.

The logic of difference and even opposition supplied by the notion of "separate spheres" has funded a feminist focus on women's lives, women's politics and women's literature since the 1960s. Reacting to historical and literary models that overwhelmingly deemed women's lives irrelevant to larger historical matters, this newer generation of women academics historicized and theorized a "world of women" that allowed us to appreciate nineteenth-century women's world, their domestic perspectives, their values, and their social and political subversiveness and opposition. Feminist historians returned to one of the most powerful early descriptions of United States democracy, Alexis de Tocqueville's *Democracy in America*, and in particular, his celebration of "The Young [American] Woman as Wife" (1835, 1840). There he describes the domestic sphere of married women as a chosen captivity: "In America, a woman loses her independence forever in the bonds of matrimony. While there is less constraint on girls there than anywhere else, a wife submits to stricter obligations. For the former, her father's house is a home of freedom and pleasure; for the latter, her husband's is almost a cloister" (592). Drawing on this powerful – and in Tocqueville's handling, *celebratory* – image of domestic captivity (and informed by Betty Friedan's powerful counterhistory of middle-class white women's domestic captivity in the 1950s and 1960s, *The Feminine Mystique*), historians and critics began investigating women's histories and writings in the nineteenth century. This massive historical and critical project redescribed middle-class women's so-called "cult of domesticity" as a negative, ideologically enforced captivity. They discovered that the "bonds of womanhood" worked to foster a self-conscious culture and a powerful counterideology of matriarchal resistance, one that revalued women's ways from inside the domestic sphere in which they were cloistered under patriarchy. This counterideology was one that contemporaries, blinkered by the same sexism that had relegated their predecessors *to* a separate sphere, had been unable to recognize and had therefore underestimated and devalued. Focusing on domestic literature – like Susan Warner's 1850 blockbuster novel *Wide, Wide World* – and culture – read through such historical records as *Godey's Ladies Book* – these new feminist scholars studied the so-called trivia of women's lives and their "formulaic" plots, finding evidence of women's complicated and sophisticated accommodations, resistances, and political agendas. This work continues to reward us with an increasingly detailed and complicated picture of women's lives and works in the private and public spheres of the nineteenth-century United States.

Additional details for that picture emerged as scholars became dissatisfied with an exclusive focus on white middle-class women. Recognizing that studying the domestic sphere as described by its middle-class inhabitants and proponents meant ignoring working-class white women and black women of the slave and free classes, many turned their attention toward the lives and writings of women "unprotected" by and largely at the margins of the so-called domestic sphere. This new layer of historical and literary recovery complicated the picture of the "woman's sphere." It enriched our understanding of women's cultures. It also challenged scholars to rethink the dimensions of white middle-class women's victimization by patriarchy, and especially to attend to how they participated in (and sometimes resisted) the victimization of fellow women in less privileged classes. Following Carroll Smith-Rosenberg's landmark theory about a "female world," this new picture of a world of women – now imagined as female worlds – was both more dimensional and more politically freighted. Now, for instance, scholars began to appreciate women like the former slave and antislavery activist author Harriet Jacobs sounding off against the exclusionary practices of middle-class women's sympathy when she offered a powerful critique of the white bourgeois "logic" of domesticity: "Reader, my story ends with freedom; not in the usual way, with marriage." Increasingly there was room to consider how women did not always identify their common interests with other women and so to study the conditions under which women could historically unite for common causes; it curbed what Ellen DuBois described in 1980 as the tendency to romanticize what women's culture did for women (31).

Sporadically throughout the feminist recovery efforts that began in the 1960s, and recently with gathering momentum, the very notion of "separate spheres" has been questioned, not just for the way it oversimplifies our understanding of literary and cultural practices as inevitably breaking down into categories of "male" and "female," but also for the way its descriptive weight overshadows texts, customs, and manners that do not reflect such clean divisions. For example, though scholars like Lucy Freibert and Barbara White, along with Cathy Davidson, gave the lie to the notion that only *women* authored sentimental fictions in the mid-eighties, it has only been most recently that any sustained treatment of male sentimentalism has been published (see Chapman and Hendler, *Sentimental Men*). Feminist critics who study sentiment have not yet spent much time studying men's sentimentalism seriously, in what we are only now beginning to recognize as its many, and arguably central, cultural manifestations – in, for instance, bachelorhood, fraternal organization and practices of patriotism.

In the last twenty years, the referents for the "spheres" have especially referred to slightly different things, depending on the orientation of the scholar using the term. Literary historians and mainstream critics have habitually used the term, following Hawthorne's famous complaint about a "damned mob of scribbling women," to refer to a divergence in the path of literary production. One fork of the path leads to "popular" or "mass literature" of sentimental, sensational, and domestic dramas, which these critics implicitly or explicitly associate with women. The other leads to elite or "literary" literature. This is the literature that rewards careful study with complexity of message and artistic design and has most often been connected with male authorship. Feminist historians and literary critics have tended, following de Tocqueville, to use the term to describe social worlds circumscribed by gender, and specifically, to a woman's domestic "world" that exists in isolation from the work-a-day business world occupied by men. Most recently, and somewhat differently, political and cultural theorists have deployed the notion of spheres, following German Frankfurt School philosopher Jürgen Habermas, to refer to a developing bourgeois political rationality, a "sphere" that developed through the medium of newspapers and print culture, one that enabled large, imagined public communities to develop through an ideal of abstracted and disinterested political critique. This sphere exists in contrast to an embodied, local investment in a private, domestic sphere, as well as to the interested sphere of marketplace competition. It was in this civic, public sphere that republicanism flourished and that revolutionary idealism took fire.

The different uses of this terminology do not, of course, invalidate its applications. But it surely indicates that readers should be careful to understand the terms of its applications when they encounter it in a critical text. Only recently, as the notion of "separate spheres" becomes more consciously problematic, have these various applications come into fruitful dialogue. For instance, as scholars have investigated the eighteenth-century emergence of the civil public sphere in the British colonies, they have discovered women assuming a public voice and public role in its early manifestations, in newspaper publications, *belles-lettres* and tearooms and salons (see for instance the work of David Shields, Carla Mulford, and Fredrika Teute). Beginning to consider the public (and not just the private) sphere as a more complicated space has allowed historians and cultural critics more carefully to appreciate the ambiguous realms of publicity that women could unofficially inhabit in social and voluntary (religious, philanthropic) organizations.

The remainder of this chapter provides a more detailed background for theoretical developments in the idea of "separate sphere" as it is relevant to contemporary literary study. Beginning with a short overview of critical attitudes toward women's writings in the early to mid-twentieth century, it outlines major trends and significant voices in the revisionist historical and literary responses of the 1960s, 1970s and 1980s, and the race-/class-informed corrective that emerged in the 1980s and 1990s. It traces developing scholarship in political and gender theory in the 1990s, and then summarizes emerging directions in the field.

Antebellum women's literature and early critics

Women's writing has always been widely read outside of academia and periodically studied as long as United States literature has been organized as a discipline in academia – since the late 1800s. As recently as the 1940s, nineteenth-century women writers were examined as central contributors to the US literary map. In fact, in 1940, two major books on nineteenth-century US literature paid close attention to women writers: Herbert Ross Brown's *The Sentimental Novel in America* and Fred Lewis Pattee's *The Feminine Fifties*. Brown focused on a novelistic subgenre, the "sentimental" novel, and traced the developing trajectory of sentimental fiction's growing female authorship with its (supposedly) intended female readership. For Brown, this relation followed the logic of the separate spheres; for instance, in outlining the supposedly natural attraction of women writers in the early nation to this genre, Brown postulates that the "atmosphere of the novel of domestic manners and morals ... was one in which the genteel female felt thoroughly at home; she might attempt it without unduly extending her 'proper sphere'" (102). For Brown, separate spheres is a commonplace, a universal fact: "every schoolboy still knows," he asserts, that "woman's place ... is the home" (101). Guided by this cliché, Brown selects passages from women writers that elaborate on the absolute gender difference that seems to confirm almost hermetically separate social worlds for the two sexes. Thus Brown, who has read extensively in women's literature (and in fact scholars today can still usefully consult his text both for its critical summaries and as a bibliographical source), pays no critical notice to a novel like E. D. E. N. Southworth's *The Hidden Hand*, a novel about a cross-dressing orphaned girl who rescues girls in distress and challenges men to duals to defend her honor. Southworth's novel challenged "separate spheres" culture in its own day and remains invisible inside Brown's taken for granted paradigm.

His "separate spheres" logic ultimately guides Brown to conclude that women's literary productions were wholly irrelevant to "more serious" literature of the period. By "more serious" he means more historically and socially relevant. Brown concludes that women's writing, with its orientation toward "pity" and "social conscience," had a "socialistic" orientation that was ultimately irrelevant to the (manful) reality of the capitalist workplace (142). But Fred Lewis Pattee, guided by Hawthorne's anguished complaint about his inability to compete with women writers in that workplace, posits those same women writers as taking over, if not an era, at least a decade. Even as Pattee castigated the decade of the American literary Renaissance – the 1850s – as "feminine" (a judgment that accumulated from his consonant descriptors: "fervent, fevered, furious, fatuous, fertile, feeling, florid, furbelowed, fighting and funny" and was summarized by Thoreau's "startling verdict" on Whitman's 1855 edition of *Leaves of Grass*: "I find reality and beauty, mixed with not a little violence and coarseness – both of which are to me effeminate" [3; 11]), he studied the productions of women with a certain degree of seriousness. He read their literature and their magazines, while he weighed the political rallying for suffrage rights in the 1850s carefully and sympathetically enough to offer another description of the decade: the decade of "Women's Rights." Though he demonstrates broad familiarity with white middle-class women's literature through the end of the century, he critically relegates most of their work to what he calls "the great mass of feminine fiction," implicitly deeming it beneath further careful study (115). This is, indeed, the pattern by which Pattee studies women's writing, becoming expert only subtly to condemn it to critical irrelevance. For instance, Pattee emphasizes that Hawthorne's famous letter to William Ticknor about the "d—d mob of scribbling women"[1] was followed shortly by a letter praising the literary talent of Fanny Fern (Sara Payson Willis Parton; see Pattee, *Feminine Fifties*, 110–11).[2] But within pages, Pattee offsets Hawthorne's praise for her work by describing Fern's most famous compilation of her newspaper columns, *Fern Leaves from Fanny's Portfolio*, as "only the beginning of the incredible vacuum in the history of American letters that we call 'Fanny Fern.'" Here he attacks Fern for precisely the aspect of her writing Hawthorne admired, accusing her of washing "a great deal of family linen in public," or, in effect, violating the protocol of the "separate spheres" by bringing the private affairs of family domesticity into the public sphere of the print market (118–20). Curiously, this division seemed less sacred for Hawthorne himself: it was precisely her willingness to violate boundaries that he found so compelling.

Against the critical trend of considering literary production broadly in its historical context, a practice that meant critics read women's and men's literature from any given period, F. O. Matthiessen's magisterial New Critical approach to nineteenth-century literature, *American Renaissance* (1941), would definitively orient critical interest away from nineteenth-century women's writing for the next twenty-some years. Focusing narrowly on five northeastern writers – Emerson, Thoreau, Hawthorne, Melville, and Whitman – Matthiessen mentions Dickinson on three pages out of more than 600, Stowe on one; though he mentions that *Fern Leaves from Fanny's Portfolio* sold 100,000 copies in its first year (x), he identifies her only as the "sister of N. P. Willis." Dismissing in a quick half-paragraph the best-selling works of Maria Cummins, Susan Warner, and E. D. E. N. Southworth, Matthiessen concludes, "But I agree with Thoreau: 'Read the best books first, or you may not have a chance to read them at all'" (xi). The most notable effect of his approach was to delineate a separate literary sphere not so much for *women*, but for (select) male writers, a rarified sphere where we could witness the production not of "fiction" but of *art*. In subsequent years, women writers like Emily Dickinson – who refused to publish her poetry – might become honorary members of this sphere, but the "mass" of "scribbling women" became literally invisible, except as a caricature against which to balance the underappreciated artistic productions of elite writers. (It is also true that the strong association of gender with domestic, sensational, and sentimental fiction had the effect of making many male writers invisible from critical consideration.)

Matthiessen's masculinist aesthetic paradigm was to have an enormous impact on US literary studies. Though Alexander Cowie still devoted entire chapters to women's contributions to the "rise of the American novel" in his major study of nineteenth-century writers in 1948, by the early 1950s,

nineteenth-century women writers became a subject apart, marked by separate spheres logic for a near-total banishment from critical study. Influential
works published by the likes of Richard Chase, R. W. B. Lewis, and Leslie
Fiedler either ignored or treated women writers only to reaffirm their "sentimental" opposition to manliness and a masculine literary tradition. When
women were studied, they were discussed as part of an entirely separate
tradition, as in, for instance, Helen Waite Papashvily's *All the Happy Endings: a Study of the Domestic Novel in America, the Women Who Wrote It,
the Women Who Read It, in the Nineteenth Century* (1956). Conceived in
the strict "separation" tradition (assuming that only women readers might
conceivably encounter women writers), Papashvily's eclectic study, a rollick-
ing, conspiratorial survey of the protofeminist and male-bashing impulses of
nineteenth-century domestic fiction, paints a world of middle-class women,
proceeds as though women's fiction has *never* been critically studied, and
only receives continued attention from women ("Now these sentimental
tales and their authors are almost, if not quite, forgotten by a new generation of readers; accorded only the briefest mention by literary historians,
banished from library shelves ... Yet a surprising number of people, princi-
pally women, still read and enjoy these relics of another world" [xiv; 210]).
Rebuking male predecessors like Vernon Parrington for dismissing women's
writing as so much "cambric tea" (see p. xvii), Papashvily herself treats it as
a kind of foxglove (a heart stimulant that in strong doses is poisonous) tea, a
formula for feminine revenge, where women's novels, far from reflecting ton-
ics for feminine submission, "reflected and encouraged a pattern of behavior
so quietly ruthless, so subtly vicious that by comparison the ladies at Seneca
[Falls Women's Rights Convention of 1848] appear angels of innocence"
(xvii).

Whether studying women writers as part of a broader United States literary
tradition or as members of an all-women's club, these treatments share basic
assumptions about these writers' emotional excess and manipulativeness,
that women only wrote for a female audience, and that writers and readers
alike were either committed to or "most at home" *in* the home, the domestic
sphere.

Historical resuscitation

Within a decade, feminist historians would begin laying the groundwork
for an explosion of interest in and a major rethinking of women's lives and
writings in the early United States. Barbara Welter and Aileen S. Kraditor introduced two new and lasting paradigms to describe women's culture: "the
cult of true womanhood" and the "cult of domesticity" in germinal late

1960s publications. A new understanding of women's history began developing, shaped once again by the metaphors of disconnection and difference. But this time, there was a sharp emphasis on the way the logic of separate spheres entailed a hierarchy oppressive for women. Elaborating on the emergence of the newly labeled "cult of domesticity," Nancy Cott's *Bonds of Womanhood* (1977) drew its metaphor of slave bondage in describing white middle-class women's culture from the writing of antislavery and feminist activist, Sarah M. Grimké, who left her South Carolina home in the 1830s with her sister, Angelina Grimké Weld, to work against slavery outside the South. This parallel between enslavement and the "cult of domesticity" or "true womanhood" marks the place where historian Cott sees an emerging feminist consciousness in the United States. According to Cott, the social enforcement of separate spheres created a group awareness that resisted the ascription of women's "inferiority" and replaced it with a notion of particularity and "difference." The space of the domestic was claimed as the place for cultivating feminine difference. This space was the "precondition" (*Bonds of Womanhood*, 201) for the organization of modern feminism but it was also a significant barrier: even as it prescribed the "home" as women's only vocation, it made it substantially harder for women to conceptualize, accept, or participate in an organized, public, political resistance.

Carroll Smith-Rosenberg had presaged Cott's analysis with her formative 1975 *Signs* essay, "The Female World of Love and Ritual: Relations Between Women in Nineteenth-Century America." There, drawing on her reading of thousands of nineteenth-century women's letters and diaries, Smith-Rosenberg depicted an emotional life where relations with other women were primary, and where "men made but a shadowy appearance" (1). She argued that a notion of "female friendship" could never encapsulate the nexus of women's relationships that "ranged from the supportive love of sisters, through the enthusiasms of adolescent girls, to sensual avowals of love by mature women," insisting that women were born into a female world. This world was one that was "closed" – women only – and "intimate" – experienced primarily with women. This was a world in which emotional, and not political concerns were tantamount, and where women did not experience their values and concerns as being subordinated or in tension with those of the public sphere. It was a world "relatively homogeneous and segregated" by gender, where heterosexual marriage was like an encounter with an "alien group" (28), and where any perceived contradictions between genders were absorbed into the rich and sustaining satisfaction of relations with other women.

Then historians Linda K. Kerber and Mary Beth Norton returned to the Revolutionary era, examining how this turbulent, productive period opened up newly politicized spaces for women's involvement in the rebellion against England and the consolidation of nation. Norton showed that though men continued in assuming that "war was theirs to make," it was also true that "war itself did speed the integration of women into the civil polity" (*Liberty's Daughters*, 8). Coining the term "Republican Motherhood" to describe an emerging political ideology for women that referenced the "public" while claiming the "private" as its sphere of virtue, action, and power, Norton and Kerber showed how women claimed a substantial *public* role through their *domestic* guardianship and cultivation of civic virtue. This model reconceived the notion that middle-class women, in all their morally pure passivity, "influenced" men's political decisions, and replaced it with a model that highlighted women's political initiative and responsibilities within the private sphere.

Thus these historians demonstrated that the precondition for the intensification of women's *domesticity* was in part a new public and *political* role for them in the United States. Mary Ryan's *Empire of the Mother* (1982) traced the progress of domesticity into its fuller antebellum articulation. Here Ryan cautioned against an overreliance on the notion that the domestic sphere was a "female world," noting that "even if the nineteenth-century home was infused with feminine values ... its fundamental structure was woven of heterosexual and heterosocial relationship." Ryan's interest in domesticity was less in tracing individual women's experiences than it was to "study the female side of one of the most significant and pervasive structures, the gender system" (8). Specifically, Ryan traces how women are enlisted as mothers whose primary job becomes the production of children who live by middle-class values. Women developed this role into a mandate with implications that reached well beyond the private sphere, a mandate that Ryan describes as a "moral empire" which is only *centered* in the home. Women's role in socializing boys and girls and their adult husbands became a mandate for their assuming a supervisory capacity with regard to social, political, and economic questions in the so-called "public sphere."

Historians were always noting contradictions, the parts of the historical record that did not confirm the ubiquity of separate spheres logic. For instance, Gerda Lerner early warned against overinterpreting middle-class white women's oppression as passive victimization (1980). In a forum on "Politics and Culture in Women's History" in 1980, Ellen DuBois presented another early critique of the emerging tendency to take language about the separateness of the spheres at "face value" (and targeting Smith-Rosenberg specifically), arguing that such work risked depoliticizing women's lives and experiences. Developing those cautions, Francis Cogan isolated and described a strongly articulated cultural alternative to True Womanhood (the teary, submissive "angel of the house"): "Real Womanhood" – one scholars had been unable to recognize because of the way the absolutism of the separate spheres blinded them. In this 1989 study, Cogan asks: "How could vast numbers of American middle-class women have clutched to their healthy bosoms an ideal of the 'submissive maiden' when that ideal was physically injurious, economically unworkable, legally contraindicated for survival within the restraints of marriage, and intellectually vacuous?" (*All-American Girl*, 3–4). Her answer? Many formulated a competing ideal, along with a competing notion of woman's sphere, where women were "biologically equal (rationally as well as emotionally)." Real Womanhood advocated self-cultivation, education, and even regular, strenuous, physical exercise, where it was women's job to maintain their health (and sometimes out-of-home employment) not just for their own sake, but also for the sake of their families. According to Cogan, it was Real Womanhood's ideal of domestic "service," however, that kept feminist historians from paying any attention to this distinctive ideology, for the way it seemingly collapsed back into True Womanhood's notion of passive self-sacrifice. But Real Womanhood helped, for instance, make sense of fictional characters like Southworth's athletic heroine Capitola who refused to stay in her room and took off daily for adventures on horseback and on foot, and in pants whenever she could!

Other historians began questioning the political and historiographical implications of focusing only on middle-class women. Christine Stansell's important study of working-class women in New York City, *City of Women*, not only elucidated the very different ideals of womanhood that guided "other" white women in urban areas, but also examined the coercive, unsisterly practices of middle-class women's philanthropy, helping to call into question the notion that "woman's sphere" functioned to consolidate women's political solidarity. At the same time scholars like Deborah Gray White and Elizabeth Fox-Genovese developed studies questioning the practice of metaphorically connecting the "bonds" of (white middle-class) womanhood to slave culture. Fox-Genovese's *Within the Plantation Household* argued that slavery did not develop sympathy between black and white women in the Old South. On the contrary, though the "domination of the master weighed on slaveholding and slave women alike," it did so with "very different consequences." Most important, Fox-Genovese argued, slaveholding women almost never saw themselves as being in a "common" relation with slave women; rather, they most frequently saw them as chattel, as sexual competition, as psychological outlets for their own sense of entrapment and frustration. Whatever the opposition to white men's power that may have developed in the slave South, it had almost nothing to do with "feminism in the Northeast" and nothing to do with abolition (*Within the Plantation Household*, 30).

Early investigation of "the cult of domesticity" was guided by the analogy between women's private sphere and the imprisonment of slavery. It argued that women's consciousness moved toward feminism as the result of a recognition of a common bondage, a common oppression, and indeed, part of the proof for the rightness of the analogy was supplied from the fact that middle-class women's involvement in antislavery protest grew from their conscious apprehension of that political analogy. But this analogy came under heavier scrutiny as historians began paying more attention to southern history in general and to African American women's history in particular.

Early historiography described the domestic sphere as preserving "traditional," older values about production and familial socialization as opposed to the rationalist, instrumentalist, modernizing bent of the marketplace. The assumption that the domestic sphere was like an underdeveloped nation, a relic of an older economic and political order, came to be questioned, though, as historians began developing analyses of working-class women's culture. These analyses helped reveal domesticity in many important respects as a counterpart to the modern marketplace, not its opposite or even a haven from it.

Literary sentimentality and the separate spheres

Drawing on the explosion of separate spheres scholarship among historians, Americanist feminist literary critics entered discussions about nineteenth-century women's culture(s) in the mid-seventies. Their most important historical referent was not Tocqueville's comments about domestic life, but Nathaniel Hawthorne's comments about women's literary productions. As Lucy Freibert and Barbara White observed in their landmark anthology of women's writings, *Hidden Hands* (titled after the popular mid-century novel *The Hidden Hand* by E. D. E. N. Southworth), "Nathaniel Hawthorne's complaint to his publisher about the 'damned mob of scribbling women' is the best-known critical statement about early American women writers" (355). By the mid-seventies, nineteenth-century women's writing was understood – despite and indeed *because* of its popular success – through Hawthorne's dismissive lens: no analysis required. Henry Nash Smith's 1974 essay on "The Scribbling Women and the Cosmic Success Story" characterized all women novelists on the basis of his reading of two of them: Susan Warner's *Wide, Wide World*, and Maria Cummin's *The Lamplighter*. Here he substitutes quotation (because "this material is quite obscure . . . I shall quote at considerable length to give the reader a sense of what it is like" [51]) for analysis, following long block quotations with such quick summary critical conclusions as "[T]he vulgarity of this passage is likely to blind the reader to historical forces that are at work in Maria Cummins's prose." The "historical forces" that Smith elucidates are those that contribute to what he describes as "the cosmic success story," where the heroine learns the personal value of and ultimate social and heavenly reward for "unquestioning conformity with received principles" (55). Women writers, and the men who supported their efforts and shared their worldview (like minister, theologian, and writer Henry Ward Beecher, and, to a somewhat lesser extent, literary figures like William Dean Howells) remained, in Smith's argument, ignorantly bound by "conventional assumptions" and "residual class consciousness" that could result only in "quaint" local color literature. Indeed, by Smith's argument, it would take Henry James the first ten years of his publishing career to free himself of the apron strings of the feminized culture of writing created by these "scribbling women!"

In *The Feminization of American Culture*, Ann Douglas confirmed and extended both Herbert Ross Brown's assertion and Smith's clear assumption that the mid-nineteenth-century literary marketplace was "dominated" by women (281). She provided an account of a debilitating cultural feminization that accompanied the "transformation of the American economy into the most powerfully aggressive capitalist system in the world" (6). In Douglas's argument, nineteenth-century American culture offset its nervousness about the developing centrality of craven and competitive economic ideals with "a perpetual Mother's day": a process of "sentimentalization" where women learned to "exploit" their emotional influence on men's public culture, with particularly wide-reaching and harmful effect in the domains of mass literature and religion. With analytic nostalgia, Douglas's book harked back to a more muscularly intellectual Calvinist theocracy, which she counterposed against a subsequent emotional culture of female writers and mass-consumers. She describes these women simultaneously as the victims and agents of a feeble but ubiquitous sentimental anti-intellectualism. Complaining that one of the faults of sentimentalism is that it did not lead to the articulation of the kind of "matriarchal values" that could actually have empowered women in the public sphere, Douglas explains the appeal of sentimentalism in the way that it promised a compensatory social power to the "cruel ... sexual stereotyping" of nineteenth-century culture. In this respect, she insists, women's seizure of sentiment "is hardly altogether their fault." But to back off from blaming women for their promulgation of sentiment in all its self-evading dishonesty would be "only to perpetuate the sentimental heresy" that Douglas framed her book to critique: to fight sentimentalism one *must* hold women accountable for the alleged sentimental diminishment of American culture in order to ascertain one's own critical distance from sentimentalism (11).

Smith, Douglas, and their predecessors provided clear examples of what Nina Baym would soon describe in an influential article as "melodramas of beset manhood": a critical faith that the best American literature establishes a central plot, where a man finds, articulates, and tests his individualism as he escapes the "encroaching, constricting, destroying" society of women ("Melodramas of Beset Manhood," 133). Baym highlighted this as a melodrama played out in criticism perhaps more than in primary texts themselves: where women are found to create stories that "conform to the expected myth," it is only (a few good) men who have the equipment necessary to effect their heroic escape from mass-cultural imperatives to conformity. As she argues, this critical myth of self-fathered artistic merit "imposes on artistic creation all the gender-based restrictions" entailed in the logic of separate spheres. It was, as she compellingly demonstrated, a critical cul-de-sac more than an accurate description of United States history or a full description of its literature, for both male and female critics.

Feminist literary critics had already begun the work of cutting through this mirage-terminus by reexamining both the local colorists and the blockbuster best-sellers. What they were finding in that study created not just a new picture of American women's writing, but new pictures and metaphors. Feminist scholars were not only reexamining women's writing, but were also making it newly available. By the mid-eighties there was a literal explosion of reprints. Susan Koppelman began publishing anthologies of women's short fiction in 1983. Judith Fetterley published an anthology of local color writers, *Provisions*, in 1985, followed soon by her coedited Norton anthology of American women regionalists, with Marjorie Pryse, in 1992. The Rutgers American Women Writers reprint series was inaugurated in 1986, and in short order had reprinted a range of novels, from frontier literature to the blockbuster best-selling novels that had been dismissed by Smith, to anti-sentimentalist novels like Southworth's *Hidden Hand*. The Schomburg Library Reprint Series of African-American Woman Writers began its 25-volume project. Henry Louis Gates presented a reprint of the first novel to be published by an African-American woman, Harriet Wilson's *Our Nig*. Oxford University Press began a reprint series of early women's novels in the early 1990s, and there were specialty series at myriad other presses.

This wave of reprints was accompanied by book-length studies of women's fiction. Josephine Donovan's study, *New England Local Color Literature*, was published in 1983, shortly followed by Annette Kolodny's provocative sequel to her landmark *Lay of the Land* (1975), a reading of women's frontier literature, *The Land Before Her* in 1984. Jean Fagin Yellin had begun presenting the results of her project to authenticate and create an authoritative edition of Harriet Ann Jacobs's pseudonymous slave narrative, *Incidents in the Life of a Slave Girl.* Carolyn Karcher was researching her monumental biography of Lydia Maria Child (1994), and publishing a series of articles on Child's individual works. In 1990, Susan Harris published her influential critical overview of nineteenth-century women's novels.

This proliferation of recovery and criticism reestablished the importance of women's literature to the developing trajectory of not just United States literary but also cultural history. Much early study confirmed feminist historiography's emphasis on the distinct social experiences and perspectives of women. For instance, Baym's 1978 reexamination of women's domestic fiction, blockbusters and otherwise, found much to confirm the assessments of Brown, Pattee, Smith, and Douglas – but provided a much more sophisticated framework for understanding. In *Woman's Fiction* she described a novelistic "overplot" – the "story of a young girl who is deprived of the supports she had rightly or wrongly depended on to sustain her throughout life and is faced with the necessity of winning her own way in the world." This is a story women write for other women, and indeed, it is through the "great vogue" of this fiction that women gained both literacy and a claim on the nineteenth-century literary marketplace. In this mode, individual authors are only distinct from one another "by the plot elements they select from the common repertory and by varieties of setting and incident with which they embellish the basic tale" (13). It is a story of women's self-education; it is "about the psychology of women" and informed by a basic "nonandrogynous certainty that men and women were essentially different" (19). These novels helped women find their own worth and self-respect in a world that, Baym insisted, opposed a mercenary world that was "neither affectional nor domestic" (20). Arguing that the term "domestic sentimentalism" overemphasized a "presumed ambience" for the novels that led critics to misunderstand these works even when they read them, Baym insisted that their domestic setting was not a form of idealism but an analysis of "social relations, generally set in homes and other social spaces" and described this mode as "simply realistic" (26). Calling attention to the misery that pervades the domestic setting in these novels, Baym outlines the way these novels counterpose a domestic morality that would transform unhappy homes into happy ones. This project converted the home into a political sphere: "to the extent that woman dominated the home, the ideology implied an unprecedented historical expansion of her influence" (27).

Reimagining the domestic sphere as a consciously political one did not lead immediately to a breakdown of the notion that men's and women's worlds were "separate" and that for middle-class white women, at least, the domestic world (however politicized) was essentially "private." Historian Mary Kelley followed Baym's plot analysis with a detailed study of what professional authorship meant for these politically domestic women writers. In Kelley's view, women's authorship entailed a painful, "inadvertent" entry into the public sphere. Profiling the careers of twelve of the most prominent women writers of the era, Kelley insisted their perspectives were uniformly "private and familial," focused not on heroic actions or public concerns but on the "quotidian of nineteenth-century women" (*Private Woman, Public Stage*, ix). Following Ann Douglas's suggestion that women's writing emerged in the "'ascendancy of commercialism over culture'" (11), Kelley emphasized the contradictions that emerged for the "literary domestics" as they emerged from the "shade" of the domestic into the "sunny place" of their incredible successes in the marketplace. The result was that these women were emotionally "torn" in ways that showed in their writing and – too often – wore on their health: "Anomalies in a man's world, they found that their ability to appreciate themselves in the public sphere was hampered by their ambiguous regard of themselves in the woman's private sphere" (xi). But soon Susan Coultrap-McQuin's study, *Doing Literary Business* (1990), offered a very different picture, arguing that women were *not* alienated by the market aspects of their business, and indeed readily found ways to exploit their simultaneous insider/outsider status in the public sphere.

In literary as in historical studies, examination of the Revolutionary era also suggested some problems with describing the "separate" spheres through categories of gender. Cathy N. Davidson's path-breaking *Revolution and the Word* (1986) paid substantial attention to women and particularly to assumptions that women formed the primary readership of sentimental and domestic novels as part of its analysis of the emerging form of the novel in the early United States. Davidson did not stop at reading early novels and analyzing their plots. She tried to figure out – from subscription lists, letters, diaries, and from the marginalia on extant novels themselves – *who* actually was reading early novels. In framing her carefully historicized account of the way the novel carried on the radicalizing, democratic energies of the American Revolution, Davidson made a startling discovery: men were avid readers of "women's fiction." They received these novels as gifts from sisters and sweethearts; they bought them for themselves. They felt passionately enough about these novels to fight about their ownership with family members, and even to identify with the heroines! Davidson's study not only debunked the "common-sense" notion that women's fiction was a social invention "by and for women," but it also insisted that, like other early novelistic forms, sentimental/domestic novels "played a vital role in the early education of readers previously largely excluded from elite literature and culture." Emphasizing the political aims of these early novels, Davidson questioned the idea that these works were produced simply as "consumable plots" – fluffy stories for leisurely diversion (79).

Davidson had traced the way that the genre ubiquitously associated with women had been written and read by men and women in the early nation. Freibert and White's important anthology, *Hidden Hands*, seconded that argument for mid-century and recounted a story in which one of the editors read a quintessentially sentimental passage from a mid-century novel and made her conference audience play "guess the author": "the guesses were reasonable enough – Susan Warner, Fanny Fern – but the passage [was] from *The Inebriate*, a temperance novel by Walt Whitman." Observing that Whitman had been *proud* of that novel, and had reprinted a passage of it as the story "Little Jane," the editors insisted on the changeable standards by which audiences and critics have judged literary value, highlighting the critical double bind to which women writers had for so long been subjected. Critics could dismiss women's writing for "just making it up" or "just telling the truth" – either way, there was no authorial vision, no writerly craft involved, and critics could tautologically assume that women's fiction was nonliterary. They introduced readers to a range of women writers, and they highlighted the fact that women wrote in *other* modes as well. Their anthology included examples of frontier romance, satirical and humorous fiction, and realism, as well as those modes conventionally associated with domestic writing: didactic, melodramatic, and abolitionist novels. Jane Curry's edition of Marietta Holley's *Samantha Rastles the Woman Question* (1983), Joyce Warren's edition of Fanny Fern's *Ruth Hall and Other Writings* (1986), and Joanne Dobson's edition of E. D. E. N. Southworth's *The Hidden Hand* (1988) provided additional hilarious examples of women's antisentimental writing.

Freibert and White's attempt to bring nonsentimentalist women writers into the spotlight was temporarily overshadowed, though, by the growing influence of Jane Tompkins's monumentally important rejoinder to Douglas, *Sensational Designs*, which included her germinal essay "Sentimental Power: *Uncle Tom's Cabin* and the Politics of Literary History." In the 1985 book, Tompkins elaborated on her arguments about sentimental power in her identification of "the other American Renaissance," arguing that contrary to the picture forwarded by Douglas, of sentimentalist women writers as "self-deluded ... manipulators of a gullible public ... the popular domestic novel of the nineteenth century represents a monumental effort to reorganize culture from the woman's point of view; that this body of work is remarkable for its intellectual complexity, ambition and resourcefulness; and that, in certain cases, it offers a critique of American society far more devastating than any delivered by better-known critics such as Hawthorne and Melville" (124). Arguing that their popularity was not the reason to ignore them, Tompkins traced out sentimentalism's matriarchal politics; its plan for changing the world by changing hearts; the critical significance of "popularity." Tompkins challenged the long-standing critical habit of prioritizing transgression, and detailed the importance of valuing subversion. Transgression was a strategy preferred by masculine culture. In the bonds of womanhood, subversion was often the only choice. As Tompkins summarizes her analysis of Warner's *Wide, Wide World*, "while the premise of Twain's novel [*The Adventures of Huckleberry Finn*] is that, when faced by tyranny of any sort, you can simply run away, the problem that Warner's novel sets itself out to solve is how to survive, given that you can't" (175).

Survival and modes of resistance and escape were important themes to a rapidly developing body of scholarship on African American women writers. It is impossible to underestimate the importance of this work for reorienting the terms of debate on sentiment and women's literary culture. In an early study, Minrose C. Gwin challenged images of interracial solidarity, the "fictional sisterhood," providing an alternative analysis of the often-violent relations between black and white women in literature of the Old South. During this same period, Jean Fagan Yellin brought her work on a study of antislavery feminists to a halt in order to follow through on leads that would result in her authentication of Harriet Jacobs's 1861 pseudonymous slave narrative, *Incidents in the Life of a Slave Girl*. This was a text long considered by white and black historians alike to be either the fabrication of a white female abolitionist – probably Lydia Maria Child whose name appeared as the editor – or of an unknown male abolitionist. But Yellin, who spent years sleuthing out information and following through a fragile chain of leads, was able to prove not only Jacobs's authorship, but also to correlate substantial details of Jacobs's life and escape from slavery to details of the narrative. This rediscovery was shortly followed by Gates's reprint of Harriet Wilson's '*Our Nig*' – written by and about a "free black woman of the north" – a startling indictment of northern, abolitionist, sentimental white womanhood.

In the chapter entitled "Slave and Mistress" in *Reconstructing Womanhood* (1987), Hazel Carby offered a landmark analysis of how black women writers had responded in their living and their writing to the powerful stereotypes generated by the white ideology of separate spheres – stereotypes which served powerfully to mystify "objective social relations" (22). The same year witnessed the publication of Hortense Spillers's germinal essay, "Mama's Baby, Papa's Maybe: an American Grammar Book" (1987), an essay that offers a counterhistory to the infamous Moynihan Report of the late 1960s and its assessments of the overly strong black women whose strength deprives black men from experiencing their manhood. In her essay, Spillers describes a "stunning reversal of the castration thematic," where African-American "Daughters and Fathers are made to manifest the very same rhetorical symptoms of absence and denial" in the symbolic structures of official US history (66). Claudia Tate and Ann DuCille offered analyses of the ways that romantic domestic middle-class norms were thematized in postwar and post-Reconstruction black women's fiction. Following Frances Smith Foster's and William Andrews's early examinations of nineteenth-century African-American women evangelists, Carla Peterson's 1998 *Doers of the Word* delivered a detailed reading of African-American women's power to respond critically and powerfully to the popular terms of sentiment and its privatizing demands on women.

In the recovery of women's literary sentimentality, the critical trend was toward revising the notion that women writers were apolitical. This body of scholarship emphasized white, middle-class women's political aims: their domestically oriented politics were millennialist, and directed by a corporatist, reformist vision. Nineteenth-century evangelism structured their belief that they could change the world by changing hearts. Growing attention to the writings and activism of African-American women in the antebellum US gradually and profoundly impacted this focus on the benevolent, reformist aspects of white middle-class women's culture. Factoring in attention to race and racial politics meant making even more complex assessments of the legacy of women's contributions to and places within the public and private spheres.

New historicism and the sentimentalist critique

In the late 1980s, a strong critique emerged within literary studies of the notion that middle-class women's literary and cultural agendas were defined by their "innocence" of or separation from the politics of the public sphere. Following the lead of Jane Tompkins's interest in analyzing the "cultural work" fiction could do, and of African-Americanist scholars who complicated the positive picture of "sentimental power," these critics found middle-class women fully invested and implicated in "public sphere" concerns as they helped in the construction of white bourgeois privilege. Developing under the critical influences of Foucauldian historiography and New Historicism, they analyzed sentimentalism as though it was continuous with, rather than isolated from or in opposition to, its larger culture. Thus this new work implied a rejection of – without always actually taking explicit aim at – separate spheres logic itself.

Karen Sánchez-Eppler's "Bodily Bonds: the Intersecting Rhetorics of Feminism and Abolitionism" (1988) heralded the New Historicist rethinking of middle-class women's role in the culture of the antebellum US. Building on a variety of critiques of the way early feminism had relied on a correlation between the "bonds of women" and the bonds of enslavement, "Bodily Bonds" developed a rhetorically nuanced account of how this correlation develops out of the particular "difficulty of representing a human body" that structures both nineteenth-century abolitionist and feminist rhetorics. Noting that the identification between the two – "of woman and slave, marriage and slavery" – can sometimes be "mutually empowering," Sánchez-Eppler documented the asymmetrical and exploitative tendencies of middle-class feminist-abolitionists' historical deployment of that metaphor. She insisted that scholarship begin accounting for how "the freedom offered by anti-slavery fiction regularly depends upon killing off black bodies," and more specifically how the "bodies feminists and abolitionists wish reclaimed and the bodies [their fiction] exploit[s], den[ies] or obliterate[s] in the attempted rescue, are the same."

Sánchez-Eppler used Harriet Beecher Stowe's *Uncle Tom's Cabin* as one of many evidentiary texts. Gillian Brown's *Domestic Individualism* made it the case text to introduce its arguments about the centrality of (women's) ideology of domesticity to (men's) developing culture of individualism. Arguing that "nineteenth-century American individualism takes on its peculiarly 'individualistic' properties as domesticity inflects it with values of interiority, privacy and psychology" (1), Brown turns to *Uncle Tom's Cabin* to show how its domesticity was implicated in the very market logic it set out to challenge. If Stowe models domesticity as a countereconomics, "an economy of abundant mother-love built on an excess of supply rather than the excess of demand and desire upon which both the slave economy and Northern capitalism operated" (24), it ultimately depends on the logic *of* slavery, where within the domestic sphere, things and people are lovingly owned. "In other words," Brown summarizes, "sentimental possession may rationalize – by personalizing – market relations" (43). Domesticity sentimentalizes – it makes personal as an affective relation – competitive, dehumanizing market conditions and thereby facilitates and strengthens the very structures it seems most to resist.

Laura Wexler's compelling analysis of domesticity's racist motives in "Tender Violence: Literary Eavesdropping, Domestic Fiction and Educational Reform" critically summarized the argument of this emerging school with its feminist literary critic predecessors. Replaying the high points of the retrospectively labeled "Douglas–Tompkins debate," Wexler called attention to how much critical ground they shared: "an agreement that instruction of the literate middle class is the chief objection as well as the chief sub-ject of domestic narrative." Their agreement prevents them from framing an argument that could look *outside* the purview of the literate middle class. Looking outside, in the specific instance of the photographic record of "be-fore and after" shots of three young Indian girls admitted to the Hamp-ton Normal and Agricultural Institute in Hampton, Virginia, Wexler iso-lates and analyzes the "imperial project of sentimentalism." As she studies the way the "after" shot of the girls normalizes their dress and posture through the conventions of a specifically white domesticity that depersonal-izes the girls, she shows how the photo reveals its own lies about its promise of acculturated literacy: the girl who "now" holds a book holds it upside down.

Wexler insisted that critics had been wrong to overlook the "sadistic" as-pects, the "externalized aggression" of sentimentalism in favor of a more comfortable analysis of its "masochistic ... flavor." Her essay became the lead in a landmark volume of essays edited by Shirley Samuels in 1992, *The Culture of Sentiment*. Samuels's editorial introduction elegantly traced the countervailing claims of sentimentalist analyses, which show that "[s]entimentality is literally at the heart of nineteenth-century American cul-ture." The essays gathered here sampled the complexity of New Historicist critiques, their aim to understand how sentimental and domestic discourse could both "produce ... and contest" its culture. Samuels labeled this the "double logic of sentiment," the way the "act of emotional response" to sen-timental works "produces the sentimental subject who consumes the work" (6). Samuels's focus, reflecting New Historicist emphases, was on discourse and rhetoric – verbal and symbolic structures of a given ideology or so-cial logic. Reading sentimentalism as a discourse allowed these critics to reassess it "not so much as a genre" but as "an operation or a set of actions" that effect readerly identifications with and across gender, race, class, and nation.

This model of analysis reads the logic of "separation" as an ideologically fictional ploy that differently enlisted white middle-class men and women for a similar class and nationalist politics, a kind of imperialist bourgeois *leger-de-gender*. Amy Kaplan's recent essay, "Manifest Domesticity" (1999) and the larger project of which it is a part, marks perhaps the culmination of this school of analysis. There Kaplan outlines domestic ideology's claims on and role within late nineteenth-century US foreign policy, the way "the idea of foreign policy depends on the sense of the nation as a domestic space imbued with a sense of at-homeness, in contrast to an external world perceived as alien and threatening" (581–2). Kaplan demonstrates the importance of contrasting domesticity not just to its familiar opposites, the marketplace or public sphere politics, but also a less intuitive opposite, the extranational, where she historicizes modern practices of philanthropy and benevolence, by locating an intricate symbiosis in the aims of domestic and Manifest Destiny discourses.

Public sphere criticism and theory

At the same time that the New Historicist critique of sentimentalism emerged, a different critical school with important implications for the study of early United States literature and culture was developing around the theories of Jürgen Habermas, a student of Theodor Adorno, and a "second genera-tion" Frankfurt School scholar. This school of criticism was not focused on women's writing or historiography, nor even the nineteenth century itself, *per se*. Rather, from various perspectives in literary, political, and cultural studies, this group of theorists and historians used Habermas's theories about the generation and "structural transformation" of the public sphere that ac-companied the western rise of market capitalism to study the social condi-tions for the democratic nation-state. Habermas's notion of the public sphere depended on the notion that it existed as a rational and critical space where private citizens could come together to discuss common, public concerns. Literary historians like Michael Warner, Larzer Ziff, Jay Fliegelman, Chris Looby, Michael Schudson, Bruce Burgett, and others productively analyzed the development of a rational public sphere in the print culture and sociopo-litical practices of the early United States.

If early public sphere Americanists did not exactly ignore gender, they did not pay much particular attention to the implications of the public sphere's gendered division of political labor, where the development of (men's) pub-lic political rationality depended on a series of private and semi-private in-stitutions like the middle-class home (with its studies, drawing rooms and parlors), salons, coffeehouses, newspapers, and novels, where they would learn to formulate their interests in the terms of privacy and individual-ity. Nancy Fraser's 1992 essay, "Rethinking the Public Sphere: a Contribu-tion to the Critique of Actually Existing Democracy," would help put the question of gender more carefully on the map for this school. Fraser cri-tiqued Habermas's model for the way it overidealized historically existing public spheres and ignored the presence of the "competing" or counter-spheres of minority groups. Lauren Berlant, a literary New Historicist, cul-tural critic and political theorist-activist, was in this same period beginning her critique of this gendered political formation, drawing on her specific ex-pertise in late eighteenth- and nineteenth-century American literature and culture.

For instance, in an influential 1988 manifesto, Berlant describes and historicizes "The Female Complaint," a feminine "self-containment" genre that serves to "mediate and manage the social contradictions that arise from women's sexual and affective allegiance to a phallocentric ideology that has, in practice, denied women power, privilege and presence in the public and private spheres" (245; 243). Originating in the emerging separate spheres culture of the 1820s, the "complaint" came into being as a "safety valve" for feminine rage, allowing them to vent their frustration at patriarchy and male privilege without leaving their protected bourgeois "private" space, allowing them to locate worldly problems and postulate solutions to them from "within" – the heart of the woman or the domestic space. Berlant's analysis of the developing genre ranges historically through examples from novels by Fanny Fern and Harriet Beecher Stowe, to the movie *Stella Dallas*, to the columns of Erma Bombeck. These various examples allow Berlant to demonstrate that while the "female complaint" has been useful for cultivating "leverage for the speaking woman: to deploy her gender to comment on and to circulate within the public sphere," it always limits the presence "woman" can have in the public sphere. Its limit is a self-imposed one (hence the "self-containing" aspect of the genre) entailed by a woman's identification with the position of the private complaining woman: "the fear that her privacy will be ruptured by something phallic like a politics, an incitement to action or a deployment of knowledge" (245; 253). Berlant proposes a counterpolitics, a movement that would aim to interrupt women's identification with a "female essence," to make "the public sphere safe for women" in all their differences, and to "intensify the rupture of the private, and inhabit, as much as we can, the constantly expanding negative terrain that will transform the patriarchal public sphere" (243–4).

Public sphere theory and historiography returned other Americanists to the rationalist political and public literature of the late colonies and early nation. David Shields's *Civil Tongues and Polite Letters* (1997) was a landmark study of the developing public sphere and its intermediary institutions in the late British colonies. His book is notable for its attention to the impact of women's practices – in tearooms and salon culture – on the expansion of the critical/rational civic sphere. Nina Baym resuscitated the historiography of early US women like Mercy Otis Warren. Other scholars like Sharon Harris and Carla Mulford concentrated important efforts on analyzing and reprinting women who participated in semi-public and public sphere discourses, like Annis Boudinot Stockton and Judith Sargent Murray.

A recent wave of scholars has begun developing an analysis not of women's role in private and public spheres but in the ideological role of gender and specifically of sentiment in developing democratic and representative practices. This new scholarship traces the developing association of sentiment with (and its assignment to) women as a national plot, where white women become the bearers of increasingly privatized virtue and of paradoxically symbolic and material bodies, as ideological supplements to the disembodied/universal white male citizen-subject. For example, Elizabeth Barnes and Julia Stern insist that sentiment is not just a political, but a nationally foundational discourse. Barnes elaborates: "American culture's preoccupation with familial feeling as the foundation for sympathy, and sympathy as the basis of a democratic republic, ultimately confounds the difference between familial and social bonds" (*States of Sympathy*, xi), thereby contributing to the affective privatization of citizenship. Somewhat differently, Stern proposes that "in the face of the overwhelming hate, anger, fear and grief that grip the nation in the 1790s, the sensationalist novelistic practices of the era constitute a form of psychic realism" (*Plight of Feeling*, 6). She reads such discourse as a democratic counternarrative that fleshes out the concerns of those elided by new, exclusionary constructions of citizenship in the early nation. More broadly, Andrew Burstein renarrates the history of the early nation as "sentimental democracy," side-stepping entirely any debate over which gender was sentimental and arguing that the US's "self-image" is sentimental.

Public spheres scholarship contributed to redirecting the terms of "separate spheres" analysis away from the subject of women's history, literature and culture, and toward the problem of gender and its role in constructing our "places" in modern life. In particular, its feminist practitioners foregrounded how separate spheres ideology simultaneously depends on the strong association of gender and space, and the ability of men and women partially and differently to transgress those boundaries.

No more separate spheres?

By the mid-nineties, scholarship was rife with suggestions that the notion of "separate spheres" was no longer a useful or even workable category for analysis. Cathy N. Davidson formulated a compendium challenge in her "No More Separate Spheres!" 1998 special issue of the journal *American Literature*, asking:

> why do literary critics and historians keep trying to move "Beyond Roles, Beyond Spheres" (the title of a 1989 forum in *The William and Mary Quarterly* that partly reprised a 1980 forum in *Feminist Studies*) and why do they so frequently return to that formulation? Finally, why is the metaphor of the separate spheres both immediately compelling and ultimately unconvincing as an explanatory device? (443–4)

Lora Romero had already hazarded an argument to answer Davidson's question. In her introduction to *Home Fronts*, Romero outlined the way "the figure of the domestic woman has haunted us for over two centuries because of her utility for overstabilizing the analytic terms 'ideology' and 'opposition'" (4). Romero argues that it is this culturally imagined figure – in "her" supposed banal popularity – that served as the stabilizing counterpart for the modern conception of the author, and "his" artistic ability to transcend or transgress the popular. "Her" consumerist complacency contrasted to "his" powerful intellectual and cultural alienation. "Her" enslavement to convention may have ensured "her" popularity, but "his" uncommon sensibility guaranteed the freedom of "his" art. Romero's reading of Hawthorne shows that these figures are not "real" but ideological, and demonstrates that Hawthorne's art in fact *depends* on the separate spheres ideology of the domestic for its own production of the uncanny, the unfamiliar, the *unheimlich* or *unhomelike* (cf. 99).

Though Romero neatly demonstrated how interdependent these seemingly "opposite" figures are, it is hard to shake the powerful association of sentiment and feminization. As Bruce Burgett has observed, the question of male sentimentalism tends to be treated in the terms of "pathology" in "its tendency to confound the homosocial worlds of (public) 'masculinity' and (private) 'femininity'" (*Sentimental Bodies* 114). Analyses of male sentimentalism have seemingly been easier to begin in eighteenth-century texts than in nineteenth-century ones. Only recently have critics begun paying sustained critical attention to male practices of sentimentalism in the nineteenth century, most notably in Mary Chapman and Glenn Hendler's *Sentimental Men* (1999). Their introductory chapter begins with the example of a 1994 *Time* magazine photo essay that chronicled – and registered surprise at – the many occasions at which George Bush had been caught crying. But as Chapman and Hendler note, presidential "blubbering is not, after all, a new phenomenon. Two centuries ago another president named George staged two scenes of tearful masculine sentimentality that solidified his position in the hearts of Americans and quickly became canonical images of masculine self-fashioning and national self-understanding" (his 1783 address to mutinous officers and his resignation from military service; see p. 2). Though sentiment became ideologically associated with femininity in the nineteenth century, the volume showed that nineteenth-century men participated in a variety of sentimental discourses and practices. This new scholarship has highlighted a number of areas for renewed investigation, from the Fireside Poets, to market practices, to the lifestyle choice of bachelorhood that Howard Chudacoff and Katherine Snyder have recently analyzed at greater length. In this same spirit, scholars like Andrew Burstein, Chris Castiglia, Russ

Castronovo, and Dana D. Nelson are studying the role of sentiment and its effect in the production of white male practices of abolitionism, citizenship, and even scientific professionalism.

In a recent essay entitled "What is Sentimentality?" June Howard surveys a range of interdisciplinary scholarship on the social production of affect and feeling, from anthropology and psychology to sociology, cognitive studies, and psychobiology. She insists on the importance of disentangling sentiment from its long association with domesticity, in order more carefully to "examine the complex historical process that weaves them together." In a world that increasingly associates individual subjectivity with particularly interiorized emotional states, Howard finds that sentimental works, however stigmatized in their association with feminized mass consumption, remain powerful to the extent that they "engage us in the intricate impasse of the public and private, proclaiming their separation and at the same time demonstrating their inseparability" (77). Howard's essay points the way less toward demonstrating that men participate in sentimentality too, than toward a more complicated analysis of emotion – the complex interface between socially produced affect and bodily, individual experience.

Much recent work suggests that the next wave of research in this area will focus on connections between emotional "states" like sentiment, and political and economic structures – like citizenship, corporations or the middle-class family, and alternatively resistant or radically different identifications. These studies historicize the development of nineteenth-century sentimentalism from its origins in Scottish Enlightenment School moral philosophy. They study its political contributions to the formation of, and practice of politics in, the early nation. They trace the sociological and political logics that linked sentiment with women, making it a personal practice, simultaneously idealizing and abjecting sentiment as women's sole sensibility, and counterposing this generic sentimental womanhood to a particularized, public, disembodied, rational male subject. It is not entirely clear that the perdurable paradigm of "separate spheres" can be overthrown by the recent trend of critical repudiation. But there are so many productive new directions emerging for inquiry that whether or not there is a definable "overthrow," there will certainly be radically different pictures to consider.

NOTES

1. Liverpool, Jany 19th, '55: "America is now wholly given over to a d—d mob of scribbling women, and I should have no chance of success while the public taste is occupied with their trash – and should be ashamed of myself if I did succeed. What is the mystery of these innumerable editions of the Lamplighter, and other

books neither better nor worse? – worse they could not be, and better they need not be, when they sell by the 100,000" (quoted in Freibert and White, *Hidden Hands*, 356–7).

2. Liverpool, Febry 2d, 1855: "In my last, I recollect, I bestowed some vituperation on female authors. I have since been reading 'Ruth Hall'; and I must say I enjoyed it a good deal. The woman writes as if the devil was in her; and that is the only condition under which a woman ever writes anything worth reading. Generally women write like emasculated men, and are only to be distinguished from male authors by greater feebleness and folly; but when they throw off the restraints of decency, and come before the public stark naked, as it were – then their books are sure to possess character and value. Can you tell me anything about this Fanny Fern? If you meet her, I wish you would let her know how much I admire her" (quoted in Freibert and White, *Hidden Hands*, 357).

WORKS CITED AND SELECTED SUGGESTED READING

Andrews, William L. *Sisters of the Spirit: Three Black Women's Autobiographies of the Nineteenth Century.* Bloomington: Indiana University Press, 1986.

To Tell a Free Story: the First Century of Afro-American Autobiography, 1760–1865. Urbana: University of Illinois Press, 1988.

Barnes, Elizabeth. *States of Sympathy: Seduction and Democracy in the American Novel.* New York: Columbia University Press, 1997.

Baym, Nina. *American Women Writers and the Work of History, 1790–1860.* New Brunswick: Rutgers University Press, 1995.

Woman's Fiction: a Guide to Novels by and about Women in America, 1820–1870. 1978. 2nd edn. Urbana: University of Illinois Press, 1993.

"Melodramas of Beset Manhood: How Theories of American Fiction Exclude Women Authors." *American Quarterly* 33 (1981): 123–39.

Berlant, Lauren. *The Queen of America Goes to Washington City: Essays on Sex and Citizenship.* Durham: Duke University Press, 1997.

"The Female Complaint." *Social Text* 19–20 (fall 1988): 237–59.

"Poor Eliza." *American Literature* 70.3 (September 1998): 635–68.

Brodhead, Richard. "Sparing the Rod: Discipline and Fiction in Antebellum America." *Representations* 21 (winter 1988): 67–95.

Brody, Jennifer DeVere. *Impossible Purities: Blackness, Femininity and Victorian Culture.* Durham: Duke University Press, 1998.

Brown, Gillian. *Domestic Individualism: Imagining Self in Nineteenth-Century America.* Berkeley: University of California Press, 1990.

Brown, Herbert Ross. *The Sentimental Novel in America, 1789–1860.* Durham: Duke University Press, 1940.

Burgett, Bruce. *Sentimental Bodies.* Princeton: Princeton University Press, 1998.

Burstein, Andrew. *Sentimental Democracy: the Evolution of America's Self-Image.* New York: Hill and Wang, 1999.

Carby, Hazel V. *Reconstructing Womanhood: the Emergence of the Afro-American Woman Novelist.* New York and Oxford: Oxford University Press, 1987.

DANA D. NELSON

Castiglia, Chris. "The Crying Game: William Lloyd Garrison's Sympathetic Address and the Whitening of the Civil Sphere." *American Literary History* (forthcoming, 2002).

"Pedagogical Discipline and the Creation of White Citizenship: John Witherspoon, Robert Finley and the Colonization Society." *Early American Literature* 33.2 (1998): 192–214.

Castronovo, Russ. *Fathering the Nation: American Genealogies of Slavery and Freedom.* Berkeley: University of California Press, 1995.

"Political Necrophilia." *boundary2* 27.2 (summer 2000): 113–48.

"'That Half-Living Corpse': Female Mediums, Séances, and the Occult Public Sphere." *Necro-Citizenship: Death, Eroticism, and the Public Sphere in the Nineteenth-Century United States.* Durham: Duke University Press, 2001.

Chapman, Mary, and Glenn Hendler. *Sentimental Men: Masculinity and the Politics of Affect in American Culture.* Berkeley: University of California Press, 1999.

Cherniavsky, Eva. *That Pale Mother Rising: Sentimental Discourses and the Imitation of Motherhood in 19th-Century America.* Bloomington: Indiana University Press, 1995.

Chudacoff, Howard P. *The Age of the Bachelor: Creating an American Subculture.* Princeton: Princeton University Press, 1999.

Cogan, Francis. *All-American Girl: the Ideal of Real Womanhood in Mid-Nineteenth-Century America.* Athens: University of Georgia Press, 1989.

Cott, Nancy. *The Bonds of Womanhood: "Woman's Sphere" in New England, 1780–1835.* New Haven: Yale University Press, 1977.

Coultrap-McQuin, Susan. *Doing Literary Business: American Women Writers in the Nineteenth Century.* Chapel Hill: University of North Carolina Press, 1990.

Cowie, Alexander. *The Rise of the American Novel.* New York: American Book Co., 1948.

Curry, Jane, ed. *Samantha Rastles the Woman Question*, by Marietta Holley. Urbana: University of Illinois Press, 1983.

Davidson, Cathy N. *Revolution and the Word: the Rise of the Novel in America.* New York and Oxford: Oxford University Press, 1986.

"Preface: No More Separate Spheres!" *American Literature* 70.3 (special issue, September 1998): 443–63.

Dobson, Joanne, ed. *The Hidden Hand, or, Capitola the Madcap*, by E.D.E.N. Southworth. New Brunswick: Rutgers University Press, 1988.

Donovan, Josephine. *New England Local Color Literature.* New York: Ungar, 1983.

Douglas, Ann. *The Feminization of American Culture.* 1977. London: Papermac, 1996.

DuBois, Ellen. "Politics and Culture in Women's History: a Symposium." *Feminist Studies* 6.1 (spring 1980): 28–36.

DuCille, Ann. *The Coupling Convention: Sex, Text and Tradition in Black Women's Fiction.* New York and Oxford: Oxford University Press, 1993.

Fetterley, Judith. *Provisions: a Reader from Nineteenth-Century American Women.* Bloomington: Indiana University Press, 1985.

Fetterley, Judith, and Marjorie Pryse. *American Women Regionalists, 1850–1910.* New York: W. W. Norton, 1992.

Fisher, Philip. *Hard Facts: Setting and Form in the American Novel.* New York and Oxford: Oxford University Press, 1987.

Foster, Frances Smith. "Adding Color and Contour to Early American Self-Portraitures: Autobiographical Writings of Afro-American Women." *Conjuring: Black Women, Fiction, and Literary Tradition.* Ed. Marjorie Pryse and Hortense Spillers. Bloomington: Indiana University Press, 1985.

Fox-Genovese, Elizabeth. *Within the Plantation Household: Black and White Women of the Old South.* Chapel Hill: University of North Carolina Press, 1988.

Fraser, Nancy. "Rethinking the Public Sphere: a Contribution to the Critique of Actually Existing Democracy." *Habermas and the Public Sphere.* Ed. Craig Calhoun. Cambridge, MA: MIT Press, 1992, 109–42.

Freibert, Lucy, and Barbara White. *Hidden Hands: an Anthology of American Women Writers, 1790–1870.* New Brunswick: Rutgers University Press, 1985.

Friedan, Betty. *The Feminine Mystique.* New York: Dell, 1963.

Gates, Henry Louis, ed. *Our Nig; Or, Sketches from the Life of a Free Black,* by Harriet E. Wilson. New York: Vintage Books, 1983.

Gwin, Minrose C. *Black and White Women of the Old South: the Peculiar Sisterhood of American Literature.* Knoxville: University of Tennessee Press, 1985.

Habermas, Jürgen. *The Structural Transformation of the Public Sphere: an Inquiry into a Category of Bourgeois Society.* Trans. Thomas Burger. Cambridge, MA: MIT Press, 1991.

Harris, Sharon M. "Hannah Webster Foster's *The Coquette*: Critiquing Franklin's America." *Redefining the Political Novel: American Women Writers.* Ed. Sharon Harris. Knoxville: University of Tennessee Press, 1995. 1–22.

Harris, Sharon M., ed. *Selected Writings of Judith Sargent Murray.* New York and Oxford: Oxford University Press, 1995.

Harris, Susan K. *Nineteenth-Century American Women's Novels: Interpretive Strategies.* New York and Cambridge: Cambridge University Press, 1990.

Herbert, T. Walter. *Dearest Beloved: the Hawthornes and the Making of the Middle-Class Family.* Berkeley: University of California Press, 1993.

Howard, June. "What is Sentimentality?" *American Literary History* 11.1 (spring 1999): 63–81.

Kaplan, Amy. "Manifest Domesticity." *American Literature* 10.3(1998): 581–606.

Kelley, Mary. *Private Woman, Public Stage: Literary Domesticity in Nineteenth-Century America.* New York and Oxford: Oxford University Press, 1984.

Kerber, Linda K. *Women of the Republic: Intellect and Ideology in Revolutionary America.* New York: W. W. Norton, 1980.

Kete, Mary Louise. *Sentimental Collaborations: Mourning and Middle-Class Identity in Nineteenth-Century America.* Durham: Duke University Press, 2000.

Kilcup, Karen L., ed. *Nineteenth-Century American Women Writers: an Anthology.* Oxford: Basil Blackwell, 1997.

Kolodny, Annette. *The Land Before Her: Fantasy and Experience of the American Frontiers, 1630–1860.* Chapel Hill: University of North Carolina Press, 1984.

The Lay of the Land: Metaphor as Experience and History in American Life and Letters. Chapel Hill: University of North Carolina Press, 1975.

Koppelman, Susan, ed. *Old Maids: Short Stories by Nineteenth-Century US Women Writers.* Boston: Pandora Press, 1984.

The Other Woman: Stories of Two Women and a Man. New York: Feminist Press, 1984.

Kraditor, Aileen S. *Up From the Pedestal: Selected Writings in the History of American Feminism.* Chicago: Quadrangle Books, 1968.

Lerner, Gerda. "Politics and Culture in Women's History: a Symposium." *Feminist Studies* 6.1 (spring 1980): 49–54.

Looby, Chris. *Voicing America: Language, Literary Form, and the Origins of the United States.* Chicago: University of Chicago Press, 1996.

Matthiessen, F. O. *American Renaissance: Art and Expression in the Age of Emerson and Whitman.* New York and Oxford: Oxford University Press, 1941.

Moon, Michael. *Disseminating Whitman: Revision and Corporeality in Leaves of Grass.* Cambridge, MA: Harvard University Press, 1991.

Moon, Michael, and Cathy Davidson, eds. *Subjects and Citizens: Nation, Race and Gender.* Durham: Duke University Press, 1995.

Mulford, Carla. *Only for the Eye of a Friend: the Poems of Annis Boudinot Stockton.* Charlottesville: University Press of Virginia, 1995.

"Annis Boudinot Stockton and Benjamin Young Prime: a Poetical Correspondence, and More." *Princeton University Library Chronicle Journal (PULC)* 52.2 (winter 1991): 231–66.

"Political Politics: Annis Boudinot Stockton and Middle Atlantic Women's Culture." *New Jersey History* 11.1–2 (spring/summer 1993): 66–110.

Nelson, Dana. *National Manhood: Capitalist Citizenship and the Imagined Fraternity of White Men.* Durham: Duke University Press, 1998.

" 'No Cold or Empty Heart': Polygenesis, Scientific Professionalization, and the Unfinished Business of Male Sentimentalism." *differences* 11.3 special issue on the Feminization of American Culture. Ed. Philip Gould and Leonard Tennenhouse. 29–56.

"Representative/Democracy: Presidents, Democratic Management, and the Unfinished Business of Male Sentimentalism." Forthcoming in *No More Separate Spheres!* Ed. Cathy N. Davidson. Durham: Duke University Press.

"Thoreau, Race and Manhood: Quiet Desperation Versus Representative Isolation." *Thoreau.* Ed. William Cain. Texts and Contexts series. Oxford: Oxford University Press, 2000. 61–93.

Newfield, Christopher J. *The Emerson Effect: Individualism and Submission in America.* Chicago: University of Chicago Press, 1996.

Norton, Mary Beth. *Liberty's Daughters.* Boston: Little, Brown, 1980.

Papashvily, Helen Waite. *All the Happy Endings: a Study of the Domestic Novel in America, the Women Who Wrote It, the Women Who Read It, in the Nineteenth Century.* New York: Harper and Bros., 1956.

Pattee, Fred Lewis. *The Feminine Fifties.* New York: D. Appleton Century, Inc., 1940.

Peterson, Carla. *Doers of the Word; African-American Speakers and Writers in the North, 1830–1880.* New Brunswick: Rutgers University Press, 1998.

Romero, Lora. *Home Fronts: Domesticity and Its Critics in the Antebellum United States.* Durham: Duke University Press, 1997.

Ryan, Mary P. *The Empire of the Mother: American Writing About Domesticity, 1830–1860.* 1982. Reprinted New York: Harrington Park, 1985.

Samuels, Shirley, ed. *The Culture of Sentiment: Race, Gender and Sentimentality in Nineteenth-Century America.* New York and Oxford: Oxford University Press, 1992.

Romances of the Republic: Women, the Family and Violence in the Literature of the Early Nation. New York and Oxford: Oxford University Press, 1996.

Sánchez-Eppler, Karen. *Touching Liberty: Abolition, Feminism, and the Politics of the Body*. Berkeley: University of California Press, 1993.
"Bodily Bonds: the Intersecting Rhetorics of Feminism and Abolitionism." *Representations* 24 (fall 1988): 28–59.
Schudson, Michael. "Was There Ever a Public Sphere? If So, When? Reflections on the American Case." *Habermas and the Public Sphere*. Ed. Craig Calhoun. Cambridge, MA: MIT Press, 1992.
Shields, David S. *Civil Tongues and Polite Letters in British America*. Chapel Hill: University of North Carolina Press, 1997.
Smith, Henry Nash. "The Scribbling Women and the Cosmic Success Story." *Critical Inquiry* 1.1 (1974): 47–70.
Smith, Stephanie. *Conceived by Liberty: Maternal Figures and Nineteenth-Century American Literature*. Ithaca, NY: Cornell University Press, 1994.
Smith-Rosenberg, Carroll. "The Female World of Love and Ritual: Relations Between Women in Nineteenth-Century America." *Signs* 1.1 (autumn 1975): 1–30.
Snyder, Katherine V. *Bachelors, Manhood and the Novel, 1850–1925*. Cambridge and New York: Cambridge University Press, 1999.
Spillers, Hortense. "Mama's Baby, Papa's Maybe: an American Grammar Book." *Diacritics* 17.2 (summer 1987): 65–81.
Stansell, Christine. *City of Women: Sex and Class in New York City, 1789–1860*. New York: Knopf, 1986.
Stern, Julia. *The Plight of Feeling: Sympathy and Dissent in the Early American Novel*. Chicago: University of Chicago Press, 1997.
Tate, Claudia. *Domestic Allegories of Political Desire: the Black Heroine's Text at the Turn of the Century*. New York and Oxford: Oxford University Press, 1992.
"Our Literary Foremother: Pauline Hopkins." *Conjuring: Black Women, Fiction, and Literary Tradition*. Ed. Marjorie Pryse and Hortense Spillers. Bloomington: Indiana University Press, 1985.
Teute, Fredrika. "In 'The Gloom of the Evening': Margaret Bayard Smith's View in Black and White of Washington Society." *Proceedings of the American Antiquarian Society* 106.1 (1996): 37–58.
Tocqueville, Alexis de. *Democracy in America*. Trans. George Lawrence; ed. J. P. Mayer. 1966. New York: Perennial Library, 1988.
Tompkins, Jane. *Sensational Designs: the Cultural Work of American Fiction, 1790–1860*. New York and Oxford: Oxford University Press, 1986.
Warner, Michael. *Letters of the Republic: Publication and the Public Sphere in Eighteenth-Century America*. Cambridge, MA: Harvard University Press, 1990.
Warren, Joyce W., ed. *Ruth Hall and Other Writings*, by Fanny Fern. New Brunswick: Rutgers University Press, 1986.
Welter, Barbara, "The Cult of True Womanhood." *American Quarterly* 18 (1966): 151–74.
Wexler Laura. "Tender Violence: Literary Eavesdropping, Domestic Fiction, and Educational Reform." In Samuels, ed., *Culture of Sentiment*, 9–38.
White, Deborah Gray. *Ar'n't I a Woman?: Female Slaves in the Plantation South*. New York: W. W. Norton, 1985.
Yee, Shirley J. *Black Women Abolitionists: a Study in Activism, 1828–1860*. Knoxville: University of Tennessee Press, 1992.
Yellin, Jean Fagan, ed. *Incidents in the Life of a Slave Girl*, by Harriet Ann Jacobs. Cambridge, MA: Harvard University Press, 1987.

Women and Sisters: the Antislavery Feminist in American Culture. New Haven: Yale University Press, 1989.

Zafar, Rafia. *We Wear the Mask: African Americans Write American Literature, 1760–1870*. New York: Columbia University Press, 1997.

Ziff, Larzer. *Writing in the New Nation: Prose, Print and Politics in the Early United States*. New Haven: Yale University Press, 1991.

3

STEPHANIE A. SMITH

Antebellum politics and women's writing

Clothes-talk

In 1851, when temperance advocate Amelia Jenks Bloomer adopted a shortened shirt worn over what were called, at the time, Turkish "trowsers," she had no idea that her married name would give to the English language a new plural noun, *bloomers*. As originally worn by suffragettes like Bloomer herself, or Elizabeth Smith Miller, Elizabeth Cady Stanton and Susan B. Anthony (among a host of other, less famous women, and not always those sympathetic to the suffragettes[1]), it was regarded as a garment that could free a woman from the confinements of more traditional styles. In the 1850s a woman's daily garb consisted of ten to twelve pounds of "starched flannel or muslin petticoats," stays, and a tightly laced corset of whalebone; these underthings were covered by full-skirted dresses "that reached to the ground, sweeping up dirt and debris from country roads and unpaved city streets" (Coon, *Hear Me Patiently*, 9). Dragging in mud, heavy as lead and hot as Hades, these confining clothes did not promote mobility; indeed, it was generally thought that trousers, when considered merely as an *item* of dress, were far more comfortable and hygienic than women's wear.[2] Certainly, trousers offered mobility, as African-American abolitionist and diarist Charlotte L. Forten (later Grimké) reported on Saturday, July 15, 1854; she donned the "'Bloomer' costume" so as to climb "the highest cherry tree ... Obtained some fine fruit and felt for the time 'monarch of all I surveyed'" (Grimké, *Journals*, 86). And as Elizabeth Cady Stanton wrote, after wearing the Bloomer for the first time, "What incredible freedom I enjoyed!" (Stanton, *Eighty Years and More*, 201; Kesselman, "'Freedom Suit'").

Soon, however, many of these women adopted the Bloomer Costume not only for the mere physical freedom it bestowed, but also as a sign they sought freedom from other, more binding social and political constraints. Thus, during both the original heyday of bloomers, from 1851 through 1854, and in their later, more widespread appearance in the 1890s as an athletic and bicycle costume, these trousers were a visual reminder that the traditional shape of emancipation in the United States might be subject to radical reform. The visual impact of these pants spoke – sometimes, although not always, more loudly than words – about the fact that many a middle-class American woman was no longer content to remain off the public stage, without a legal voice, a juridical presence, or a vote in a democracy that claimed to provide equality for all (Kelley, *Private Woman, Public Stage*).

But, if bloomers served as a reminder that the concept of freedom was being pressured from several quarters to reform in the United States during the latter half of the nineteenth century, the costume also had the power to suggest that the natural itself might be unstable and subject to interpretation because it suggested that gender, generally understood as part of the natural order, might not be rigidly fixed. Since the dominant sex–gender system of most cultures is rendered legible, in part, through the language of clothing, to tamper with clothing signifies potential changes – tantamount, perhaps, to tampering with the natural order of things. In fact, although a number of women had either worn or adapted trousers for a variety of uses – as play clothes for young girls, as underwear, as spa clothing or as working clothes, worn mostly by working-class women – for many years,[3] "panting" in public still signified masculinity to the middle class. Exceptions might be made for a variety of reasons, but pants on women were generally considered lower class, risqué or shocking.[4] Such firm associations between class, gender, and dress remain evident in certain lingering prejudices about dress, or in commonplaces such as "who wears the pants in this family?"[5]

By wearing pants in public, the Bloomerites implicitly threw the door open to questions that had often gone unasked, the simplest of these being: if women could wear pants, what else might they do, or be? Would such wearing of pants allow masculinity to be usurped, even destroyed? Weren't trousers on women indecent, unnatural – weren't they suggestive? The very possibility that "natural" sexual signification, like clothing itself, might be altered, or the idea that their girls might "pant" in public, gave parents pause: what did it mean? Would women become as overtly sexual as men – or prostitutes? As historian Gayle Fischer writes, "it is difficult to determine if the general public's resistance to female trousers stemmed more from the fear that women would seize male power or from the fear that pants-clad women would be unabashedly 'sexy'" ("'Pantalets' and 'Turkish Trowsers,'" 113). This potential for modification to which the bloomers pointed, along with the prospect of overt female eroticism and gender confusion, rattled the middle class.

Clearly, a "panting" girl was trouble. She would have to be managed. Such management is not only evident in the historical vicissitudes and ultimate fate of the New Costume, as Amelia Bloomer's trouser-set was called, but also in the linguistic fate of a once familiar, once household word, *bloomer*. A highly public, publicized, and political "statement" when Amelia Bloomer first wore the design in 1851, bloomers were parodied, criticized, and finally ridiculed to death by 1854. According to Elizabeth Cady Stanton, the word *bloomer* itself had come into being as an epithet designed to belittle the women's movement.[6] However, as the historical record shows, many women adopted both the costume and the name of Bloomer(ite) with pride and with defiance in the face of such ridicule; in fact, Amelia Bloomer held it as a point of personal pride to have given her name to the Bloomer Costume, and she wore the trousers until she retired from public speaking. But by 1854, other women in the movement had ceased to wear the garment as streetwear, and so it vanished for a time. According to Gerda Lerner, the costume "soon became a symbol of revolt against all the senseless restrictions imposed on women and was worn with grim persistence in the face of ridicule, abuse and public censure" (*Grimké Sisters*, 335–6). But women like the Grimké sisters did finally give it up; "Sarah gave the costume up gladly, for she had worn it only from conviction; Angelina did so with the understanding that in time a better and more attractive dress for women would be developed and accepted" (Lerner, *Grimké Sisters*, 336; Birney, *Grimké Sisters*). In the 1870s, however, bloomers reemerged as a topic of dispute in the discourse of a scientific dress-reform movement. This reform, bolstered by the claims of burgeoning fields in health science, eventuated in the far more acceptable version of the fabled emancipation drag. The new bloomers were designed as an aid to physical activity, specifically for cycling. But even this new version faded over time. No longer considered indecent, although still eroticized, trousers for women were relegated to sportswear, or shortened, or made only for children, and so became specialized, stuffed back up under skirts from whence pantaloons had once descended, returned by custom and fashion to the realm of the private underthing, those unmentionables that girls were supposed to blush over. Estelle Ansley Worrell's comment about children's clothing is apt here; she observes that

> how a nation's children are treated and educated reveals much about its atti-
> tudes towards its citizens . . . Evidence shows that American children's clothing
> utilized new European styles and daring or even "shocking" new ideas sooner
> than did the fashions of adults. Apparently we dress our children in new styles
> that we ourselves are not always ready to accept. In recent history, young chil-
> dren wore bikini bathing suits before their parents did. The same was true with
> pantaloons at the beginning of the nineteenth century . . . Girls wore trousers
> or pantalets before their mothers did and made bloomers part of their regular
> wardrobe before their mothers did. (*Children's Costume in America*, 4)

And as Valerie Steele notes, in Paris, "Even feminine underpants were regarded as 'demi-masculine' apparel, and it was only gradually over the course
of the century that they entered the respectable woman's wardrobe. At mid-
century, they were still mostly worn by little girls, sportswomen, and *demi-
mondaines*. Dances like the *can-can* and the *cahut* exploited the 'naughty'
image of underpants, as dancers raised their legs to display kneelength *pan-
talons*" (*Paris Fashion*, 164). In fact, although middle-class women did wear
trousers, until the late twentieth century all female trousers had particular
uses or meanings and, when women wore them, what they wore had more
than likely been made for a man, or else tailor-made for a particular woman.
For example, during the First World War, the women who were recruited to
work in the factories, particularly munitions factories, often wore what their
men had worn, trousers or boilersuits, although it was considered daring.[7]
In the Second World War, many women, from Rose Will Monroe, better
known as Rosie the Riveter, to Norma Jeane Dougherty, later known as
Marilyn Monroe, donned workmen's jumpsuits, overalls, and blue jeans,
again to help the war effort. But, although trousers for women did gain increasing acceptance as appropriate clothing, it was not until the dust raised
by the social upheavals of the 1960s settled that trousers truly became part
of any middle-class woman's *public* wardrobe. Even so, questions about the
propriety of when and how and why pants should be worn can still haunt
job-seekers, professionals (especially politicians), and the fashion pages.[8]

Meanwhile, even if, by the 1940s, women could wear pants, the word
bloomers had ceased to signify a feminist politics. It was no longer a word
that made a political statement about women's freedom. In fact, in colloquial
use, the once adult, once political word *bloomer* signified babyhood more
than anything else. Children wore bloomers, even though the pantaloons
that girls had worn as early as the 1820s had never been called bloomers,
and would not be called such until well after the heyday of Betty Bloomer's
bicycle costume.[9] And the association between infancy and femininity that
had been foisted upon "bloomers" in the wake of what has since been called
the First Wave of feminist agitation in the United States was to reemerge
during the 1960s, just as the Second Wave began to surge. While protests
against the Vietnam War and racial inequality began to turn violent, as the
sexual revolution heated up and bras were about to burn, and as the parental
complaint "you can't tell a boy from a girl anymore" grew into a howl of
unrest, bloomers were introduced by the world of *haute couture* as a pert,
sex-kittenish little item for the hip young thing, particularly in England and
France.[10]

Thus did this completely *American* English word lose its ability to index an
intense and prolonged moment of nineteenth-century political conflict about

gender in the United States (and elsewhere), as reflected in most American desk-top dictionaries of the late twentieth century, which, when they list *bloomers* as something other than the plural of a flowering plant or, significantly, as slang for a *blunder*, list the word as: n. 1. bloomers, a. loose trousers gathered at the knee, formerly worn by women as part of a gymnasium, riding, or other sports outfit. b. a woman's undergarment of similar, but less bulky design and c. the trousers of a bloomer (costume). Only rarely does the now secondary meaning, 2. a costume for women, as advocated about 1850 by Mrs. Amelia Jenks Bloomer (1818–94) of New York, appear ("Bloomer"). Often the dictionary will offer no explanation as to what Mrs. Bloomer was advocating, besides the costume itself.[11]

But, one might ask, why notice such a small matter as this single word's definition and common use? In fact, common sense might tell the persons availing themselves of these aforementioned dictionaries that any woman advocating the wearing of pants in the mid-nineteenth century was no doubt an agitator for other, presumably more substantive political and emancipatory, projects. Historically, however, this would not be true, for, as Gayle Fischer has shown, the women of the Oneida Perfectionist Community in Oneida, New York adopted trousers for rather different reasons than the Bloomerites did, reasons that had very little to do with emancipation politics. "In contrast to mainstream critiques," writes Fischer, "Oneida Community criticism of clothing focused on the way dress made the 'distinction between the sexes vastly more prominent and obtrusive than nature [made] it'" ("'Pantalets' and 'Turkish Trowsers,'" 130). To these women, trousers signified both nature – after all, women, like men, had legs – and the virginity of youth – a submissive, girlish state. "The style unquestionably made Oneida women appear infantile or childlike" (132), writes Fischer, and the Oneida women were encouraged to remain girlish.

But historical accuracy and the Oneida Community aside, why should a dictionary be politically specific, if it cites historical information – names, dates, and so forth? In this chapter, I wish to propose an answer to such a question by using this entirely American neologism "bloomer" to show how common usage and the production of common sense are linked. By doing so, I will explore the ways in which common usage can help to alter the shape of what is generally recognized and understood as common sense. I do this in order to argue, in turn, that common sense drives the tenor of everyday life where feminism finds both the deepest resistance and yet, paradoxically, also a home, because it is primarily in the commonplaces of language – in the sayings and in the things we all just know – that common sense is both composed and torn asunder, both sustained and belied. I will also show that compressed within the history of this one word *bloomers* is the story of how our underlying common sense about such things as birth, breeding, or brawn was challenged by social, medical, and political changes that, in turn, affected our language. To be more specific, if *bloomer* was once a commonplace watchword that signified women's emancipation, it did so by being caught between conflicting and changing versions of common sense: it was a term that could conjure up the common-sense belief that mobility meant practicality, and that the physical health and well-being of wives, sisters, and daughters was important enough to warrant dress reform movements in the 1850s and again in the 1870s. But it was also the watchword for commonsense assumptions about frailty and femininity that endured throughout the nineteenth and into the twentieth century, assumptions which suggested that masculinity and patriarchal authority were under siege the minute women wore pants. By 1854, however, despite the rational common-sense arguments in favor of trousers set forth by those women who proudly called themselves Bloomers or Bloomerites, the Bloomer Costume was judged indelicate, indecent, and overly masculine by the prevailing tide of another kind of common sense, the common sense of tradition and religion, as set forth by antisuffrage, antireformists. And yet, by the 1890s a new kind of common sense about gender had begun to take hold and to prevail. By 1895, bloomers were thought, by some, to be appropriate to the growing social mobility of the soon-to-be explosive phenomenon of the "New Woman." Certainly young women just coming into their own donned bloomers and went biking in numbers. Furthermore, if, by the 1940s, bloomers had become primarily children's underwear, by the 1960s and 1970s, bloomers reappeared as hip fashion, adapted by designers such as Yves St. Laurent and Mary Quant, and as such signified a "new" sexual era.

Such changes in the signification of one word, I will argue, can serve as an index to the shifts in commonly held cultural attitudes not only toward dress or hygiene but also to sociopolitical changes in the domain of sexuality. My point here is that if the word *bloomer* was once part of the everyday political language in the 1850s, and tied, then, to what the Bloomerites saw as a rational logic of practical common sense about women's clothing and thus also women's place in the world, prevailing modes of common sense would also turn the Bloomer Costume into bloomers as we now know them: a quaint, picturesque sartorial feature of the past linked to childhood, underwear, and fashion fads, with perhaps a sketchy relationship – and certainly an underreported one, if the dictionary is any indication – to political events. And yet, along the historical and linguistic way, an American common sense about femininity was also radically altered.

A picture may very well be, as the common saying goes, worth a thousand words, but a word can also paint a thousand pictures. So loudly did the picture of a "panting" girl speak, in fact, that women who wished to tether the power of language to their own purposes finally gave up on trousers. But although bloomers, as a costume, had a visual impact that spoke louder than words, I think it also worth seeing what other pictures a history of the word can paint. Women in antebellum America sought to forge new meanings and so to make a new home in the world for themselves. Indeed, reformists and abolitionists sought nothing less than to remake constitutional law, and while bloomers are only indirectly linked to the fight against legalized slavery, women like Amelia Jenks Bloomer – who was also a writer, an editor, and a public speaker – did seek to change the meaning of another common word for which the United States stood and for which it would presently hurtle itself, sundered in two, into war: *freedom*. The larger public issues at hand for Amelia Jenks Bloomer in 1851 were temperance, abolition, and women's rights. But the underlying question – what is literally meant by freedom? – was at stake.

To put this claim another way, if clothes are like words, words are like clothes; each speaks a cultural language; each has a gendered grammar; they are subject to interpretation, remotivation, and misunderstandings. The "Bloomer," as both an American neologism and as an American experiment in dress reform, offers us the site of a unique historical convergence of *political language* and *material object*, from which to examine the ways in which American women tried to alter the ways of their forefathers, and thus to alter common sense. They would try to change the vocabulary of their everyday lives and the political life of the nation; they would try to make politics "mean" in a new fashion, one more suited to tell them of a future in which they, and their children, would have more mobility, more possibility. Or as Susan B. Anthony said, in a counter-centennial address in Philadelphia on July 4, 1876, "Woman's wealth, thought and labor have cemented the stones of every monument man has reared to liberty ... We ask justice, we ask equality, we ask that all the civil and political rights that belong to citizens of the United States, be guaranteed to us and our daughters forever" (Franklin, *American Voices, American Lives*, 435–40).

Panting girls

Common sense. Most Americans are proud of it. Many will appeal to it in order to further a political goal. Certainly the women who were called Bloomerites used the logic of common sense when they spoke of their costume as the rational dress. How, they asked, could one properly care for children, bound by the frivolous dictates of French – *foreign* – fashion? Was it not easier to lift a child, or perform other womanly tasks, unburdened by whalebone? Pragmatically speaking, why constrict the human body so cruelly that bruising, broken ribs and intestinal injury result? Some doctors agreed. But health was not the only issue. The Bloomer soon had ardent adherents who saw the garment as a means to signify changes to both their physical well-being *and* their mental health, if not also their social condition. As Anne C. Coon notes, factory girls in Lowell, Massachusetts organized a Bloomer Institute to help them achieve two stated objectives: "Mutual Improvement – in Literature, Science and Morals" – and "Emancipation" from the thralldom of fashion and other unnatural or unhelpful trappings (*Hear Me Patiently*, 12).

On July 4, 1853, for the occasion of an address entitled "Mothers of the Revolution" given in Harford, New York by the then popular temperance speaker and editor of an internationally known women's newsletter called *The Lily*, Amelia Jenks Bloomer, this toast and poem was delivered by a contingent of young women who were "tastefully attired in the Bloomer Costume" (*Hear Me Patiently*, 62):

> The Bloomer Costume – The most appropriate as well as the most convenient dress for ladies – May it soon become their universal costume.

> Let sickly ladies talk and flirt
> And tell their paper passion,
> Amid those trailing, draggling skirts
> Because it is the fashion;
> But give *me* the gay and sprightly lass
> Who "*pants*" for health so blooming,
> For her I'd fill the flowing glass
> And shout, "huzza! for bloomers!"

Some two years prior to this address, in 1851, Amelia Bloomer and Elizabeth Cady Stanton had designed their rational costume for women. They were goaded on by an opponent of women's rights, who had jestingly endorsed dress reform as a means to ridicule those agitating women of Seneca Falls – women like Bloomer, Stanton, and Anthony – who had stirred up such a fuss in 1848 when they met at the first women's liberation conference ever to be held in the United States, and where they had drafted the famous document, "The Declaration of the Rights of Women." Bloomer and Stanton responded by adapting a costume that Stanton's cousin, Elizabeth Smith Miller, or Libby Miller, the daughter of dress reform abolitionist Gerrit Smith, had worn in European spas: a shortened skirt worn over large, so-called "Turkish trowsers," gathered in at the ankle with a string or button.[12]

Such a costume was not wholly unfamiliar to many middle-class women, who might have worn pantalets or pantaloons as children. Certainly, many had heard of or perhaps had fantasized about the harem and the seraglio, where "Oriental" women wore voluminous pantaloons and veils – thus the epithet "Turkish." Dropping pounds of muslin, while also obviating the need to corset tightly, the new costume was hailed by some women and their male supporters as more sane and sanitary than the fashions then current. Amelia Bloomer, who took up the dress with relish and dedication, soon found her name bowdlerized into a plural noun, *bloomers*, and bestowed on a garment that was also referred to in the popular press as the Camilla, the Tom-Boy, Turkish trowsers, the Oriental Costume or that indecent dress. A British broadsheet in 1851 lampooned the attire thus:

> Listen, females all
> No matter what your trade is,
> Old Nick is in the girls,
> The Devil's in the ladies!
> Married men may weep,
> And tumble in the ditches
> Since women are resolved
> To wear the shirts and breeches.
>
> Ladies do declare
> A change should have been sooner,
> The women, one and all,
> Are going to join the Bloomers.
> Prince Albert and the Queen
> Had such a jolly row, sirs;
> She threw off stays and put
> On waistcoat, coat and trousers.
>
> The world's turned upside down,
> The ladies will be tailors
> And serve Old England's Queen
> As soldiers and as sailors
> Won't they look funny when
> The seas are getting lumpy,
> Or when they ride astride
> Upon an Irish donkey?
> (Gattey, *Bloomer Girls*, 75)

Some forty-two years later, on January 17, 1895, about two weeks after the 76-year-old Amelia Jenks Bloomer had died in Council Bluffs, Iowa, the

New York Truth ran a "suggested epitaph" for her:

Here lies
(Quite safe at last from reckless rumors)
The erst well-known and
Well-abused Miss Bloomer.
Living too long,
She saw her once bold coup
Rendered old-fashioned by the Woman New.

By noisy imitators vexed and piqued,
her fads outfadded and her freaks out-freaked
She did not die till she had seen and heard
All her absurdities made more absurd.

In short,
She found Dame Fortune but ill-humored,
And passed away
In every point out-Bloomered.

And so it might have seemed to Amelia Bloomer herself, for although she had seen the cause of colleagues Frederick Douglass, Angelina and Sarah Grimké, and Lucretia Mott change the nation through Civil War, neither her own treasured cause of temperance nor a woman's right to vote became constitutional amendments before she died.

Yet the dismissive mockery of the aforementioned epitaph serves also to indicate that the "bloomer craze" caused more disturbance than *Truth's* biting humor suggests. Not only does the epitaph nervously record the growing visibility of the New Woman, whose agitation would finally lead to women's suffrage in 1921, but in the heyday of the Bloomer Costume more than simply a *few* sprightly, scandalous gay lasses, as the first poem coyly names them, panted in the public eye. Despite ridicule and censure, the Bloomer as a public, day dress for middle-class women, rather than as an immodest, private dress donned at spas, had spread quickly from Seneca Falls – where Bloomer lived and worked as an editor and speaker – to Scotland, England, Canada, and Australia – all across the fractured British Empire. It spread by word of mouth, through correspondence and through *The Lily*, where Bloomer offered free patterns for the costume in return for subscriptions (11). There was "Bloomerism in Picadilly," "Bloomerism at the Crystal Palace," and Madame Tussaud and Son's exhibition offered the public the "Bloomer Costume: Five beautiful varieties by which the public may judge if this dress may ever become popular" (Gattey, *Bloomer Girls*, 67–72).

Moreover, as the rational dress craze spread, it carried with it implications that would soon erupt in other debates that, at the end of the twentieth century, are often considered more serious than either prohibition or dress reform. Advocates claimed that the costume freed the *natural* form of a woman's body from the unnatural constraints of fashion. Despite Amelia Jenks Bloomer's belief in temperance, Bloomerites were ready to "fill the flowing glass / And shout 'huzza! for bloomers!,'" presumably with all the (masculine?) gusto of their new-found health. Aghast at such a picture, opponents cried that panting girls were unnatural, that only men were naturally suited to the suit. And so the nature of woman herself, a question that Sigmund Freud would soon spend his life attempting to answer, was up for debate. Bloomers became a referendum on nature. But what such an argument about the naturalness of trousers also suggests is that "nature" was not a transparent or immutable category, but one that indeed might have to be shaped, written, or even theorized, in order to be seen – or read – at all. What is natural – natural clothes, a natural sexuality? How should the natural be handled or determined, if it is not, well, natural? If Charles Darwin set the term "natural selection" into motion in 1859 upon the publication of *The Origin of Species*, the scientific, public, and legal debates that raged in the wake of Darwin's work would set the stage for the infamous *Tennessee* v. *John Scopes* or the "Monkey Trial" of 1925, in which high school teacher John Thomas Scopes had been charged with illegally teaching evolution, a *cause célèbre* later dramatized in the play and film, *Inherit the Wind*. Two famous legal minds, Clarence Darrow and William Jennings Bryan, squared off in the courtroom, Darrow for the defense, Bryan for the state of Tennessee. Such conflict about the nature of the natural reerupted in the summer of 1999, when the Kansas state school board ruled that Darwin should be stripped from public school curriculum because evolution is not a fact, but a theory. It would seem that the nature of nature remains a site of conflict. And certainly any theory about nature – whether biological, religious, or psychological – will help to shape ruling common-sense ideas about sex, race, and gender.

In July 1851, *Harper's New Monthly Magazine* reported that "there appears to be a decided and growing tendency on the part of our countrywomen to wear the trowsers" (288). So *Harper's* kindly offered to the "practical reformers, bold as Joan d'Arc" a "sketch of Oriental Costume, as a model for our fair reformers," which they titled the "Turkish Costume" (288; see figure 1). The next month, *Harper's* ran a page entitled "Woman's Emancipation. Being a letter addressed to Mr. Punch, with a drawing, by a strong-minded American Woman" (424; see figure 2). A cruel if acute parody of

Figure 1   *Turkish Costume: Harper's New Monthly Magazine*, July 1851.

Figure 2   Illustration from *Harper's New Monthly Magazine*, August 1851.

American reformist tracts, whether antislavery, temperance, or suffragist, this letter, signed by Theodosia Eudoxia Bang, M.A., MCP Phi, Delta, Kappa, KLM &c.&c. (of Boston, US), reads:

> We are emancipating ourselves, among other badges of the slavery of feudalism, from the inconvenient dress of the European female. With man's functions, we have asserted our right to his garb, and especially to that part of it which invests the lower extremities. With this great symbol, we have adopted others – the hat, the cigar, the paletot or round jacket. And it is generally calculated that the dress of the Emancipated American female is quite pretty – as becoming in all points as it is manly and independent. I inclose a drawing made by my gifted fellow-citizen Increasen Tarbox of Boston US for the *Free Women's Banner*, a periodical under my conduct, aided by several gifted women of acknowledged progressive opinions. (424)

I quote *Harper's* at length because this paragraph, and the sketch, tell a tale of what was to be almost a century-long resistance to the politics of female suffrage. Independence was first and foremost a white man's prerogative, and had been since the Founding Fathers signed the Constitution into law. Until 1921, the vote, as a sign of that independence and freedom, was a man's civil prerogative as a citizen. Progressive opinions about changing

Figure 3   The "New Woman" and her bicycle from the 1890s.

the vote, and about female suffrage in particular, were deemed silly, ugly, and indecent – as evident in the name Increasen Tarbox, perhaps an allusion to the supposed perils of racial intermingling or to the outrageous indelicacy of women smoking cigars, wearing hats, their ankles scandalously exposed.

Another month later, in *The Lily* of September 1851, Bloomer published an engraving of herself. Neither as dainty and fantastically Orientalized as Harper's first version nor as short and as fantastically masculinized as the second version, this Bloomer Costume is presented as serious, sober, and decidedly female, according to the gender norms of the day. Intriguingly, though, the engraving does not refuse to suggest that the Bloomer might speak of something else, for this fashion is clearly not the fashion and if, in one hand, Mrs. Bloomer holds a fan, the other rests pointedly upon an uncorseted and generous – but not too! – waist. Demure *and* defiant, she counters the other versions. The Bloomer would return in several forms (figure 3).

It should be noted here that Bloomer herself seldom wrote or spoke about her clothes. She never gave a public lecture on dress reform, for example. She preferred to let the Bloomer costume speak for itself – and evidently, for a few years, it spoke quite loudly and contradictorily. There were Bloomer polkas, waltzes, theatrical productions; there were songs like "I want to be a Bloomer." But there were also Staffordshire china figures made of Mrs. Bloomer, one showing her wearing a man's collar and holding a cigar (Gattey, *Bloomer Girls*, 73). And there were those Lowell factory girls, who in working in the mills or in the garment industry, were among the most poorly paid laborers in the United States, a fact that Amelia Bloomer, who did speak about women and labor, never forgot. And in 1852, in Montreal, women reenacted a mild version of *Lysistrata*, using the Bloomer: they threatened *en masse* to don the new outfit if the city did not immediately take measures to clean the streets.

However, in that threat one can see the beginning of the Bloomer's political decline: the ladies of Montreal did not, in fact, don the Bloomer *en masse* and by 1854, few besides Amelia Bloomer herself still wore the costume in public. The sheer dailiness of wardrobe began to blast away at the women's resolve.[13] "We put the dress on for greater freedom," lamented Elizabeth Cady Stanton, "but what is physical freedom compared with mental bondage? ... It is not wise ... to use up so much energy and feeling that way" (Stanton *et al.*, *History of Woman Suffrage*, 890). In March 1856, Charlotte Forten reported that she was persuaded to go to a party dressed "in full Bloomer costume, which I have since had good cause to regret" (151). As Susan B. Anthony said, the Bloomer had become something of "an intellectual slavery; one never could get rid of thinking of herself, and the important thing is to forget self. The attention of my audiences was fixed on my clothes instead of my words" (quoted in Barry, *Anthony*, 82).[14]

Anthony's and Stanton's sense that their words and their clothes were in competition for meaning, and that by adopting clothes – and then, finally, political positions – more in keeping with majority expectation, one could forget oneself, is a forcible reminder that appearances speak and that they do not always say what was intended, nor do they guarantee the meaning of the message. As Joan Blumberg notes, for women in the nineteenth century, appearance was linked to moral character – "becoming a better person meant paying *less* attention to the self ... When girls in the nineteenth century thought about ways to improve themselves, they almost always focused on their internal character and how it was reflected in outward behavior" (*Body Project*, xxi). So although appearance was supposed to be a matter of indifference, and although excessive frippery was seen as a moral failing in a woman, ironically, it mattered very much what Susan B. Anthony wore – her appearance played a large part in how an audience would respond to her, and she was perhaps the most public figure of the women's rights movement. Some of the reports she received about the Bloomer were not encouraging.

Among the most virulent was the claim that the Bloomerites were "a hybrid species, half-man, half-woman, belonging to neither sex" (Gattey, *Bloomer Girls*, 85). Such descriptions hounded those women who felt impelled to speak in the public sphere, no matter what clothing they wore, because like it or not, appearance figured as part of the conflict.

Dress was a persistent topic of concern for women in the nineteenth century, whether or not they were of the middle class, whether or not they advocated temperance, abolition, or women's rights. If the Bloomerites went too far in the direction of "masculinization," the increasingly seductive dictates of fashion, often seen, as I mentioned earlier, as a foreign French import, threatened to enfeeble, degrade, and imperil womanhood – or as Sara Parton (a.k.a. author Fanny Fern) wrote in "To the Ladies: a Call to be a Wife," a woman who thought "more of her silk dress than her children" was an abomination (307–8). Not surprisingly, the kind of rhetoric used against the enfeebling effects of fashion mirrors that launched in the early nineteenth century at the supposedly ennervating effects of "silly" novel-reading. Indeed, as historian Mary Kelley notes, when novelist Caroline Howard Gilman (a.k.a. Clarissa Packard) recounted the events surrounding her first publication, in 1810, she recalled that she had wept bitterly about it because it seemed shameful to her at the time, "as if I had been detected in man's apparel" (*Private Woman, Public Stage*, 180).

But despite the fear and the warnings, the novel gained a place in the household, and as the nineteenth century progressed, more and more women turned to writing as a means to support themselves; meanwhile, more and more magazines like *Godey's Ladies Book* entered the home carrying images of, and patterns for, the latest styles. Riotous fashion was winning out over sober maternity, and although Amelia Jenks Bloomer saw her invention as a "modest proposal" on behalf of sobriety in dress, other women, like Fanny Fern, could only see it as an even worse alternative to frippery – a coarsening of womanhood's true grace and beauty. And sadly, as late as 1963, when Betty Friedan wrote *The Feminine Mystique*, part of what she sought to correct was a then still-prevalent notion that the women of the suffragette movement had been coarse and unfashionable: "These women," she felt compelled to write, "were not man-eaters" (86). Common knowledge, however, said otherwise: in the early 1960s, the feminism of the nineteenth century, as well as the soon-to-come second feminist movement, was generally thought to be a dirty joke, perpetrated by hard-faced, humorless, embittered, unfashionable, sex-deprived or alien, i.e. lesbian, lower-class, foreign, hybrid, shrews. Never mind that both Anthony and Stanton had been of the middle class, white "ladies" of their time. And never mind that both knew full well the impact of appearance, using it, when expedient, to further their own cause. Early supporters of the rational dress, they dropped it in 1854 when it began to become a source of such persistent abuse that it was a political liability.

And then, in 1868, Stanton and Anthony undertook a rather more radical, conservative, and distressing campaign. With the Civil War over and the cause for women's equality no further along than it was in 1848, they found themselves faced with the fact that abolitionists like Frederick Douglass had turned their attention to getting freedmen the vote. Outraged, Stanton and Anthony severed their ties with what was left of the abolitionist movement by forming the National Woman's Suffrage Association, and later began to court southern politicians by claiming that a white woman's racial superiority outweighed the claims of freedmen. The proposed constitutional amendment that would grant "Manhood Suffrage" was, wrote Stanton, "an open, deliberate insult to the women of the nation." Universal male suffrage would allow men of the "lower orders, natives and foreigners, Dutch, Irish, Chinese and African" (quoted in Newman, *White Women's Rights*, 64), to legislate for white women and this, she argued, was an abomination, much to the horror and dismay of many former abolitionist colleagues, like the Grimké sisters, who stayed with the Women's Suffrage Association because it continued to support the fight for African-American emancipation and equality (Birney, *Grimké Sisters*, 333). Finally, by 1881, when Stanton and Anthony wrote the first volume of the still yet to be achieved *History of Woman Suffrage*, certain alliances were downplayed or scripted out. As historian Anne C. Coon notes, "references to Bloomer and the *Lily* in the *History* were minimal, and Bloomer's chapter on Iowa was heavily edited" (*Hear Me Patiently*, 30). Their mutual association, it is true, had never been an easy one, given Bloomer's far more tentative and sometimes conservative approach to the issues that motivated Stanton and Anthony. But the Bloomers had also moved. In 1853, they moved to Ohio, where Amelia tried to keep *The Lily* alive. But later, after they moved on to Council Bluffs, Iowa – at that time still a frontier town – she was forced to give it up. In Iowa, although she continued to work on behalf of women and temperance, she was removed from "the geographical, emotional and political center of the woman's movement" (ibid.). In addition, she had always been somewhat of a difficult colleague, shy but outspoken, often irritable and well aware that she had neither the class privilege nor the education nor social position of either Anthony or Stanton (ibid., 31). In fact, some commentators at the time blamed the failure of the Bloomer on class prejudice. "Mrs. Merrifield, whose *Dress as a Fine Art* (1854) is one of the most enlightening books on fashion at this time, says: 'We are content to adopt the greatest absurdities in dress when they are brought from Paris or recommended by a French name, but American fashion has no chance of success in aristocratic England'" (64).

Thus did the story of Amelia Jenks Bloomer, and the Bloomer Costume to which she had given her name, begin to shrink. As Anne C. Coon writes:

> In histories of the early feminist movement, Amelia Bloomer's contributions are often summarized in a brief reference to the garment that bears her name. While her support of dress reform did indeed focus national attention on the "Bloomerites," and did result in a sweeping, yet fleeting, national preoccupation with a new style of dress, Amelia Bloomer has left us with much more than a "costume." Still, the substance of her work has been eclipsed by the image of the "Bloomer" as a "shocking" and "immoral" costume in the nineteenth century and, in later years of "bloomers" as frivolous or "unmentionable" undergarments. Thus, our memory of Amelia Bloomer has regrettably been reduced to caricature. (*Hear Me Patiently*, 16)

Bloomers crept back into the closet in 1854, and vanished from the streets until the 1890s. In fact, their disappearance was helped along by the way in which the suffragettes themselves used the prejudice of appearance, and responded to the pressures of everyday abuse and ridicule. Although some, like Gerrit Smith, Elizabeth Smith Miller's activist father, remained adamant that dress reform was a necessary and integral part of any movement that would emancipate women, others – and significantly, those politically prominent, white, middle-class women who had attempted to wear the garments – found the daily grind of being associated with children, the working class, or simply sticking out like a sore (masculine) thumb amongst their peers, too dispiriting and physiologically taxing. As J. C. Flugel reports in his curious, oft-cited study, *The Psychology of Clothes*, issued 1930 by the Hogarth Press:

> Of course there is such a thing as negative prestige. A fashion may be killed in its infancy by being adopted by persons whom it is considered undesirable to imitate. The classical instance of this was the sudden disappearance of "bloomers" in 1851 when a London brewery dressed all their barmaids in nether garments of this type. Another (and in a sense more literal) method of killing fashions was by associating them with public executions – in the persons either of the executed or the executioner. In Queen Anne's reign there was considerable pother about women appearing in the street in their nightgowns. But this fashion speedily came to an end when a woman was executed in a garment of this description. In the terminology of the behaviourist, the habit was "deconditioned" by being thus brought into association with an event of such a painful character. (152 n. 2)

It would seem, then, that until the latter half of the twentieth century, middle-class women who panted in public found not freedom, but rather associations that were too painful and counterproductive to endure.

Cycles

Thus does appearance speak louder than words. And yet, the word *bloomer* itself remained in the vocabulary, and in use – or as Charles Nelson Gattey wrote in 1967, "Mrs. Bloomer has indeed had her revenge and we should be grateful to this singular woman who gave the world so useful a plural" (*Bloomer Girls*, 14). Furthermore, by 1873–4, dress reform once again became an issue for widespread public debate, first in Boston and then in other cities, when Abba Louisa Goold Woolson, a teacher, popular literary essayist, and an officer of the New England Women's Club sponsored a series of lectures about dress.

This is not to say that the *issue* of dress reform had died out utterly in the intervening years; but these lectures were offered so frequently, and became popular enough that Woolson collected and published them. The lecturers were four women doctors – Mary J. Safford-Blake, Caroline E. Hastings, Mercy B. Jackson, and Arvilla B. Haynes – and Woolson herself, and the lectures were designed to convince the general public that "the whole structure and the essential features of our present apparel are undeniably opposed to the plainest requirements of health, beauty and convenience" (Woolson, *Dress Reform*, vi). These women saw to it that an "accessible and attractive room, which is intended to serve for a bureau of information on all matters connected with dress reform," was set up at "25 Winter Street, over Chandler's dry-goods store, room 15." They also provided, at the lowest cost possible, garments and patterns for garments designed on "strict hygienic principles."

Although she seldom said so in public, Woolson herself favored pants; but in 1874, "bloomers" were still seen as far too radical a move. Overly heavy skirts, corseting, flimsy materials: these might all prove to be physically dangerous. Yet the doctors who agreed to help Woolson still had rhetorically to manage the tradition of the "American Costume" by designating it as a brave, intelligent attempt, but one which both delayed true dress reform and, in the end, had given too much credit to what Woolson termed "thoughtless women." Because the Bloomer

sought to accomplish an immediate result by ill-considered and inadequate means ... to the majority of thoughtless women it remained an object of indifference or of ridicule ... Men sneered at the costume without mercy, and branded it hideous. As made and worn by many of its followers, it was certainly not beautiful: but had it been perfection itself, it would have utterly perished; for arrayed against it were the force of ignorance and of habit . . . [even] had the costume succeeded in establishing itself as our permanent and recognized dress, it would not have rendered further reform unnecessary . . . So long as the trunk of the body is girded in the middle by bands, with too little clothing above and an excess of it below, so long will the greatest evil of our present dress remain untouched. (*Dress Reform*, x–xi)

The doctors had changed tactics. Rather than cite the rational politics of emancipation which had been the clarion call of the mid-century suffragettes, they chose to use moral patriotism and the science of hygiene to argue the same things their predecessors had argued: that fashion was a foreign import, thereby un-American; that women of the upper classes had a moral duty to dress with less ostentation; that American women should begin a gradual shift towards a more healthful style befitting the natural shape of a woman's childbearing form. They had, they said, a far more scientifically sound version of *common sense* than that of either the radical Bloomerites or previous doctors, and they offered a series of talks which presented what they saw as up-to-date medical and historical evidence to prove that women's fashionable clothing was physiologically dangerous and morally repugnant, a threat to the life of the (white) woman, her child, and the future of the nation.

"In presenting to you some thoughts upon the subject of dress," says Mary J. Safford-Blake, M.D., "I do not desire you to accept my *ipse dixit* of right or wrong; but I hope you will probe the facts presented, and, if they appeal to your common sense and reason as truths, that you will heed them, not alone for your own good, but that your influence may go forth as a help and guide to others" (*Dress Reform*, 5). Mercy B. Jackson, M.D. goes further. "We are a republican nation," she says,

at least in form, and have no distinct classes where the lines are so tightly drawn that citizens cannot pass from one to the other . . . We should therefore, as good citizens and as Christian women, do all we can to foster self-respect . . . Is not society accountable in a great measure for . . . breaches of trust in private citizens and public servants? And who but women control the customs of society, and make them either prudent, wise, and moral, or extravagant, foolish and immoral? I appeal to the moral sense of the ladies present, and I ask them if they are willing, by their example and influence, longer to countenance a mode of dress which is so little fitted to answer the reasonable demands that should be made upon it, and so destructive of health and morals? (*Dress Reform*, 91–5)

In other words, according to these female physicians, *their* mode of rational dress reform was more scientifically and medically rational than the previous rational dress; their garments would not speak so directly of anything like "emancipation," as the famous failure had, but rather of moral strength and scientific fact. Significantly, almost none of the physicians use the term *bloomer* when describing the various costumes that they urge their middle-class audiences to adopt, even when the item in question looked a lot like, well, pants. Yet a corset and hoops remained, to many, indispensable; a "lady" in 1874 was hooped and the persistence of the corset and hoop shows that the women physicians ran into at least as much resistance as their misguided mothers. It should be noted, too, that many of the physiological, hygienic and antifashion arguments would continue to be made over and over again, as in, for example, Miss Ada S. Ballin's *The Science of Dress in Theory and Practice*, published in 1885. Miss Ballin thought the Bloomer had failed because it was too violent a change from tradition. She promotes the demure divided skirt.[15]

Still, as I have noted, most middle-class women continued to tight-lace and hoop. The general public resisted dress reform, and the idea of the Bloomer as a radical, unfeminine costume remained to haunt any type of so-called rational alteration, especially one that included pants. Very few middle-class women, even if persuaded that their health might be at risk, took heed of medical or scientific common sense because ladies were made, and middle-class women wanted to be seen as genteel, white ladies, not as something other or darker. If that meant corsets and hoops, so be it. Otherwise, what you had was not a "natural" (white) lady. Fashions that signified gender, race, and class, through the material means of laces and stays, held sway and so did the taint of past ridicule and caricature, which kept gay and panting lasses straight-laced and off the streets.

Then, fifty years or so after the initial failure of bloomers, the bicycle arrived and bloomers finally came into their own. "Women began riding bicycles and for this new sport, they wore bloomers. Soon after that bloomers became the name of a style of feminine drawers or knickers which had a great vogue in the early twentieth century, especially under sports clothes and schoolgirls' gym tunics" (Ewing, *Dress and Undress*, 64). Sometimes also called knickerbockers, but more often and more generally named bloomers, the cycling costume spread with the bicycling craze.[16] Like the bicycle itself, Betty Bloomer had arrived. And so had changes in the manufacture of clothing. Beginning as early as the 1830s, but culminating in Isaac Merrit Singer's patent in February of 1854, the sewing machine greatly aided in the mass production of men's clothing, but as the twentieth century came into view, more and more clothes were being made for women "ready-to-wear." As Nancy L. Green remarks, "the masculinization of certain feminine styles encouraged the transfer of ready-made techniques to women's wear

(*Ready-to-Wear, Ready to Work*, 27). Therefore, even if "Betty Bloomer was ahead of her time in pushing pants" (27), her ubiquity and familiarity, along with changes in manufacturing, labor practices and technology, paved the way for the public's acceptance of trousered women. This was particularly so in France. As Valerie Steele notes, "Bloomers indeed seem to have been far more commonly worn in Paris than in England or the United States ... and this was the case despite the fact that many fashion writers strongly disliked the costume, regarding it as ugly and unfeminine. But ... everyone wore bloomers ... Very likely this was precisely *because* bloomers were presented in France as a fashionable item (rather than as a quasi-feminist statement)" (*Paris Fashion*, 76). Thus, by 1895, many middle-class girls in the United States had not only adopted the bike and the Bloomer, they also began to adopt the epithet the "New Woman," and so ushered in the twentieth century. This is not to say that the New Woman was without controversy; sharp battles were still being fought over woman's proper place, and as Marta Banta remarks:

> Consider what it meant to be a feminist at the turn of the century in light of the problems of identification created by her ideological position. A woman who elected to advance a body of social and political principles was compelled to resolve the question of how to embody those abstract values pictorially ... Somehow the feminist had to *dress* her ideas and her inner convictions in order to let them be expressed, however inadequately, by the surface she presented. Only then would "society's" perception of her image translate into collective conduct that would advance her principles and protect her from hostility and ridicule. (*Imaging American Women*, 78)

And it should also be noted that although bloomers had gone public, they were increasingly understood as a *specialized* costume. So if bloomers no longer bore the same stamp of a colonialist seraglio erotic fantasy that the original spa clothing of Turkish trowsers might have borne, they did retain the eroticism of gender transgression that had made George Sand so infamous. Furthermore, as bloomers moved farther and farther into the realm of the narrowly particularized – as they became more of what we might think of as a true "costume," for gymnastics, for bathing, for biking or for titillation, rather than as an every-day *habit* donned socially in lieu of a dress or skirts – what they took with them was their history of female political resistance to patriarchal domination.

Common sense about women, however, had been changed. Although the athletic woman was undoubtedly the subject of scoffing throughout the 1890s and into the early part of the twentieth century, by the 1920s the athleticism of girls was generally considered more natural and healthy. A story published in *McClure's* magazine in June 1922 illustrates such changes to a woman's common sense about herself, as well as the ambivalence with which those changes were received. The story is a satire entitled "She Didn't Have Any Sense" by Scammon Lockwood, and tells us that "the chief reason all the women had for saying that Allegra Bascom didn't have any sense was because she laced. This, to a strong-minded, sensible lady who believes in suffrage and the equality of the sexes is the very last word in female folly." But Allegra is still the heroine of this piece.

Nevertheless, slowly and surely, the Gibson Girl gave way to F. Scott Fitzgerald's Jazz Age flappers with their bobbed hair. Trousers for women were no longer a complete outrage and no longer viewed with as complete a popular disdain as they had been in 1851. A new common sense about femininity was burgeoning, helped along by the bloomer girls, the New Woman, and by medical and scientific reforms regarding hygiene and gynaecology, or as Joan Blumberg notes, by 1913,

> American middle-class women were developing a heightened sensibility about issues of feminine hygiene. They found the new disposable napkins extremely desirable because they promised less work, more comfort, greater mobility and a germ-free environment. The new hygiene also provided middle-class mothers with a safe script for their private conversations with their daughters. Instead of talking about the "curse of Eve" or "nerve stimulation" (which they could not see), they focused on the logistics of "sanitary protection." (*Body Project*, 40)

By the 1920s, the American middle-class woman had, after a long and bitter struggle, gained the vote. But she did not gain, nor has she gained, the equal rights amendment early suffragettes sought. Still, more and more girls, despite discouragement, took to the sports field; more changes to the common-sense understanding of femininity were introduced, through new scientific fields like psychology and gynaecology, and if some of that new common sense looks questionable by the standards of the late twentieth and early twenty-first century, it also shifted the sphere of woman's influence.

At the same time, bloomers, as an item of clothing, were being thoroughly tamed, stripped, as it were, of their emancipatory meaning. Once made into a semi-acceptable costume, their brashness and their anger seemed less brazen. The vote achieved, the point of "bloomers" was less sharp. Soon, these pants would be relegated to childhood, and to the past. The word *bloomer* would reflect such a change because as the pants themselves were translated from the rude, the revolutionary, and the indecent to the practical, pragmatic, and finally to the childish, no longer was the word able to signify anything like a bold new (feminist) tongue.

Feminism and fashion

By the 1940s and 1950s it was not unusual for women to wear trousers or slacks as they were called for a host of particular reasons. They did not, however, don anything like the suffragette bloomers. Meanwhile, generally speaking, men still wore the pants. As noted earlier, during both the First and Second World Wars, women who worked wore boilersuits and blue jeans. Between 1915 and 1954 skirts lengthened and shortened according to the dictates of fashion and need, while the feminine profile went from the corseted hourglass to the pencil-thin flapper and back again to the hourglass, at least as that hourglass was constructed through those binding but flexible girdles and bras that had been made possible by the wartime inventions of nylon, rayon, and polyesters.

But all this time, only children were dressed in bloomers or knickers. And although actresses such as Marlene Dietrich and Katherine Hepburn or fashionable, infamous women like Coco Chanel might wear trousers in public, in *general*, the middle-class woman wore some variation of a dress: from the Chanel suit to the Dior "New Look," they wore skirts, house and cocktail dresses or evening-gowns. By the late 1950s, if certain types of pants had come into vogue – such as the tapered ski-pant or stirrup pant – slacks, as the name implies, were still considered leisurewear. A working woman would seldom, if ever, wear pants to the office. Indeed, when Capri pants became fashionable in the late 1950s, some fashion magazines once again lamented the sheer ugliness of trousers on women, a lament reminiscent of the fashionable disdain for bloomers that helped to drive the garment off the streets nearly 100 years earlier.[17]

But by the late 1950s, continuing into the early 1970s, significant alterations were underway. These alterations of the *social* order began to be reflected in, and, indeed, managed by, the fashion pages. And in 1967, an old familiar word was dusted off and made its way back into use, at least briefly. As the Paris *Evening News* reported, "Bloomers peep boldly beneath the hemlines of short as ever smocks and shifts … beguiling bloomers in acid colors, aimed at the young and gay … miniskirts are dead, long live bloomers" (Gattey, *Bloomer Girls*, 177-8). Although the concept of Parisian *haute couture* had existed for years alongside the always increasing mass production of ready-to-wear lines, the late 1960s and early 1970s saw resistance, subversion, and nostalgia inundate fashion. Widespread demand for the unique, for the ethnic, the hand-made and the antiestablishment made a significant impact on what women wore and how they wore it. Thus the late 1960s and early 1970s was a period in which "personal" or "individualistic" styling, as it was called, went hand in hand with more traditional modes. Both saw rapid change. But it was the "London Look" that took off, and "took off" in more ways than one. After years and years of covering themselves head to toe, young women ditched the yardage for skin. This "look" was dominated by the mini-skirt, introduced in 1966, and by Mary Quant's bell-bottoms covered by a tunic that sometimes doubled as a mini-skirt. Such comparative nudity was followed by a rage for culottes, hot-pants, micro-mini-skirts and a bashful little pair of panties called bloomers. Even Turkish trousers came back, as an "ethnic" item. Midi and maxi lengths also appeared, but from 1966 on, young, carefree and childish held sway and "the glossy magazines went overboard with the new fashion mood ... It began to mean that you could wear anything anywhere" (Ewing, *History of Twentieth-Century Fashion*, 200). But by insisting on fantasy and *youth*, girlhood as sexy, fashion played down political revolution. Young and individualistic, these were the terms being marshaled to both describe and in effect contain the "youth revolution" or "youth explosion." Of course, the "erotic child," the sex-kitten, the "nymphet," as Humbert Humbert put it,[18] had enjoyed – and continues to enjoy – a long history in the United States. This kind of eroticism – especially the eroticization of little girls – is evident in popular American culture in figures like Little Eva and Shirley Temple, Lolita and Jon-Bennet Ramsey. Part of Marilyn Monroe's appeal was her combination of childlike innocence and overt sexuality.[19] The Oneida Perfectionist Community had known full well that women adopting the fashions of girlhood took on an attractive, virginal glow (Fischer, "'Pantalets' and 'Turkish Trowsers,'" 134). But the contrast between the vision of femininity that appeared on the fashion pages of the 1960s and the images of the women who took part in various social or political rebellions is nevertheless a marked one. That is, despite wild oscillations in image and fashion, in 1972, as Elizabeth Ewing notes, most middle-class "women still derived their position mainly from their relationships with men, so fashion aimed to attract men and in its development the 'seduction principle' was closely bound up with the hierarchic or status one" (*History of Twentieth-Century Fashion*, 229). The predominance of this pattern was no doubt under siege. Divorce rates spiked; Second Wave feminist activism took shape. Meanwhile, however, the fashion pages put women in pigtails and baby dolls, knee socks and bloomers. Thus, for example, although Motown might have been changing the face, race, and sound of popular music, the fact that *The Supremes* had a breakthrough hit single in 1964 with *Baby Love* is suggestive. And yet, although the predominance of the Baby Doll over and against the Bra Burner may seem to belittle the angrier aspects of the youth revolution, at the same time, a new common sense about sexuality was being forged, one in which it was no longer wholly unusual or "unnatural" for a woman to "wear the pants." Such a new common sense about femininity has not been achieved without pain, of course, nor without struggles that look to continue on into the twenty-first century.[20] It was, however, a new way of understanding one's place in the world and a far cry from the last turn of the century, when, even after fifty-two years of agitation, women were still unable to vote as fully fledged American citizens.

The word *bloomer*, however, after its brief fling as mod style for the hip flower-child of the 1960s, and perhaps in part *because* of that fling, still refers to undergarments or children's clothes. If mentioned at all, the Bloomer Costume is most often deemed a failure that had politically bankrupt – or at least counterproductive – colonialist effects. Cultural critic Marjorie Garber's narrative about the ill-fated costume is a typical one:

> As an innovation, unfortunately, the Bloomer Costume ranks with the Susan B. Anthony silver dollar; only a few convinced individuals, and some utopian communities, adopted the style. The Turkish connotations attracted some unfavorable attention, despite the rage for artifacts *à la Turque* ... a writer to the New York Tribune pointed out the lack of freedom of Middle Eastern women compared to Americans, and suggested that the spectacle of female reformers in Turkish trousers was properly a cause for cultural irony. (*Vested Interests*, 314)

Not only has Garber reduced the number of people who wore the Bloomer to "a few convinced individuals" – a description that contradicts the historical record – but she also insists, here, upon the Oriental aspect of the dress.[21] However, while it is certainly true that critics of the costume at the time pointed out the Bloomer's association with things Oriental and Turkish, it is equally true that the Bloomer Costume was neither called nor conceived of as precisely Turkish or Eastern by many who *adopted* Amelia Jenks Bloomer's particular version. To these women, Bloomer had made "panting," a male prerogative, female. The alterations made to the Turkish idea had Americanized it, had made the Bloomer as American as apple pie, and, as Gayle Fischer has persuasively demonstrated, the "complexities of cultural borrowing within fashion" ("'Pantalets' and 'Turkish Trowsers,'" 123) are profound in the case of bloomers. As she argues, "[I]f the women's rights dress reformers chose Turkish trowsers in order to distance their costume from male dress and make it more palatable to the general public, then they failed. Although many disliked the freedom dress because of its Eastern origins, they were far outnumbered by those who simply felt that women dressed in 'Turkish' pantaloons looked like men" (129).

To a contemporary cultural critic, the *seeming* refusal, on, say, Amelia Bloomer's part, to fully acknowledge or understand the irony of bloomers may, of course, read like another indication of the imbalances of colonialism, as Garber suggests. But again, the historical record suggests otherwise, inasmuch as the abolitionist and suffragette women in the nineteenth century knew full well that their so-called rational garment had an erotic and exoticized irony. Debates about "other" cultural practices of female oppression, from the so-called slavery of Eastern women to the practice of Chinese foot-binding, raged in the pages of *The Lily* and in other emancipation or abolitionist newspapers.[22] What the dress reformers *believed* they were seeking, by adopting bloomers, was a common-sense dress, one that was based upon logical arguments regarding the natural shape of the female body, just as dress reform physicians believed they did in the 1870s.

However, history, as surely every historian must know, is seldom recounted or recalled with an accuracy that reflects archival records. Similarly, rationality and common sense often have *nothing* to do with one another. And clothes, as women from the Bloomerites to the bra burners knew only too well, often speak more loudly and far less rationally than the person wearing them. Clothes will tell tales – or have tales told of them – and there is no lack of idiomatic or historical evidence to prove that clothes are made to tell particular, common-sense stories (seldom rational) about politics and everyday life. For as historian Kathy Peiss notes, it was not just bloomers that spoke of politics:

> Women strikers in a thread-mill (1890s), for example, linked fashion – wearing bonnets – to their sense of American identity and class consciousness, contrasting their militancy to Scottish scabs who wore shawls on their heads. Believing in the labor movement's ideology of self-improvement, organization, worker's dignity, these women devoted their leisure to lectures, evening school, political meetings and union dances. (*Cheap Amusements*, 64)

Furthermore, at the end of the twentieth century, idiomatically, one can still be told that "clothes make the man," and that women "dress to kill." Indeed, although the stricter *Man in the Gray Flannel Suit* dress codes for men and women did give way to the pressure of love-beads, *Hair*, and the wilder extravagances of Glam Rock or disco, women are often counseled to wear something "appropriate" to an interview; rape cases are won or lost depending on the victim's choice of underwear. Cross-dressing on the job, unless it is your job, can get you fired. Because, as Roland Barthes reminds us in *The Fashion System*, clothes signify. Like words, they are subject to both vastly different interpretations and changing mores. In 1902, when Theodore Dreiser made clothes speak in his novel *Sister Carrie* – as if to ratify Karl Marx's theory of commodity fetishism, first published in 1867 – clothes spoke with both a "moral significance" to the wayward Carrie, and with the pressure of a desire not to be withstood. As Carrie wanders through the new-found glories of an urban department store, she finds fine clothes "a vast persuasion; they spoke tenderly and Jesuitically for themselves," in a voice that a shoe fetishist might have longed to hear: "'Ah, such little feet,' said the leather of the soft new shoes, 'how effectively I cover them'" (98). Despite her sense that she ought to be or to get married, rather than living as a kept woman, Carrie's desire for nice clothes overwhelms all other considerations.

Indeed, clothes speak to us of ourselves as we exist in a dense cultural web of multiple class boundaries, ethnic or racial heritages, and sexual dimorphism, as well as changes made to those systems over time. Clothes and fashion can serve to code what is now called "sexual orientation" – as in, for example, the green suits and red ties of men seeking the company of men during the 1930s[23] – and sexual availability – as in the variety of statements the wearing of a ring can make, although jewelry is technically not clothing and I could no doubt fill the pages of an entirely different chapter than this one about it. My point here is that the politics of the everyday makes clothes speak and that clothes speak to us of the dailiness of our politics, as this brief history of "panting" girls demonstrates.

If the social upheavals during the 1960s and 1970s ushered in distinct changes to the sociopolitical landscape for the average American woman, fierce arguments, both private and public, about the significance of so-called "traditional" women's accouterments *still* rage – should one wear lipstick? under what circumstances? should one shave one's legs? wear high-heels? is one oppressed if one does so? The choices made are politically inflected and received as such, whether one follows a conscious feminist politics or not. According to Kath Weston, for example, "many feminists regarded traditionally feminine dress as impractical, uncomfortable attire that objectified women and rendered them vulnerable to sexual attack. Skirts, heels, long hair, and makeup were the first to go. A woman who walked into a lesbian bar in a dress ... was likely to have her lesbian identity questioned and unlikely to have anyone ask her to dance" ("Do Clothes Make the Woman?," 15). Impractical, uncomfortable, oppressive: are these not the same commonsense terms by which the mid-nineteenth-century Bloomerites condemned corsets and the yardage of crinoline they were supposed to wear? And those who donned the more practical, less oppressive, more rational Bloomer costume, as we have seen, also had their femininity questioned – sometimes humorously, sometimes vilely and violently. One thus might be tempted to conclude, along with both Gayle V. Fischer and Marjorie Garber, that what "bloomers" speak about is failure. The bloomer may be merely a demonstration of another common-sense adage – that everything changes and everything stays the same. However much we know that clothes speak a multitude of conflicting meanings, we also always already know what they say.

And yet, as the history of the word *bloomer* sketched out in this chapter suggests, such stasis hardly reflects the historical record because, over time, common sense about femininity, repeatedly challenged by new social practices, new medical and political understandings, *was* and is changed. The history of the word *bloomer*, then, can serve as an index not only to a certain kind of failure, but also as a testament to the changes made in commonly held cultural attitudes and to the sociopolitical domain in which women live out their lives. Rather than lay blame for the failure of bloomers at the feet of Amelia Jenks Bloomer herself, or on the concept of frivolity, or at the doorstep of a misguided Western colonialism, I want to argue that what failed was not bloomers, not really, because eventually, in changing, they helped to accomplish change. What failed was, rather, the suffragettes' reliance on the idea that rationality was equal to common sense, and that both would prove persuasive enough to produce the political changes they sought. Because common sense is not simple, or plain, or rational. It is fickle, variable and crazy. The problem with the Bloomer Costume was the problem of common sense. Logically, Amelia Jenks Bloomer, Libby Smith, Elizabeth Cady Stanton, and Susan B. Anthony were being rational. Everyone knew that trousers were more convenient and comfortable than a dress. To wear a garment that increased one's mobility was not a mere frivolity, and they designed one along the lines of women's garments with which they were already familiar. The problem with the Bloomer was that it interfered with a common sense about that most irrational of domains, sex, and sexual desire. Until and unless common sense is altered, no amount of "panting" will change the general public's mind.

Furthermore, in hindsight, much of what these women *wrote* about their hopes and ideals seems today not only movingly eloquent, but also sounds remarkably, resoundingly like *current* common sense. Here is Amelia Jenks Bloomer, speaking in the 1870s:

> We are not content that the universities at Ithaca, Ann Arbor and Iowa City should open their doors to the equal admission of both sexes to the advantages of collegiate education, but we would have the same generous policy control all the colleges and universities in the country. The doors of Harvard, Yale, and Union, in this country, and of Oxford and Cambridge, in England, should be also open to woman and the contest will not be ended until this is accomplished.

Everywhere, in every form, the just claims of woman to equal educational privileges must be ultimately acknowledged. And not only this, but we claim that she shall nowhere be debarred from any form of industry or any sphere of labor for which she has capacity, and when she accomplishes as much by her day's work as a man does by his, that she shall be paid the same price. (Coon, *Hear Me Patiently*, 183)

In effect, then, if bloomers failed, Amelia Jenks Bloomer did not, entirely, even if many are still waiting to be paid the same wage as a man. However, to create a new politics and a new political language – whether of dress or of words – is next to impossible if a common usage does not take hold. And as the activist women of antebellum America also knew, one must repeat oneself, wearily, over and over again, to be heard through the din of common sense. Therefore, if the domain of the everyday – in language or in dress – remains one of the most resistant to political agitation, it is also the place wherein the politics of change eventually comes to reside. It should not be surprising, then, to find that voice and image have long been the staging ground from which American social activism such as the feminist movement – First, Second or Third Wave – have launched campaigns. Thus it might be wise indeed to insist that the *entire* history of a word like *bloomer* be noted, that is, to insist that the infantilization of this American *political* neologism not be forgotten. For in the historical process of such linguistic change is visible an on-going struggle over the nature of nature. Women in the nineteenth century did make a bold bid to tether the power of language to their own purposes; they sought to forge new meanings, in clear, eloquent, and rational arguments which were nevertheless received by many as gibberish. Still, through persistence and the repetition of such so-called female blather, everyday common sense did change, and if the Bloomer became bloomers, we would be wise to at least try to remember how and why.[24]

NOTES

1. See Fischer, "'Pantalets' and 'Turkish Trowsers,'" on the degree to which dress reform preoccupied a number of women for different and often conflicting reasons.
2. On the general preferability of male attire, see ibid., Coon, *Hear Me Patiently*, and Steele, *Paris Fashion*.
3. As Fischer remarks, Lady Mary Wortley Montagu famously wore trousers in her travels in Turkey ("'Pantalets' and 'Turkish Trowsers,'" 116). See also "Costumes." For a more extensive history of trousers as underwear, see Ewing, *Dress and Undress*.

4. In any history of the Bloomer costume, the question of decency is always an issue. For discussions of eroticism and trousers, see: Steele, *Paris Fashion* and *Fashion and Eroticism*; Ewing, *Dress and Undress*; Fischer, "'Pantalets' and 'Turkish Trowsers'"; Kesselman, "'Freedom Suit'"; Craik, *Faces of Fashion*; Gaines and Herzog, *Fabrications*; and Byrde, *Nineteenth-Century Fashion*.

5. See also Peiss, *Cheap Amusements*; Garber, *Vested Interests*; Barnes and Eicher, *Dress and Gender*; and Lurie, *Language of Clothes*.

6. See Coon, *Hear Me Patiently*, 12–14; see also Stanton, *History of Woman Suffrage*, 890, and Lerner, *Grimké Sisters*, 335.

7. See Ewing, *History of Twentieth-Century Fashion*, 81–2, and Green, *Ready-to-Wear, Ready to Work*, 26–7.

8. Such questions are reflected in incidents such as the blue jean scandal in Italy, in 1998, when the courts ruled that a woman who wore blue jeans could not legally be raped.

9. See also Martin, *The Way We Wore*.

10. See Ewing, *History of Twentieth-Century Fashion*. See also Baines, *Fashion Revivals* and Gattey, *Bloomer Girls*.

11. Other dictionaries consulted were *The American Heritage Dictionary*, *Webster's Dictionary*, and *The Dictionary of American Slang*.

12. The story of the Bloomer's genesis has been recounted both by the participants themselves, and by various histories of the movement. See Coon's "Introduction," *Hear Me Patiently*, Kesselman, "'Freedom Suit,'" Stanton, *History of Woman Suffrage*, and Lerner, *Grimké Sisters*.

13. As Fischer, "'Pantalets' and 'Turkish Trowsers'" notes, even the women of the Oneida Community gave up wearing it outside the confines of their own community walls.

14. Barry is quoting a letter from Elizabeth Cady Stanton to Susan B. Anthony, February 19, 1854, Library of Congress.

15. As quoted in Martin (*The Way We Wore*, 100–1), Miss Ada S. Ballin thought the Bloomer died because it was "too violent" a change.

16. See also Gattey, *Bloomer Girls*, Steele, *Paris Fashion* and Ewing, *History of Twentieth-Century Fashion*.

17. See Ewing and Garber, *Vested Interests*.

18. Borrowing from Vladimir Nabokov's *Lolita*.

19. See also Dyer, *Heavenly Bodies*.

20. As Coon notes, the so-called "bra burners" also suffered the same kind of ridicule as Bloomerites. The press seized upon dress as the issue and thus dismissed the other, more radical and political claims of feminism (*Hear Me Patiently*, 35 n. 4).

21. See also Lurie, *Language of Clothes*, who insists that bloomers did not enjoy any widespread attention until the 1890s.

22. As I have written elsewhere (*Conceived by Liberty*, 54), abolitionists like Lydia Maria Child often referenced other cultural practices to which they took exception when attempting to talk about the condition of women. Chinese footbinding was a favorite example; so was the seraglio. That they were unware of the irony they invited by wearing something like Turkish trowsers, or by being uninterested in the suffering of their "sisters," despite the evident and often virulent racism that ran through the women's movement, is unlikely, particularly given

the following poem that Gayle V. Fischer quotes, noting how it "compares the 'inhuman' 'Turkish' harem with the 'inhuman' Western practice of wearing physically restrictive clothing: 'Talk of Turkish women / In their harem-coop, – / Are we less inhuman, / Hampering with a hoop?'" ("'Pantalets' and 'Turkish Trowsers,'" 123).

23. See Garber, *Vested Interests*, and Chauncey, *Gay New York*.

24. I wish to dedicate this chapter to Professor Louise Newman and all my feminist colleagues.

WORKS CITED

Baines, Barbara Bruman. *Fashion Revivals: From the Elizabethan Age to the Present Day*. New York: Drama Book Publishers, 1981.

Banta, Martha. *Imaging American Women: Idea and Ideals in Cultural History*. New York: Columbia University Press, 1987.

Barnes, Ruth, and Joanne B. Eicher, eds. *Dress and Gender: Making and Meaning*. New York and Oxford: Berg Publishers, Inc. (St. Martin's), 1992.

Barry, Kathleen. *Susan B. Anthony: a Biography of a Singular Feminist*. New York: Ballantine, 1988.

Barthes, Roland. *The Fashion System*. Trans. Matthew Ward and Richard Howard. New York: Hill and Wang, 1983.

Birney, Catherine. *The Grimké Sisters: Sarah and Angelina Grimké: the First Women Advocates of Abolition and Woman's Rights*. Boston: Lee and Sheppard, 1885.

Blumberg, Joan Jacobs. *The Body Project: an Intimate History of American Girls*. 1997. New York: Vintage Books, 1998.

Byrde, Penelope. *Nineteenth-Century Fashion*. London: Batsford, 1992.

Chauncey, George. *Gay New York: Gender, Urban Culture, and the Making of the Gay Male World, 1890–1940*. New York: HarperCollins, 1994.

Coon, Anne C., ed. *Hear Me Patiently: the Reform Speeches of Amelia Jenks Bloomer*. Westport, CT: Greenwood Press, 1994.

"Costumes of All Nations: the Toilette in Turkey." *Godey's Magazine and Lady's Book* 45 (January 1852): 45.

Craik, Jennifer. *Faces of Fashion: Cultural Studies in Fashion*. New York: Routledge, 1994.

Dreiser, Theodore. *Sister Carrie*. 1900. Harmondsworth: Penguin, 1994.

Dyer, Richard. *Heavenly Bodies*. New York: St. Martin's Press, 1986.

Ewing, Elizabeth. *Dress and Undress: a History of Women's Underwear*. London: Bibliophile, 1981.

History of Twentieth-Century Fashion. London: Batsford, 1974.

Fischer, Gayle. "'Pantalets' and 'Turkish Trowsers': Designing Freedom in the Mid-Nineteenth-Century United States." *Feminist Studies* 23.1 (spring 1997).

Flugel, J. C. *The Psychology of Clothes*. 1930. International Psycho-Analytical Library 18. London: Hogarth Press and the Institute of Psycho-Analysis, 1966.

Franklin, Wayne, ed. *American Voices, American Lives*. New York: W. W. Norton, 1997.

Friedan, Betty. *The Feminine Mystique*. New York: Dell, 1963.

Gaines, Jane and Charlotte Herzog. *Fabrications: Costume and the Female Body*. New York and London: Routledge, 1990.

Garber, Marjorie. *Vested Interests: Cross-Dressing and Cultural Anxiety*. New York: HarperPerennial, 1992.

Gattey, Charles Nelson. *The Bloomer Girls*. New York: Coward-McCann, Inc., 1967.

Green, Nancy L. *Ready-to-Wear, Ready to Work: a Century of Industry and Immigrants in Paris and New York*. Durham: Duke University Press, 1997.

Grimké, Charlotte L. Forten. *The Journals of Charlotte L. Forten Grimké*. Ed. Brenda Stevenson. Schomburg Library of Nineteenth-Century Black Women Writers. New York and Oxford: Oxford University Press, 1988.

Harper's New Monthly Magazine (July 1851): 288; (August 1851): 424.

Kelley, Mary. *Private Woman, Public Stage: Literary Domesticity in Nineteenth-Century America*. New York and Oxford: Oxford University Press, 1984.

Kesselman, Amy. "The 'Freedom Suit': Feminism and Dress Reform in the United States, 1848–1875." *Gender and Society* 5 (December 1991): 495–510.

Lerner, Gerda. *The Grimké Sisters From South Carolina: Pioneers for Woman's Rights and Abolition*. New York: Schocken Books, 1971.

Lockwood, Scammon. "She Didn't Have Any Sense." *McClure's* (June 1922).

Lurie, Alison. *The Language of Clothes*. New York: Random House, 1981.

Martin, Linda. *The Way We Wore: Fashion Illustrations of Children's Wear 1870–1970*. New York: Scribner's, 1978.

Newman, Louise. *White Women's Rights: the Racial Origins of Feminism in the United States*. New York and Oxford: Oxford University Press, 1999.

Parton, Sara [Fanny Fern]. "To the Ladies: a Call to be a Wife." *Fresh Leaves*. 307-8.

Peiss, Kathy. *Cheap Amusements: Working Women and Leisure in Turn-of-the-Century New York*. Philadelphia: Temple University Press, 1986.

Smith, Stephanie A. *Conceived by Liberty: Maternal Figures and Nineteenth-Century American Literature*. Ithaca and London: Cornell University Press, 1994.

Stanton, Elizabeth Cady. *Eighty Years and More – Reminiscences 1815–1897*. 1898. New York: Schocken Books, 1971.

Stanton, Elizabeth Cady, Susan B. Anthony, and Matilda J. Gage. *History of Woman Suffrage*. 6 vols. New York: Fowler and Wells, 1881–1922.

Steele, Valerie. *Fashion and Eroticism*. New York and Oxford: Oxford University Press, 1985.

Paris Fashion: a Cultural History. New York and Oxford: Oxford University Press, 1988.

Weston, Kath. "Do Clothes Make the Woman?: Gender, Performance Theory, and Lesbian Eroticism." *Genders* 17 (fall 1993): 1–21.

Woolson, Abba Goold, ed. *Dress Reform: a Series of Lectures Delivered in Boston, On Dress as it Affects the Health of Women*, with illustrations. 1874. Reprinted in *Women in America: From Colonial Times to the Twentieth Century*. Series Eds. Leon Stein and Annette K. Baxter. New York: Arno Press, 1974.

Worrell, Estelle Ansley. *Children's Costume in America, 1607–1910*. New York: Scribner's, 1980.

2
GENRE, TRADITION, AND INNOVATION

4

KATHRYN ZABELLE DEROUNIAN-STODOLA

Captivity and the literary imagination

In *Playing in the Dark: Whiteness and the Literary Imagination*, Toni Morrison argues that the central themes of American literature – "autonomy, authority, newness and difference, absolute power" – are engendered, molded, and "activated by a complex awareness and employment of a constituted Africanism."[1] Morrison contends that race undergirds even much classic American literature because consciously and unconsciously nineteenth- and twentieth-century American authors dramatized and narrativized the essence of slavery through the trope of the "civilized" free (masters) and the "savage" unfree (slaves). Arguing against overly conservative or literal readings, she concludes, "It would be a pity if the criticism of that literature continued to shellac those texts, immobilizing their complexities and power and luminations just below its tight, reflecting surface. All of us, readers and writers, are bereft when criticism remains too polite or too fearful to notice a disrupting darkness before its eyes" (Morrison, *Playing in the Dark*, 90–1).

Complementing this postcolonial response is Sandra M. Gilbert and Susan Gubar's classic feminist interpretation of the nineteenth-century American female Gothic as employing the archetypal symbol of the "madwoman in the attic."[2] These cooped-up women subjects in the literature – perhaps best exemplified by the unnamed narrator in Charlotte Perkins Gilman's famous short story "The Yellow Wallpaper" – are physically confined by their surroundings, but they are also confined by other forms of oppression, including the psychological, sexual, and social. Indeed, in that regard, the pun on the meanings of "confinement" as enslavement and also childbirth is highly significant.

Taking primarily Morrison's and secondarily Gilbert and Gubar's studies as inspiration, this chapter proposes that nineteenth-century American women's writings reveal a particular preoccupation with captors, captives, and the rhetoric of captivity as women explored potential identities and roles in the new century. Sometimes overtly, but often covertly, these women's writings draw on the experience of slavery, mainly from the slave narrative, and the experience of captivity, mainly from the Indian captivity narrative. While these two forms probably did not originate in the United States, they certainly flourished there and were published in larger numbers than elsewhere. As more and more nineteenth-century women became authors themselves rather than merely subjects for male authors, they experimented with the captor–captive paradigm in different texts and contexts, both nonfictional and fictional.

The five works under consideration span the early to late nineteenth century, include white, black, and Native American voices, and represent considerable generic variety. They are Mary Jemison's Indian captivity narrative, *A Narrative of the Life of Mrs. Mary Jemison* (1824), incorporating the voice and persona of its Native American subject, who was interviewed for the book by author/editor James E. Seaver; Lydia Maria Child's frontier romance-cum-captivity narrative, *Hobomok* (1824); Maria Monk's *Awful Disclosures of the Hotel Dieu Nunnery of Montreal* (1836), a fiction masquerading as fact in the genre called the convent captivity narrative; Elizabeth Stoddard's short story in the realistic mode, "Lemorne *versus* Huell" (1863); and finally, a post-Civil War slave narrative calling for black pride and self-empowerment, Lucy Delaney's *From the Darkness Cometh the Light; or, Struggles for Freedom* (1891).[3] These texts all examine captivity as a dynamic cultural trope in which racial and gendered borders are simultaneously constructed and transgressed.

But why would the concept of captivity have such a hold on the literary imagination of women? To gain some insight into the potential for radical social change initiated during the Revolution, we might consider the famous epistolary interchange between Abigail and John Adams, in which Abigail asked her husband to "Remember the Ladies" in "the new Code of Laws" being drafted (March 31, 1776), and John responded that while he knew Revolutionary fervor had made schoolboys, apprentices, Indians, and slaves rebellious, he did not realize it had affected women too (April 14, 1776).[4] When it became clear, especially in the nineteenth century, that Revolutionary rhetoric and reality applied mainly to white males, some women allied themselves with other oppressed groups to show their disillusionment or voice their disapproval. They were aided both by the cultural reality of enslavement and Indian captivity and by the literary treatment of these oppressive conditions in the genres of the slave narrative and the Indian captivity narrative. Specifically, women's writings often implied that perhaps another revolution was needed in which a female ideology, with its emphasis on family and feeling, would depose a male one, with its emphasis on society and intellect.

Over and over again, women writing of bondage in the form of captivity or slavery pitted vulnerable young females – often cast as daughter figures – against tyrannous older males – often cast as fathers, suitors, husbands, or other authority figures (for example, the lawyer in "Lemorne *versus* Huell" or the priests in *Awful Disclosures*). When the plot involved sundering the family unit early on, these texts often concluded by reuniting relatives, especially daughters, sisters, and mothers, as in Delaney's slave narrative, and showing the power of generational continuity, as in Jemison's text and *Hobomok*.

Two issues need clarification before the five works can be examined individually. First, just as the captive paradigm often literally involved a male captor and a female captive, so a woman's oral or written text might be "captured" by a male editor or author and the woman's words themselves held hostage to a more powerful agenda.[5] Sometimes the male author or editor even stepped into the first person and impersonated his subject.[6] Such mediation occurred mainly, of course, in the fact-based captivity or slave narratives, represented here by James E. Seaver's story of Mary Jemison; Lucy Delaney's slave narrative, which bears the editorial mark of some unknown person, presumably male; and Maria Monk's *Awful Disclosures*, written mostly by the anti-Catholic cleric J. J. Slocum – with help from others – but purportedly from Monk's own oral testimony.[7] Yet we should not assume that the woman's voice was always muted. Certainly in the Jemison narrative, for example, Jemison herself appears to have preselected information to give Seaver and oriented her story toward a positive presentation of her Seneca family and culture.[8] Texts with several voices are termed multivocal, heteroglossic, or palimpsestic because they involve narrative strains that can be discussed but not always separated.[9] In such texts, it may be impossible to distinguish where one voice stops and another begins.

The second issue concerns the extent to which texts of captivity or slavery were propagandist. In its most neutral sense, "propaganda"means disseminating or promoting particular ideas. According to Jacques Ellul, in his classic study of the subject, propaganda encompasses four major areas: reeducation and brainwashing; psychological action; public and human relations; and psychological warfare.[10] Additionally, it can be categorized into three basic types: "white," in which the information is basically accurate; "gray," in which the information's validity is questionable; and "black," in which the information is flagrantly false. As later discussion will clarify, all the texts under consideration are propagandist to a greater or lesser degree: *Awful Disclosures* is the most propagandist and "Lemorne *versus* Huell" is probably the least.

In all events, the texts provide their own answers to such questions as: How does a woman select a good husband? Is it socially and economically feasible for a woman to remain single if she chooses? How can a woman be a good daughter, wife, and mother? How can a man be a good son, husband, and father? How can Americans, especially American women, fulfill both their private and public roles and responsibilities? What recourse does a woman have if she is provoked into rebelling or escaping from oppression? How does she do so? What is a good Christian? Does the definition of a good Christian vary according to race and gender? When – if ever – does a slave have the right to escape bondage? What models form the best basis for relations among races?

The first literary use of captivity in this study concerns the Indian captivity narrative, which refers to texts featuring non-Indians, usually whites, captured by Native Americans. While the form originated in factual – or at least fact-based – narratives written or dictated by the captives themselves, fictional and propagandist elements were evident early on. In the historical record, it is probably true that more women than men were captured by Indians; still, in the narrative record, a disproportionate number of the best-known accounts concern females. Two of the most famous fact-based Indian captivity narratives feature the Puritan women Mary Rowlandson and Hannah Dustan, whose stories first appeared in 1682 and 1697 respectively. Both Rowlandson and Dustan exemplify two standard narrative roles for women in the captivity literature as victims and avengers. Not until the eighteenth century, however, paralleling the rise of the novel, could the Indian captivity narrative sometimes refer to a wholly fictional account. By 1824, when *A Narrative of the Life of Mrs. Mary Jemison* and *Hobomok* were published, both factual and fictional Indian captivity narratives coexisted comfortably in the literary marketplace. Moreover, the Indian captivity narrative had evolved to the point where it more freely complicated the main characters' roles of victim and victor and showed generic variation, experimentation, and even parody.

American Indians took captives for various reasons including ransom, adoption, trade, enslavement, and revenge. The fate of a hostage depended partly on luck, partly on age and gender, and partly on the practices of a particular Indian people. Revenge for continued white encroachment into western Pennsylvania seems to have been the impetus for Mary Jemison's capture on April 5, 1758 by a Shawnee and French raiding party who killed the rest of her family. However, two Seneca women soon adopted her to replace a lost relative. As a Seneca, Jemison took the name Dehgewanus, which means "Two Falling Voices," but she continued to use her British name when appropriate and gave her children both Indian and British names too.

The binary names of Mary Jemison/Dehgewanus and of her eight children showed that while she certainly crossed cultures and considered herself a Seneca, she understood that her culture of origin continued to have an impact on her affairs which she could use to her own benefit. Unlike many captives, then, Jemison continued to live close to whites, who eventually accorded her a kind of celebrity status as a cultural oddity, "the white woman of the Genesee," as they called her. For Jemison was a white woman who chose to remain with the Indians even when able to return to European ways and who cemented her identity by marrying twice within her adopted culture. Thus Jemison plays the complex role of an empowered, shrewd woman who transculturated to Seneca life and then manipulated her captivity narrative despite the efforts of the author, James E. Seaver, to exert his own textual hegemony.

Let us look a little more closely at the unlikely pairing of Mary Jemison, transculturated Seneca woman, and James E. Seaver, local doctor and amateur author. In 1823, the octogenarian Jemison agreed to a series of interviews with Seaver, who had been hired by antiquarians to write her life story. To protect her own interests, Jemison astutely insisted on being accompanied by her white legal adviser, protector, and friend, Thomas Clute. As Seaver admitted in his introduction, if Clute had not been there, Jemison probably would have told a lot less. Presumably, Seaver's influential white male backers instructed him to maintain control over the text, and this may explain the book's elaborate apparatus. A certain amount of textual apparatus is typical of captivity narratives in which the author/editor is male and the subject female, and this structure encloses, and often diminishes, the narrative itself in favor of the controlling editorial presence. However, *A Narrative of the Life of Mrs. Mary Jemison* is heavily encumbered by an unusual amount of prefatory and concluding material. It begins with the "Author's Preface," including Seaver's observations on biography in general and on his own particular methodology; next comes the "Author's Introduction," covering historical background, the three-day interview, and his impressions of his elderly Seneca subject; then the narrative itself follows, which takes up the bulk of the book and is written in the first person, though some of the information Seaver acknowledges did not come directly from Jemison; and finally, the book concludes with a long appendix of other source material.

Given Seaver's prominent narrative presence, it is sometimes disconcerting for readers to note the textual "gaps" through which Jemison's voice and views appear to come. Jemison had lived as a Seneca woman for over sixty years when she met Seaver, so inevitably the story she told him was at least informed by "Native American oral traditions ... perspectives and autobiographical forms," some of which Seaver – perhaps unwittingly – preserved

(Walsh, "'With them was my home,'" 67). Throughout the narrative, comments recur that discredit American culture (for example, the evil effects of white-induced alcoholism among Indians) and that dignify Native American culture (for example, the kindness and nobility of Jemison's husbands: Sheninjee, who died young, and Hiokatoo, with whom she lived for fifty years). In addition, the weight given certain characters or incidents suggests a greater manipulation of white readers by a Native American subject than the bookish editor Seaver apparently detected. A good instance occurs in chapter 8, which tells of a man who was Jemison's neighbor for a while, one Ebenezer Allen, a Tory but also a bigamist, thief, murderer, and outlaw. Perhaps Seaver included this chapter thinking his readers would enjoy the adventures of a scoundrel. But presumably he obtained his information from Jemison, and perhaps *she* told him so much because she wished to criticize white culture as a whole through the acts of a single white man. This strategy falls into the Seneca "oral tradition of the self-vindication narrative" (Walsh, "'With them was my home,'" 60).

Also, Jemison attempts to bridge the two cultures that she signifies by emphasizing points of contact: temperance, hard work, and most of all, love of family. Thus she concludes her narrative by stressing the strength of generationality and mentioning her three surviving daughters from the eight children she bore, her thirty-nine grandchildren, and fourteen great-grandchildren, all living near her in Buffalo or on the banks of the Genesee River, New York. "Thus situated in the midst of my children," she says in her final paragraph, "I expect I shall soon leave the world, and make room for the rising generation" (Seaver, *Narrative*, 160).

From Seaver's apparatus in the first edition, as well as much of his text, we see him overtly reinforcing negative stereotypes of Native Americans, for example in the title page's blurb on the contents of the book: "An Account of the Murder of her [i.e. Jemison's] Father and his Family; her sufferings; her marriage to two Indians; her troubles with her Children; barbarities of the Indians in the French and Revolutionary Wars; the life of her last Husband, &c; and many Historical Facts never before published. *Carefully taken from her own words.*" But counteracting this negative propaganda is Jemison's covertly positive propaganda. Thus Seaver's claim that the text was "*carefully taken from her own words*" has a double edge, for Jemison's subversive persona and agenda show through more clearly than Seaver could have intended.

The second variation on the captivity text lies in the fictionalized, sentimentalized, Indian captivity narrative. In the white world, more and more women were becoming authors – particularly of fiction – and exerting greater control over their texts; ironically, under the guise of the novel, they were able to voice their views on gender roles and race relations more openly than Jemison could. One such author was Lydia Maria Child, whose first novel, *Hobomok*, appeared in 1824, the same year as *A Narrative of the Life of Mrs. Mary Jemison*. Published when she was only twenty-two, Child's novel made her famous and initiated a lifelong literary career devoted to abolitionism, feminism, and Indian rights. *Hobomok* was inspired by *Yamoyden*, a narrative poem in the genre of the Indian captivity narrative published in 1820 and written by James Eastburn and Robert Sands. She combined elements of this poem with her own historical research in reaction against her contemporary and compatriot James Fenimore Cooper's prototype of white/Native American interaction – war and conquest. Instead, "conspicuously flouting patriarchal authority and revising patriarchal script," Child indicated that interracial marriage was a better model for race relations (Child, *Hobomok*, xi).

Set in Salem in 1629, the novel focuses mostly on Mary Conant, who rebels against her strict Puritan father by choosing unconventional spouses: initially Hobomok, an Indian, and then Charles Brown, an Episcopalian. The novel complicates the traditional Indian captivity narrative by showing that Mary Conant is held captive by her father's bigotry and inflexibility, but that when she escapes by choosing to marry Hobomok, she experiences a sense of freedom she had never felt before, even though both her father and most of the Puritan community of Salem ostracize her.

Mary Conant's rebelliousness is first signified when – recalling the girls involved in the real Salem Witch Trials in 1692 – she casts a spell at night in the forest to determine who her husband will be. She is startled when first Hobomok and only later Brown step into her magic circle because she is in love with Brown, not Hobomok. The plot proceeds with Mary Conant's continuing sense of paternal oppression, so that when she receives news of Brown's presumed death at sea and recalls Hobomok's appearance in her magic circle, she agrees to marry the Indian from "a sense of sudden bereavement, deep and bitter reproaches against her father, and a blind belief in fatality" (121). As with the women in the Salem Witch Trials, Mary's complex behavior indicates her desire to be visible and vocal, not invisible and silent as required by Puritan patriarchy. Mary achieves happiness outside European American culture, then forces greater tolerance from the symbol of Puritan rigidity, her father, when she reenters Puritan society after Brown reappears and Hobomok sacrifices his own happiness by ritually divorcing her and disappearing from view, thus allowing her to marry Brown and fulfill the magic spell.

Child makes Brown and Hobomok best friends and alter egos, so that although Mary is married to one at a time, in essence she is simultaneously wed to both (xxix–xxxiii). Mary's marriages connect the Puritan, Episcopalian, and Indian worlds, signaling Child's wish for greater tolerance among races and religions. Readers who might have read both *A Narrative of the Life of Mrs. Mary Jemison* and *Hobomok* in 1824 would have been struck by the inversions and ironies of a fact-based and a fictional treatment of marriage between white women and Native American men (the situation for white men and Native American women was somewhat different, of course). Like other narratives concerning transculturated captives, Jemison was initially captured unwillingly but then exchanged cultures and refused to return to white society even when able to do so. However, Mary Conant willingly left white culture but returned within its fold through the agency and generosity of another. Child presents Hobomok's and Mary's marriage as one of mutual affection and respect as indicated by the most natural manifestation of such feelings: the birth of a child and establishment of a new family. Yet when Charles returns, Hobomok sacrifices his son and his own happiness for what he takes to be the greater happiness of his wife, Mary, and his best friend (and her first love), Charles.

Although Child has Hobomok leave New England, he does not take his son with him. Instead, by the end of the novel, the extended family consists of Charles and Mary Brown; Mary's considerably chastened father, who accepts his mixed-blood grandson and Episcopalian son-in-law; and Charles Hobomok Conant, the child of Mary and Hobomok, whose names unite his stepfather, father, and grandfather. Together, these characters form a harmonious microcosm of what multicultural America could be if women had greater control over the course of gender and race relations.

Following in this fictional tradition, but eschewing religious tolerance, anti-Catholic convent captivity narratives appeared in the American press from 1835 or so until the beginning of the Civil War. These wildly popular, sensational accounts – almost invariably fictional – featured young, idealistic, Protestant ingenues who joined a convent only to find drudgery, sadism, corruption, and sexual perversion there. The publication in 1836 of Maria Monk's *Awful Disclosures of the Hotel Dieu Nunnery of Montreal* cemented interest in this literary form, which was considerable: like many of the other convent captivities, Monk's work was a best-seller, with sales of approximately 20,000 in the first week and 300,000 by 1860. As Susan M. Griffin points out, elements of the convent captivity narrative were familiar to American readers through other literary traditions such as the gothic novel and the Indian captivity narrative, and they also tapped into a widespread insecurity that increased immigration and a growing Catholic population threatened America's WASP identity.[11] The emphasis on young women in these accounts also played into the sense that the traditional roles of nineteenth-century white Protestant women were being further destabilized by different cultural encounters, with Roman Catholicism, for example. Yet the threat of Catholicism was not as new as it might have seemed, nor was its yoking with the victimized woman and the narrative of captivity. In the historical record, especially during Puritan times, Indian captivity narratives stressed not only the secular danger of being captured by Indians and tempted to transculturate but also the spiritual danger of succumbing to French Catholicism, since many New England captives were marched to New France (Canada) for ransom. In an effort to brainwash such captives and literally break their spirit, the French authorities tried many strategies and often found that the socialized passivity of young girls and women made them especially vulnerable. One of the most famous instances of such culture crossing concerns Eunice Williams, daughter of the Puritan minister John Williams, who was captured with her family in 1704 in the famous attack on Deerfield, Massachusetts. Taken to Canada, Eunice became a Kahnawake Indian and a Catholic convert, much to the anguish of her family, who believed her damned in this life and the next. When young girls did not remain with their Indian captors in Canada, they sometimes took refuge in convents, converted to Catholicism, and stayed in Canada as nuns for the rest of their lives.

Hence the cultural link between the earlier Indian captivity narratives and the nineteenth-century convent captivity narratives: young girls like Maria Monk were seduced and captured by a sham religious culture that denied them their prime social roles of marriage and motherhood within a traditional family unit. In convent life, perversions of the marriage and family contract were everywhere, from the nun's being "the bride of Christ," to her wealth/dowry going to the Catholic Church rather than to her husband, to fathers (i.e. Catholic priests) who behaved not like paternal protectors but like seducers and thus committed not only rape but a form of incest, and to young girls who were impregnated and, if they resisted the priests' subsequent advances, murdered along with their newly delivered – and newly baptized – babies.

Awful Disclosures tells the story of Protestant-born Maria Monk, who first attends a convent school and then resolves to become a nun, partly to rebel against her mother. While the text is rife with the rhetoric of captivity and enclosure, at critical times Monk appears freer than the narrative conventions would suggest to make her own decisions and follow through on them. Thus she leaves the convent as a novice and marries a ne'er-do-well, but seeks readmittance and takes vows shortly thereafter, adopting the name St. Eustace, and, after several years, she is able to escape from the convent with relative ease. While there, she admits to observing, participating in, or being subjected to a number of tortures including the murder of three babies, the solitary confinement and disappearance of many novices and nuns, rape, and the use of such penances as a leather gag, a cap that burns the head, and a belt stuck with sharp, inward-turning points. During the story, Monk introduces many characters in passing but only one that she dwells on – a rebellious and heterodox nun named Jane Ray, who is prone to trickery and who seems present, rather bizarrely, for semicomic relief.

The first edition of *Awful Disclosures* ended abruptly with the pregnant Monk's escape from the Hotel Dieu convent, but the book's popularity and the public's desire for more information led almost immediately to a second edition. Here, a sequel detailed Monk's harrowing experiences as a fugitive nun sought by the Catholic authorities, and other paraphernalia, such as "Reception of the First Editions," "Review of the Whole Subject," and "Supplement" with a ground plan of the convent, appeared to corroborate Monk's initial revelations. Yet all these documents – including the original *Awful Disclosures* – were in fact propagandist fabrications put out by members of the Protestant Reformation Society as part of the "No-Popery crusade" (Billington, *Protestant Crusade*, 98–9).

There really was a woman named Maria Monk who lived in Canada and who fled to the United States, but her own mother claimed that a childhood brain injury caused her daughter's confinement in a Catholic mental asylum near Montreal from where she escaped with a former lover (not a priest) who was the father of her illegitimate child (Billington, *Protestant Crusade*, 101). Yet the testimony of Monk's mother, as well as early inspections of the Hotel Dieu convent whose architecture bore no resemblance whatsoever to Monk's description, was largely ignored at first; instead, Monk's rabidly anti-Catholic backers and the "real" authors of her text put her on the lecture circuit from 1836 to 1837 and reaped huge profits from the sale of *Awful Disclosures*. Finally, a series of lawsuits confirmed the deception, and Monk's own waywardness involving another illegitimate child, drunkennesss, prostitution, and imprisonment for theft led to her final downfall and death in about 1850 (Billington, *Protestant Crusade*, 108).

As a propagandist publication created and marketed by men impersonating a woman, *Awful Disclosures* raises important questions about female authorship, a woman's body, and a woman's text. Like the other convent captivity narratives, Monk's book signals "a cultural anxiety about the new generation of daughters" and "discloses not only priests' plots and women's prisons but also the fundamental weakness of the female self on which the future of American Protestantism rests" (Griffin, "Awful Disclosures," 104–5). In other words, a woman who is vulnerable to captivation – spiritual, emotional, physical – is also vulnerable to captivity.

The next variation on captivity narratives extends to short fiction and shows the dual dangers of domestic captivation and captivity. Margaret Huell, the heroine of Elizabeth Stoddard's short story "Lemorne *versus* Huell," is only too aware of these perils and does her best to resist them, though she is unsuccessful. Margaret Huell is one of a series of female characters Stoddard wrote about who dramatize tensions between the social expectations of marriage, motherhood, and dependency (slavery) and the individual search for selfhood and independence (freedom). Indeed, these characters also represent their creator's difficulty in being accepted for the original, unconventional artist she really was and her bitterness at being denied the literary recognition she deserved. Further, Stoddard's recasting of a domestic tale as a kind of slave narrative recalls feminist Elizabeth Cady Stanton's defense of another sentimental fiction with a twist, Fanny Fern's novel *Ruth Hall* (1855). Stanton ordered, "'Read "Ruth Hall," as you would read the life of "Solomon Northrup," a Frederick Douglass, as you would listen to the poor slaves in our anti-slavery meetings.'"[12] Thus, both Stanton and, later, Stoddard equate "gender oppression with racial oppression" (Grasso, "Anger in the House," 255).

Narrated by Margaret Huell, "Lemorne *versus* Huell" tells of a lawsuit and a love affair. Margaret Huell, an unmarried music teacher of forty, lives in genteel poverty with her widowed mother. Shrewd, unpretentious, and outspoken, Margaret accepts that while she is economically deprived because she is single, she has other freedoms. Margaret's wealthy aunt Eliza Huell, also unmarried, sends for her niece to attend her as she takes a salt-water cure in Newport, Rhode Island, and while there Margaret is courted by Edward Uxbridge, the struggling lawyer of Eliza Huell's opponent in the lawsuit of the story's title. Mutually attracted to each other, the couple are also social equals. Edward claims to admire Margaret's "courage, fidelity, and patience" and also her "passionate soul" (825), and Margaret allows her feelings to prevail although she immediately discerns Edward's "domineering disposition" (818). Aunt Eliza bribes Edward with $60,000 to lose the lawsuit for his client, Mr. Lemorne, on the understanding that when she dies, she will leave the land which is the object of the original lawsuit to Margaret – which is to say to Edward, since nineteenth-century property laws usually did not recognize a wife's separate claim. Aunt Eliza and Edward Uxbridge get what they want, but the story ends with Margaret's sudden, terrifying insight into how she has been used by her aunt and husband and how marriage has trapped and disempowered – not freed – her.

Let us examine more closely the captivity rhetoric of this story, which is carried forward by the metaphor of "the contract." Most obviously, contractual obligations apply to the lawsuit Eliza Huell has brought against

Lemorne, but they also apply to the marriage contract between Margaret and Edward, which enables Aunt Eliza to win the legal claim. Litigation and marriage involve two parties, and in the nineteenth century those parties took the roles of dominance (the lawsuit's winner/the husband, i.e., the captor) and submission (the lawsuit's loser/the wife, i.e., the captive).

Throughout the story Margaret defines herself and others in contractual terms. For example, according to her aunt's instructions, Margaret goes out in the carriage every day while in Newport because she "considered the rides a part of the contract of what was expected" during her stay (816). On one occasion, Margaret sets out for church one Sunday as directed by Aunt Eliza but, struck by "the consciousness of being *free* and alone" (821), takes a walk instead. Unexpectedly encountering Uxbridge, she admits, "'I am a runaway. What do you think of the Fugitive Slave Bill?'" to which he tellingly responds, "'I approve of returning property to its owners'" (821). At the end of the conversation, they agree to see each other again and Margaret returns home, "forgetting the sense of liberty [she] had started with" (822) because of her submissive position *vis-à-vis* both Aunt Eliza and Uxbridge, her future husband.

As the courtship proceeds, Margaret's rhetoric of captivity continues to reveal her underlying understanding of her future role, which she tries to repress because of her genuine affection for Uxbridge. When he admits he loves her, Margaret asks herself, "Why should this have happened to me – a slave? As it had happened, why did I not feel exultant in the sense of power which the chance for freedom with him should give?" (825). The answer, as she comes to realize, is that the freedom seemingly offered by marriage is illusory. Willing to give herself to Edward, she wants him to give himself to her also, but there is no mutual giving; instead, as she interjects in her narrative, "I was not allowed to *give* myself – I was *taken*" (826). Captivated by Edward, Margaret is blinded to her true position – captivity – until it is too late.

Perhaps it is the ultimate irony that the character with the most power in the tale is Eliza Huell, who never marries. Thus she retains control of her life and her inherited wealth, unlike her brother (Margaret's father), who married a woman beneath him and ran through his fortune, then died and left his wife and daughter virtually penniless and powerless. Yet Eliza Huell's guilty conscience at having manipulated her niece will not allow her to rest completely easy, nor will she be able to exploit Margaret's services, as in the past, because Margaret's new status as Edward's wife requires her to attend to him. And so this sardonic story ends.

Finally, we come to the last example of captivity and the literary imagination, Lucy Delaney's autobiography *From the Darkness Cometh the Light* or *Struggles for Freedom*, which appeared very late in the formal history of the genre known as the slave narrative. The slave narrative (or, as scholars Charles T. Davis and Henry Louis Gates prefer, "the slave's narrative," a term giving the enslaved person ownership of his or her own story) refers to the written or dictated testimony of individuals held under the chattel slavery system.[13] Most of these accounts were published from the late eighteenth century to the end of the Civil War as weapons in the abolitionist arsenal, with the most produced from about 1830 to 1860. The prototypical women's slave narrative is undoubtedly Harriet Jacobs's *Incidents in the Life of a Slave Girl*, which came out in 1861. While Jacobs's literary skills give her an identity and an agency uncommon for either an African American or a white woman in the mid-nineteenth century, the prevailing image that she presents is of the victimized woman harassed by her master and forced to incarcerate herself in her grandmother's attic for seven years while awaiting a break for freedom. Jacobs is a different kind of "madwoman in the attic" from the type envisaged by critics Gilbert and Gubar, but for much of her narrative she is an enclosed woman nonetheless, having been physically confined for seven years and having been legally confined until her manumission at the end of the book. Rather than choose this extensively examined text, however, I have opted for a lesser-known, post-Civil War slave narrative stressing assertive black women willing (and able) to work the system to obtain their rights. In some ways, *From the Darkness Cometh the Light* can be seen as a continuation of or sequel to the story in *Incidents in the Life of a Slave Girl*. In the latter, Jacobs ends her account with the termination of her legal status as a slave, although historically many years of life and activism followed for Jacobs; in the former, Delaney provides a longer, more comprehensive view of her family's and her own life and activities.

From the Darkness Cometh the Light turns on both the justice and injustice of the American legal system. Like many slave narratives, it details the complex genealogies of slaves and the precariousness of their lives as property. A careful overview of the plot stressing the particulars of Lucy Delaney's individual story reveals these themes. The story begins with the abduction of Lucy Delaney's mother, Polly Crocket, from the free state of Illinois to Missouri, where she is illegally sold into slavery. Clearly, the legal system fails Polly at this point. Purchased by Major Berry for his wife, Polly falls in love with the major's servant Apollo, and they have two children, Nancy and Lucy. Major Berry dies in a duel, but his will specifies that his slaves pass to his wife and that they be freed upon her death. Mrs. Berry eventually remarries and becomes the wife of a lawyer, Robert Wash, who, when she dies, ignores the terms of Major Berry's will and sells Apollo "way down South," as the narrative states (14). Again, the American legal system is flaunted by its representative, lawyer Robert Wash. Major Berry's daughter Mary Cox and her husband take Nancy with them to Niagara Falls where – advised by Polly not to return to the South – Nancy plans her escape, coolly crosses the border into Canada, and makes a good life for herself there. When Mr. and Mrs. Cox return to St. Louis, they take Polly and Lucy as their slaves. Polly stands up to Mrs. Cox one day and finds herself on the auction block for her boldness. She escapes and stays on the run for several weeks but finally turns herself in for fear that the Coxes will revenge themselves on Lucy.

But Polly has had enough. Instead of escaping and continuing to evade the issue of her status as a free woman, she decides to take legal action, knowing that God is on her side. She employs a good lawyer and sues for her freedom. "She had ample testimony to prove that she was kidnapped, and it was so fully verified that the jury decided that she was a free woman, and papers were made out accordingly" (24). If Polly is a free woman, then of course so is Lucy, and her mother immediately begins further proceedings to remove Lucy from her position as slave to Major Berry's other daughter, Martha Mitchell, and her husband, who have mistreated her. Lucy goes into hiding, but to ensure her safety before and during the trial, the sheriff places her in jail after Polly reveals Lucy's whereabouts. Major Berry's daughters throw many hurdles in the way, but after seventeen months in jail, Lucy is finally freed after a jury trial. As she says, "My only crime was seeking for that freedom which was my birthright!" (35). Ironically, incarceration becomes the means by which Lucy ultimately changes her status from slave to free woman.

Again employing a strategy typical of many slave narratives, *From the Darkness Cometh the Light* next turns to further reunification of the sundered slave family. Through Polly's work as a laundress and Lucy's as a seamstress, they save up enough money for Polly to visit her daughter in Canada. The narrative tells its readers that only "By exercising rigid economy and much self-denial" can mother and daughter accumulate the needed funds for Polly's "hard-earned and long-deferred holiday" (53). Although Nancy invites her mother to stay in Canada, Polly decides to return to St. Louis. In 1845, Lucy marries Frederick Turner, but he dies shortly afterwards in a steamboat explosion. Lucy is grief-stricken, but her mother only tells her, "'Cast your burden on the Lord.' *My* husband is down South, and I don't know where he is; he may be dead; he may be alive; he may be happy and comfortable; he may be kicked, abused and half-starved. *Your* husband, honey, is in heaven" (56). Suitably chastened, Lucy agrees that her mother's burden is heavier than her own.

Four years later, Lucy remarries and remains the wife of Zachariah Delaney for forty-two years. During that time they establish their own family as a counterbalance to slavery's domestic destructiveness, but none of the four children survives their parents, two dying in infancy and two in their twenties. Still, once again, Lucy consoles herself by acknowledging, "Our children were born free and died free! Their childhood and my maternity were never shadowed with a thought of separation" (58). Lucy's next sorrow is the death of her mother, yet once again Lucy displaces her sadness by interpreting her mother's life and death as triumphant, "She had lived to see the joyful time when her race was made free, their chains struck off, and their right to their own flesh and blood lawfully acknowledged" (59). Lucy has only one piece of unfinished family business left: trying to discover the whereabouts of her long-lost father. Through lengthy inquiries, she finds out that her father has always lived on a plantation near Vicksburg, and she arranges a reunion between her father, herself, and her sister, Nancy, in St. Louis. But the rigors of a hard life have left Apollo "prematurely old" and, feeling "like a stranger in a strange land," he longs to return to the only home he has known for forty-five years in Mississippi (61). Lucy feels she cannot hold him, and he does indeed return South.

As a representative of the ex-slave, the free woman, what does Lucy do with her life after all its physical, emotional, and legal turbulence? She moves inward to develop her spirituality and outward to serve her people, pointing with pride to her membership in the Methodist Episcopal Church and her position as "Most Ancient Matron of the 'Grand Court of Missouri,' of which only the wives of Masons are allowed to become members" (62–3). For her presumably mostly white readers, Lucy Delaney ends her autobiography with the crux of the matter: that her story should settle in readers' minds the question, "'Can the negro race succeed, proportionately, as well as the whites, if given the same chance and an equal start?'" (63–4).

This chapter proposes that a greater sensitivity to the tropes of captivity and enslavement can help readers better understand the concerns of nineteenth-century American women writers. In Morrison's terms, readers must be willing to interpret American literature in more radically political ways, not to "shellac" it so its "complexities and power and luminations" cannot be penetrated (Morrison, *Playing in the Dark*, 91). The first two texts in my chapter are manifestations of the different cultural work performed by the early nineteenth-century Indian captivity narrative. Though heavily editorialized, Seaver's *A Narrative of the Life of Mrs. Mary Jemison* nevertheless incorporates – and perhaps is even substantially controlled by – the voice and ideology of its Native American subject, Mary Jemison/Dehgewanus herself. But in *Hobomok*, a novel of Indian captivity, author Lydia Maria Child could express her views on racial intermarriage as freely as she thought her readers would tolerate without (male) intervention. *Awful Disclosures of the Hotel*

Dieu Nunnery of Montreal moves away from Indian captivity to a woman's purported incarceration in a convent. This propagandist convent captivity narrative, actually written by rabidly anti-Catholic men, was grafted onto a real woman's biography for credibility. In the short story "Lemorne *versus* Huell," published during the Civil War, Elizabeth Stoddard reveals the marriage contract to be a form of legalized captivity with the woman-wife as slave and the man-husband as slavemaster. Thus Stoddard uses the captivity trope to question that most sacred of nineteenth-century institutions, marriage. Last, *From the Darkness Cometh the Light* is a slave narrative whose message is victory, not victimization, as evidenced by Lucy Delaney's continued development into a self-actualized woman. The slave narrative's early cultural work as abolitionist propaganda has been replaced by a sense of individualism. Toni Morrison would appreciate the irony that perhaps the freest woman in the five texts under consideration is the ex-slave.

NOTES

1. Toni Morrison, *Playing in the Dark: Whiteness and the Literary Imagination* (New York: Random House, 1993), 44.
2. See Sandra M. Gilbert and Susan Gubar, *The Madwoman in the Attic: the Woman Writer and the Nineteenth-Century Literary Imagination* (New Haven: Yale University Press, 1979).
3. The texts, from which all subsequent quotations are taken, are as follows: James E. Seaver, *A Narrative of the Life of Mrs. Mary Jemison*, ed. June Namias (Norman: University of Oklahoma Press, 1993); Lydia Maria Child, *Hobomok*, ed. Carolyn Karcher (New Brunswick: Rutgers University Press, 1986); Maria Monk, *Awful Disclosures of the Hotel Dieu Nunnery of Montreal* (New York, 1836); Elizabeth Stoddard, "Lemorne *versus* Huell," in *The Norton Anthology of Literature by Women*, ed. Sandra Gilbert and Susan Gubar (New York: W. W. Norton, 1985); Lucy Delaney, *From the Darkness Cometh the Light or Struggles for Freedom*, in *Six Women's Slave Narratives*, ed. William L. Andrews (New York and Oxford: Oxford University Press, 1988).
4. *The Letters of Abigail and John: Selected Letters of the Adams Family, 1762–1784*, ed. Lyman H. Butterfield (Cambridge, MA: Harvard University Press, 1975), 121 and 122–3.
5. See Gary Ebersole, *Captured by Texts: Puritan to Postmodern Images of Indian Captivity* (Charlottesville: University Press of Virginia, 1995).
6. See Lorrayne Carroll, "'My Outward Man': the Curious Case of Hannah Swarton," *Early American Literature* 31 (1996): 45–73.
7. Ray Billington, *The Protestant Crusade, 1800–1860: a Study of the Origins of American Nativism* (New York: Macmillan, 1938), 101.
8. See Susan Walsh, "'With them was my home': Native American Autobiography and *A Narrative of the Life of Mrs. Mary Jemison*," *American Literature* 64 (1992): 49–70.
9. See Tara Fitzpatrick, "The Figure of Captivity: the Cultural Work of the Puritan Captivity Narrative," *American Literary History* 3 (1991): 1–26.

10. Jacques Ellul, *Propaganda: the Formation of Men's Attitudes* (New York: Knopf, 1965), 133.
11. Susan M. Griffin, "Awful Disclosures: Women's Evidence in the Escaped Nun's Tale," *PMLA* 111 (1996): 93–107.
12. Quoted in Linda Grasso, "Anger in the House: Fanny Fern's *Ruth Hall* and the Redrawing of Emotional Boundaries in Mid-Nineteenth-Century America," in *Studies in the American Renaissance*, ed. Joel Myerson (Charlottesville: University Press of Virginia, 1995), 255.
13. See Charles T. Davis and Henry Louis Gates, *The Slave's Narrative* (New York and Oxford: Oxford University Press, 1985).

WORKS CONSULTED

Burnham, Michelle. *Captivity and Sentiment: Cultural Exchange in American Literature, 1682–1861*. Hanover: University Press of New Hampshire, 1997.

Castiglia, Christopher. *Bound and Determined: Captivity, Culture-Crossing, and White Womanhood from Mary Rowlandson to Patty Hearst*. Chicago: University of Chicago Press, 1996.

Derounian-Stodola, Kathryn Zabelle, ed. *Women's Indian Captivity Narratives*. Harmondsworth: Penguin, 1998.

Drinnon, Richard. *Facing West: the Metaphysics of Indian-Hating and Empire Building*. Minneapolis: University of Minnesota Press, 1980.

Faery, Rebecca Blevins. *Cartographies of Desire: Captivity, Race, and Sex in the Shaping of an American Nation*. Norman: University of Oklahoma Press, 1999.

Gould, Philip. *Covenant and Republic: Historical Romance and the Politics of Puritanism*. Cambridge and New York: Cambridge University Press, 1996.

Jacobs, Harriet. *Incidents in the Life of a Slave Girl*. Ed. Jean Fagan Yellin. Cambridge, MA: Harvard University Press, 1987.

Jones, Jacqueline. *Labor of Love, Labor of Sorrow: Black Women, Work, and the Family From Slavery to the Present*. New York: Basic Books, 1985.

Harris, Susan K. *Nineteenth-Century American Women's Novels: Interpretive Strategies*. Cambridge and New York: Cambridge University Press, 1992.

Karcher, Carolyn L. *The First Woman in the Republic: a Cultural Biography of Lydia Maria Child*. 1995. Reprinted. Durham: Duke University Press, 1998.

King, Wilma. *Stolen Childhood: Slave Youth in Nineteenth-Century America*. Bloomington: Indiana University Press, 1995.

Mills, Bruce. "Lydia Maria Child and the Endings to Harriet Jacobs's *Incidents in the Life of a Slave Girl*." *American Literature* 64 (1992): 255–72.

Tompkins, Jane. *Sensational Designs: the Cultural Work of American Fiction, 1790–1860*. New York and Oxford: Oxford University Press, 1985.

Zagarell, Sandra A. "Elizabeth Drew Barstow Stoddard: a Profile." *Legacy* 8 (1991): 39–49.

5

ELIZABETH PETRINO

Nineteenth-century American
women's poetry

The study of nineteenth-century American women's poetry is undergoing a renaissance. Aside from Emily Dickinson, nineteenth-century female poets were largely forgotten until the archival investigations of the 1970s, when they were rediscovered and examined by several critics.[1] Despite the already extensive effort to reprint women's poems, write their critical biographies, pioneer new and more useful anthologies, and compile lengthy and inclusive encyclopedias, scholars have only begun to examine critical approaches to women's poems and the assumptions they bring to bear on reading and teaching women's writing. What do these anthologies tell us about nineteenth-century American women's writing? How should we judge their poetry?

In "Nineteenth-Century American Women Poets Revisited" (1998), Cheryl Walker contends that women's writing contains more stylistic variety and vocal complexity than previously ascribed. In *The Nightingale's Burden* (1982), she identifies several persistent types of poems: the "sanctuary" poem, in which the protagonist finds freedom in a shelter; the power fantasy; the "free bird" poem, in which the speaker identifies with a bird in flight and symbolically imagines freeing herself; and the marriage poem. Although her essay still identifies generic features in women's poems, Walker advocates dividing women's poetry into four temporal and stylistic categories: early national, romantic, realist, and modern. Early national poets, like Lydia Sigourney, appeal to piety and reason, praise decorum, and base their belief in human dignity on democracy. Romantics, like Frances Osgood, writing in the early to mid-nineteenth century and including transcendentalists, explore extreme psychological states and emotions rather than the effects of injustice on the individual. Slavery and Indian rights are abstractions. Realists, like Alice and Phoebe Cary, on the other hand, are poets who "take up the political challenges of the romantics but devote themselves to portraying the conditions of everyday life" (Walker, "American Women Poets Revisited," 232). Finally, moderns resist sentimentalism, refuse to come to tidy conclusions about moral dilemmas, use fractured language, and challenge any belief system that dictates a single view of the world. Both Helen Hunt Jackson and Lizette Woodworth Reese employ language that is free of archaisms, highly imagistic, and portrays a subjective view of life.

Walker's categories provide a useful way to explore the variety and complexity of nineteenth-century American women's poetry. Walker admits that women's poems are hybrids, often combining more than one style and literary movement. Thus, reading nineteenth-century women's poems presents the difficulty – and the pleasure – of reading them outside of traditional categories. Sentimentalism – the expression of unwarranted emotion in decorative, florid language – presents an obstacle for modern readers, who are more comfortable with spare language and checked feelings. Sentimentalism, according to M. H. Abrams, applies to "an excess of emotion to an occasion, or, in a more limited sense, to an overindulgence in the 'tender' emotions of pathos and sympathy" (*Glossary of Literary Terms*, 156). Since Abrams's *Glossary of Literary Terms* was published, critics have redefined the term to include a range of emotional responses once defined as "excessive" and now viewed as a style, strategy, or other device. Although reading their poetry may go beyond our taste, the expression of emotion in many women's poems may lead us to reconsider the portrayal of them as "angels in the house," and, simultaneously, to reconsider our definition of sentimentalism. No saccharine expression of emotion, nineteenth-century women's lyrics portray lust, greed, and anger openly. Although they cultivated a public persona and were widely known for poems that appealed to the masses, many female poets also wrote lyrics that expressed emotions barely considered printable in their eras. Adah Isaacs Menken (1835–68) and Emma Lazarus (1849–87), whose "The New Colossus" was inscribed on the Statue of Liberty, for example, both stake out new emotional territory by using strong female characters, invoking Old Testament locales, and expressing their emotions in florid language. Known widely for her popular "The Battle-Hymn of the Republic," Julia Ward Howe (1819–1910) in her book *Passion Flowers* (1854) challenged the prevailing image of women's private lives, even though she felt that home life was sacred and that women should build upon that foundation rather than disturb the basic institution of society. A lesser-known poet, Rose Terry Cooke (1827–92) portrays in "Blue-Beard's Closet" and "Semele" the threat of seduction and rape. Not accepting the conventional formula of piety and overblown grief, these poets use excessive emotion in part to signal their willingness to go beyond the constraints of their era. Finally, their commitment to causes of social injustice reveals their similarity to male writers and leads us increasingly to question a false division between the sexes.

Writing in an era of political, religious, and artistic ferment, nineteenth-century American women writers were vitally engaged in bringing about social and political change. Despite their domestic themes, writers were committed to abolition, Indian rights, pacifism, temperance, suffrage, education, and the environment, to name a few.[2] Recently, new revisions by social historians and literary critics have sought to qualify the doctrine of "separate spheres" – the belief that men's and women's realms of action belonged to work and the home respectively and were mutually exclusive. They demonstrate that the boundaries between these "spheres" were more fluid than previously gathered. Despite their often troubled personal lives, female poets hinted at no discord, using Mary Kelley's terms, between their "private" selves and "public stages."[3] Furthermore, male and female poets appear to have interacted more than once thought. In *Doing Literary Business: American Women Writers in the Nineteenth Century* (1990), Susan Coultrap-McQuin argues that the so-called "Gentleman Publishers" – men like Thomas Bailey Aldrich, who performed personal favors, advanced money, and edited women's literary works – encouraged trust and loyalty among their female authors. This aura of gentlemanly courtesy, as well as the popularity of literary salons, like those of Alice and Phoebe Cary in New York City and Annie Fields in Boston, allowed writers to interact and learn from each other. Male and female writers shared their literary milieu and their works resemble one another in style and content.

Nineteenth-century American women's poetry has been derided by the aesthetic values of its own and a later age; today it is challenging the norms by which we judge literary texts. Between 1820 and 1885, editors often characterized women's verse as affective, "natural," and spontaneous and portray women as unconscious wellsprings of emotion. The aesthetic criteria employed by nineteenth-century editors who judged women's "effusions" – insisting that they speak about pious and domestic topics in a smooth-flowing, untroubled meter – also prompted late nineteenth-century and early twentieth-century critics' vehemence against sentimental verse. Like Mark Twain's sentimental versifier, Emmeline Grangerford, the poetess became humorists' stock-in-trade. Except for Dickinson's crucial example, nineteenth-century American women's poetry was thought until only recently to be more conservative and less varied stylistically than the fiction, and to be intellectually dull. A sensitive reader, Louise Bogan in her *Achievement in American Poetry* (1951) delineated an "authentic current" of emotion and technical simplicity in the poems of Lizette Woodworth Reese (1856–1935), Louise Imogen Guiney (1861–1920), and Dickinson, yet she rejected sentimental poetry as a caricature against which early twentieth-century writers needed to define themselves. Male poets like Edwin Arlington Robinson (1869–1935), according to Bogan, "twist[ed] the clichés of sentimental poetry to a wry originality" and heralded a new era in American poetry, revealing a heightened realism, laconic speech, and dry humor (21). On the other hand, women poets, whose methods "proved to be as strong as they seemed to be delicate," were responsible for the important task of "revivifying warmth of feeling" (22–23). Bogan dates the beginning of this new era of genuine feeling and technical simplicity from the publication of Wilcox's *Poems of Passion* in 1886 and Reese's *A Branch of May* in 1887. Despite their achievement, however, she deems the high emotionalism and formulaic techniques of women's verse responsible for the drop in quality of Victorian poetry. Although in many ways she belittles women's verse by inscribing it within a sentimental frame, Bogan also pays tribute to the first appearance of genuinely realistic and adventurous poets who were Dickinson's contemporaries: "It is all the more remarkable, in view of this redoubtable and often completely ridiculous record of sentimental feminine attitudinizing in verse, that true, compelling, and sincere women's talents were able to emerge. Sentimental poetry on the middle level was never destroyed – it operates in full and unimpeded force at the present day; but an authentic current began to run beside it" (24).

The women poets Bogan singles out for praise might aptly be termed "proto early-modernist," as Paula Bennett argues, for they bridge the heightened sentimentalism of mid-nineteenth-century America and the imagism, particularity, and aesthetic restraint of the modernists. In contrast, modernist writers divorced themselves from the exaggerated emotion and simple narratives about domestic life of the Victorian era and advocated instead restrained feeling and a highly imagistic style. The imagist poem finds its roots in late nineteenth-century women's nature poems, which often reflect "a movement . . . toward greater concrete detail, more ambiguous and flexible stylistic expression, and toward a much wider – and more disturbing – range of themes and voices than high-sentimentalism, with its commitment to religiously based domestic and cultural values, allowed."[4]

Unlike Bogan, who dismissed sentimental writing as the unwarranted expression of emotion, many critics are seeking to recuperate sentimental literature. It relies on a deeply entrenched set of communal values and the conventions of religion and family life. Engaging the reader in a heightened display of feeling, sentimental texts "work" when they succeed in moving the reader. In *Sensational Designs: the Cultural Work of American Fiction, 1790–1860* (1985), Jane Tompkins contends that, unlike modernist writers who value unique language, sentimental novelists use commonplace language to appeal to the reader's emotions. Rather than extol the works of Stowe and other female writers over those of their male contemporaries on aesthetic grounds, she contends that the neglected tradition of women's literature should be judged according to its political or moral objectives. In

The Culture of Sentiment: Race, Gender, and Sentimentality in Nineteenth-Century America (1992), Shirley Samuels similarly argues that sentimentalism engages readers in a complex network of emotional issues. Not purely aesthetic in nature, sentimental literature for Samuels is permeated with political meanings that range across race, class, and gender lines.

Sentimental writers might be read to excavate political and social values of the period, but their works also yield pleasure based in rhetorical and linguistic complexity and stylistic eloquence, certainly objectives as important as their political motivation. Doing "cultural work," as Tompkins puts it, in a way that is not reductive or crassly materialistic means we must account for the rhetorical power and artistic achievement of texts. In one of the first essays to address how we might more profitably read sentimental poetry, Joanne Dobson stresses the shared values and generic features by which sentimental literature succeeds or fails on its own terms. In "Reclaiming Sentimental Literature," she writes: "Literary sentimentalism . . . is premised on an emotional and philosophical ethos that celebrates human connection, both personal and communal, and acknowledges the shared devastation of affectional loss" (Dobson, "Reclaiming Sentimental Literature," 266). Their clichés – the "crystal drop" for a tear or "curtaining lids" for closing eyes – are euphemisms for grief and death, and the degree to which they can convey real emotion using such trite expressions demonstrates their consummate artistry. Innovative writers, through the brilliant use of conventional language, can secure for sentimental literature a place in the literary canon: "As a body of literary texts, sentimental writing can be seen in a significant number of instances to process a conventional sentimental aesthetics through individual imagination, idiosyncratic personal feeling, and skilled use of language, creating engaging, even compelling fictions and lyrics – as, for example, in works by Alice Cary, Harriet Jacobs, Frances Sargent Osgood, Lydia Sigourney, and Harriet Beecher Stowe, to name a few" (265).

In "Teaching Nineteenth-Century Women Writers," Paul Lauter challenges the formal and conceptual standards we apply to canonical literary works and explains the traditional devaluation of nineteenth-century women's literature.

> If we accept the definitions of literary excellence constructed in significant measure from the canonical works and used to perpetuate their status, we will inevitably place most of the fiction by nineteenth-century white women and black writers at a discount, and view them as at best elegaic local colorists, at worst, domestic sentimentalists. Indeed, we will not see what these writers are attempting to accomplish, much less how well or poorly they do what Jane Tompkins calls their "cultural work." (Lauter, "Teaching," 128)

For Lauter, accepting the definition that a classic transcends its time prevents us from appreciating the qualities that make nineteenth-century women's writing distinctive. Texts are historical agents that encode and transmit ideas pervading their culture. If we accept only the standards of self-containment, metaphysical ambiguity, and irony extolled by the New Critics, we will appreciate neither the authors' stated or implicit intentions nor their relative success or failure, much less their ability to affect social change.

Although Dobson, Tompkins, and Lauter argue that sentimentalism requires we shift our standards to appreciate the criteria by which these works were originally judged, I would argue that a comparison of men's and women's verse deepens our understanding of their poetic achievement. Like their male counterparts, female poets adhere to family values, elevate the roles of mothers, grieve over the deaths of children, press for abolition, and so on. Male poets, such as Longfellow, Whittier, Freneau, and Emerson, also inscribe sentimental moments or at least reflect beliefs in family and religion that female poets share. Both men and women use stylistically similar features in their poems. They differ, however, in the density of detail with which they represent domestic matters (Walker, "American Women Poets Revisited," 234). Women, whose lives revolved around the home and family life, rendered the day-to-day behaviors of their children in more detail than men. Sentimentalism's appeal to shared values becomes a means for understanding and ultimately changing the world.

Poetry of the early national period: Lydia Sigourney and Philip Freneau

A writer of the early national period, Lydia Huntley Sigourney exemplifies in her writing the sentimental appeals that pervade early nineteenth-century protest literature. Sigourney embodies the conflict typical for women writers in this period: her life conforms in every respect to the social standards of her age, except that she writes professionally. Her lyrics, too, reflect the dilemma of most women's work: on the one hand, she elevates a mother's union with her infant as a means to connect with women from every nation and race and, as a sentimentalist, to evoke sympathy. On the other hand, she addresses issues of Indian rights, environmentalism, the effect of westward expansion on the landscape, women's maltreatment, abolition, education, and pacifism. According to Bennett, "she can be written off as the archetypal nineteenth-century poetess, a writer whose obsession with death, especially child death, makes her the foremother of an entire century of Emmeline Grangerfords. Conversely, she can be viewed ... as a basically political writer, whose particular concerns – Indians, women, the environment, peace, etc. – make her a highly sympathetic figure for audiences today" (Bennett, *Anthology*, 3–4). In fact, such views are not mutually exclusive. As a popular nineteenth-century writer, Sigourney employed all the sentimental poetic conventions of her day. What is remarkable is the extent to which, within the dominant rhetoric, she was able to challenge political injustices.

According to Walker, Annie Finch's watershed article, "The Sentimental Poetess in the World: Metaphor and Subjectivity in Lydia Sigourney's Nature Poetry," contends that Sigourney "defied the conventions of romantic poetry, which were premised on a male view of subjectivity and individualism, substituting instead a female 'sentimental' ethic based on shared communal values" (Walker, "American Women Poets Revisited," 233). Rather than present a model of subjectivity standing apart from the world, the female poet, according to Finch, lacks a privileged central self and relies instead on shared values, such as family love and religion, to bond with others. If, as Finch posits, female poets give nature equal rank as an independent entity, then Sigourney portrays nature as standing above human concerns, testifying to the injustices perpetrated upon oppressed peoples.

One can usefully compare Sigourney's elegy for the dispersed Indian peoples whose names have been preserved on the landscape with that of another writer who also eulogizes their passing – Philip Freneau. Philip Freneau's "The Indian Burying Ground" memorializes the traces of the Indian landscape and describes a fantasy of the Indians who have passed away but still haunt their land:

> In spite of all the learned have said,
> I still my old opinion keep;
> The *posture*, that *we* give the dead,
> Points out the soul's eternal sleep.
>
> Not so the ancients of these lands –
> The Indian, when from life released,
> Again is seated with his friends,
> And shares the joyous feast.
>
> His imaged birds, and painted bowl,
> And venison, for a journey dressed,
> Bespeak the nature of the soul,
> ACTIVITY, that knows no rest.
>
> His bow, for action ready bent,
> And arrows, with a head of stone,
> Can only mean that life is spent,
> And not the old ideas gone.
>
> Thou, stranger, that shalt come this way,
> No fraud upon the dead commit –

Observe the swelling turf, and say
They do not *lie*, but here they *sit*,

Here still a lofty rock remains,
On which the curious eye may trace
(Now wasted, half, by wearing rains)
The fancies of a ruder race.

(lines 1–24)

Although the Indians have died, they are still present to the speaker's mind; despite the passage of time, the natural features of the landscape – "the swelling turf," "a lofty rock," "an aged elm" – all signal the continuation of the Indians in the observer's mind. Freneau compares the forest to a sylvan utopia, replete with a "shepherd" who observes the scene and an "Indian queen" named "*Shebah*," evoking the Old Testament kingdom. If, as Walker contends, sentimentalism occurs when feeling predominates over reason, then Freneau's closing stanza celebrates the power of the "fancy" over "reason" and, by extension, of "fancy" over the poetic imagination: "And long shall timorous fancy see / The painted chief, and pointed spear, / And Reason's self shall bow the knee / To shadows and delusions here" (37–40). However, in relegating the Indians to "shadows" and "delusions," Freneau avoids the political imperative to protest the Indians' disappearance. As Susan Gilmore has argued, "Freneau's poem serves as a eulogy – one which elides the Indian's on-going presence as well as poetry's political impact. 'Reason' can afford a cursory 'bow' to sentiment in a poem which buries even as it resurrects its subject" (Gilmore, "'Ye May Not Wash It Out,'" 6).

In "Indian Names," Sigourney points out the persistence of vanished Indian nations in the nation's cultural memory through their place names. Like many women's poems, Sigourney's lyrics can be usefully compared to those of men who address the same concerns. Sigourney's "Indian Names" openly protests the excision of Indians, rather than naturalizing their passing into the landscape:

Ye say they all have passed away,
That noble race and brave,
That their light canoes have vanished
From off the crested wave;
That 'mid the forests where they roamed
There rings no hunter shout,
But their names is on your waters,
Ye may not wash it out.

(lines 1–8)

Sigourney objects to the forgetfulness of the white settlers who ignore Indian names, and accuses the nation of breaking its pact with the Indians. The most impressive metaphor of the poem is water, symbolizing both Christian succession and the white settlers' desire to cleanse the Indian from the land. The Indian's name "is on your waters," and "Ye may not wash it out" (6–7). Indeed, the names of the "everlasting rivers" eloquently express in a "dialect of yore" a reminder of this truth. Yet the paradox of the poem lies in the futile desire on the part of the white settlers to Christianize and erase any traces of the Native peoples from the land. Sigourney's choice of a domestic metaphor to protest against the erasure of the Indians from our history suggests just how closely she believed disenfranchised women could be aligned with, and speak for, the dispossessed Indians. According to Gilmore, "as the essence of baptism and the conduit for exploration and commerce, water becomes the medium of colonial annihilation and forgetfulness" ("'Ye May Not Wash It Out,'" 7). European explorers to America have inscribed the Indians and their tragic history onto the landscape permanently by keeping the original Native names for our lakes, streams, and mountains.

Nineteenth-century American women poets: romantics

Unlike Sigourney, who finds in Christian succession and democracy ample reason to protest the attempted erasure of the Indians from the landscape, romantic poets base their objection to injustice on philosophical grounds. Cheryl Walker notes that "the American romantics . . . revel in their emotions and explore extreme psychological states; they defy conventions, even praising sexual excess, and their work is notable for its lack of balance and its dark implications about the human psyche" (Walker, "American Women Poets Revisited," 232). Whereas early national poets celebrate democratic ideals and elevate the individual based on equality, romantics redress attacks on individual liberties in more abstract terms. Margaret Fuller, writing her poem "Governor Everett Receiving the Indian Chiefs" in 1837, attacks not so much the Jacksonian policy of forced Indian removal but the overblown, sentimental treatment of the Indians in novels and poems: "American romance is somewhat stale. / Talk of the hatchet, and the faces pale, / Wampum and calumets, and forests dreary, / Once so attractive, now begins to weary" (8–11). Fuller turns to nature for inspiration throughout the poem and to revivify the dead language of poetry. Yet she praises the power of Everett's speech when she notes that it moves even the most stoic to shed "some natural tears" (101). The closing stanza ambiguously endorses a vote in favor of the power of words to move the viewer: "'Twas a fair scene – and acted well by all; / So here's a health to Indian braves so tall – / Our Governor and

Boston people all!" (152–4). Given Fuller's initial critique of sentimental language and her evocation of the same description, she may well have meant to parody the rhetoric of sentimental novelists, like James Fenimore Cooper and Catharine Sedgwick: "But every poetaster scribbling witling, / From the majestic oak his stylus whittling, / Has helped to tire us, and to make us fear / The monotone in which so much we hear / Of 'stoics of the wood,' and 'men without a tear'" (14–18). The power of speech to move the listener to moral actions is perfectly in keeping with the power of sentiment to change the nation.

Among the poets of the romantic era, Frances Sargent Osgood flaunts convention and explores men's and women's emotions in the social world. Osgood deals with social life and courtship in her witty, urbane poems of the 1840s and 1850s. Certainly, a number of romantic writers, such as Edgar Allan Poe, Harriet Prescott Spofford, Rose Terry Cooke, Margaret Fuller, and Emily Dickinson, long for a realm of plenitude that may never have existed or is irretrievably lost. As a romantic, Osgood elevated love as an unattainable ideal, while she wittily portrayed the actual dealings between men and women. As Joanne Dobson has argued, Osgood's manuscript poems reveal an irreverence that was perhaps too challenging for her to consider publishing them. As a sentimentalist, moreover, she extols fancy or imagination over reason. "A Flight of Fancy," for example, portrays a case between two litigants, Fancy, portrayed as a colorful, light-hearted bird, and dour old Reason. They appear before the bar of Judge Conscience. Despite the judgment in Reason's favor, Fancy appeals to everyone, and, ultimately, she lulls reason to sleep and escapes through the "hole in the lock" of the cell door. Walker describes this poem as a "power fantasy" in which the female speaker seeks to exert control by escaping from the patriarchal order: "She claims the right to her freedom but in doing so she subverts the reigning order" (Walker, *Nightingale's Burden*, 39–40). If Fancy is associated with women's freedom and sexuality, then women can escape the domination of Reason only through "the very image of their sexuality" (Walker, *Nightingale's Burden*, 40).

Written perhaps as a response to Poe, "The Lily's Delusion" epitomizes Osgood's witty, rebellious revision of sentimental language:

> A cold, calm star look'd out of heaven,
> And smiled upon a tranquil lake,
> Where, pure as angel's dream at even,
> A Lily lay but half awake.

> The flower felt that fatal smile
> And lowlier bow'd her conscious head;
> "Why does he gaze on me the while?"
> The light, deluded Lily said.

Poor dreaming flower! – too soon beguiled,
She cast nor thought nor look elsewhere,
Else she had known the star but smiled
To see himself reflected there.

Close in form and sentiment to Poe's "Evening Star," Osgood may have
meant to comment sarcastically on her perceived betrayal. His poem "Evening Star," written in 1827, might have been the basis for Osgood's "The
Lily's Delusion." Poe recounts a romantic disillusionment. In the middle
world, between day and night, the speaker observes the "cold moon" (5),
surrounded by her "slaves" (6), the planets, but notes that she exhibits only
"her cold smile" (10). Disappointed by her lack of feeling, the speaker turns
to the evening star and extols her pride twice as well as the distance from
earth that makes the star appear more attractive to the speaker. Osgood's
poem creates a dreamy netherworld ruled by moonlight and its deceptions
rather than by the light of day, symbolizing full consciousness. The Lily's
semiconsciousness hints that, not yet fully initiated into the deceptions of
love, she must undergo a romantic betrayal. Innocent and flattered by the
apparent constancy of the "cold, calm star," the Lily does not see its vanity
until too late. Aptly titled, "The Lily's Delusion" turns the tables on writers
who portray women as vain creatures and chastises women for not realizing
the true object of men's attachment.

Nineteenth-century American women poets: realists

Whereas romantics elevate the emotions and human psyche, realists accu-
rately depict the conditions under which people live. As Cheryl Walker notes,
"realists take up the political challenges of the romantics but devote themselves to portraying the conditions of everyday life. Alice Cary and Lucy
Larcom might be classified as realists insofar as they make available the detailed struggles of common people of the working class" ("American Women
Poets Revisited," 232). Donald Pizer notes that one hallmark of nineteenth-
century realism is verisimilitude of detail derived from observation and documentation, as in the case of photography and journalism. Such writing
"is an effort to approach the norm of experience – that is, a reliance upon the
representative rather than the exceptional in plot, setting, and character"
(Pizer, *Realism and Naturalism*, 1–2). According to M. H. Abrams, whereas
romantic literature often presents "life as we would have it be, more picturesque, more adventurous, more heroic than actual," realism presents "an
accurate imitation of life as it is" (Abrams, *Glossary of Literary Terms*, 140).

Far from elevating the lives of its characters, as does romance, realistic writing portrays the average, commonplace person who has ordinary experiences. Although the characters' lives may be ordinary, they may display, under special circumstances, heroism. Cary and Larcom rose from the lower and middle classes and devoted themselves in their work to depicting the lives they knew. Both writers were influenced by another poet who idealized the plight of the working classes: John Greenleaf Whittier. In fact, Whittier attended the Carys' salons in New York City, and Phoebe so idealized his talent that she extolled him in one poem as "Great master of the poet's art!" In a letter to John Greenleaf Whittier about her book, which she had just sent him, Cary notes "it is made of what I myself have seen and felt and known – I have tried to depict the scenes I am familiar with, and have not tried to pen what was foreign to my experience" (MS BMS AM 1844 [69]; Sept. 28, 1866). Although she notes that she wishes to discuss spiritualism and other topics with him, her writing is drawn from the actual circumstances of her life. Not only were Whittier's poems thought worthy of emulation, they also reflected political views shared by other liberal northern intellectuals; as an abolitionist, a Quaker, and a defender of the working class, Whittier wrote poems that elevated the life of the average laborer. As Walker notes, it would be very difficult to tell Whittier's poems from Alice Cary's or Lucy Larcom's, both of whom wrote poems sympathetic to the lives of working-class women. Not only do Whittier's poems concern the virtues of heroism (as in "Barbara Frietchie"), they also portray stalwart New Englanders who enforce a strict code of ethics on others, as in "Skipper Ireson's Ride," in which the women of the town of Marblehead tar and feather the captain for sailing away from his sinking ship and leaving the townspeople to drown.

Another writer who portrays middle-class life, Henry Wadsworth Longfellow, depicts the heroic stoicism of the lower classes in the poem "The Village Blacksmith." Unlike Cary, Longfellow celebrates the stoicism that allows the blacksmith to continue on in life, despite his many losses. Given the blacksmith's centrality in his village, he becomes an emblem of stoicism and the power of sentiment to transform human lives into something greater:

> Week in, week out, from morn till night,
>   You can hear his bellows blow;
> You can hear him swing his heavy sledge,
>   With measured beat and slow,
> Like a sexton ringing the village bell,
>   When the evening sun is low.

And children coming home from school
Look in at the open door;
They love to see the flaming forge,
And hear the bellows roar,
And catch the burning sparks that fly
Like chaff from a threshing-floor.
(lines 13–24)

Extolling the blacksmith's simple life and remarking the regular sound of his
hammer, which marks time for the village like a sexton ringing "the village
bell," Longfellow naturalizes the blacksmith's description and hearkens to
the season of change and death: the boys gather round the smithy in the after-
noon to see the sparks that fly from the anvil like "chaff from a threshing
floor." Free of debt, the blacksmith embodies a natural dignity and meets the
world head on: "And looks the whole world in the face, / For he owes not
any man" (11–12). Furthermore, in the face of seasonal change, Longfellow
portrays the way women can connect the blacksmith with emotion: listening
to his daughter's voice makes his heart "rejoice" (30–6), and imagining it
resembles his deceased wife's voice brings him to tears.

Read against the heroic stoicism and pervasive sentimentalism in the
depiction of lower-class life in Longfellow's "The Village Blacksmith," Cary's
"The Washerwoman" portrays the tragedy of a woman's plight by sentimentally placing her disappointment in the context of her failed social ambitions,
which were typically fulfilled for women through marriage. Instead, Cary's
poem indicts classicism by portraying the way the villagers misjudge Rachel's
life based on her appearance. Cary alludes to the story of disappointed love
between Rachel and "old crazy" Peter. Although the speaker nostalgically
recalls Rachel's place in the village, she conveys the ennui her actions create
in those around her. The children count the shirts to be cleaned as they pass
by and find it "weary work / Only to hear her rub" (19–20). The blacksmith,
too, jokes that he wishes he had her never-tiring hands and her back as an
anvil. Finally, the housewives, who might be thought to understand, only
ask Rachel "with a conscience clear and light" (33–4) to come at night to
wash. The last stanza holds out the possibility that Rachel and Peter's love
might be consummated in heaven: "Her heart had worn her body to / A
handful of poor dust, – / Her soul was gone to be arrayed / In marriage-
robes, I trust" (65–8). The last line comments on their possible marriage in
heaven, yet its ambiguous tone suggests that the outcome may differ from
her expectations. Despite her hard life, Rachel is worn down by her "heart."

Fully immersed in the language of sentimentalism, women writers adopted
what Alicia Ostriker has called the "voice of duplicity" to acquire more

freedom in print than otherwise might have been imagined possible. We might classify the voices of Cary's poems as mimetic: as Mary Jacobus explains, a mimetic voice imitates women who, unable to write outside the patriarchal tradition, must adopt its vocabulary and stylistic techniques in order to undo it ("Question of Language," 210). In "The Bridal Veil," Cary depicts a woman who differentiates between the socially sanctioned view of marriage and her personal viewpoint: marriage does not imply possession of her soul and emotion. Rather than support the bodily and legal possession of women in marriage, the speaker challenges the groom to "grow to new heights if I love you to-morrow" (12). The crux of the poem's ambiguity lies in the image of the veil: symbolically dividing the past from the present, girlhood from married life, it simultaneously signals her role as wife and hides her real emotions. Beneath her veil, the bride has "wings," which may be angelic or presage her desire for flight. "And spite of all clasping, and spite of all bands," she warns, "I can slip like a shadow, a dream, from your hands" (16–17). "Bands," of course, implies marriage banns or a wedding band as well as manacles. Building on the common idealization of women, the speaker reveals the choice that lies before the married couple: the veil serves as a remnant of "peace that is dead" or the sign of "bliss that can never be written or spoken" (23). The bride may conform publicly to the socially sanctioned role in marriage, but in private she responds to her husband's caresses or chiding, leaving the veil to symbolize either the consummation of their union or its division.

Nineteenth-century American women poets: modernists

Modernist writers appear toward the end of the century and diverge from the literature of protest. Bennett argues that a modern sensibility emerged in women's nature poetry.

> On the basis of the poems I have collected, I now believe that a direct line can be demonstrated between women poets writing in the late nineteenth century and the major women poets of early modernism. More than that, it can be shown that stylistic and thematic changes in women's poetry between the late 1850s and 1890 – changes that, among other things, help account for the surprisingly positive reception Dickinson's poetry enjoyed in 1890 on its first publication – are basic to the evolution of the early modernist poem. ("Nature Poetry and the Imagist Poem," 89–90)

Among the features she identifies is a movement away from archaic language and communal values and toward a personal, idiosyncratic viewpoint. The personal and idiosyncratic style includes a more ambiguous, complex, and less conventional point of view than that of sentimental poets, with their reliance on religious and home life. I would argue that the modernism in imagist poets, such as Amy Lowell and H. D., who stress imagery, aesthetic restraint, and an increasingly open poetic form, is already evident in poets from the 1870s and 1880s. Helen Hunt Jackson's alienated subjectivity, linguistic complexity, and heightened sense of imagery set her apart from many of her precursors to become a hallmark of the modernists. Like several of her contemporaries, Jackson was a traditionalist who used the sonnet to express her innermost feelings in a detached way. Frequently, her speakers comment on the lives of women whose existences are portrayed through alien settings, such as polar seas, deserts, or tropic oceans.

In "Poppies in the Wheat," the speaker displays astute awareness of nature that goes beyond a farmer's materialism:

> Along Ancona's hills the shimmering heat,
>   A tropic tide of air with ebb and flow
>   Bathes all the fields of wheat until they glow
> Like flashing seas of green, which toss and beat
> Around the vines. The poppies lithe and fleet
> Seem running, fiery torchmen, to and fro
> To mark the shore.
>   The farmer does not know
> That they are there. He walks with heavy feet,
> Counting the bread and wine by autumn's gain,
> But I, – I smile to think that days remain
> Perhaps to me in which, though bread be sweet
> No more, and red wine warm my blood in vain,
> I shall be glad remembering how the fleet,
> Lithe poppies ran like torchmen with the wheat.

Portraying the port city of Ancona, Jackson preserves the memory of the field and contrasts her awareness with the farmer's dull, plodding nature. This poem compares the heat to "a tropic tide of air" and the fields to "flashing seas of green," where the red poppies resemble "running, fiery torchmen" who mark the shore. Another poem, "Tidal Waves," published in the *Atlantic Monthly* in 1881, recounts the tidal waves that "In cruel clutch the mightiest ships they take, / Tossing them high in fiendish jubilee; / Leaving them far inland, stranded hopelessly" (3–5). Awakening "strange fancies" in the speaker, she compares these tidal waves to "brave women's souls" that are borne "To barren inlands, where, too strong to die, / Even of thirst and loneliness and scorn, / Like ghastly stranded wrecks, long years they lie!" (12–15). Whereas in "Tidal Waves" Jackson explicitly connects the women's stalwart lives to their inward exile, "Poppies on the Wheat" omits any discussion of women's lives. Unlike the farmer, who is caught up in the world of loss and gain, "counting the bread and wine," the speaker's memory when "bread be sweet / No more, and red wine warm my blood in vain" (12–13) will serve as consolation. Ultimately, the poem celebrates the power of imagination over actual life: the poet creates flowers for eternity through her beautiful imagery, whereas all the farmer can do is make dry bread. The allusion to Ancona, a busy port city, explains the farmer's commercialism and confirms the speaker's alienation – albeit silent – from the mercenary civilization of gain and loss.

Similarly, Lizette Woodworth Reese's "August" uses imagery to depict a vivid contrast between blazing lilies and their parched surroundings. Reese's poem marks her from her precursors: she does not append a moral. Instead, although she portrays the landscape in detail, the poem conveys a feeling of emptiness and absence: left on the scene, a rose bush with "not one / Rose left," and a spider lying in wait for its prey. In contrast to the absence of movement and signs of life, she highlights the contrast between the dry land and the wild lilies, ablaze with color, lit like "saffron torches through the hush" (7). The impression of death overall is enhanced by the spider's web, the "rank scents" on the air, and the stillness of the scene appears in the final image: "Upon the hill / Drifts the noon's single cloud, white, glaring, still" (13–14). Emptying her poem of emotion, Reese accentuates the existence of nature apart from human concerns and uses imagery to create an atmosphere of silence and solitude in an amoral universe.

Emily Dickinson shares many of the characteristics of nineteenth-century American women's poetry, while at the same time she exceeds her contemporaries. Recently, the vein of criticism that sees Dickinson as a scribal publisher raises provocative issues about her absorption of the standards of verse as well as her process of composition. In *Open Me Carefully: Emily Dickinson's Intimate Letters to Susan Huntington Dickinson*, Ellen Louise Hart and Martha Nell Smith contend that Dickinson exchanged poems throughout her life with her sister-in-law, Susan, creating a poet's workshop in which each writer edited and influenced the other. Far from atypical, however, Dickinson's compositional process resembles the exchange of poems and letters among many women writers. The idea that verse should remain private was a convention that kept genteel women from publishing and, simultaneously, necessitated the development of a network of professional relationships among other women. While they held the most powerful roles in the publishing industry and established criteria for judging women's verse, influential women, like Annie Adams Fields, acted as literary advisors, surrogate publishers, and salon holders to female authors like Louisa May Alcott, encouraging them to make the acquaintance of other writers. Dickinson uses several methods – circulating manuscripts among friends, visual effects, and the genre of the "letter-poem" – adapted by other women writers to build community among their literary counterparts and circumvent the rigors of publication. Given that many women writers needed to discover a means to distribute their writing, they mildly accepted the dictates of the publishing world while their subtle and ambiguous lyrics challenge the status quo.

Like the modernists, Dickinson resists the religious and philosophical systems that are hallmarks of the Victorian age. Like Jackson and Reese's poems, Dickinson's lyrics reveal the individualism, fractured syntax, and relativism that is more characteristic of the modernists than the Victorians. As Christopher Benfey notes about the poem beginning "Four Trees – upon a solitary Acre" (J 742), "The question of placement – the place of the four trees in the general nature, the place of human beings with regard to them – is for Dickinson, and for other American writers, a serious question. The poem is about giving place. 'Why do precisely these objects which we behold make a world?' Thoreau asked. Dickinson's concern with objects – with how they are placed, and 'give place' to one another – seems to pose the same question" (Benfey, *Emily Dickinson*, 115). Dickinson's canon is built around poems like this one that address the way objects in the world gain meaning depending on their placement with respect to other objects. The lyric beginning "Each Life Converges to some Centre –" (J 680) conveys the syntactical ambiguity and lack of a perceived philosophical or religious center:

> Each Life Converges to some Centre –
> Expressed – or still –
> Exist in every Human Nature
> A Goal –
>
> Embodied scarcely to itself – it may be –
> Too fair
> For Credibility's presumption
> To mar –
>
> Adored with caution – as a Brittle Heaven –
> To reach
> Were hopeless, as the Rainbow's Raiment
> To touch –
>
> Yet persevered toward – surer – for the Distance –
> How high –
> Unto the Saints' slow diligence –
> The Sky –

Ungained – it may be – by a Life's low Venture –
But then –
Eternity enable the endeavoring
Again.

(J 680)

Although the design may be unperceived, Dickinson argues that there is still a "Centre" to which "Expressed – or still – " each human life "converges." The indeterminacy of where or what that center might be and its inability to be articulated argue for the poet's modern sensibility: rather than view the goal as attainable, its meaning is tantalizingly distant to the speaker, who compares it to a "Brittle Heaven." Replacing the off rhymes of the first three stanzas with full rhymes, the poem implies that some conclusion may be attained with effort: like "the Saints' slow diligence," perseverance may allow those on earth to attain their goal. Paradoxically, although the goal may be unattained in one lifetime by a single "Life's low Venture," eternity ensures that the pursuit will continue again and again.

Jackson's and Reese's poems are typical of the modern poems by late nineteenth-century American women writers, who refine the language of sentimentalism and omit the didacticism and piety that so many writers cleaved to earlier in the century. Reese portrays the land in the absence of human beings, downplaying the religious and communal values important to the sentimentalists. Jackson, on the other hand, adheres in her poems to the activism and Christian values of mid-nineteenth-century writers, yet she underscores her detachment from the world of commercialism that Dickinson detested as well, elevating art above daily life and betraying the individual's alienation that becomes standard in modern poetry. Reese and Jackson extend the achievement of women's poetry beyond protesting injustice or redefining women's roles to a self-conscious assertion of their poetic artistry. In doing so, they forecast the writings of modernists who are increasingly concerned with creating images that, as T. S. Eliot claimed, provide an "objective correlative" to specific emotions. More than any other poet, Dickinson uses indeterminacy and ambiguity to question the predominant mode of belief while maintaining a radically open poetic form. And Jackson, Reese, and Dickinson bring the lyric to the threshold of the twentieth century by using a conversational style, common language, and frequent enjambment, all features that are synonymous with a more contemporary sensibility.

Sentimentalism is only one of the strains of literary styles used in nineteenth-century America. Traditionalism, modernism, imagism, didacticism, symbolism – even as we refine our understanding of sentimentalism, we should take account of the extraordinary range and variety of styles of women's poems. Only by acknowledging that men and women influenced one another's poetry as well as demonstrating the particular ways that women's poems differ can we begin to see the unique and important contribution nineteenth-century American female poets have made to our changing literary tradition.

NOTES

1. In particular, the publication of Cheryl Walker's *The Nightingale's Burden: Women Poets and American Culture before 1900* (1983) broke ground for other works that sought to expand the American literary canon. In addition, Emily Stipes Watts's *The Poetry of American Women from 1632–1945* (1977) and Alicia Ostriker's outstanding *Stealing the Language* (1989) have broadened the range of poets under discussion, and a number of once popular but long neglected poets, such as Lydia Sigourney, Frances Osgood, Alice Cary, Helen Hunt Jackson, and Lizette Woodworth Reese, are now discussed in college classrooms, critical articles, and popular scholarly debate. Within the past few years, anthologists have begun to revise the canon first selectively sketched by Cheryl Walker's *American Women Poets of the Nineteenth-Century: an Anthology* (1992). Karen Kilcup's *Nineteenth-Century American Women Writers: an Anthology* (1997) organizes a variety of texts organized chronologically, thematically, and generically to expose the cross-cultural implications of women's lives. Similarly, Janet Gray's anthology, *She Wields a Pen: American Women Poets of the Nineteenth Century* (1997), reframes American literature as a comparative discipline comprising heterogeneous cultures. And Paula Bennett's *Nineteenth-Century American Women Poets: an Anthology* (1998) creates a taxonomy of writers who represent racial and regional differences. She divides the volume into "principal" and "secondary" poets of "regional, national, and special interest."
2. Paula Bennett notes that Lydia Sigourney, a writer of books of etiquette, wrote poems that demonstrate a wide variety of political concerns. Bennett, *Nineteenth-Century American Women Poets*, 3.
3. The title of Mary Kelley's book (see below) alludes to the split between women's public and private personae in nineteenth-century America.
4. See Paula Bennett, "Late Nineteenth-Century American Women's Nature Poetry and the Evolution of the Imagist Poem," *Legacy: a Journal of American Women Writers* 9 (1992): 92.

WORKS CITED

Abrams, M. H. *A Glossary of Literary Terms*. 3rd edn. New York: Holt, Rinehart and Winston, 1971.
Benfey, Christopher E. G. *Emily Dickinson and the Problem of Others*. Amherst: University of Massachusetts Press, 1984.

Bennett, Paula (Bernat). "Late Nineteenth-Century American Women's Nature Poetry and the Evolution of the Imagist Poem." *Legacy: a Journal of American Women Writers* 9 (1992): 89–103.

Bennett, Paula Bernat, ed. *Nineteenth-Century American Women Poets: an Anthology*. Malden, MA: Blackwell, 1998.

Bogan, Louise. *Achievement in American Poetry, 1900–1950*. Chicago: Henry Regnery Co., 1951.

Coultrap-McQuin, Susan. *Doing Literary Business: American Women Writers in the Nineteenth Century*. Chapel Hill: University of North Carolina Press, 1990.

Dobson, Joanne. "Reclaiming Sentimental Literature." *American Literature* 69.2 (1997): 263–88.

Finch, Annie. "The Sentimental Poetess in the World: Metaphor and Subjectivity in Lydia Sigourney's Nature Poetry." *Legacy: a Journal of Nineteenth-Century American Women Writers* 8 (1988): 3–18.

Gilmore, Susan. "'Ye May Not Wash It Out': Women Poets, Native Subjects, and Sentimental Resistance." Unpublished paper, delivered at the Race, Gender and Sentimentality in Nineteenth-Century American Literature Conference, Cornell University, March 29–31, 1990.

Gray, Janet, ed. *She Wields a Pen: American Women Poets of the Nineteenth Century*. Iowa City: University of Iowa Press, 1997.

Hart, Ellen Louise, and Martha Nell Smith, eds. *Open Me Carefully: Emily Dickinson's Intimate Letters to Susan Huntington Dickinson*. Ashfield, MA: Paris Press, 1998.

"H.H." *Nation* 13. 298 (March 16, 1871): 183–4.

Howe, Julia Ward. *Passion Flowers*. 1854.

Jacobus, Mary. "The Question of Language: Men of Maxims and *The Mill on the Floss*." *Critical Inquiry* 8. 2 (winter 1981): 207–22.

Kelley, Mary. *Private Woman, Public Stage: Literary Domesticity in Nineteenth-Century America*. New York and Oxford: Oxford University Press, 1984.

Kilcup, Karen, ed. *Nineteenth-Century American Women Writers: an Anthology*. Oxford: Basil Blackwell, 1997.

Lauter, Paul. "Teaching Nineteenth-Century Women Writers." *Canons and Contexts*. Oxford: Oxford University Press, 1991. 114–32.

Ostriker, Alicia Suskin. *Stealing the Language: the Emergence of Women's Poetry in America*. Boston: Beacon Press, 1986.

Pizer, Donald. *Realism and Naturalism in Nineteenth-Century American Literature*. Carbondale: Southern Illinois University Press, 1984.

Reese, Lizette Woodworth. *A Branch of May*. 1887.

Samuels, Shirley, ed. *The Culture of Sentiment: Race, Gender, and Sentimentality in Nineteenth-Century America*. Oxford: Oxford University Press, 1992.

Tompkins, Jane. *Sensational Designs: the Cultural Work of American Fiction, 1790–1860*. Oxford: Oxford University Press, 1985.

Walker, Cheryl, ed. *American Women Poets of the Nineteenth Century: an Anthology*. New Brunswick: Rutgers University Press, 1992.

The Nightingale's Burden: Women Poets and American Culture Before 1900. Bloomington: Indiana University Press, 1982.

"Nineteenth-Century American Women Poets Revisited." *Nineteenth-Century American Women Writers: a Critical Reader*. Ed. Kilcup, 231–44.

Watts, Emily Stipes. *The Poetry of American Women from 1632 to 1945*. Austin: University of Texas Press, 1977.

Wilcox, Ella Wheeler. *Poems of Passion*. 1886.

Manuscript of Alice Cary's letter to John Greenleaf Whittier appears courtesy of the Houghton Library, Harvard University.

6

SHIRLEY SAMUELS

Women at war

Recent attention to women's roles in the Civil War has uncovered several stories of women who dressed as men in order to fight in battle, such as Sarah Wakefield on the Union side. The Confederacy had female warriors as well. One Union soldier remembered how "Another She-Devil shot her way to our breastworks with two large revolvers dealing death to all in her path. She was shot several times with no apparent effect. When she ran out of ammunition, she pulled out the largest pig-sticker I ever seen ... she stabbed three boys and was about to decapitate a fourth when the Lieutenant killed her."[1] The terrifying specter of such heroism may have affected the difficulty warrior women who survived faced in receiving antebellum pensions. However many cases may eventually be documented, the murderous intentions behind such a rampage were hardly confined to participation in battle. The northerner Gail Hamilton's "A Call to My Country-Women," for example, complains that "stitching does not ... hew traitors in pieces before the Lord" (*Atlantic Monthly*, March 1863, p. 346). And in a response to Hamilton's piece, an anonymous writer for the Loyal Publication Society declared that "many a Southern woman, during this war, has written to husband, brother or lover, to bring home with him 'a dead Yankee, pickled,' or 'a hand, or an ear, or a thumb, at least'" (New York: May 1863). While such extreme manifestations serve as commentary, they also situate the unease of fictional examples. Marion Harland's *Sunnybank* (1867) has southern women writing to their soldier boyfriends to ask for "rings, and charms, and watch-chains made of the bones of Federal soldiers slain in battle" which might then be "displayed exultingly by Southern *ladies* as trophies of their lovers' valor" (165).

Not, or not only, for sensational effect do these anecdotes appear here. Nor merely do they serve to bring into relation the emotional violence I will argue underlies relations between women in domestic fiction with the sensational bloodiness of war fiction. In these accounts, from the intimate possibilities for consuming a pickled Yankee to the implied transformation between needle and sword, we can see how the Civil War externalizes in extraordinary ways how an image of home might appear. While men were making such intimate gestures on the battlefield as picking up body parts and sewing them back together, the domestic gestures alluded to here – sewing, nursing – become involuted and interpellated as violence. To consider both emotional violence and bloody dismemberment is to imagine that the overwrought emotional anxieties expressed in narratives like Susan B. Warner's mid-century narrative of a dysfunctional childhood, *The Wide, Wide World* (1850), are part of the generalized sense of threat characterized by broken families, betrayed hierarchies, and vehement longings for a restored order. Therefore while the Civil War may provide the most visible location for such disruptions of families and such rearranging of family ties, I propose that its narratives are contiguous with such stories of tension and desire between women as M. E. Holmes's later nineteenth-century melodrama *Woman Against Woman* (1880).

Even as the terrible violence of the Civil War displaced women of all races and classes, it also provided a disquieting liberation from previously rigid roles. In its extreme form, such liberation may appear in the fiction of the period as an assumption that women can fight in battle. In less extreme, but still disconcerting ways, the transformation of women's roles occurs through their intimacies or, paradoxically, through the failed intimacies between them. This chapter proposes to take on, first, the unsettling antagonisms in women's relations, or women at war with each other; and second, the unsettling intimacy in women's relations as they stand together facing war. Looking at women and violence in novels written by women after 1860,[2] the first section examines works by Susan Warner and Marion Harland for tense dynamics between women whose relations are often expressed in violent terms. The next section reads novels by Augusta Evans and E. D. E. N. Southworth for how they elaborate the relation of women to war. Although these categories suggest an opposition between home and world, I want to resist such binaries. That violence within the home might mirror or present a complicated engagement with violence outside the home appears explicitly in war fiction, but the domestic fiction that less explicitly refers its wars to the outside world still locates its violence in a complicated uneasiness about women's roles within the home. In looking at women's roles, I will examine what the Civil War discloses rather than what this fiction reflects about the Civil War. That is, borrowing the familiar language of the house divided, I want to look at what women do when the domestic as well as the national house falls.

I

Domestic fiction employs violence in a curious form. While many novels describe an orphan girl making her way in the world, what makes that scenario possible is the mother's disappearance or desertion. Whether by death or, as in the wildly popular novel *The Wide, Wide World*, by illness which leads first to separation and then to death, such desertions betray a strong ambivalence about the figure of the mother.[3] Although the heroine in these novels frequently calls upon the memory of her mother to sustain her, the enemies she encounters are often mother substitutes. The violence of their oppression and of her antipathy towards them might suggest that she suppresses violent memories of her mother.

Behind this treatment of mothers, I argue, is a shift from how women were depicted during the American Revolution (repeatedly as licentious or bad mothers) through models of congruence and reciprocity between world and home in the historical novels of the early republic. These fictions figure a circular or even tautological relation between the familial and the sociopolitical (where women are presented in isomorphic relation to "worldly" or sociopolitical concerns). In the later sentimental and domestic novel there is a virtual disappearance of the worldly or sociopolitical, or rather an absorption of these concerns within the domestic sphere. Such absorption appears, for instance, in novels like Marion Harland's *True as Steel* (1872) and Susan B. Warner's *Diana* (1877). Both portray mothers who resent their daughters. In *True as Steel*, the mother appears as a novel-reading, opium-taking alcoholic whose notions of sentiment are utterly destructive and whose invocation of the necessary bond between mother and daughter becomes the weak excuse for the damage she does to her daughter's marriage. In *Diana*, the mother has no such vices; indeed, she is an exemplary housekeeper. But the vengeance she carries out on her daughter is no less harmful; while invoking a model of housekeeping rather than of mother–daughter love, she burns the letters from her daughter's fiancé. As a result, thinking her first love untrue, her daughter marries another man. Even as the novel has a rather amusing take on fine ladies and what they might do, it reasserts matrimonial destiny. The heroine announces, "I can only fire a pistol and leap a fence on horseback and dance a polka," and is asked "Can you make butter and bread and pudding and pies and sweetmeats and pickles and all that sort of thing?" (90). In treating their daughters as property, these mothers use the language of sentimental investment to disrupt the expectation of maternal care. That is, as the familiar language of maternal love comes into play, there is a subtle but terrible doubt introduced that it protects daughters.

As they act to procure the marriages they believe appropriate, such mothers expose the emotional violence inside a sentimental model of maternal love.

In a chapter called "Documentary Evidence," near the end of *True as Steel*, the heroine reads a letter her mother wrote a dozen years previously to the man her daughter loved:

> She has never whispered it (even to me, her devoted Mother!) in her conscious moments, but the *Hapless Idolatry is undermining* her constitution . . . From her earliest youth, you have been her *Ideal*, her HERO. Too proud to show this, she has let 'Concealment, like a worm in the Bud,' gnaw heart and Brain until she is now a Total *Wreck*! . . . I, only, the helpless, *agonized* Mother, have penetrated the depths of her Heart . . .! On my knees I implore you to rescue my tender, fond, high-spirited Daughter, who adores you in secret, yet who would expire of *Shame* did she suspect that another possessed the Knowledge of that Adoration. Should I apologize for revealing the secret she would guard with *her life* if need were? I know you to be an honorable Gentleman – . . . I trust you to keep it! (281–82)

The recipient of this letter keeps the secret, but the mother does not. Extending the contest with her daughter, she shows her the letter: "With one spasm of fury, Hadassah rent the sheet from top to bottom and threw it into the fire. 'Mother!' her hand high in the air, as if taking an oath, 'do you think that Heaven or I can ever forgive you this thing?' "

For what "thing" is it that Hadassah's mother can never be forgiven? Not only does she violate the conventions of the sentimental novel in speaking, for her daughter, the love that is unsought, but her speech succeeds: the man she addresses proposes to Hadassah and they have been married for the past twelve years. In writing a letter declaring her daughter's love, the mother brings about the marriage that her daughter desires. But it was precisely that secret that Hadassah had taken pride in controlling. While in a delirious fever she has repressed speech (*"silence à la mort"*) in order to keep from betraying herself. Thus her insistence that she can never forgive her mother has several sources. In the context of nineteenth-century sentimental constructs, to be exposed as loving before such love has been solicited is a horrifying betrayal. In this case, moreover, she feels her husband has been blackmailed into marriage. Most monstrous, by the perspective of this fiction, it is the mother who has "penetrated the depths of her heart," a penetration weirdly sexualized and perhaps even more strangely associated with a potentially fatal invasion. A category of secrecy that both she and her mother have associated with life – "the secret she would guard with *her life*" – has been revealed in terms of sentimental maternal love. Seeking to effect a "Revolution" in her daughter's feelings, the mother instead speaks the revolution of those feelings: she expresses what her daughter cannot express, yet does so explicitly as a way of betraying her daughter.

Hadassah's mother repeatedly invokes parenting to suggest the motive for her revenge: "There are many things I could have told you if you had relied upon my judgment, confided your sorrows and joys to me as other girls do with their mothers" (278). The worst sin appears as a "hapless Idolatry," as though the religion of home and the family were being cast aside for this strange and forbidden sexual desire. Resentment of her desiring and capable daughter goads the mother: "Hadassah's stirring housewifery [was] a jagged thorn in [her mother's] side ... Moreover, the father's partiality for this one of his children irked the mother unreasonably" (51). Her mother complains, "You worship her as you never did me when I was in my prime – much less now. She is the rising, I am the setting sun" (51). Hadassah aggravates the role reversal by describing her mother in terms that suggest parental despair: "She would suffer less if she ate less rubbish [and] if she did not devour such heaps of indifferent novels." "Constant study" of "trashy books" and "sensational periodicals" by her mother "must produce mental dyspepsia and by overheating the imagination render everyday life stale and distasteful" (88–9). The struggle against mothers that preoccupied writers of the early republic in such works as Rebecca Rush's *Kelroy* (1812) seems displaced here by a generation whose relation to parents has become a form of inverted and agonized parenting.

The fashioning of the female subject produces highly conflicted relations between women, and especially between mothers and daughters. Competition between mother and daughter has more benign manifestations, but its culminating force appears as the mother's fear of being sexually as well as socially supplanted by her daughter. Perhaps the disappearance of the conflict between the political and the familial – and even the reciprocity between them – means not simply a disappearance, not simply a translation into a conflict between home and world, but a conflict between women that quite explicitly (even transparently) involves the formation of rival female identities. In *True as Steel*, the allusions to Shakespeare that invoke the love declaration of the cross-dressing Viola in *Twelfth Night* bring in extraordinary tensions about gendered identity and sexual violence. This literature presents a fashioning of selves densely conflicted by problems of language and sexual difference and especially by violence. This is not to recuperate these novels for their modernity, but perhaps to indicate what is being missed in dismissing domestic novels as unworldly – or, paradoxically, ignored by celebrating them as an embodiment of female sentimental power. The embarrassment of sentimentality is perhaps that it too obtrusively keeps repeating "secrets" – like that of *True as Steel*. And this secret may be how much violence occurs between women in this fiction, and how much that violence becomes associated with disturbances in the social structure. The major disruption of such structures caused by war provokes even more dramatic shifts in expected roles for women. As violence reorients women's sphere, so too the energy of new conflicts about gender and race is mapped on to how and whom to desire.

II

For women characters as well as writers, the war raises such questions as what can be done at home and how the idea of home "fits" with ideas about the nation. Battlefield and home appear tensely joined, each unsettling the role of the other. Women emerge from the extension of domestic duties – sewing and nursing among them – taking elements of nurture and using them as weapons of war. The popular magazine *Godey's Lady's Book* ignores the war but begins a column for widows. Distinctions between younger and older widows are marked by different issues that take up each of their roles separately (younger widows will want to attract another husband, for example). In other publications, rumors float about women who write to their soldier brothers, lovers, or husbands asking to have body parts collected from enemy soldiers and mailed to them or who pose as nurses in order to poison the food of invalid soldiers in hospitals. As war provokes risks, it also releases women from ordinary social roles. Yet what makes boundary crossing and transgression interesting in this fiction often appears as the staged attraction between women over the body of a fallen hero.

Stories about the Civil War, most notably in the yearning poetry of Walt Whitman, have prompted literary critics to examine the relation between male battlefield vulnerability and homoeroticism. Drawing on this work, I want to suggest that fictional battle pieces at once feminize vulnerable male bodies and release the often stunningly erotic energies of women. However historically notable women were as nurses, or by their sewing and relief work through the Female Sanitary Commissions, the libidinal pleasure expressed through these literary works is found in how the situation of the war allows and indeed promotes the love of women for each other. As battlefields have famously allowed men to express their love for each other, so for women to love other women becomes integral to how this fiction promotes national loyalties.

To allude to unions between women as patriotic is not to overlook the obvious consideration of what unions might have been available with so many men dead. Nor do I mean to trivialize these deaths with the supposition that they provide a convenient means by which to imagine women's ability to form new relations with each other. At the same time I want to suggest that the vulnerability of wounded male bodies might enable such links between women, especially when presented as a visual cue. Women in this fiction are repeatedly shown bending over recumbent men, often in their hospital beds, as in Louisa May Alcott's *Hospital Sketches* (1863). Portrayals of erect women leaning over weakened or dying men reverse roles and offer an implied critique of the more repressed resistance to heterosexual marriage as well as pointing to an even rarer topic, slavery. Few of these works mention slavery. The most peculiar effect of this absence in Civil War women's writing may be that it reappears in the resistance to marriage that battlefield erotics encourages. As such fiction recruits nationalism to new declarations of independence, it also shows women how to love each other through loving the nation.[4]

Nineteenth-century fiction retains the capacity to stage surprises. Nowhere is this more true than in the novels of E. D. E. N. Southworth. In an otherwise benign scene of imperializing domesticity – a conversation between two women bound on a missionary voyage around the horn of Africa – sentiments such as the following call attention to the relation between the ship's physical location and the more usual direction of such transatlantic crossings during the Middle Passage. Echoing the language of the free love advocate John Humphrey Noyes in his dialogue of slavery and marriage, the ardent Britomarte of *Fair Play* declares of "woman's position in marriage" that she becomes a "slave, since she lapses into the personal property of her husband" (185, 184). Her newly married companion resists in the language of southern apologists: "I *like* the idea of belonging to my husband and having him to love me and take care of me" (185). The routes of love and possession that were initially disrupted by the passage of ships bearing goods and bodies across the Atlantic during the slave trade are never mentioned in this novel that explicitly traces the story of the Civil War as a story about how white women may dispose of their bodies. And yet the version of domesticity that it at once challenges and enacts rewrites the nation's still dominant conflict as one about the erotics of possession. The displacement of the hidden subjects of race, class, and servitude on to sexuality makes women and their bodies the source and the destiny of the irrepressible conflict.

Despite the range of settings and characters in her sixty or so works of fiction, Southworth's writing has one basic tendency: all of her houses are haunted.[5] Almost invariably, they are haunted by women who seek redress for a lost inheritance. In the case of her Civil War novels, the inheritance is national destiny – the home under siege is the national house divided. What such hauntings provide are opportunities for Southworth to show the home as a site of battle rather than retreat, a place where women make homes, in Lora Romero's evocative phrase, into home fronts. This section will explore some routes that such battle lines traverse. As texts, I will use the paired novels *Fair Play* and *How He Won Her* (1868 and 1869), and the paired inversions I would like to trace in these novels are the emphatic displays of patriotism in home settings and the eroticism between women that another form of inversion permits, even as the novels work inexorably toward satisfactory heterosexual coupling.[6]

Because Southworth never saw a plot she did not like, I will resist summary and will only touch on three of the novel's four women characters. We are introduced to "the four orders of female beauty – the blue, gray, hazel, and black-eyed woman" (28) in *Fair Play* as they prepare to graduate from Bellemont College for Young Ladies. Unsettling the oppositional excitations that would have been aroused for contemporary readers attuned to every mention of the blue and gray are the modifications of hazel and black. The question of what marriage each desires becomes settled ineradicably within the first 40 of 1,000 narrative pages. War operates as an effective delay as the women find distinctive methods for entering into patriotic service – and yet the delays of extended plots may also be seen to defer the anticipated marriages in ways that provide another form of satisfaction. That is, the romantic thrust of the book seems first about relations between women. The story promotes a romantic attachment between Britomarte and Erminie. Erminie loves Britomarte "with a devotion approaching idolatry. And it was probable the masculine element in the character of the beautiful young amazon that so powerfully magnetized the maiden" (30–1). Yet even as these bonds between amazon and maiden will keep the women weaving in and out of each other's homes and beds, the warp and woof of the novel's proclaimed romantic entanglements will be heterosexual. That the novels end with marriage after 1,000 pages may not be as significant as that the resolution through marriage is deferred for 1,000 pages occupied by the interruptions of war.

When the four "belles" discuss marriage, Britomarte inveighs against its laws. Foreshadowing her later work in battle, Britomarte's rage against patriarchy means that, "like Judith, she could have cut off the head of Holofernes without relenting" (29). Using the language of the forthcoming war, Elfie wants to determine "the best means of *of*fence and *de*fence against our natural enemies, meaning our future hubs" (36). Marriage appears as a battlefield in which matters of offence and defense preoccupy the combatants. Such violence may be just as significant if less visible in the traditional account of merging woman's identity with man's in marriage: Erminie wants to "lose SELF in the one great vital love a true wife finds in a true husband" (37–8). Yet it is to Britomarte that Erminie talks "as a girl talks to her accepted lover," and to her she promises to "be as constant to you as ever woman was to man!" Britomarte responds that "if I were a man" she would marry her "immediately" (46). Using a rather violent acknowledgment of gendered restrictions, she continues: "Not being a man, however, I shall not hate you for loving me, nor kill you for serving me. Being a woman I shall love you truly all your life, and shield you carefully from all men" (47). This violent imagining of heterosexual marriage suggests that women must be extremely well armed to engage in such combat.

The combat preparations that the young women facing marriage undertake come in handy as they find themselves facing military conscription. The first female recruit who attempts to enter the battle is the impish Elfie, who fools the draft into inducting her by using her masculine middle name. As "Sydney Fielding" she shows up for boot camp and is furious at the response: "Women have enlisted, and have served; but always when disguised as men. I never in my life heard of a woman being drafted" (57). And yet, "Sydney Fielding is at present at home, and not in the service, is white, is twenty years old, and sound in mind and body" (59). Elfie continues, "I am not an alien, nor an invalid, nor an idiot ... I am a native born citizen of the United States, aged twenty years, sound in mind and body, wind and limb, single, and with no one but my country depending on me for support" (61). In her idealism, Elfie sulks when not accepted. The violence she cannot express on the battlefield finds another form when, seeking to convert her forcibly at once to his political cause and to marriage, her lover abducts her. Leaving bloody traces on his body in the form of scratches and bites, Elfie later gives him her hand, though not her political allegiance, when she finds him dying in a Washington, DC hospital. And such violence surrounds or enables many scenes of tenderness between men and women not only in Southworth's fiction but also in that of her contemporary women writers.

III

The languishing male heroes of one of the best-selling Civil War novels, Augusta Evans's *Macaria* (1864), provide the occasion for a southern elegy for the sundering of the nation seen through the conflicted courtships of two vibrant women. This novel also shows women characters expressing affection when confronted with prone masculine bodies, even as such eroticized and vulnerable male bodies leave women in charge. The women left standing over the bodies of dead or dying men, bodies they then commemorate, must provide a new understanding of what relation there might be between their homes and national destiny. That is, although they celebrate male heroics, the relation between patriotism and coupling they express finds them yoked to each other.

Toward the novel's end, the two women who have survived the loss of all available male partners stand together viewing an epic painting one has just completed. The painting is crowded with allegory and tragicomedy: "a torn, stained battle-field" shows "mangled heaps of dead." Different generations and generative possibilities have been cut short: "Among the trampled, bloody sheaves of wheat, an aged Niobe mother bent in anguish, pressing her hand upon the pulseless heart of a handsome boy of sixteen summers, whose yellow locks were dabbled from his death wound. A few steps farther, a lovely young wife, kneeling beside the stalwart form of her husband, ... lifted her woeful, ashen face to Heaven in mute despair, while the fair-browed infant on the ground beside her dipped its little snowy, dimpled feet in a pool of its father's blood, and, with tears of terror still glistening on its cheeks, laughed at the scarlet coloring." The gruesome blood in this landscape is unimaginably made absurd by the playfulness with which it is treated as color. Over and over, the red or crimson or scarlet seems more emphatically present than the loss of life. And yet the clichéd language seems also to erase the impact of what might otherwise appear as starkly visual violence: "Just beyond these mourners, a girl of surpassing beauty whose black hair floated like a sable banner on the breeze, clasped her rounded arms about her dead patriot lover ... Neither blue shadows nor wreathing, rosy mists, nor golden haze of sunset glory, softened the sacrificial scene which showed its grim features strangely solemn in the weird, fading, crepuscular light" (415).

The point here is not just the unbearable alliteration, nor the promiscuous use of adjectives, nor even the cartoon figures, but that all of this vivid bloodiness is once again turned to the question of women's rights. The women and children who survive the story of sacrifice witness at once the loss of men and the need to imagine a destiny outside of marriage and the family. Following their attention to this lurid landscape, the heroines Electra and Irene debate their roles as single women, since "upon the purity, the devotion and the patriotism of the women of our land, not less than upon the heroism of our armies, depends our national salvation" (417). Their desire for patriotism gives way to a more familiar note. As Irene explains, "when disposed to lament the limited sphere of women's influence, I am reminded of Pascal's grand definition: 'A sphere of which the center was everywhere, the circumference nowhere'; and I feel encouraged to hope that, after all, woman's circle of action will prove as sublime and extended" (318). The circle of women's influence is a familiar tenet of the cult of domesticity. Invoking Pascal on the concept of limitless circumference makes ambition an honored and yet ordinary inhabitant of women's separate sphere. Lofty ambition as an ordinary inhabitant of a "sublime" hearth challenges the gendered separations invoked while in the midst of upholding them. The absence of men makes women's sphere of influence necessary and heroic as well as dominant. There may be other forms of identification imagined through such cathartic attention to wounded male bodies and the implied morality of political affect they enforce. As gestures toward a private morality, they also make citizens identify with pain as patriotic. What formal features of sensational fiction might follow? Such fiction is roped by the bonds of womanhood, by normative processes of heterosexual coupling, *and* by the passionate identifications with state or nation that bring women together. In Southworth's novels, "state" and "nation," often conflated or staggered in critical citation, remain doggedly opposed. All the characters travel north from the Mason–Dixon line, yet to be from the south of Washington and Jefferson can mean either the new nation of the Confederacy or the State of Virginia that has in its significant history as the source of US presidents mattered vividly as a source of the northern sense of nation. The excitations new nationalisms can produce leak through the novel's attempt to seal in national affect for the northern cause. Three of the four women in the novel love southern rebels, and their protests about divided loyalties have suspicious echoes. Indeed, the protests may be appropriately inadequate, since they fracture the assumed relation between satisfactory marital liaisons and declarations of loyalty to the union. For nation or state to appear as a third term in erotic relations brings politics into the state as well as eroticizing politics. Consequently, like proclamations valorizing heterosexual union in fiction that promotes or enables the coupling of women, the outsized assertions made on behalf of the union appear to produce conflagration as much as a way to be at home in the nation.

Nationalism and romance recur as tensely imbricated in each other's structures. A further resistance to marriage insists that it line up with political affiliation, a dismissed evocation of divided political loyalties. When her secessionist lover proposes, for example, Elfie refuses him, saying, "I mean to be true to my country!" He replies, "Your native *state* is your country! To her alone is your allegiance due" (429). Taking patriotic duty back home, she responds, "if a state has the right to secede from the Union, a county has the same right to secede from a state; [and] the husband from the wife, and the child from the father!" (429). Realigning secession with rebellion against the father and loyalty as the extension of the lessons learned from the mother, she continues: "The Constitution of the United States is written in just about the plainest English that I have ever read and I claim to understand my mother tongue!" (430). Yet she at once recovers national loyalties for women's sphere and denies their applicability. Although she participates in political intrigue, Elfie goes on to protest: "why I or any woman should make any sacrifice for the sake of the country. What have *we* to do with the country? Why should we devote our time, labor, money, life, health and happiness to the country, as many of us *will* do, if this comes to a civil war? *We* have no share in the administration of the government, no voice in the election of its officers! I declare it is a burning shame to the manhood of America" (438–9). Reminiscent of Frederick Douglass's protest about liberty in "What to the Slave is the Fourth of July?" (1852), her protest performs another silent link between the situation of women and the unnamed struggle against slavery.

That protest, that shame called down on the manhood of America, appears as a challenge to womanhood. Incorporating domestic acts of resistance, Elfie causes trouble in secessionist Virginia by sewing a huge flag to hang in front of her house: "It was twenty-four feet long by eight broad. It had forty-eight stripes and a hundred stars . . . ! When it was done, I had a misgiving that it was over regulation size, and that there were more stripes than was lawful, and more stars than states; but I wasn't sure, for I had forgotten all about my geography and history; and besides, I thought if I had made a mistake it was certainly on the right side, and at worst, it was only a prophecy of the future, for the dear old flag is bound to grow and increase; and if she isn't entitled to a hundred stars now she will be when we have annexed South America and the rest of creation!" (406). Turning domestic feats into imperialist claims, this outsized flag mounted in front of a loyal but undefended Virginia home provokes rebel wrath as expansionist and imperialist dreams collide violently with a more limited nationalism.[7] As Elfie demonstrates, to believe in the destiny of the United States is to produce the home as a battlefield.

More than the cross-dressing violence of Britomarte, who appears in protean form as a variety of male military figures, Elfie's act shows domestic and war narratives in dialogical relation. Having cut and sewn her political loyalty, Elfie explains: "The first public act of my life resulted in getting our house burned over our heads!" (404). When a mob approaches to tear down the flag, she stations herself at a window and fires at them (413–15). Her aim appears unnervingly good – she shoots a man out of the tree to which she has attached her enormous flag. When reproached for how narrowly she misses killing him, she retorts, "And suppose I had? It would have been very shocking to a new recruit like me, just at the first go off; but, bless you! It would not have weighed on my conscience very heavily" (410). Such assertions bring us full circle to how demonstrations of political loyalty can literally burn down the house. The novel cannot end by bringing the women together and instead moves their passion for each other and for the national enterprise on to a fantastic conjoining of domestic and patriotic enterprises through this conflagration.

In burning down the house, the national as well as the particular home burns. What then is it to be at home in this America? By Elfie's assertion, it is at once to stitch your political loyalties on to an outsized flag and to have fantasies about imperialism. If the "dear old flag is bound to grow and increase," then a form of organic nationalism brings home-making and patriotism together. What women produce when they couple, as well as when they attach the flag to the home, is to annex the rest of creation. This purer form of domesticity, this fantasy of women's sphere, makes all of creation an annex for the national home.

NOTES

1. The first letter is reproduced in *A Woman's War*, p. 93. Notable recent work on this topic includes Elizabeth Young's absorbing account of cross-dressing women in the Civil War.
2. Such an overview would include early works like Tabitha Tenney's *Female Quixotism* (1802). Here the presence of vagrant soldiers enables a well-intentioned young woman in a settled bourgeois neighborhood to impersonate a soldier in order to pretend a seduction. Her cross-dressing disguise leads to a humorous entanglement when she must learn to wield the weapons of war as well as words of love to become an all too plausible suitor. It might also include works like Catharine Sedgwick's *Hope Leslie* (1826). In a different wartime situation – the colonial violence with dispossessed Pequots – both of the major female characters, Magawisca and Hope, wear disguises to intercede in dramatic scenes of imprisonment and escape.
3. See Nina Baym on typical scenarios and Sheila Rothman on illness in nineteenth-century America. She argues that the invalid was expected to demand separation from familial duties and responsibilities in order to follow up on the moral demands of getting better, often by physical separation and traveling to a different climate. Such a scenario appears in *The Wide, Wide World*.
4. How the Civil War affected gender and class distinctions has preoccupied historians only fairly recently. I have in mind historians like Drew Faust and Catherine Clinton and literary critics like Elizabeth Young. Theoretical works that have become classics, works such as Eve Sedgwick's *Between Men* or Klaus Theweleit's *Male Fantasies*, have also influenced me.
5. Before going further, I want to acknowledge briefly that drawing obscure authors or texts into critical conversation invariably arouses dilemmas. If we attribute to rather unknown works the status of representative texts, the question arises about how much the popular literature that unseats contemporary conventions provides pleasure for escaping or for reinforcing the boundaries of understood propriety. In conducting a critical discussion of lesser-known works, it can be difficult to find salient details without the dread staging of plot summary. For authors as manically prolific as E. D. E. N. Southworth, who profitably spent almost fifty of her eighty years publishing fiction, new novels may be "recovered" for some time to come before critics will have the comfortable luxury of assuming audience familiarity. *The Hidden Hand, or Capitola the Madcap* has crossed over into the canon via a paperback edition for classroom use. Others, ranging from the wildly popular novels *The Deserted Wife* and *Ishmael, or the Self-Raised*, to the collection of stories *The Haunted Homestead*, will probably emerge more slowly.

6. Cf. Karen Tracey's account of the "double proposal" excoriated by Wilkie Collins as well as the forthcoming work by Anne Ingram on these novels, which she refers to under their serial title *Britomarte the Man Hater*. This work has led her to a series of other fictional works with cross-dressing women, work she has kindly shared with me. Among other works she has located, *Remy St. Remy, or the Boy in Blue* carries out a provocative story of cross-dressing and crossed lovers.
7. Amy Kaplan has recently proposed such a relation between domesticity and imperialism.

WORKS CITED

Baym, Nina. *Woman's Fiction: A Guide to Novels By and About Women in America, 1820–1870*. New York: Cornell University Press, 1978.
Clinton, Catherine. *The Other Civil War: American Women in the Nineteenth Century*. New York: Hill and Wang, 1984.
Faust, Drew. *Mothers of Invention: Women of the Slaveholding South in the American Civil War*. Chapel Hill: University of North Carolina Press, 1996.
A Few Words in Behalf of the Loyal Women of the United States. New York: May 1863.
Hamilton, Gail. "A Call to My Country-Women." *Atlantic Monthly* (1863): 345–49.
Harland, Marion. *Sunnybank*. New York: Carleton, 1873.
Kaplan, Amy. "Manifest Domesticity." *American Literature* (September 1998): 581–606.
Loyal Publication Society. Wm. C. Bryant & Co. New York: May 1863.
Romero, Lora. *Home Fronts: Domesticity and its Critics in the Antebellum United States*. Durham: Duke University Press, 1997.
Rothman, Sheila. *Living in the Shadow of Death: Tuberculosis and the Social Experience of Illness in American History*. Baltimore: Johns Hopkins University Press, 1995.
Sedgwick, Catharine. *Hope Leslie*. New York: White, Gallaher, and White, 1826.
Sedgwick, Eve. *Between Men: English Literature and Male Homosocial Desire*. New York: Columbia University Press, 1985.
Southworth, E. D. E. N. *The Deserted Wife*. New York: Appleton, 1850.
Fair Play. Philadelphia: T. B. Peterson, 1868.
The Haunted Homestead. Philadelphia: T. B. Peterson, 1860.
The Hidden Hand, or Capitola the Madcap. New York: G. W. Dillingham, 1888.
How He Won Her. Philadelphia: T. B. Peterson, 1869.
Ishmael, or the Self-Raised. Philadelphia: T. B. Peterson, 1876.
Tenney, Tabitha. *Female Quixotism*. Boston: I. Thomas and E. T. Andrews, 1801.
Theweleit, Klaus. *Male Fantasies*. Translated by Stephan Conway *et al*. Minneapolis: University of Minnesota Press, 1987.
Tracey, Karen. *Plots and Proposals: American Women's Fiction, 1850–90*. Urbana: University of Illinois Press, 2000.
Warner, Susan B. *The Wide, Wide World*. London: T. Nelson, 1852.
A Woman's War: Southern Women, Civil War, and the Confederate Legacy. Richmond, Va.: Museum of the Confederacy.
Young, Elizabeth. *Disarming the Nation: Women's Writing and the Civil War*. Chicago: University of Chicago Press, 1999.

7

SUSAN GRIFFIN

Women, anti-Catholicism, and narrative in nineteenth-century America

Where was religion in nineteenth-century American women's writing? Every-where.[1] Especially with the ideological shift from a patriarchal-centered Calvinism to a more "feminized" nonsectarian Protestantism (see works cited below: Cott, Douglas, Sklar), women were given warrant to write on religious matters. At times, this writing took the form of overtly theologi-cal texts, some conventionally pious, others, like Mary Baker Eddy's 1875 *Science and Health* and Elizabeth Cady Stanton's 1895 *The Woman's Bible*, radical and revolutionary. More widespread was the way that religion as a topic pervaded virtually every genre of women's (and for that matter men's) writing from Sarah Grimké's abolitionist *An Epistle to Christian Women of the South* (1836) to Emily Dickinson's intensely spiritual – and skeptical – poetry.

Perhaps the most striking component of nineteenth-century religious writ-ing was the development and proliferation of religious fiction. In 1871, Harriet Beecher Stowe described the current craze for narratives that "teach[] by parables":

> It is now understood that whoever wishes to gain the public ear, and to pro-pound a new theory, must do it in a serial story. Hath any one in our day, as in St. Paul's, a psalm, a doctrine, a tongue, a revelation, an interpretation – forthwith he wraps it up in a serial story, and presents it to the public ... We have Romanism and Protestantism, High Church, and Low Church and no Church, contending with each other in serial stories, where each side converts the other, according to the faith of the narrator. (*My Wife and I*, 2)

Although Stowe images the writer as male here, she, along with count-less other female authors, were major purveyors of theologies through the medium of polemical fiction. The novel had come to be popularly perceived as woman's proper pulpit.[2]

Changes within the scholarly disciplines in recent years have legiti-mated religious writings as objects of study: feminist rediscovery of texts by nineteenth-century women; the reclaiming – in the wake of modernism – of religion as an appropriate realm of critical study; new historical, sociological, and cultural studies work; interest in polemical, popular, and sensational writing. The next task in our study of religion's role in nineteenth-century writing and culture needs to be an exploration of its theological and political heterogeneity. Growing recognition of this multiplicity can be seen in the new editions of writings by Jewish and Native American women, for example.[3] What also needs scholarly work, however, is the variety within American women's Christianity and its texts.[4]

This chapter looks at an enduring thread in nineteenth-century American women's writing: that of anti-Catholicism. Anti-Catholicism informs women's fiction in a variety of ways and takes a number of forms: stock characters and sensational gothic plots, nativist attacks on immigrants, theological debates. As Jenny Franchot and others have cogently argued, nineteenth-century American anti-Catholicism also, and importantly, provides a means of critiquing Protestantism itself. In addition, anti-Catholic narratives serve to push the borders of what can be "decently" written about. As Richard Hofstader says, "Anti-Catholicism has always been the pornography of the Puritan." Depictions of Catholicism become a legitimating realm for depicting female action, mobility, and sexuality.[5]

Studying the case of anti-Catholicism helps us to recognize the generic complexity of nineteenth-century women's writings, the ways in which the sensational penetrates the domestic. These examples illustrate as well the fact that women's writing is not immune to nor apart from the ideologies of the time. That is, religious fiction is not only not exclusively women's, but women's religious writing does not represent a separate, morally superior female world apart from the political, theological, economic, and racial tensions of the period. The fact that intertextuality extends across sexual lines is vividly rendered by the ways in which women incorporate male documents and signatures within their texts and by examples of men purporting to speak in women's voices and even under women's names. Anti-Catholic writing is also international in its intertextuality – American Protestantism reads and borrows from that of Britain, even as its most sensational narratives become best-sellers overseas. Finally, looking closely at the particulars of this specific case of women's Protestant polemical writing reveals a diversity of political and theological stances, helping to deconstruct the idea of a singular and single nineteenth-century female culture of letters.

The literature of anti-Catholicism, which dates to the beginnings of Protestantism in the sixteenth century, is vast and varied. Anti-Catholicism played an important role in the inception of Anglo-American fiction itself, especially in the gothic tales of the British novelist Ann Radcliffe (1764–1823).

Elements of that tradition endured: sometimes used explicitly and delibe-rately as part of a Protestant polemic; sometimes as narrative elements, which, while carrying a related ideological freight, are nonetheless not pri-marily theological in aim. Recent recognition that the gothic in America is not solely a male realm has, in stressing the liberatory aspects of women's participation in this "subversive" genre, tended to downplay the intimate and enduring connection between the gothic and anti-Catholicism. Yet, as the examples below illustrate, this connection typically obtains, as when we see the fictions of women writers who have been perceived as defenders of domesticity, like Sarah Josepha Hale and Harriet Beecher Stowe, infu-sing their religious arguments for Protestant hearth and home with narrative elements that are recognizably both gothic and anti-Catholic.

Anti-Catholic writing almost invariably recycles certain standard elements and assumptions. Familiar figures are the crafty Jesuit, the lascivious monk, the sadistic Mother Superior, the innocent young woman beguiled into the convent. Anti-Catholic polemics portray lower-class Catholics as being kept by their priesthood in primitive ignorance and poverty, forbidden to read the Bible, deprived of their own wills and consciences by the confessional. In America in particular, Catholicism is seen as threatening to democratic citi-zenship. And anti-Catholicism becomes intertwined with nineteenth-century nativist fears about the waves of Irish and German immigrants, as well as the Spanish-speaking inhabitants of the American Southwest.

If the Catholic immigrant is perceived as threateningly poor, the Catholic Church itself is depicted as a repository of untold riches and a space of gor-geous sensuality: beautiful music, elaborate vestments, flickering candles, intoxicating incense, arcane ritual. At the center of this luxury is the Pope, a power-hungry despot, dispatching Jesuits worldwide as part of a conspiracy to fill his coffers and extend his political dominion. By the 1830s, for exam-ple, American fears about the papacy centered around the West, in particular the Mississippi valley, which was seen as what Ray Allen Billington, captur-ing the nineteenth-century millenial tone, calls "the scene of the death strug-gle between Protestantism and Catholicism" (*The Protestant Crusade*, 119).

This chapter surveys some of the uses to which different nineteenth-century American women writers put the structures and stories of anti-Catholicism, focusing, in particular, on the cultural work done by figures of the Catholic woman and her counterpart, the Protestant girl. In varying forms, the Catholic woman appears in works as diverse as the escaped nuns' tales of the thirties and forties, Hale's republican reworking of these sensational nar-ratives, Orvilla S. Belisle's nativist *The Archbishop* (1854), Augusta Evans Wilson's depiction of the racially inflected differences between Protestant and Catholic young women in her tale of the Alamo, Stowe's historical fiction set in the Renaissance, and Pamela Cowan's 1870 *The American Convent as a School for Protestant Children.*

The most famous and influential anti-Catholic narratives of the nineteenth century were nominally written by women: Maria Monk's *Awful Disclosures of the Hotel Dieu Nunnery of Montreal* (1836) and Rebecca Theresa Reed's *Six Months in a Convent* (1835). These were phenomenally popular books. Some 200,000 copies of *Awful Disclosures* were sold within a few weeks; 300,000 by 1860. It has been frequently reprinted into the twentieth century. *Six Months in a Convent* sold 10,000 copies in the first week and an estimated 200,000 within a month. In both of these sensational narratives, like the many others that followed, a woman tells of her escape from imprisonment in a convent. The case of these two is typical as well in that their "true" stories seem to have been recorded – or perhaps created – by the male sponsors of the escaped nun (Franchot calls *Awful Disclosures* "an intriguing example of collaborative writing" [154]). Rather than attempting to decide on the vexed status of Monk's and Reed's tales as "women's writing," it may be profitable to turn to two other examples of the "escaped nun's tale" whose authorship is less contested: Lucinda Martin Larned's *The American Nun* (1836) and Josephine Bunkley's *The Testimony of an Escaped Novice* (1855).

Bunkley's narrative was published by the mainstream Harper and Brothers. (Although Harper's had turned down Maria Monk's *Awful Disclosures* as too sensational, James Harper, who was a prominent nativist, published a number of other anti-Catholic books.) Bunkley writes her narrative, she says, in order to set the record straight, to counter other versions of her story that have been circulating. She incorporates a number of these in her text (including letters from her former Mother Superior and a Father O'Donnell, as well several anonymous "vulgar and threatening" missives) and includes, in addition, her own supporting documents: an editorial introduction and conclusion; "factual" notes that purport to quote from Church authorities like Ligouri; and examples of other women's convent experiences.

Bunkley's example is typical in its dual focus. On the one hand, her purpose is to reveal and detail the horrors of convent life – the deceitful ways young women are lured into nunhood, the confessor as sexual predator, convents as "priests' prisons for women," the Mother Superior as petty, vindictive despot, the deliberate attempts at breaking inmates' wills, the pervasive Catholic spying and deceit. Only the escaped nun – the renegade – can tell this true story, can reveal to Protestants the hidden truth of Catholicism.

On the other hand, as Bunkley's frantic efforts at justification and verification demonstrate, the escaped nun is also suspect, compromised as to her virginity and her verity. How can a woman who has been in a convent be an "honest woman"? Along with the other antebellum escaped nuns' stories, Bunkley's narrative suggests a cultural anxiety about women's newly dominant role in religion – what has been called "the feminization of American culture" (see works cited below: Cott, Douglas, Ryan, Sklar).

Lucinda Larned also expresses what is clearly a timely anxiety about the new generation of American women and their shaping influence on American Protestantism. *American Nun* represents a variation on the novel that warns against reading novels, a genre that, in America, dates back to the eighteenth century (see Baym, *Novels, Readers, and Reviewers*; Davidson, *Revolution and the Word*). Here the narrative technique is used for theological purposes: novel-reading, which her mother teaches her to love, so incapacitates Larned's heroine Anna Howard for everyday life and love that she rejects her fiancé and runs away from home to take up what she believes will be the romantic life of a nun. She is, of course, soon disabused of these fancies and eventually escapes from the convent. But Anna's troubles are not over, for she finds that hers is the suspicious status of the renegade. The virtuous clergyman with whom she takes refuge hesitates to help her, declaring that "'a runaway nun is not exactly such a companion as a clergyman of my age ought to be seen with.'" Anna recognizes her fallen state: "A deep flush overspread the wan face of Anna, and for a time she remained silent; then said, 'It is true, I have no vouchers for the truth of my story'" (117). Having been seduced by Catholicism, the Protestant girl proves her unworthiness to be trusted.

Unlike Bunkley and Larned, whose writerly achievements are largely – and understandably – forgotten, Sarah Josepha Hale, whose status as an author and editor was unprecedented in American literary history, has received twentieth-century critical appreciation, particularly in Nina Baym's recent work. Hale was the long-time editor of *The Ladies' Magazine* (1827–36) and *Godey's Lady's Book* (1837–77), among the most widely read and influential magazines of the period. She wrote indefatigably both for what Nicole Tonkovich Hoffman reminds us was known as "Mrs. Hale's magazine" and independently in a variety of genres. Surprisingly, she also wrote a variation on the escaped nun's tale in "The Catholic Convert," published in 1835 in *Traits of American Life*. An ardent proponent of domesticity and gentility, who took seriously what she saw as the shaping of a middle-class republican sensibility, Hale seems an unlikely candidate for the sensational matter and methods of anti-Catholic polemic.

Nonetheless, in "The Catholic Convert" Hale uses familiar images and narrative structures drawn from anti-Catholicism to deliberately turn some of Protestantism's favorite attacks on Rome back on to American Protestants themselves. She employs a standard anti-Catholic story and types less to attack Catholics than to foster national allegiances and cultivate middle-class culture among Yankees. If the escaped nun's tale provides a way to indirectly question the feminization of American religion and culture, "The Catholic Convert" critiques the soulless and self-interested Protestantism that Hale feared was coming to dominate post-Revolutionary America. She accuses her representative Protestant figures, the Redfields, of adhering only to the letter of Christian law: "[W]hile they kept the Sabbath day with pharisaical strictness, the other six days were their own," days in which their lives are guided solely by the selfish standard of "'pecuniary profit'" (53, 52). It is Catholicism, of course, that Protestants have traditionally seen as a rule-bound religion of surface compliance. Lacking the inner light and individual faith of Protestantism, Catholics, it was argued, fanatically follow the letter of the law and are satisfied with ceremonial mummery.

Into the "pharisaical," market-driven Redfield household, Hale introduces a runaway nun of sorts. Mary Marshall's education has been neglected by her father, a grieving widower. Left in the charge of a Catholic woman, Mary is beguiled by a Jesuit who convinces her that her father is a heretic and that she belongs in a convent. Participating selectively in the rhetoric of anti-Catholic literature, Hale invokes the sensational language of sadism and torture to describe the way that "religious bigotry and fanaticism ... binds the soul in chains, which rust and canker, till a moral paralysis ensues, and all the natural and innocent feelings of the heart are turned to vile and cruel purposes" (86). Discovering his daughter's disaffection, Mr. Marshall spirits Mary away in the dead of night, bringing her incognito to the Redfields. Mary is saved from unnatural Catholic celibacy by the local young Protestant minister who awakens her to love and life.

The Redfields, in turn, are reformed and refined by their encounter with Mary and her romantic story. "The Catholic Convert" ends with a vision of marital happiness, of a unified Republic, of a middle-class household refined by female gentility; it ends, that is, as domestic fiction. Yet that vision rests on its author's and the audience's knowledge of sensational and anti-Catholic characters and plots.

Hale's warning in "The Catholic Convert" about the dangers of neglecting American daughters' religious training is part of her continuing public campaign to raise the standards for female education. Anti-Catholicism also served as an occasion for such arguments in 1834 when Hale wrote of her reactions to the burning of the Ursuline convent in Charlestown, Massachusetts. This time she attempts to delineate the "Traits of American Life," not through a gothic/domestic tale, but with a series of articles analyzing a national scandal.

The perceived dangers of Catholic education played a prominent role in the nineteenth-century campaign to institutionalize a system of public schooling that would form America's youth into responsible US citizens. Historians have focused primarily on the nineteenth-century public school controversy as a dispute about the education of American boys (see works cited below: Nasaw, Tyack and Hansot). The nineteenth-century educator Horace Mann argued successfully that the way to socialize immigrant boys – particularly the Irish – into American citizenship was through public schooling. Mann and other educators deliberately sought to break the influence of Catholic families and of parochial schools. However, the education of Protestant girls in Catholic convent schools was a secondary source of controversy, as reactions to the Charlestown burning – Hale's among them – make vivid.

The Ursuline convent on Mount Benedict, which housed a fashionable school for wealthy Protestant girls, was attacked by a mob, an action that reverberated nationally. Rebecca Reed's *Six Months in a Convent* is only one of the many popular narratives that told and retold this story. Hale used the Charlestown burning as an occasion to argue, in three articles in the *American Ladies' Magazine*, that Protestant schools were neglecting the important education of middle- and upper-class American girls. Rather than framing this as a special interest issue, Hale argues that America's national destiny is at stake. The titles for her essays – "The Ursuline Convent," "How to Prevent the Increase of Convents," and "Convents are Increasing" – successively up the ante, as Hale insists that female education is the key to "Saving the West from the Pope" (Billington, *Protestant Crusade*). Hale argues that male missionaries bent on converting the immigrants who were quickly settling the American West will labor in vain without female helpmates. But if only Catholic convents educate young women, then those missionary wives will be Catholic. In short, unless American women are offered an educational alternative, "convents will increase, and Catholicism become permanently rooted in our country" (564).

Later in the century Pamela H. Cowan's *The American Convent as a School for Protestant Children* (1870) again takes up the issue of religious institutions and the education of America's females. *American Convent* was published by the Protestant Episcopal Society for the Promotion of Evangelical Knowledge, located in New York. A notice in the opening pages tells us that the volume is being published "by Special Contribution" for the Sunday Schools of St. Paul's Church, Boston, and St. John's Church, Jamaica Plain, Massachusetts, signaling American children's contribution to the fight to save their peers.

What Cowan's novel shows is that children must rescue children because of the dangerous state of American parenting. Like Larned's Mrs. Howard, whose own novel-reading and lax parenting lead to her daughter's "romantic" immurement in the convent, and Hale's Mr. Marshall, who drastically underestimates the importance of his daughter's religious education, Cowan describes parents who are too busy pursuing wealth, too self-indulgent, too swayed by fashion and fine manners, to recognize the dangers that the convent school holds for their daughters. Typical is Mr. Chamberlain, who adheres to a "system of false economy which led him, while indulging his family in all the elegancies of life, to endanger the welfare of his children for a paltry consideration" (81).

Cowan calls into question the entire enterprise of "the American Convent as a School for Protestant Children." Why do Catholics leave their own children in ignorance, expending their efforts and funds on Protestant youth, Cowan asks. Her answer is that Catholic convents are not educational institutions at all but spaces of indoctrination. Cowan shows crafty nuns enticing Protestant parents by offering to educate their girls cheaply and reassuring them that no proselytizing will take place. In truth, these girls – especially heiresses – are constantly pressured to convert. Parents are deliberately deceived until it is too late. Two of Cowan's Protestant girls manage to emerge from these trials relatively unscathed, but the destruction of two others devastates their families. Cowan adds her voice to "the cry from many a violated hearthstone, as from many an *auto-da-fé*," that has gone up against the priests and nuns who seek to substitute convents for American homes (327).

Despite Cowan's warnings about convent education and its effects, the stories of mistreatment and deceit that she recounts in *American Convent* are relatively mild. Not so with the sensational nativist novels of the fifties. For example, Orvilla S. Belisle, a polemical Protestant writer, authored two novels: *The Prophets* (1855), an attack on Mormonism, and *The Archbishop; or Romanism in the United States* (1854), on Roman Catholicism, pornographically mix violence and sexuality.

The Archbishop is a nativist attack on the outspoken John Hughes, archbishop of New York, the first foreign-born American Catholic bishop (1797–1864). In this book Belisle supports contemporary nativist male associations like the "Know-Nothings." These brotherhoods of "real" Americans – that is, native-born whites of Western European descent – saw themselves as defending American liberty and democracy against "foreign influence." Catholic immigrants were perceived as participants in Rome's campaign to take over the country, establishing the papacy as a religious and secular power in America.

The Archbishop is a novel about male rivalry, but central to that rivalry are women. Belisle describes young American republicans deprived of the girls they love by unnatural foreign fathers. However, in addition to being the object of generational male warfare, the novel's three main female characters represent three of the most common trajectories for women's stories in the literature of anti-Catholicism.

Isabel marries in her youth an ambitious man who puts her aside in order to rise in the Catholic clerisy, becoming "The Archbishop," and, he hopes, eventually, the Pope. She dies of a broken heart. However, the Archbishop's inhuman and unmanly actions towards his wife come back to haunt him throughout the novel, in which "Isabel, you are fearfully avenged" becomes the repeated refrain.

Enna, the innocent daughter of the Archbishop and Isabel, is ignorant of her parentage. In order to preserve her purity the Archbishop secretly raises her in his own house according to Protestant principles. As she grows into womanhood, she is insulted by men who assume that any young woman who lives in a priest's house is a whore. *The Archbishop*, like a whole group of nativist novels written in the 1850s, alludes to the well-known narratives of incestuous relationships between priests and their daughters. Incest does not, in fact, take place in Belisle's novel. Nonetheless, other characters are vocal in their suspicions and Enna is clearly her mother's representative, insofar as she physically resembles Isabel, and, as the object of her father's only "human" emotion, is the recipient of his caresses and affection. Enna eventually escapes into Americanness and marriage with the former lover of Irene Freeman.

Irene Freeman, the fiancée of a young American patriot, is the victim of a Catholic priest who lusts after her. Kidnapped from the confessional, locked in a cell, drugged and raped, her existence is such that she would be, as the Protestant male characters repeatedly insist, better off dead. She finally escapes from the church during a conflagration only to die, apparently of shame.[6]

One might argue that there is nothing particularly "female" about Belisle's anti-Catholic polemic. In fact, *The Archbishop* is one of a group of remarkably similar nativist novels written by men and women at mid-century. However, focusing on Belisle's female characters allows us to recognize how religion not only reflects but also inflects nineteenth-century constructions of the feminine.

Isabel, Irene, Enna – the similar names encourage us to see these women as different versions of "the female." This nominal connection appears even stronger when we recognize that the name "Inez," with which they resonate, apparently comes to be associated in mid-nineteenth-century America with a stock character of Catholic womanhood. The primary example here is Augusta Evans Wilson's *Inez; a Tale of the Alamo* (1855).

Augusta Evans Wilson was a popular southern writer, famous for her best-seller *St. Elmo* (1867) about an independent young woman who refuses numerous offers of marriage, succeeds as a writer, and eventually reforms the Byronic man who pursues her throughout the novel. *Inez* was Wilson's first novel, written when she was just twenty. The figure of the Catholic girl – Inez – allows Wilson to develop the character of an independent, sexualized young woman that she is later able to transfer to the white American girl.

The main female characters of *Inez; a Tale of the Alamo* are white, Protestant young women, Mary Irving and Florence Hamilton. The title character, Inez de Garcia, is a Mexican Catholic whose story is a variation on the Pocahontas narrative which, as Mary Dearborn has shown, is central to American national mythology. The "eroticized and exoticized ethnic woman" (*Pocahontas's Daughters*, 10) risks her life to rescue the white Anglo man. The result may or may not be her rescue into (miscegenous) marriage. (The Pocahontas figure has also been known in American literary criticism as "the dark woman" familiar to readers of Cooper and Hawthorne as the sexualized, ethnic other.)

Dearborn's *Pocahontas's Daughters* looks at the Pocahontas story as it is retold by ethnic women writers – the ways in which these women "write back" to the white male patriarchal rendering of the story. *Inez*, in contrast, serves as an example of the other female version of the Pocahontas story: that told by white women, in this case specifically a white Protestant Southern woman. This woman writer employs neither of the strategies Dearborn associates with works by women of color and ethnicity, neither the Cinderella story of marriage to the WASP who raises up the ethnic woman, nor the dolorous tale of victimization and rape. Instead, the woman writer, in showing the Pocahontas figure as sexualized and aggressive, participates in and furthers the ideology of white male writers. However, rather than simply condemning this "other" behavior or using it strictly as a foil to set off the virtues of white women (though she does do this), Wilson employs the dark maiden as offering a noble alternative not accessible to her white heroines.

Part of what is at stake in this story is sexuality, as can be seen in the following passage in which Mary, the faithful Protestant, discovers that her cousin has been perverted into Catholicism by her father's (extorted) deathbed request.

> The cousins stood up, and each gazed full upon the other. Mary's face was
> colorless as marble, and her hands were tightly clasped as she bent forward

with a longing, searching, eager look. A crimson glow rushed to Florence's very temples; then receded, leaving an ashy paleness. "I am a member of the Church of Rome." Mary groaned and sank back into her chair, at this confirmation of her fears. (*Inez; a Tale of the Alamo*, 115)

The alternating blushes and paleness, the suspicions and secret, the confessional mode, all point to what Wilson's readership would have understood as the sexualized nature of Catholicism (later, Florence must make the same confession to her horrified and disgusted husband). However, in Wilson's novel, we do not see the plot of priestly rape/seduction played out with the white Protestant heroine, but rather with the dark girl. The threat to Florence is articulated through the lascivious designs of Father Mazzolin, an Italian Jesuit, on Inez and her fortune.

Inez is certainly the most powerful character in the novel, a woman of physical courage, disregard for convention, and capacity for selfless love. All three of the novel's female characters suffer silently in their love for a man. The most virtuous woman – Mary – actually dies because she is too "feminine" to speak her love for Dr. Bryant. Just as Inez enacts the dangerous sexual encounters with the priest that are only imagined for Florence, so too the unrequited love for Dr. Bryant that she shares with Mary drives the Catholic girl, not to languorous death, but to action. As a Pocahontas figure, she first attempts to save the white man she loves, then, when she cannot, Antigone-like, she risks her life and defies the powers that be in order to recover and bury his body. Inez dies of the infection that she contracts on the battlefield strewn with dead bodies. Unlike Mary, who succumbs to the beautiful death of the girl-too-good-to-live, standard to nineteenth-century Protestant fiction, Inez ends her life cursing the priest who has destroyed her religious beliefs and is interred during a tempest in unhallowed ground. Nonetheless, Wilson hints at the power of this "other" woman's passion when, echoing the lovers' end in Emily Brontë's *Wuthering Heights* (1847), she has Dr. Bryant's body secretly reburied with that of Inez. This gothic moment of triumph for the Catholic woman of color glances at narrative possibilities that Wilson will explore – albeit in limited ways – with her white Protestant heroines in later novels.

Wilson's Inez is not alone in American fiction at mid-century, as I have suggested. For example, an Inez appears importantly in *Stanhope Burleigh: the Jesuits in Our Homes* (1855) by Helen Dhu. "Helen Dhu" is a pseudonym used by Charles Edwards Lester, a prolific and well-known writer of history and biography, as well as a translator. All of his other works were written under his own name, suggesting that this sort of fiction would have been perceived as more palatable coming from a woman's pen.

In "Dhu"'s novel Inez is an Italian Catholic who is, like Belisle's Enna, the secret daughter of a powerful Catholic cleric. When the daughter discovers her father's identity, she turns against him and plots to help the young American man whom she has come to love, but who, like Wilson's Dr. Bryant, is reserved for the weak, feminine, white girl, Genevra. Passive and "feminine," Genevra endures her persecution by Catholic fathers (lay and clerical), eventually dying of her trials. Genevra's death scene is instructive: the Protestant girl is forced to become a nun in a ceremony represented as simultaneously a virgin sacrifice, a deflowering, a wedding, and a funeral. As the Abbess reaches to shear off Genevra's hair in preparation for her veiling her, the young woman shrieks "'Spare me! ... Save me! – Save me! – Inez! Stanhope!'" (399). The Protestant girl calls for rescue first to the powerful and resourceful Catholic female, then to her male lover. Her estimation of their relative powers is astute, as Stanhope ends up tossed out of the chapel into the street, whereas the last we see of Inez is her escape from the convent chapel dressed as a boy.

Recurrent in these stories is the religious cynicism created by Catholicism's deceitful and manipulative training. As the Inez character shows, the young woman raised as a Catholic loses all faith when she discovers the truth of the Roman Church and clerisy's hypocrisy and corruption. Her choices are to become corrupt, to go mad and/or die, or to rebel and lose faith. The formerly Protestant girl who has been seduced into Catholicism – like Larned's Agnes or Hale's Mary or Wilson's Florence – can always revert to her (the) true faith – although she often pays the price with her health and sometimes her life. But for a Catholic, especially a Catholic of Latin ethnicity, to convert to Protestantism is rare in these texts. These are not narratives of assimilation.

In part, this authorial refusal to allow the Catholic girl to assimilate is symptomatic of these women writers' feelings towards recent immigrants to America. However, the very attractiveness of characters like Inez suggests that the trajectory of her narrative(s) is more powerful when its sensationality is preserved intact, rather than being dissipated into domesticity.

There is another version of the Inez character, and she is named Agnes (the English equivalent – by way of Latin – of the hispanized name). Associated by name both with St. Agnes, a virgin martyr of the Catholic Church, and Christ, the *Agnus Dei*, the Lamb of God, a virtuous Agnes serves as a minor female figure in many nativist novels of the period (including *Stanhope Burleigh* and *The American Convent*). Agnes is more prominent as the title character in Harriet Beecher Stowe's *Agnes of Sorrento* (1864). Stowe sets her historical fiction in fifteenth-century Florence, depicting the Catholic Church as torn between the proto-Protestant reformist wing, represented by the Dominican monk Savonarola, and the more familiarly corrupt papal and papist Church of Rome. Like Hale, who uses the mirror of Catholicism as a way for American Protestants to see their flaws, Stowe writes not primarily to attack Catholicism but to reform Protestantism by offering Catholic history as a reflective text in which Protestantism itself can read.

The innocent, childlike Agnes is entrammeled in what she does not even recognize as a sadomasochistic relationship with her confessor. More normal (and normalizing) is the mutual love between Agnes and young Prince Agostino. Stowe revises the nativist plot of male rivalry between sons and fathers insofar as in *Agnes* the young man finally saves the girl from the perversely sexualized father figure. And, passive as Agnes appears throughout the novel, she is nonetheless herself a powerful religious rescuer of others. As Franchot points out, the childlike Agnes resembles Stowe's most famous girl heroine, Eva St. Clare, insofar as her natural holiness not only protects her from corruption but also inspires and reforms those around her. Although this fifteenth-century Agnes is, necessarily, Catholic, not Protestant, the Protestant millennial history in which Stowe's text participates regards Protestantism not as representing a break in religious history but as the true continuation of Christ's church. It is the Church of Rome which, by choosing corruption, becomes deviant. Thus Stowe's Agnes is a Protestant maiden *avant la lettre*, a girl whom Franchot calls "the spiritual ancestress of America" (249).

There are, of course, other versions of the Catholic woman depicted in nativist literature, most prominently the slovenly, defeminized Irish harridan. The cultural threat that Irish and German immigration posed to nineteenth-century Protestant America made Catholic women's failures to meet accepted standards of domesticity and femininity a major topic of discussion (see McDannell,*Christian Home in Victorian America*). Since, unlike Protestant prayer, Catholic worship was not home-based, Irish women and their homes were seen as miserably, even criminally, lacking. This was part of a transatlantic Protestant discourse, as demonstrated by Henry Mayhew's influential ethnography of *London Labour and the London Poor* (1861–2), which describes at length the distinctive (and inferior) nature of Irish women and their homes.

If Catholic homes failed to be sacred spaces for family prayer, Catholicism was also depicted as destructively infiltrating the inner sanctums of the Protestant domesticity. The paranoid image of the Catholic servant as spy conceives the German, or more commonly, Irish hireling as privy to all the most intimate secrets of home and family which she reports faithfully to her confessor. Belisle warns against this nationwide information network: "This lurking of spies around our firesides, even in our chambers in the silent watches of the night, extended all over the Union" (180). Novelists describe American families who benightedly believe in religious tolerance hiring these "Bridgets," excusing them from family prayers and permitting them to attend mass and confession. Polemical writers argue that this benignity is really only foolish naïveté. Too trusting Americans find themselves the victims of intrigue, their children corrupted into popery, their homes violated. Even those families who think they are hiring Protestant servants must be on their guard: the Vatican's plan to turn the United States to popery depends upon a deliberate campaign that scruples at neither theft nor deceit.

If lower-class Catholic women servants are represented as advance scouts for the Old World's campaign to conquer the New, Protestant women writers, as the examples of Bunkley, Larned, Hale, Wilson, Belisle, Cowan, and Stowe demonstrate, position themselves squarely in the front lines of the battle against Rome, seeing the defense of Protestant America as appropriately fought in the pages of fiction. Speaking of the fiction writer "Charlotte Elizabeth" (Elizabeth Tonna, 1790–1846), the narrator of Wilson's *Inez* declares: "The Pope of imperial Rome, surrounded as he is with luxury, magnificence, and hosts of scarlet-liveried cardinals, who stand in readiness to convey his mandates to the remotest corners of the earth, has been made to tremble on his throne by the pen of feeble woman" (154). Through writing, a woman can be powerful enough to threaten the world's wealthiest and most insidiously powerful despot.

"Charlotte Elizabeth" was a British writer, popular on both sides of the Atlantic. But Wilson's recognition of her as a role model should not be taken as a demonstration that influence in anti-Catholic writing was simply one way. Monk's *Awful Disclosures*, for example, was an international best-seller, much cited and imitated in Britain. What Wilson's invocation of "Charlotte Elizabeth" reminds us of is the international nature of nineteenth-century American literary culture.

The variety of women's religious writing within that culture is suggested by the differing ways that, for example, Belisle's virulent nativism and Stowe's liberal Protestantism make use of the narrative traditions of anti-Catholicism. American women writers also drew on anti-Catholic tropes, rhetoric, and characters in fiction that was pointedly not religious in nature. Works that are completely unconcerned with Protestantism's battle to save America from Rome nonetheless attempt to manipulate readers' knowledge of anti-Catholic writing for their own sensational ends.

A case in point is Louisa May Alcott's 1866 *A Long Fatal Love Chase*. Rejected by her publisher, Alcott's "lost" novel was not published until 1995. Alcott's other "thrillers," republished in anthologies like *Behind a Mask* (1975) and *Plots and Counterplots* (1976), altered twentieth-century readers' sense of the writer of *Little Women* (1868–9) and have been important in understanding American women writers' participation in the sensational. *A Long Fatal Love Chase* can help to suggest the pervasiveness and usefulness of anti-Catholic traditions.

A Long Fatal Love Chase's generic aspirations are clearly indicated by its title. This tale of passion tells the story of Rosamond Vivian, a bold, beautiful girl, seduced by the satanic Phillip Tempest. Most of the novel describes Rosamond's pursuit across Europe by the man whom she desires despite herself. Halfway through the narrative, the Protestant Rosamond takes refuge in a convent, disguising herself as Sister Agatha. The religious implications of this action are treated lightly by Alcott: "vigils and prayers, penances and confessions had a charm for her now" (123). The convent appears to be a space of tranquillity and good works.

However, it turns out that Rosamond has, in fact, entered the traditional convent of anti-Catholic fiction. Kind Mother Ursula is replaced by a new Superior, the jealous and petty Mother Magdalene, who makes the Protestant heroine's life a misery; Father Dominic probes Rosamond's secrets in the confessional and sells them to her demon lover; and young Father Ignatius falls in love with Rosamond and "haunts her like a shadow" (125). The names of these religious characters point to their associations with stock figures: the virginal Ursula v. Magdalene, the nun as fallen woman; the inquisitorial Dominic[an]; the namesake of Ignatius Loyola as gliding Jesuit. In a scene cinematic in its staging, Rosamond enters the confessional and reveals her continuing love for Tempest, only to have "a burst of exultant laughter startle ... her like a thunderclap, the curtain was pushed aside and through the grating looked the dark face of Phillip Tempest!" (130).

In Protestant polemic, the confessional is traditionally the space where Catholic priests reveal their true selves, corrupting their female penitents with insinuating questions (Protestant heroines typically return from their first confessions with cheeks indignantly "ablaze" at the priest's sexual questioning), a place of kidnapping and even rape. Here Alcott invokes those associations by putting the satanic man in the priest's place. Titillating too are Rosamond's relations with Father Ignatius, who helps her flee secretly from the convent. *Love Chase*, *Thorn-Birds*-like, teases readers with the possibility that Ignatius will break his vows, as when Rosamond finds the book that he has been reading about Martin Luther's marriage. Alcott also flirts with the incestuous implications of priestly sexuality, when she calls attention to Rosamond and Ignatius's habit of referring to one another as "father" and "daughter." In short, Alcott uses Protestant and gothic representations of the Church of Rome in order to ratchet up her narrative's sexual tension. This secularized escaped nun's tale passionately climaxes in the two men's final encounter over Rosamond's dead body. When Father Ignatius exults that he will be reunited with his love in heaven, Tempest, jealous and competitive to the last, stabs himself, defiantly declaring, "Mine first – mine last – mine even in the grave!" (241). Alcott revises even as she spectacularly literalizes the conventional struggle between the Catholic cleric and the secular man for the woman's body and soul.

The effect of *Love Chase*'s outrageous ending depends, of course, on readers' recognition of its sacrilege. We can never know exactly how a nineteenth-century audience would have read this unpublished fiction, but Alcott's strategy seems clear. Assuming a shared knowledge, not of Catholicism, but of its representations in Protestant narratives, Alcott attempts to put that knowledge to work, to take advantage of the associations invoked in her readership by "the confessional," "the convent," and "the priest."

Nineteenth-century women writers' religiosity, like their domesticity and sentiment, has been a vexed subject for twentieth-century readers and critics. Feminist work, beginning with that of Nancy Cott, has allowed the reclaiming of what was once a source of embarassment – or even point of derision – helping readers to recognize this important women's sphere as a site of female power. What women learned in church organizations, they went on to apply to secular purposes: abolition, temperance, and suffrage. Jane Tompkins has taught us to see the "sentimental power" of the religious writings of Stowe and others. What looking at the specific case of women's anti-Catholic writing demonstrates is the heterogeneity of that power, as well as its entanglement with the theological, political, and cultural tensions of the day. The escaped nuns that flee across the pages of nineteenth-century women's fiction represent complex and shifting constructions of womanhood. The figures of Mary, Grace, Inez, Agnes, and Agatha work variously to anxiously limit and to actively liberate what it means to be American and female.

NOTES

1. My question echoes Nina Baym's in *Novels, Readers, and Reviewers*: "Who, then, as the reviewers saw it, read novels? In the broadest sense, everybody" (47).
2. See Helsinger, Sheets, and Veeder's useful analysis (*The Woman Question*, 183–91) of the way Elizabeth Stuart Phelps employs fiction to tell the story of a woman preacher in her 1870 "The Woman's Pulpit."
3. See, too, recent work on women and spiritualism during the period, for example, Andrews, *Sisters of the Spirit*, and Braude, *Radical Spirits, Spiritualism and Women's Rights*.
4. Bibliographic work by Billington, Franchot, Griffin, and Reynolds details this variety.

5. In the hands of some male – and a few female – writers, this actually looks more like a chance to depict sadism, masochism, and misogyny.
6. Irene Freeman's fate is similar to that of Cecelia, the young heiress, who is seduced by her priestly guardian, cheated of her inheritance, and condemned to imprisonment. She, too, dies while escaping her priestly tormentors.

WORKS CITED AND SELECTED SUGGESTED READING

Alcott, Louisa May. *Behind a Mask: the Unknown Thrillers of Louisa May Alcott.* Ed. Madeline Stern. New York: William Morrow, 1975.
A Long Fatal Love Chase. New York: Random House, 1995.
Plots and Counterplots: More Unknown Thrillers of Louisa May Alcott. Ed. Madeline Stern. New York: William Morrow, 1976.
Andrews, William L., ed. *Sisters of the Spirit: Three Black Women's Autobiographies of the Nineteenth Century.* Bloomington: Indiana University Press, 1986.
Baym, Nina. *American Women Writers and the Work of History, 1790–1860.* New Brunswick: Rutgers University Press, 1995.
Feminism and American Literary History. New Brunswick: Rutgers University Press, 1992.
Novels, Readers, and Reviewers: Responses to Fiction in Antebellum America. Ithaca: Cornell University Press, 1984.
Woman's Fiction: a Guide to Novels by and about Women in America, 1820–1870. Ithaca: Cornell University Press, 1978.
"Onward Christian Women: Sarah J. Hale's History of the World." *New England Quarterly* 63 (1990): 249–70.
Belisle, Orvilla S. *The Archbishop; or Romanism in the United States.* Philadelphia: William White Smith, 1854.
The Prophets; or Mormonism Unveiled. Philadelphia: William White Smith, 1855.
Billington, Ray Allen. *The Protestant Crusade, 1800–1860: a Study of the Origins of American Nativism.* New York: Macmillan, 1938.
Braude, Ann. *Radical Spirits, Spiritualism and Women's Rights in Nineteenth-Century America.* Boston: Beacon Press, 1989.
Women and American Religion. New York and Oxford: Oxford University Press, 1999.
Bunkley, Josephine M. The *Testimony of an Escaped Novice: From the Sisterhood of St. Joseph, Emmettsburg, Maryland, the Mother-House of the Sisters of Charity in the United States.* Philadelphia: Harper and Bros, 1855.
Cott, Nancy. *The Bonds of Womanhood: "Woman's Sphere" in New England, 1780–1835.* New Haven: Yale University Press, 1977.
Cowan, Pamela. *The American Convent as a School for Protestant Children.* New York: Protestant Episcopal Society, 1870.
Davidson, Cathy N. *Revolution and the Word: the Rise of the Novel in America.* New York and Oxford: Oxford University Press, 1986.
Davis, David Brion. "Some Themes of Counter-Subversion: an Analysis of Anti-Masonic, Anti-Catholic, and Anti-Mormon Literature." *Mississippi Valley Historical Review* 47 (1960–61): 205–24.
Dearborn, Mary V. *Pocahontas's Daughters: Gender and Ethnicity in Early American Culture.* New York and Oxford: Oxford University Press, 1986.

Dhu, Helen [pseud.]. *Stanhope Burleigh: the Jesuits in Our Homes*. New York: Stringer, 1855.

Douglas, Ann. *The Feminization of American Culture*. New York: Knopf, 1977.

Eddy, Mary Baker. *Science and Health*. Boston: Christian Science, 1875.

Franchot, Jenny. *Roads to Rome: the Antebellum Protestant Encounter with Catholicism*. Berkeley: University of California Press, 1994.

Griffin, Susan Mary. "Awful Disclosures: Female Evidence in the Escaped Nun's Tale." *PMLA* 111 (1996): 93–107.

"'The Dark Stranger': Sensationalism and Anti-Catholicism in Sarah Josepha Hale's *Traits of American Life*." *Legacy* 14.1 (1997): 13–24.

Grimké, Sarah Moore. *An Epistle to the Clergy of the Southern States*. 1836.

Hale, Sarah Josepha. *Traits of American Life*. Philadelphia: Carey, 1835.

"Convents are Increasing." *American Ladies' Magazine* 7 (December 1834): 560–4.

"How to Prevent the Increase of Convents." *American Ladies' Magazine* 7 (November 1834): 517–21.

"The Ursuline Convent." *American Ladies' Magazine* 7 (September 1834): 418–26.

Helsinger, Elizabeth, Robin Lauterbach Sheets, and William Veeder. *Social Issues*. II. *The Woman Question: Society and Literature in Britain and America, 1837–1883*. Chicago: University of Chicago Press, 1989.

Hoffman, Nicole Tonkovich. "*Legacy* Profile: Sarah Josepha Hale, 1788–1874." *Legacy* 7.2 (1977): 47–55.

Hofstader, Richard. "*The Paranoid Style in American Politics*" *and Other Essays*. 1965. Chicago: University of Chicago Press, 1979.

Larned, L[ucinda Martin]. *The American Nun; or, The Effects of Romance*. Boston: Otis, 1836.

McDannell, Colleen. *The Christian Home in Victorian America, 1840–1900*. Bloomington: Indiana University Press, 1986.

Monk, Maria. *Awful Disclosures of the Hotel Dieu Nunnery of Montreal, Revised, with an Appendix*. 1836. New York: Arno, 1977.

Nasaw, David. *Schooled to Order: a Social History of Public Schooling in the United States*. New York and Oxford: Oxford University Press, 1979.

Phelps, Elizabeth Stuart. "A Woman's Pulpit." *Atlantic Monthly* 26 (1870): 11–22.

Reed, Rebecca Theresa. *Six Months in a Convent, or, The Narrative of Rebecca Theresa Reed, Who was Under the Influence of the Roman Catholics About Two Years, and an Inmate of the Ursuline Convent on Mount Benedict, Charlestown, Mass., Nearly Six Months, in the Years 1831–1832 With Some Preliminary Suggestions by the Committee of Publication*. 1835. New York: Arno, 1977.

Reynolds, David S. *Beneath the American Renaissance: the Subversive Imagination in the Age of Emerson and Melville*. Cambridge, MA: Harvard University Press, 1988.

Faith in Fiction: the Emergence of Religious Literature in America. Cambridge, MA: Harvard University Press, 1981.

Ruether, Rosemary Radford, and Rosemary Skinner Keller, eds. *In Our Own Voices: Four Centuries of American Women's Religious Writings*. New York: Harper and Row, 1995.

Women and Religion in America. New York: Harper and Row, 1981.

Ryan, Mary P. *Cradle of the Middle Class: the Family in Oneida County, New York, 1790–1895.* Cambridge and New York: Cambridge University Press, 1981.

Sklar, Kathryn Kish. *Catherine Beecher: a Study in American Domesticity.* New York: W. W. Norton, 1976.

Stanton, Elizabeth Cady. *The Woman's Bible.* European. 1895.

Stowe, Harriet Beecher. *Agnes of Sorrento.* 1862. Boston: Houghton Mifflin, 1896. *My Wife and I.* New York: Ford, 1871.

Tompkins, Jane. *Sensational Designs: the Cultural Work of American Fiction, 1790–1860.* New York and Oxford: Oxford University Press, 1985.

Tyack, David, and Elizabeth Hansot. *Managers of Virtue: Public School Leadership in America, 1820–1980.* New York: Basic Books, 1982.

Wilson, Augusta Evans. *Inez; a Tale of the Alamo.* 1855. New York: Harper and Bros, 1864.

8

PRISCILLA WALD

Immigration and assimilation in nineteenth-century US women's writing

Lamenting the discrepancy between her vision and her experience of America, the young protagonist of Russian immigrant Anzia Yezierska's short story "How I Found America" seeks out her sister's teacher as a potential confidante. She pours out the story of her immigration from Russia and of her disappointment at the hardship and poverty, but most of all at the loneliness and alienation she has experienced in the New World. She is amazed at the depth of understanding manifested by this "born American," whose ancestors came over on the Mayflower. The teacher, bemused by the intense young girl's amazement, reminds her that "The Pilgrim Fathers" were themselves "immigrants two hundred years ago," and she goes on to quote the words of celebrated man of letters Waldo Frank: "We go forth all to seek America. And in the seeking we create her. In the quality of our search shall be the nature of the America that we create."[1] In the exchange, the protagonist believes that she has "found the soul – the spirit – of America!" (Yezierska, "How I Found America," 297).

If the questing protagonist of the story did not quite find the soul and spirit of America, she had at least discovered a dominant theme of immigrant stories – some written by immigrants, but many by the numerous public figures and settlement workers who wished to legislate immigrant policy and to define, in order to shape, "the immigrant experience." The theme would be picked up and institutionalized subsequently by many historians of immigration in the second half of the twentieth century, who argued that the immigrant experience was central to – and even constituted – America and that each generation of immigrants reinvigorated the spirit of the nation. The protagonist of *Bread Givers*, a loosely autobiographical novel Yezierska would publish in 1924 (four years after the collection of short stories in which "How I Found America" appeared) would find the spirit celebrated by her predecessor much more elusive. The difficulties that Sara Smolinsky encounters as she negotiates life in the New World, from New York's Lower East Side to an unspecified small town and back again, are more familiar to readers of the fiction and memoirs of nineteenth-century American women immigrants. While the nature of those difficulties varies widely with the writers' motivations for immigrating, historical moment, places of origin and embarkation, class, ethnic and racial identities, the struggle to adjust to the new place and the ambivalences about doing so are common to most such accounts. These stories bear witness, moreover, to another struggle: the tension between the emerging genre of an "immigrant narrative" and the lived and recounted experiences of women who immigrated. Common to many of their works is the effort to reconcile their experiences with the expectations and conventions of the genre. These works often manifest their writers' desire both to depict the often painful struggle to negotiate two cultures and to demonstrate their cheerful conformity with the terms of Americanization.

Central to the shaping of the immigrant narrative is the term *immigrant* itself. Migrations and movements of human populations have characterized the human experience, but the experience connoted by the term *immigration* is a relatively modern phenomenon, and it suggests the relocation of individuals, alone or in small groups, from one community to another. On the surface, the term does not seem to distinguish among the many motivations for immigration, yet not all those who become "Americans" – or whose descendants do so – are labeled "immigrants." The distinctions between those who are and those who are not thus labeled help to elucidate the cultural assumptions implicit in the "immigrant narrative." The notorious slave trade, for example, was responsible for the alienation of countless Africans from their homes. The fact that "immigration" does not typically evoke the experience of those who survived the Middle Passage attests to the element of choice that is inscribed in the word: immigrants putatively have chosen to make the journey. Yet we need to consider how, why, and with what consequences the word *immigration* has evolved to exclude the experience of entire populations who have been thus forcibly transplanted. With what words do we describe the experience of enslaved Africans who came to live in an alien culture? Or that of the Amerindians who were "removed" from their lands by European settlers in the United States under the terms of the early nation's "Indian Removal policy"? Or even of Mexicans who, without moving, suddenly found themselves "foreigners" on the land on which their ancestors had lived for generations because a border had moved? In this chapter, I will consider the stories told not only by and about women who would traditionally define themselves as "immigrants" to the United States, but also by others who clearly experience themselves as cultural outsiders. The resonances among their accounts attest to the ambivalence that all of these women experienced – internally and externally – as they encountered the expectations and conventions of American culture. From the confluences and variations among these stories, a picture emerges of the factors, including but not limited to race and gender, that complicated the ready assimilation into American culture that was a central feature of the generic "immigrant narrative."

As the teacher in Yezierska's short story seems implicitly to understand, the conceptual importance of the idea of immigration in the United States stems from the logic of the nation's founding. One of the most striking differences between English common law as codified by William Blackstone in his mid-eighteenth-century *Commentaries on the Laws of England* and its adaptation in the United States during the Revolutionary period is the disappearance of the category of *denizen*. The term describes someone who is foreign-born, an alien, but who by royal prerogative has been granted the status of English subject. The status, however, does not carry with it the full rights and privileges of a native-born English subject: no one born an alien can ever attain the full status of the native-born English subject. As Blackstone notes, "a denizen is in a kind of middle state between an alien and natural-born subject, and partakes of both of them" (Blackstone, *Commentaries*, 302). A child born on English soil of an alien father (even if the status of denizen is subsequently conferred on the father) can also never be entitled to the full status of English subject.

The absence of the category of denizen in the United States marks an important change in the understanding of citizenship in the new republic. For the framers of the Constitution, the change was as pragmatic as it was ideological. The settler colony was not old enough to have a population entitled to full subjecthood under the terms of British common law that would be sufficiently sizable to constitute a community equal to its founders' ambitions. Many of the leaders of the Revolutionary government would be denizens under British common law. And what sense would it make to restrict membership in a land that needed to be populated? We could say that the framers made a virtue of necessity when they eliminated the category of denizen and adopted the French term *citoyen* rather than the British *subject*. To them, the change marked a dramatic break with the very terms through which the English nation constituted itself. The body they called into legal existence with the Constitution was going to shift the terms of national belonging subtly, to borrow the words Theodore Roosevelt would use a century later, from "birthright" to "faith."[2] The conception that the United States was a nation of immigrants, which remains a popular belief to this day, arguably has its roots in the eradication of the category of denizen.

From the outset, the new government was to be a model nation, forged out of the theories of the Enlightenment, "conceived in liberty" as Abraham Lincoln would intone nearly a century after the founding moment, "and dedicated to the proposition that all men are created equal." America, in other words, was to be more an idea than a place. The men who set out to found the nation were conscious of the gravity of their project and of the difficulty of the task. The war that had been fought and won on the battlefields had only set the scene for the work of nation-building. The policies and goals of the new republic had to be articulated and made to permeate every level of existence. Noah Webster, whose spelling and grammar books were familiar to the nation's earliest schoolchildren and whose dictionaries continue to line the shelves of classrooms, libraries, and private homes, sought to impress upon the legislators of the new government the need for an "America . . . as independent in *literature* as she is in politics, as famous for *arts* as for *arms*" (Webster, *Letters*, 4). Out of a political entity and a concept, an American culture needed to be shaped. Hence the particular pressure on writers and artists of the period to constitute America and the special importance of education in that process.

For Webster, as for many of his most prominent contemporaries, education was intrinsic to the task of nation-building. Following Enlightenment theories, he believed that "education, in great measure, forms the moral characters of men, and morals are the basis of government. Education should therefore be the first care of a legislature" (Webster, *On Being American*, 83). But beyond these general moral and political principles, the classrooms in the new republic were to be the sites of cultural articulation. Not just gentlemen, but Americans emerged from the schools of Webster's imagination, with knowledge of the new nation's history, geography, and, if the most outspoken among the educational reformers had their way, even distinct orthography and prosody upheld as sacred principles. And the young American would also graduate with a clear sense of his or her role in the emerging nation. Webster and his colleagues argued over how to shape programs of study and curricula to instantiate not only the role itself but also the conviction that the welfare of the nation depended upon his or her continual performance of that role.

The proposals and debates surrounding pedagogy offer perhaps the clearest articulation of gender roles in the new nation. If, after all, education provided the blueprint of national belonging, then surely girls needed instruction in their roles as much as their brothers needed to be prepared to assume theirs. Writing of the "separate and peculiar mode of education proper for women in a republic," medical doctor, man of letters, and celebrated educator Benjamin Rush contended that "they should not only be instructed in the usual branches of female education, but they should be taught the principles of liberty and government; and the obligations of patriotism should be inculcated upon them" (Rush, "Of the Mode of Education Proper," 19).

As helpmates and mothers, women would tender their most important contributions to the nation, since "the opinions and conduct of men are often regulated by the women in the most arduous enterprises of life, and their approbation is frequently the principal reward of the hero's dangers, and the patriot's toils. Besides, the first impressions upon the minds of children are generally derived from the women. Of how much consequence, therefore, is it in a republic that they should think justly upon the great subjects of liberty and government" (19). Historian Linda K. Kerber coined the term "republican motherhood" to describe the role that white women forged for themselves in the nation's founding years.[3] Their patriotic duty consisted in reproducing citizens in every sense of the word, populating the nation with boys trained to uphold the ideals of the nation through civic and economic participation across a wide range of occupations and with girls prepared to support them by turning their domestic duties themselves into civic virtues. Thus they sketched the contours of "the American woman."

While the curriculum varied across class and gender lines, non-Europeans (indigenes and Africans) were conspicuously absent from most of their proposals. In that absence, these figures haunted the democratizing project and national ideals from the outset. In the earliest stories of immigration, they characteristically embody the tensions implicit in the strategies of homogenization embraced by the educators and other advocates of nation-building.

Relationships between white women and indigenes are at the heart of two romances that are not typically thought of as immigrant narratives, but, again, that Yezierska's wise teacher would be likely to recognize as such. Both Lydia Maria Child and Catharine Maria Sedgwick were born in the US, but both Child's *Hobomok* (1824) and Sedgwick's *Hope Leslie* (1827) feature female protagonists who journey from England to make their homes in colonial New England. By the middle of the nineteenth century, political resistance to immigrants as expressed, for example, in the anti-Irish and anti-German, and, more broadly anti-Catholic sentiments of the notorious Know-Nothing Party of the 1850s would implicitly configure Anglo-Americans as natives. Yet these historical novels of the 1820s remind us that immigration was indeed the formative experience of Anglo-America. They offer important insight into the genealogy of the immigrant paradigm.

Through their female protagonists' immigrant experiences, both Child and Sedgwick sketch out the features of a (white) American national character. The authors are explicit in their frame stories about the importance of history-writing to their fictional tales. Adopting the persona of a male author in her preface, 22-year-old Lydia Maria Francis (she was not yet married to David Lee Child) has the putative author explain his motivation for writing

Hobomok as the call to arms of cultural nationalists who have sparked in him the "'desire to write a New England novel'" (Child, *Hobomok*, 3). The tale itself begins with yet another fiction: the author claims to have unearthed the manuscript of an ancestor that might help to disclose "the varying tints of domestic detail [that] are already concealed by the ivy which clusters around the tablets of our recent history" (6). Three years later, Sedgwick would locate her own motivation in the ambition "to illustrate not the history, but the character of the times" (*Hope Leslie*, 3). Both women saw their tales as important contributions to the project of shaping a national character and the national history that was its prerequisite.

Their stories of female protagonists who are brought to live in the New World allow them to explore the terms by which the immigrant is integrated into the community; the immigrant's assimilation enacts, and thereby makes visible, the features that make someone "American." Both protagonists elect to become "American," although it is important to remember that both stories are set in a historical period in which the colonists still consider themselves English. In fact, the heroines as well as the benevolent patriarchs with whom they interact reflect US values in the early nineteenth rather than the seventeenth century. The anachronisms bear witness to the writing, during the nationalist 1820s, of a retroactive national history that superimposes "American" values and gender roles on the social landscape of an earlier moment and that "resolves" (or avoids) the complications of contemporary Indian policies with the depictions of Amerindians who bestow their blessings on the nation-to-be as they relinquish their own claims. Writing their stories distinctly from a white woman's point of view, both Child and Sedgwick offered paradigms of assimilation that underscored the possibilities of agency and importance of compassion to white women and the nobility of character but inevitability of "removal" of indigenes.

Child's Mary Conant, who has been raised by her Royalist maternal grandfather in England, is brought to the colonies to live with her parents following her brothers' deaths and the onset of her mother's ultimately fatal illness. The tension between her and her austere Puritan father, whose politics have estranged him from Mary's beloved grandfather, finds its fullest expression in his rejection of her Royalist fiancé, Charles Brown, who has followed her from England. Expelled from the colony, Charles undertakes a long sea voyage from which he vows to return to Mary. News of his death by drowning, following her beloved mother's death, sends Mary into despair, and she marries the Amerindian Hobomok, who has befriended the fledgling community partly because of his devotion to Mary. When Mary realizes what she has done, she accepts her exile from her community, believing that her wedding vows are nonetheless binding for not being Christian. She feels bound to

Hobomok, moreover, both because of his kindness to her, and because of their child, Charles Hobomok. When Charles Brown's death proves to have been a mistaken rumor and he returns for her, however, Hobomok gallantly relinquishes his claim to her and goes "'far off among some of the red men in the west'" (139). Charles and Mary marry, but they remain in the colonies since, as Mary explains, she cannot go to England because her son would disgrace her; Mary's father, softened by the loss of his daughter and grateful for her return, is reconciled with Charles, and Charles Hobomok is gradually assimilated into the community, as "his father was seldom spoken of, and by degrees his Indian appellation was silently omitted" (150). They become, in other words, an "American" family, their internal quarrels displaced on to externalized and ostensibly resolved (although actually repressed) racial tensions.

Sedgwick's Hope Leslie does not marry an Amerindian, but her sister does. Moreover, Hope's friendship with Magawisca, the daughter of a Pequod chief, is a key feature in Hope's assimilation into her New England community. Hope, her mother, and her sister Faith set out for the New World upon the death of her English father, Hope's mother having been physically prevented from emigrating with her Puritan fiancé by her own father. The passing of the years and their marriages to other people have not dulled their love, and Hope's mother commits her daughters to the care of William Fletcher when she dies onboard ship. The Fletcher household includes Magawisca and her younger brother Oneco, who had been captured during a massacre of Pequod women and children by the colonists. During a raid to rescue his children, Magawisca's father and a band of Mohawks attack the Fletcher home, and the family members are slaughtered, with the exception of Mr. Fletcher and Hope, who are not there, and young Everell and Faith, who are spared (although captured) because of the interventions of Magawisca and Oneco respectively. Magawisca subsequently saves Everell's life and facilitates his escape, losing an arm in the process.

While Everell is sent to complete his studies in England, Hope becomes increasingly assimilated into the wilderness of western Massachusetts, where William Fletcher has made his home. When she helps an unjustly accused Indian woman escape from a Puritan jail, however, her spirit is perceived to be in need of taming, and she is accordingly sent to Boston to live with Governor John Winthrop. The grateful Indian woman repays Hope's kindness by promising that she will get her word of her long-lost sister, and the messenger who undertakes that task is none other than Magawisca. In the graveyard where their mothers are buried – side by side – Magawisca tells Hope that her sister has married Oneco and is fully assimilated into an Indian life from which she has no wish to return to English society. From the perspective of the early nineteenth century, in which the successful colonization of the United States had already transpired, Sedgwick can safely have Magawisca remonstrate with a horrified Hope that "the Great Spirit looks down on these sacred spots, where the good and the peaceful rest, with an equal eye" (197). With Magawisca's departure, Hope can even contemplate the "mysterious" interweaving of their destinies that had brought their mothers "from a far distance to rest together here – their children connected in indissoluble bonds!" (201). The spatial and spiritual connections, however, signal an absorptive rather than an inclusive vision; Sedgwick's depiction of the Great Spirit that Magawisca worships is derived from the beneficent deity of early nineteenth-century New England, and Magawisca is at once physically excluded and spiritually assimilated into that culture, which is configured through the alleged postmortem maternal bond.

At what was to be the sisters' final meeting, Magawisca and Faith are captured by the English (Hope having been followed without her knowledge), and the second half of the novel recounts the rescues that restore the community's stability by returning everyone to their rightful place: Faith to her husband, Magawisca to her father, and a newly domesticated Hope to Everell. The Indians remain only in spirit. For, as Magawisca assures her idealistic friends, "the Indian and the white man can no more mingle, and become one, than day and night" (349). While individuals can intermarry (like Faith and Oneco), they move into one or the other world. But Magawisca leaves Everell and Hope with a blessing of their union, which she sanctifies and which stands in for her actual presence. In their marriage, as in the neighboring graves of Hope's and Magawisca's mothers, a spiritual connection replaces an impossible cultural one. The "America" that is their legacy is thereby depicted as consecrated by Magawisca and by her Great Spirit.

Both stories retell the history of the settlement of New England with a defiant female immigrant protagonist at the center; Mary Conant and Hope Leslie more fully embody the spirit of America envisioned by their creators than the rigid Puritan fathers with whom they struggle. These are stories of domestication. The girls' nobility and their figurative deaths (Hope disappears and is presumed dead after Magawisca's capture) soften the hearts of those Puritan fathers as they reconstitute their families. At the same time, Mary and Hope relinquish their defiant spirits and are reborn into the roles of wife and mother through which they are fully integrated into communities whose reproduction they will ensure. The history of colonial New England, invoked in the intense spirit of nationalism that followed the War of 1812, is here filtered through the domestic vision of the 1820s. The stern Puritan patriarchs are reincorporated as benevolent and indulgent fathers, more in line with an Enlightenment model of the family, and they unite with spirited young women to form a nation predicated on that model.

Of course, that family is conspicuously white. Neither Sedgwick nor Child, who would become a powerful abolitionist, can imagine a place for the indigenes. Out of love for Mary, Hobomok obligingly removes himself west, while the act of forgetting through which Charles Hobomok becomes American conforms to Thomas Jefferson's fantasy of an intermingling of blood through which Indians could be assimilated (as individuals) into American culture.[4] Going native, moreover, enables Mary's conversion, but only after, unlike Faith Leslie, she eagerly returns to the settlers' community. Hope's and Magawisca's bonding over their mothers' graves similarly enacts Hope's conversion and her attachment to the land. Yet Magawisca's insistence on the fundamental incompatibility of their cultures prompts her to refuse Hope and Everell's offer to join their family, and, with the few remaining members of her tribe, she, like Hobomok, removes herself to the western wilderness. Indigenes, in other words, symbolically enact Europeans' transformation into Americans: they literally inspire them and then conveniently concede Anglo-America's victory and, implicitly, their right to the land. While the state was struggling in the courts and on the battlefields over tribal land rights, these novels imagine a resolution to the problem of the clash of cultures in which the nobility of indigenes is equaled only by the inevitability of their disappearance. The white heroines of these novels show their "benevolence" by championing these noble savages, but they show their putative "good sense" by being disgusted by the prospect (or realization) of intermarriage with them and by accepting the sad inevitability of their disappearance. Their recognition of the differences between cultures that they cannot fully bridge attests to their fitness to represent the true spirit of America.

Subsequent immigrant narratives record their protagonists' struggles precisely with the paradigm that *Hobomok* and *Hope Leslie* offer: the female immigrant makes choices – and displays a heroism – that attest to her fitness not just to become American, but actually to embody and reproduce America. While stories written by women who actually immigrated to the US vary in tone from celebratory to critical of the nation, they tend – across cultural and historical differences – to register some kind of ambivalence, or at least difficulty, concerning the immigrant protagonist's efforts to negotiate cultural differences and prescriptions as well as the particular gender roles that she must assume as she becomes an American.

The largest groups of immigrants during the first of what historians typically describe as the three great waves of immigration (1830–1860; 1880–1920; 1965 to the present) (Gabaccia, *From the Other Side*, 3) hailed from Western Europe. Characteristically, they came from middle- or lower-middle income families and from agricultural regions where the beginnings of industrialization or natural disasters such as drought had made family farms harder to maintain. While from our contemporary perspective it may seem that they should have had less culture shock moving to early nineteenth-century America than, for example, an Italian peasant who left a family farm for Mulberry Street in the 1890s, diaries and letters from these women regularly speak of the alienation they felt in the very landscape in which they had to make their homes. Late eighteenth-century English immigrant and pioneer Rebecca Burland, for example, disembarks at her new home only to be "utterly confounded" at the discovery that "there was no appearance of a landing place, no luggage yard, nor even a building of any kind within sight." She and her husband "looked at each other till [they] burst into tears, and [their] children observing [their] disquietude began to cry bitterly." In a plaintive question that will become something of a refrain in such narratives, she wonders, "Is this America?" (Burland, "Time Picture of Emigration," 45–7). Many among them settled, alone or with families, on the frontiers of the west, and the want of companionship is a frequent complaint, although it is also typically expressed in the letters and diaries of the native-born women who shared their migration. The personal accounts of women on the frontier are filled with reports of the sheer difficulty of the work and of simply getting through the day. For immigrants, those hardships were compounded by the strangeness of customs, and their accounts take on an ethnographic tone as they attempt to describe their lives to their chief audiences: their families back home. Mid-nineteenth-century Norwegian immigrant Gro Gudmundsrud Svendsen writes home that "one must readjust oneself and learn everything all over again, even to the preparation of food. We are told that the women of America have much leisure time, but I haven't yet met any woman who thought it so! Here the mistress of the house must do all the work that the cook, the maid, and the housekeeper would do in an upper-class family at home. Moreover, she must do her work as well as these three together do it in Norway."

For women immigrating alone, farming and homesteading was a far less likely occupational choice than domestic service, factory work, or even prostitution, all of which took them more frequently to cities. Yet, again, the experience of a foreign-born woman (especially if she emigrated from an English-speaking country) did not differ significantly from that of her native-born coworker, although industrialists often distinguished among them, and encouraged nativism, by reserving the supervisory positions for the native-born. All the same, any woman who worked or otherwise entered the public sphere in competition with men violated important gender prescriptions, and accounts from both groups attest to these women's awareness of their exclusion from the full terms of American womanhood embodied in the figure of the "True Woman."

The nineteenth-century heir of the "Republican Mother," the "True Woman" represented an allegedly national ideal of womanhood to which white upper- and middle-class women had almost exclusive access. She embraced and transmitted the virtues of piety and sobriety, creating an environment in which her husband and children would be inspired to embrace those virtues as well. She was paradoxically submissive and in absolute control of the domestic arrangements and the moral well-being of her family. With their different ideas about women's work and women's roles – from food preparation and homemaking to child-rearing and domestic gender arrangements – immigrant women frequently failed to meet the requirements of True Womanhood. But the terms of True Womanhood were equally elusive for the numerous native-born women excluded on the basis of class and race. Living in an environment very different from the New England world of Sedgwick and Child, these women had nonetheless to conform their homes and themselves to the values and culture of upper- and middle-class New England, which offered the prototype for the American nation in the early nineteenth century.

Perhaps no one so poignantly represents the nature of that exclusion as well as African-American writer Harriet Jacobs, whose *Incidents in the Life of a Slave Girl* (1861) describes how she was nearly silenced by the shame she felt (and that others encouraged) because of the terms of her enslavement that led her to surrender a chastity that was a non-negotiable mark of womanhood in mid-nineteenth-century white America. She recounts how her master's sexual advances and his jealous refusal to give her permission to marry the man she loved drove her into the arms of a powerful white man who could protect her. But, as she surmises, many of her white interlocutors and potential readers find evidence not of her oppression, but of her depravity in this choice. As Jacobs's account makes clear, not everyone was eligible for "True Womanhood," but since it was into this ideal that a woman was "Americanized," many immigrant women and others marginalized by race and class, like the native-born Jacobs, found themselves thereby excluded from the full terms of American personhood. For Jacobs, as for many marginalized women, the discrepancy led them to question the professed ideals of America and ultimately to begin to change the definitions of "woman" and "American."

By contrast, the "cultured, talented and beautiful" (as well as fair-skinned) Cuban exile/immigrant Evangelina Cisneros would come to embody the spirit and soul of the nation, in the late nineteenth century, when her plight (she was imprisoned because she resisted the advances of an ill-intentioned

Spaniard) and her daring rescue from a prison in Cuba (presented in a dramatic scene worthy of *Hope Leslie*) were published in a volume designed to help her earn her living (Cisneros, *Story*, 41). Significantly, among the letters to Maria Cristina, queen regent of Spain, written on Cisneros's behalf by "the women of America" and featured as the first chapter of her personal narrative, is one penned by Varina Jefferson Davis, the widow of the President of the Confederacy.[6] By class and by appearance, Cisneros, like the fair-skinned and wealthy Spanish heroine of Maria Amparo Ruiz de Burton's *Who Would Have Thought It?* (1872), fit the ideal. While even less cultured, talented, and beautiful fair-skinned immigrants could certainly expect better treatment than the enslaved (or even free) African-American population, a woman who had to work or who simply could not afford domestic help could not maintain herself, her family, or her home according to the prescriptions of True Womanhood. Yet, in many foreign-born women's narratives, dismay at the treatment of women was rivaled by – or perhaps displaced by – shock at the blatant injustices suffered by the nation's nonwhite populations. Scottish missionary Sue McBeth, for instance, is astonished, in the 1860s, by the nation's failure to honor its treaties with indigenous tribes.[5]

Such critiques extended to the general treatment of the working-class immigrants as well, and for some authors they proved the grounds upon which to assert the superiority of a natal culture. The dominant theme in the works of prolific Irish Catholic writer Mary Anne Sadlier is the difficulty of maintaining the values and cultural integrity of the homeland in the bigoted and materialistic United States. The noble-hearted Bessy Conway, the heroine of *Bessy Conway; or the Irish Girl in America* (1863), is shocked by the profligacy and failure to uphold their religious convictions of her fellow immigrant servants. An immigrant priest remarks on " 'the calm repose, so to speak, that pervades Irish life, the contentment which springs from true religion, and is altogether opposed to that feverish whirl of excitement in which people here are perpetually engaged: – honor seeking! – money-seeking! – office-seeking! – progress! – utility!' " (Sadlier, *Bessy Conway*, 124). And, upon having saved up enough money to return (gratefully) home, Bessy cautions others contemplating the journey that " 'there's many a girl that … leaves home a simple country girl with the fear of God in her heart, and the blush of modesty on her cheek, that turns out very bad and very indifferent in America' " (295). Like any young woman going from the country to the city, she risks falling prey to the urban corruptions and anonymities – to the temptations of "dress and finery, and balls and dances" (295). But for Sadlier, the threat is compounded by the danger of falling in with "Protestants and Jews, and everything that way," that seems to represent not just urban America, but the large mobile, tradition-resistant culture that is America itself.

Assimilation is the greatest danger in her novels. The materialistic Blakes in *The Blakes and the Flanagans: a Tale Illustrative of Irish Life in the United States* (1855) destroy their family by sending their children to be educated among the Protestants while their religious relatives, the Flanagans, thrive by attending more to their faith than to their pocketbooks. Another victim of assimilation, the protagonist of *Confessions of an Apostate* (1864), converts to Protestantism to marry his bewitching beloved, appropriately named Eve. Although he starts out happy with his wife and five children, he is forced to live with a steady stream of bigotry not only from strangers in his adopted land but also from his own wife and her family. Since he keeps his roots a secret from his associates and even his children, he is forced to endure the anti-Irish, anti-Catholic slander that they learn from his wife's aunt. Sadlier suggests that he is suffering divine retribution when his four youngest children die, leaving only a spoiled and bigoted oldest son whom he nearly kills in an incident that also brings on Eve's death. In the end, disgusted by and estranged from his son and rejected by his natal family, he returns to his hometown in Ireland to die, a lonely but repentant stranger, leaving his life's story to the townspeople to warn them about the dangers and consequences of apostasy.

Sadlier documents the best opportunity that America offers those Irish immigrants who do decide to remain in *Con O'Regan; or, Emigrant Life in the New World* (1864), when a community of emigrants migrates to rural Iowa to start their own farming community.[7] There the children are saved from exposure to the corrupting influence of American youth, who teach them to disrespect their parents and despise their roots. Young Patsey (Patrick) Bergen, for example, has become nearly unmanageable for his parents, and he talks continually about changing his "nasty Irish name" to Jake or Jeff the first chance he gets (203). Immersion in Iowa's Irish emigrant community, however, restores his filial sense of duty and his pride in his Irish name. Sadlier's novels are particularly exceptional documents, since many of the earliest women immigrants were not literate, especially in English, and even those who were did not have the access to publication in any form that their late nineteenth-century counterparts might find. Most of the firsthand documentation of their experiences survives in the form of letters and diaries. For wealthier and more established women, like the Jewish Emma Lazarus, the world of letters was somewhat more hospitable, and it offered the possibility to try to reclaim or at least reshape "the immigrant narrative." Despite her wealthy background and her apparent assimilation, Lazarus's Judaism and her artistic ambition prevented her from settling as comfortably into the domestic expectations of the True Woman as, for example, Mary Conant and Hope Leslie. Although she was not an immigrant, her experience of anti-Semitism complicated her American identity and even led her to advocate a Jewish homeland in Palestine, since, as she wrote,

> Even in free America, we have not yet succeeded everywhere and at all times in persuading the non-Jewish community to accept or reject us upon our personal merits, instead of condemning us as a race for the vices and follies of individual members. This species of injustice, from which we occasionally suffer, in common with some other races, is the inevitable consequence of our representing an unpopular minority in opposition to a dominant and numerically overwhelming majority. (Lazarus, "The Jewish Problem," 608)

Yet Lazarus also considered herself very much an American, and she was simultaneously troubled by and in sympathy with critics, both domestic and foreign, who did not understand that the nation needed time to realize its ideals. She explored her own ambivalence through the male immigrant protagonist of one of her two works of fiction, "The Eleventh Hour," which chronicles the frustration of a Romanian artist who emigrates in search of freedom of body and soul only to find himself disappointed in both the nature of freedom in the US and the absence of artistic achievement and value. In this story, ambivalence about the US is registered in the debate between Sergius Azoff, the immigrant, and Dick Bayard, the husband of one of Sergio's students, who reminds Sergio of the newness of the nation and urges him to be patient and wait to see what forms art and beauty will take in this brave new world.

Lazarus is best known to contemporary readers for her poem "The New Colossus," which helped establish the particular symbolism of the Statue of Liberty. Inscribed at the base of the statue, the words of this poem celebrate "A mighty woman with a torch, whose flame / Is the imprisoned lightning, and her name / Mother of Exiles" (Lazarus, "The New Colossus," 40). Into this Mother's lips, Lazarus puts the words that have come to embody the professed creed of America:

> Give me your tired, your poor,
> Your huddled masses yearning to be free,
> The wretched refuse of your teeming shore.
> Send these, the homeless, tempest-tost to me,
> I lift my lamp beside the golden door!

In "The New Colossus" Lazarus affirms the American ideal of democracy in the Mother of Exiles' welcoming words and underscores the possibilities for greatness and national realization embodied by the "huddled masses yearning to be free." Enjoining the "ancient lands" to keep their "storied pomp," the Mother welcomes her new children as the new nation's future.

Yet, significantly, they are children, and it is the Mother's job to turn them into Americans. In its maternal incarnation, the statue welcomes her immigrant children in conformity with the precepts of "The Cult of True Womanhood," in which this mother safeguards the sanctity of the home and thereby the nation through a paradoxically firm docility expressed by the statue's commanding mild eyes. Although the poem expresses Lazarus's vision of the ideal into which she hopes the nation will grow, the discrepancy between the ideal and the immigrant experience, as well as the ambiguity of the statue's maternal role, was not lost on her: her work with Russian Jewish immigrants had made her well acquainted with their daily struggles.

The Mother of Exiles would have her counterparts in the settlement workers, many of them second- and third-generation immigrants themselves, who, in response to the massive influx of emigrants from southern and eastern Europe between 1880 and 1920, established their residences in immigrant neighborhoods and assumed the task (and the rhetoric) of "mothering" the immigrants. The settlement house was designed to be a place where immigrants could congregate and socialize, while receiving medical advice, education, and treatment. Those who ran the houses, typically women, directed particular attention to the immigrant mother, who remained in her community, unlike her children and husband, whose school and work lives often exposed them at least to the values of mainstream America. Seen as the center of familial socialization, she was therefore a crucial target for their Americanization efforts. Classes in American cooking and housekeeping were among the staples of the settlement houses. While the settlement workers characteristically championed the immigrants against outspoken nativists who advocated legislation restricting who and how many could enter, their efforts to discourage women's Old World customs met with ambivalence if not outright hostility. Accounts written by settlement workers like the second-generation (German) Jewish American Lillian Wald reveal the kinds of ambivalence that Lazarus also showed towards more recent immigrants with whom she worked, although in a different capacity. The settlement workers took their maternal roles seriously, at once protecting their new American pupils from the perils of an unsympathetic, even bigoted, bureaucracy and expressing frustration at their intractable clinging to their old ("un-American") ways. Many teachers in New York's immigrant neighborhoods themselves had grown up in those neighborhoods; the protagonist of Yezierska's *Bread Givers*, Sara Smolinsky, experiences her own ambivalent assimilation in relation to her young pupils, while the narrator of second-generation Irish American Myra Kelly's *Little Citizens: the Humours of School Life* (1902), one of several novels the author based on her own experiences as a teacher on New York's Lower East Side, implicitly comes to terms with her own Americanness as she prepares her Jewish students for life in their adopted land.

For their part, the immigrant mothers may not have been much more likely to commit their thoughts to the page than their predecessors, but their daughters were, and the ambivalence toward both their old world and their "American" mothers found powerful expression in their work. On one hand, the daughters had pressure from the settlement workers and others who sought to enlist them as more Americanized allies in their efforts to wean the immigrant mothers of their Old World "superstitions" (like breastfeeding) in favor of the customs and conventions of their adopted lands. On the other hand, the daughters lived with parental expectations that they would inherit from their mothers the role of culture bearer, carriers of the sacred traditions in which they were raised. So the daughters found themselves at once parented and parenting. As Russian Jewish immigrant Mary Antin explained in the introduction to *The Promised Land* (1911), the book-length account of her immigration that she dedicated to the memory of Josephine Lazarus, Emma's sister, her parents were

> partners in the generation of my second self, copartners with my entire line of ancestors. They gave me body, so that I have eyes like my father's and hair like my mother's. The spirit also they gave me, so that I reason like my father and endure like my mother. But ... I soon chose my own books, and built me a world of my own.
>
> In these discriminations I emerged, a new being, something that had not been before. And when I discovered my own friends, and ran home with them to convert my parents to a belief in their excellence, did I not begin to make my father and mother, as truly as they had ever made me? Did I not become the parent and they the children, in those relations of teacher and learner? And so I can say that there has been more than one birth of myself, and I can regard my earlier self as a separate being, and make it a subject of study. (xi–xii)

The strangeness of parenting one's parents is a common theme of the personal narratives of women who came not only from abroad, but also from any culture perceived to be in need of "Americanization." Because of the expansion of the publishing industry and of public education at the turn of the twentieth century, the period witnessed a veritable renaissance of writing by women whose chronicling of their experience as cultural outsiders found their way to a curious American public in the pages of such widely circulating periodicals as the *Atlantic Monthly* and even on the newly emergent silver screen. The account penned by Amerindian Gertrude Bonnin (Zitkala-Sa) of her journey from a childhood in her western village to an Indian school and eventually to the east to become a writer was serialized in the *Atlantic Monthly* in 1900. She describes how she decided, against her mother's objections, to accompany missionaries back to their Indian school both because of their stories about "the great tree where grew red, red apples: and how [she] could reach out [her] hands and pick all the red apples [she] could eat," and because she wished to follow her brother who had already been attending their school for three years (Zitkala-Sa, "Impressions of an Indian Childhood," 46). But her retrospective narration prepares the reader for the alienation of the experience, which she describes as her "first turning away from the easy, natural flow of [her] life" (45). Already her brother's education had begun to "civilize" her mother first to "change from the buffalo skin to the white man's canvas that covered [their] wigwam" and then to give up the "wigwam of slender poles, to live, a foreigner, in a home of clumsy top" (45). From her own blissful unselfconsciousness, the narrator moves into the identity of "Indian" in a white and hostile world.

Brutalized by an "iron routine" that it was "next to impossible to leave . . . after the civilizing machine had once begun its day's buzzing," the narrator finds herself alienated from home and family, a dilemma familiar both in immigrant narratives and in other stories in which children from a marginalized culture are forcibly socialized into a cultural mainstream (Zitkala-Sa, "School Days of an Indian Girl," 190). "Even nature seemed to have no place for me," she laments. "I was neither a wee girl nor a tall one; neither a wild Indian nor a tame one. This deplorable situation was the effect of my brief course in the East, and the unsatisfactory 'teenth' in a girl's years" (191). For her, the restlessness that is intrinsic to coming of age is inseparable from – and possibly the result of – the alienation that accompanies her vexed assimilation. But the ensuing conflict with her mother is unmistakably the outcome of her education.

Impossibly liminal, she continues to move forward into the ambiguity reflected in the title of the last of three instalments, "An Indian Teacher Among Indians." When she accepts a position teaching in a school like the one she had attended, she is forced to wonder whether she is a teacher who is an Indian or a teacher of Indians, to wonder, that is, whether she is somehow relinquishing her past. Alienated from one world, she finds no place in the other, but the ambiguity becomes insupportable when she is asked to serve as a missionary and bring others into a fate like hers. "Like a slender tree," she observes, "I had been uprooted from my mother, nature, and God. I was shorn of my branches, which had waved in sympathy and love for home and friends. The natural coat of bark which had protected my oversensitive nature was scraped off to the very quick. Now a cold bare pole I seemed to be, planted in a strange earth" (386). The image summons the telegraph pole that is the one familiar object the narrator sees as she looks regretfully and fearfully out of the window on her first journey east with the missionaries. Very near her mother's dwelling, similar poles "had been planted by white men" ("Impressions," 37), and the poles represent at once the denaturing effect of white culture and the one link to home that the alienated young girl has.

In her moment of crisis, the narrator resigns from her job as a teacher of Indians, but she does not return west. Rather, she goes further east and takes up a pen. Exchanging the role of teacher for that of writer, she need no longer facilitate the process of assimilation but can now describe and analyze it. The narrator of this autobiographical account does not note that her father was white and that she had been born outside the reservation and had moved there with her mother after her father's departure. Significantly, Bonnin assumes the *nom de plume* Zitkala-Sa when she moves more fully into her father's culture to become a writer. As a writer, in other words, she moves geographically further from her mother, but returns to that culture with her pen. Like the telegraph pole, the writer is harbinger at once of an encroaching civilization and of the possibility of communication, connection and perhaps even return. As a writer, she can express and possibly even, to some extent, bridge the cultural gulf she is forced to inhabit.

The writer who assumes the task of describing the strategies and consequences of Americanization initiatives characteristically describes herself as being between cultures, an interpreter and a participant. In that role, she finds the emblem and the expression for her daily life. The writer is often seen as betraying her family and is cast as unfeminine. Interestingly, nearly the whole of the first half of the personal narrative of the hyperfeminized Cisneros is written by other people, including Julian Hawthorne, son of the famous author, who introduces the volume, and Karl Decker, her rescuer, who narrates the entire story of her dramatic liberation. And Cisneros ostensibly writes not so much to tell her story, but, at the behest of the journal that had first publicized her plight, to support herself in her exile. Her own half of the volume opens with an account of her dutiful efforts on behalf of her unjustly condemned father and her (enforced) heroism (no willing heroine she) in the face of her father's death and her own orphanhood.

For Eurasian writer Edith Maud Eaton (Sui Sin Far), by contrast, the first effort to understand and describe the cultural gulf marks her precisely as "a storyteller," as she explains in the autobiographical essay, "Leaves From the Mental Portfolio of an Eurasian," which she published in *The Independent* in 1909. She opens her account with a memory of overhearing her nurse, when she is four years old, gossiping about how her young charge's mother is Chinese. When she tries to report the incident to her mother, she is not fully intelligible, and her nurse brands her a "storyteller," for which her mother slaps her. Storytelling is itself henceforward connected in her account with prejudice and with the uncomfortable position she occupies as an Eurasian woman, and intelligibility becomes an important theme in her account of life between cultures. In England, Canada and the US, she consistently encounters a racism born of ignorance and, once established as a journalist, she is "often called upon to fight [the] battles [of Chinese persons] in the papers" (Sui Sin Far, *Leaves from the Mental Portfolio of an Eurasian*, 128). As a short story writer, she turns those battles into accounts of the struggles – and triumphs – of life in a world that had legally closed its doors to her mother's people with a series of Chinese Exclusion Acts beginning in the early 1880s.

Sui Sin Far evinces her ambivalence by simultaneously embracing her mother's race and denouncing the intrinsic bigotry of racialism: "My mother's race is as prejudiced as my father's," she observes. "Only when the whole world becomes as one family will human beings be able to see clearly and hear distinctly. I believe that some day a great part of the world will be Eurasian" (129). Like Zitkala-Sa, she reports restlessness: when she is East she longs to be West and in the West, she yearns for the East. No place is quite home. "After all," she begins her concluding paragraph, "I have no nationality and am not anxious to claim any. Individuality is more than nationality" (132). Espousing the theory of the American melting-pot, she embodies the lived experience of its ambiguities: she is an uncanny subject, unintelligible to Eastern or Western analysis alone and exposing the contingency of the idea of "home."

The storyteller is bemused, she reports, by the orientalism of people who advise her "to 'trade' upon [her] nationality" and who explain that if she wants literary success in America she "should dress in Chinese costume, carry a fan in [her] hand, wear a pair of scarlet beaded slippers, live in New York and come of high birth" (132). She should replace her contemporary Chinese American companions with an acquaintance with Chinese ancestors and should continually profess the undying wisdom of Confucius. She does indeed quote Confucius at the end of her account, but not, as her orientalist advisors have counseled, for an exotic effect. Rather, into Confucius's words she puts the putatively *American* credo of individualism – an individualism that lies at the heart of the melting-pot: "'You are you and I am I,' says Confucius." And, accordingly, the narrator writes, "I give my right hand to the Occidentals and my left to the Orientals, hoping that between them they will not utterly destroy the insignificant 'connecting link.' And that's all" (132). Like Zitkala-Sa's telegraph pole, she is a connecting link, and like Zitkala-Sa, she also understands that her writing might effectively negotiate the more painful connection between cultures that has been inscribed on her body. She is careful to establish her chosen profession as an alternative to the roles of wife and mother. The daughter once punished for her story-telling views her own role in reproducing the "human family" as ideological rather than biological.

While Zitkala-Sa and Sui Sin Far explicitly incorporate their ambivalence about Americanization into their personal narratives, Antin offers an ostensible paean to her chosen home in *The Promised Land*. Emigrating, as she did, to escape the infamous pogroms and enforced migrations that Jews suffered in tsarist Russia, Antin is motivated to forget a troubled past. Whatever disappointments the New World presented to her and her family, the past offered no nostalgic respite even for her imagination. Antin claims to record her acculturation experiences not to return to or to analyze her past, but to exorcise it. That is not to say that the account of her Polotzk childhood and her subsequent journey, which occupy half of the book, is not as full of the frolics of childhood – including a sumptuous description of cherries and strawberries, the taste of which she has never since been able to duplicate – as it is of the abuses that she suffered as a Jew. But her translation to America and her American education are far more joyful experiences than those of Zitkala-Sa and far less uncomfortable than those of Sui Sin Far. Indeed, the account Antin offers in her aptly titled volume conforms neatly, at least on the surface, to the prescriptions of the immigrant narrative offered by mainstream America. In the middle of the book, when she finally lands in Boston, she even adopts the primary metaphor of late nineteenth-century immigration: "The process [of becoming American] is spontaneous on all sides, like the education of the child by the family circle" (*Promised Land*, 180).

Yet Antin's exuberance is tempered from the outset by a curious pain that she expresses in the last paragraph of her introduction. "I want to forget – " she expostulates, "sometimes I long to forget. I think I have thoroughly assimilated my past – I have done its bidding – I want now to be of to-day. It is painful to be consciously of two worlds. The Wandering Jew in me seeks forgetfulness. I am not afraid to live on and on, if only I do not have to remember too much. A long past vividly remembered is like a heavy garment that clings to your limbs when you would run. And I have thought of a charm that should release me from the folds of my clinging past. I take the hint from the Ancient Mariner, who told his tale in order to be rid of it. I, too, will tell my tale, for once, and never hark back any more. I will write a bold 'Finis' at the end, and shut the book with a bang!" (xiv–xv). A book written in order to help her to forget? Coleridge's Ancient Mariner did not forget his woes in their telling; rather, he is perpetually compelled to repeat his story. Into the telling of this happy American tale, Antin weaves the ambivalence that so thoroughly characterizes the immigrant narrative. The

Wandering Jew evokes the curse – the Jew wanders because he is welcome nowhere – and Antin's story becomes an emblem of her wandering. Inscribed in Antin's story, as in Zitkala-Sa's and Sui Sin Far's, are both the return and the assimilation that cannot be completed. Although they represent three different experiences of migrations to and within "America," all three are painfully conscious that they live in two worlds, that their selves, as Antin describes it, cannot be fully reconciled. And all three seek solace, if not full resolution, in the act of writing, of telling a story that may impose some kind of order on the past and effect some kind of change in the present and future.

Whether expressed as forcefully as in Zitkala-Sa's and Sui Sin Far's work or less explicitly as in Antin's, the ambivalence of all three accounts attests to the ambiguities of the places they occupied in mainstream America. After all, an "*immigrant*," like a "convert," by definition carries the reminder of an alternative past; an "immigrant," by definition, is not "at home." In turn, their stories, like those of others like them uncannily underscored the contingency of home and the inevitability of migrations and change. In response, "Americanization" programs were stepped up, as legislators and educators, journalists and politicians sought to define "Americanism" and supervise its reproduction. These variously motivated programs combined benevolence with bigotry, and the implicit violence of the ideology of assimilation did not escape prophet of cultural pluralism Horace Kallen, who insisted that people "cannot change their grandfathers" and that "Jews or Poles or Anglo-Saxons, in order to cease being Jews or Poles or Anglo-Saxons, would have to cease to be" ("Democracy Versus the Melting-Pot," 220). Indeed, to the violence of assimilative strategies we might trace the tragic fates of so many nineteenth-century literary heroines marginalized by their racial, ethnic, or class backgrounds, especially when they venture out of their immediate environs. For if the difficulties of assimilation registered by women authors from these groups do not differ radically from their male counterparts, the women seem to pose much more of a threat to nineteenth-century white (especially male) authors. Characteristically viewed in this period as carriers of culture, (white) women literally embodied the future of the Republic. Other women, frequently eroticized in nineteenth-century literature, embodied a threat vaguely defined but nonetheless haunting. So, from Cooper's Cora, Hawthorne's Miriam, and Melville's Isabel to Stephen Crane's Maggie and Kate Chopin's Desirée, exoticized and desired women had to die.

The literary fate of one of the most celebrated exoticized woman has inscribed her neither as an "American woman" nor as a survivor, yet in her earliest incarnation, Cho-Cho-San, better known as "Madame Butterfly," sheds important light on the fate of the immigrant woman.[8] Originally a character in an 1898 short story by John Luther Long, Cho-Cho-San strikingly embodies the potentially tragic fate of the Americanized woman. In his exploration of an American naval officer's seduction and abandonment of a young Japanese girl who believes they are married for life, Long, a self-proclaimed "feminist," sets in Japan a story that could well be read as an allegory of Americanization. Lieutenant Benjamin Franklin Pinkerton sets out to turn his young Japanese "wife" into an "American woman." He belittles her traditions and alienates her from her relatives. In true American fashion, he replaces descent with consent, telling her that she will have to "get along without ancestors" and that he "shall have to serve in the capacity of ancestors" (Long, "Madame Butterfly," 6). The consequences of this alienation – Cho-Cho-San has no one to whom she can turn when she realizes that she has been abandoned – offer a material analogue to the psychological burdens of assimilation; Pinkerton, in effect, allegorically embodies the ideology of assimilation and the chauvinistic beliefs that it can entail. He calls her "an American refinement of a Japanese product, an American improvement in a Japanese invention" (13). The extent of her alienation is captured as she contemplates suicide. The sword "was the one thing of her father's which her relatives had permitted her to keep. It would have been very beautiful to a Japanese" (83), a phrase that ambiguously positions Cho-Cho-San as possibly no longer Japanese. Strikingly, Cho-Cho-San's very ambivalence keeps her alive. As she begins to make the incision, "she now first knew that it was sad to die" (85). She fails to complete the act, and her maid comes out to bind up her wounds. The story ends with Pinkerton's blonde wife coming to ask for Cho-Cho-San's baby but finding the house empty. The story does not resolve with her death or with a departure that accommodates white America. It is interesting, in fact, that subsequent versions – Belasco's stage adaptation and Puccini's opera – witnessed her death. Her survival is an important feature of Long's allegory.

Among the exoticized heroines' real-life counterparts who also survived, some chose to tell their stories, to recount the struggles and record the changes that they witnessed. Their stories explore not only the psyche of the marginalized writer or narrator, but also the social structures that preserve their marginality, that maintain the term *immigrant*, for example, many generations beyond its descriptive accuracy. Their stories are testaments to their survival and to their insistence on telling their stories against the many stories told about them. In telling them, they have contributed to changes in the definition of *America* and *American* and they witness the full strength of that survival.

NOTES

1. The citation is from Waldo Frank's *Our America*.
2. Roosevelt uses these terms in his essay "True Americanism."
3. See Linda K. Kerber's *Women of the Republic: Intellect and Ideology in Revolutionary America*.
4. The clearest articulation of that fantasy is in the speeches Jefferson delivered to predominantly Amerindian audiences.
5. See "The Diary of Sue McBeth – A Missionary to the Choctaws, 1860–1861."
6. The quotation is from the prefatory documents, "Protests and Petitions," entitled "The Women of America," pp. 31–55.
7. The earliest edition of *Con O'Regan* is not dated; the first dated edition is 1864.
8. I wish to thank Arthur Groos and Alexandra Suh for calling my attention to this story.

WORKS CITED

Antin, Mary. *The Promised Land*. Boston and New York: Houghton Mifflin, 1912. Originally published in 1911 by the Atlantic Monthly Company.

Burland, Rebecca. "A True Picture of Emigration." *Immigrant Voices: Twenty-Four Narratives on Becoming an American*. Ed. Gordon Hutner. New York: Signet, 1999. 40–55.

Blackstone, William. *Commentaries on the Laws of England*. A facsimile of the first edition of 1765–1769, vol. L, *Of the Rights of Persons*. 1765. Chicago: University of Chicago Press, 1979.

Child, Lydia Maria. *Hobomok and Other Writings on Indians*. Ed. Carolyn L. Karcher. New Brunswick: Rutgers University Press, 1986.

Cisneros, Evangelina. *The Story of Evangelina Cisneros (Evangelina Betancourt Cosio Y Cisneros), Told By Herself Her Rescue by Karl Decker*. New York: Continental Publishing Co., 1897.

"The Diary of Sue McBeth – A Missionary to the Choctaws, 1860–1861." Ed. Anna Lewis. *Chronicles of Oklahoma* 21 (June 1943): 186–95.

Eaton, Edith Maud (Sui Sin Far). The *Independent* 66 (January 21, 1909): 125–32.

Gabaccia, Donna. *From the Other Side: Women, Gender and Immigrant Life in the US, 1820–1990*. Bloomington: Indiana University Press, 1994.

Jacobs, Harriet. *Incidents in the Life of a Slave Girl*. 1861. Ed. Nellie Y. McKay and Frances Smith Foster. New York: W. W. Norton, 2001.

Kallen, Horace. "Democracy Versus the Melting-Pot." *Nation* 100. 2509–91 (February 18 and 25, 1915): 190–4 and 217–20.

Kelly, Myra. *Little Citizens. The Humours of School Life*. New York: McClure, Phillips and Co., 1902.

Kerber, Linda K. *Women of the Republic: Intellect and Ideology in Revolutionary America*. New York: W. W. Norton, 1986. Originally published by the University of North Carolina Press, 1980.

Lazarus, Emma. "The Jewish Problem." *Century* 25 (February 1883): 602–11, 608. "The New Colossus," *Emma Lazarus: Selections from her Poetry and Prose*. Ed. Morris U. Schappes. New York: Book League, Jewish People's Fraternal Order of the International Workers Order, revised and enlarged edition, 1947.

Long, John Luther. "Madame Butterfly." *Madame Butterfly, Purple Eyes, A Gentleman of Japan and A Lady, Kilo, Glory*. New York: Century Co., 1898. 1–86.

Roosevelt, Theodore. "True Americanism." *The Works of Theodore Roosevelt*. New York: Scribner's, 1926. 13–26.

Ruiz de Burton, Maria Amparo. *Who Would Have Thought It?* Ed. and introduced by Rosaura Sanchez and Beatric Pita. Houston: Arte Publico Press, 1995.

Rush, Benjamin. "Of the Mode of Education Proper in a Republic." *Essays, Literary, Moral, and Philosophical*. Philadelphia: Printed by Thomas and Samuel F. Bradford, no. 8, South Front Street, 1798. 6–20.

Sadlier, Mrs. J. *Bessy Conway: or The Irish Girl in America*. New York: P. J. Kennedy and Sons, 1863.

The Blakes and the Flanagans. New York: D. and J. Sadlier and Co., 1855.

Con O'Regan or Emigrant Life in the New World. New York: D. and J. Sadlier and Co., 1864.

Confessions of an Apostate. New York. P. J. Kennedy, 1903.

Sedgwick, Catharine Maria. *Hope Leslie, or, Early Times in the Massachusetts*. Ed. Carolyn L. Karcher. Hammondsworth: Penguin, 1998.

Svendsen, Gro Gudmundsrud. "Frontier Mother." *Immigrant Voices*. Ed. Gordon Hutner. New York: Signet, 1999: 69–84.

Webster, Noah. *Letters of Noah Webster*. Ed. Harry R. Warfel. New York: Library Publications, 1953.

Selections from *The American Magazine, 1787–88. On Being American. Selected Writings, 1783–1828*. New York: Frederick A. Praeger, 1967. 78–92.

Yezierska, Anzia. "How I Found America." *Hungry Hearts and Other Stories*. New York: Persea Books, 1985. 250–98.

Zitkala-Sa. "Impressions of an Indian Childhood." *Atlantic Monthly* 85.507 (January 1900): 37–47.

"An Indian Teacher Among Indians." *Atlantic Monthly* 85.509 (March 1900): 381–6.

"The School Days of an Indian Girl." *Atlantic Monthly* 85.508 (February 1900): 185–94.

3
CASE STUDIES

9

FREDRIKA J. TEUTE

The uses of writing in Margaret Bayard Smith's new nation

When Margaret Bayard Smith wrote the words "let this book speak for me," she offered a potent proposition (October 1, 1804, diary). With this declaration, she claimed meaning for her writing and significance for herself. Implicitly, she was asking, not asserting, and she was proposing that "this book" was to say what she felt she could not speak. The proposition was fraught with the complications of the post-Revolutionary era in which she lived and of her ambitions, which the age inspired. She employed different writing formats, diaries, letters, publications, to voice her intellect and feelings, as she sought to authenticate her experience to herself, to her children, and to others. Her claim was ultimately historical, for she meant, like others of her generation, to convey her life and her vision of American society to posterity. At her most ambitious, the "me" spoke for the nation (Baym, *American Women Writers*, 1–9, 11–45, 92–103, 214–39; Ziff, *Writing in the New Nation*, 28–9, 144–5; Gould, *Covenant and Republic*, 14–16, 61–132). She offered in her writings an expansive definition of what it was to be an American. And in her silences can be found the silences in America's history.

Margaret Bayard Smith's life spanned the transformative period of the new nation. Born during the Revolution (1778) outside of Philadelphia, she died in Washington, DC, in 1844. Her father was Colonel Jonathan Bayard, a prominent merchant, Patriot, legislator, and jurist in Pennsylvania and New Jersey; she grew up in the midst of a well-connected network of mercantile and landed elite families of the mid-Atlantic region. She received an excellent education within the Bayard households and at the Bethlehem Moravian Female Seminary. Marrying her second cousin Samuel Harrison Smith in 1800, she moved with him to Washington, where he published the *National Intelligencer*, the organ of the Jefferson administration. Fascinated with politics, inspired by ideals of social improvement, Bayard Smith sought to achieve intellectual expression and self-fulfillment. In her critical engagement with the dominant establishment, she exercised power in structuring a national political culture. Nevertheless, even as an elite white woman, she experienced the limitations of the republican system in circumscribing access to America's promise.

She matured in a period under the sway of forces unleashed by the Enlightenment and American and French Revolutions. Women, like many other groups, gathered empowerment from the ideologies of individual self-realization and independence. As Mary Wollstonecraft came to personify, though, women who enacted ideals of self-fulfillment and social liberation were doubly exposed to criticism. Intellectual women who appropriated the freedom to express their own ideas and desires ran the risk of being construed as both an "unsex'd female" (having a manly mind) and an oversexed female (consuming with lust). The intersection of reason and feeling became a crucial site in the struggle over controlling women's will in the reaction at the end of the eighteenth and into the nineteenth century (Barker-Benfield, *Culture of Sensibility*, 368–95; Brown, "Mary Wollstonecraft"). Bayard Smith registered the contests of the era.

During the 1790s, Margaret Bayard Smith imbibed a strain of sensibility espoused by contemporary radicals in Europe. Building on the belief that man had innate moral sentiments in sympathy with other human beings, they imagined improving society through critical judgment. Bayard was part of a heterosexual circle of young intellectuals in New York City including Margaretta Mason, Maria Nicholson, and Maria Templeton; Elihu Hubbard Smith, Charles Brockden Brown, William Dunlap, Samuel Miller, and Samuel Latham Mitchill (members of the all-male Friendly Club) (Cronin, ed., *Diary of Elihu Hubbard Smith*). These men and women read and discussed together Rousseau, William Godwin, Wollstonecraft, Erasmus Darwin, Coleridge, among other contemporary authors. Bayard took inspiration from the intellectual ferment and universalist ideals to which she was exposed. She absorbed Godwin's and Wollstonecraft's ideas of sensibility. They informed Bayard Smith's perceptions of justice and individual freedom well into the next century.

Over the course of the eighteenth century concepts of sensibility ratified man's natural feelings, conditioned by reflection, as the source for both social bonds and individual judgment. Containing both conservative and liberal dynamics, the culture of sensibility by the end of the century had taken on radical egalitarian implications in the Revolutionary movement and writings of people like Godwin and Wollstonecraft. They insisted on the exercise of reason in directing passions toward benevolent goals. Educable faculties were to critique human affections in relation to larger social goods, exposing established institutions and obligations, including domestic relations, to scrutiny. The equilibrium between reason and feeling proved unstable in the heated ideological debates of the 1790s. However uneasily balanced, the coordination of individual imagination and sympathy with individual improvement and a just society inspired Bayard Smith's own actions and her judgment of the society in which she lived (Jones, *Radical Sensibility*, 6–18, 101–4). Her sensibility was the wellspring of creative tensions between her desires, her duties, and her social vision.

Through her writings, she sought to reconcile the conflicting impulses exerted by her aspirations and by societal strictures. In each of three different formats, diaries, letters, and print, she expressed competing sides of herself. The diaries contained representations of a divided self for her posterity's edification. Her publications projected a public sensibility on which to model American life. Her family letters, primarily to her sisters in New Jersey, Philadelphia, and New York, were her most intensely personal revelations about herself. In her journals of the 1800s directed to her progeny, she struggled to justify herself, alternately mobilizing her conscience and her soul. Her argument with herself emanated from the ideological contests of the 1790s between conserving social cohesion and liberating human potentiality. In representing herself to her children, she crafted a version of herself as mother and wife that her own words belied. She vented her frustrations, then wrote herself into submission. The gesture of submission, however, undermined the social system to which she deferred (Greenblatt, *Renaissance Self-Fashioning*, 254). Her underlying resistance revealed prescriptions of moral duty to be proscriptions of individual freedom. In her disruptive assertions, she recognized soul mates in her hired enslaved servants.

She carried over her debate concerning white women's and blacks' social roles and autonomous desires in her anonymous publications. Over the first four decades of the nineteenth century, in magazine articles, poetry, children's stories, and novels she proffered an American sensibility emanating from shared feelings and reason stimulated by free social exchange. Questioning normative bonds of marriage and family, she raised the possibility of individual fulfillment and social affections grounded in a moral apprehension of liberty. Cutting across gender, status, and racial lines, her narratives of an emergent American society portrayed both elite white women's public role and racial amalgamation. Her printed works transmitted to a public audience her historical and critical vision.

In the early 1800s she wrote out of the conflicting strains of conservative and radical sensibility to imagine a more capacious social system in the United States. Under Thomas Jefferson's and James Madison's presidencies, she allied with Dolley Madison and other elite women in Washington to form an expansive public culture. In their drawing rooms, they forged a continental leadership and projected a national political society. During the War of 1812, with the fears of black insurrection, the national retreat from antislavery, and the Smiths' own purchase of blacks, Bayard Smith went silent on the wrongs of enslavement. As she began her publishing career in earnest in the first half of the 1820s, she returned to formulating an American sensibility that recognized all groups' claims to the social goods of freedom. In the aftermath of the war and the Missouri Compromise, though, political concerns over territorial expansion and social devolution transmuted white Americans' Revolutionary idealism of equality into nationalist expediency of differentiation. Democratic politics had the effect of cutting across class lines and domesticating women (Nelson, *National Manhood*, 35–8). The American Colonization Society and Indian removal both sought to consolidate national unity around the exclusion of nonwhites. Underlying these policies were fears of female independence, class solidarity, and racial amalgamation. When Bayard Smith attempted to publish her most important novel "Lucy" in 1824/5, she found that her project to articulate affinities and aspirations shared between lower-class whites and blacks, women and men, was unprintable. Her earlier silence had become the nation's silence.

When she announced "let this book speak for me," she was addressing her daughters, aged four months and three years, in her diary (October 1, 1804). In opening a conversation with them, she also initiated a conversation with the future. Imagining her own death, she wished to be known. She wanted to leave an impression of her experience and care. If she should die, then, "let this book speak for me my children, in these pages you may converse with your Mother; here you shall find a true history of my life, a transcript of my heart." By implication, she could inscribe in the record the truth that was hidden from sight. Knowing that "you shall be the confidants of every thought of every feeling, of every circumstance," would be "an irresistible inducement...always to adhere to the right, & avoid the wrong." In her promise to confess "every notion" of her life, "good or bad, right or wrong," she proposed that her writing would be a transparency of herself, revealing the conflicts within. She was admitting that she had not been living solely for her daughters and that her temptations were strong. Through her diary-keeping, she intended to transmit to a larger audience her sensibility, her thoughts and feelings, and at the same time to discipline them. As both a record and a projection of identity, such written explorations were a form of power, controlling a sense of self and shaping it for self and others. She wrote what she could not speak. In her texts, she carried on a dialogue that she wished posterity to hear (Kelley, "Designing a Past for the Present," 315–46; Kelley, "Reading Women/Women Reading," 414–19; Lockridge, *On the Sources of Patriarchal Rage*, 1, 69).

In the first decade of the nineteenth century, Bayard Smith published three small pieces, an essay and a poem in the *Monthly Magazine, and American Review* (1800) and her children's story *The Diversions of Sidney* (1805). These, her first known assays in print, carried the stamp of sensibility that would mark her subsequent publications. Drawn from her personal experiences, they objectified her felt tensions between individual aspirations and societal roles. Packaged within a seeming promulgation of social prescriptions and literary conventions were projections of liberated human capacity and harmonious social relations. At the very heart of her writings were her own discontents with the lot society had cast her and her desires to transcend quotidian restraints.

All three pieces dealt with women's passions and intellect in relation to marriage; entwined in the children's story was the enslaved black's potential in relation to white dominion. All three indirectly challenged the marital confines placed upon women. Her published writings, in conjunction with her diaries and letters, suggested that the ideal of affective family ties was a form of social control over autonomous impulses. The presence of enslaved blacks within the household highlighted family authority as problematic. Basing obedience on moral grounds of affection and duty shifted the basis of male claims to dominance from hierarchical rights of rulership to personal consent. Paternal authority depended on dependents' willingness to submit. Prescriptions of the moral obligations of women, servants, and children elided the discrepancy between representations of families and practices occurring within them. Founding governance on feelings set authority on unstable footings in the new nation. If the American Revolution proved anything, it demonstrated that affections could be alienated (Fliegelman, *Prodigals and Pilgrims*, 9–12, 83, 123–54; Lewis, "The Republican Wife," 689–721).

Before their marriage in 1800, Samuel Harrison Smith and the then Margaret Bayard carried on a three-year courtship. This was the period during which she spent time in the New York circle of young intelligentsia. Under the influence of late Enlightenment ideas discussed with her friends, Bayard expounded her goals for herself and her ideals for marriage in a series of letters to her fiancé between 1797 and 1800. The vision elaborated by Bayard was that of a companionate relationship (Jabour, *Marriage in the Early Republic*, 10–11). In explaining her views, she probed the heart of affectional marriage. She found at its core inequities of power. To Smith she expostulated a model of sensibility that allowed the full flowering of intellectual and emotional capacity of both partners. On the eve of her marriage to Smith, Bayard read portions of her commonplace book to three of her New York intimates, Maria Templeton, William Johnson, and

Charles Brockden Brown. One of the essays read, "The Evils of Reserve in Marriage," the men selected for publication in Brown's new periodical, the *Monthly Magazine, and American Review*. Praising its "just" sentiments, her friends valued her essay for its Godwinian analysis of the requisite sensibility brought to bear on the married state (May 23, 1800 to Samuel Harrison Smith).

Interpreting her piece as an admonishment to Samuel Harrison Smith and as prescience about the future is hard to avoid. It appeared in the June issue of the *Magazine*. The theme was not propitious for a couple soon to be married. Its intent was to set out the recipe for felicity in marriage, in a word, "candour. All reserve, obscurity, or disguise, are productive of indifference, suspicion, or distrust." Presented as a narrative by a widow, her monologue held her mistakes up to a younger woman as an example "of the necessity of perfect candour, and unbounded confidence in the conjugal union" (409). Although Bayard may have meant to purvey positive advice (to herself, as well as to others), this preface, and an even briefer perfunctory two-sentence conclusion, ended up as mere brackets to her cautionary tale. Her imagination expanded on a morose story concerning the dangers of withholding love and support from one's spouse out of an excessive sensibility to the other's reserve. If Bayard was lecturing herself, she was also prodding Smith. The husband, though "of a thoughtful disposition, and tender heart," was distant and uncommunicative, preoccupied with his business at the center of the city far from their home on its outskirts. His silence and indifference caused the wife disappointment and distrust. And so the cycle spiraled downward. At base, the subject was the potential for disappointment and alienation in the married state when feelings were not mediated by reason.

Rather than promoting the ideal of companionate marriage, Bayard's "Evils" achieved the reverse. It deconstructed the premises of affectional marriage and exposed the unequal power equation underlying it. Although both the wife and husband suffered hurt feelings at the hand of the other, the wife experienced total social isolation within the home, while the husband circulated in society. The lack of children signaled the barrenness of their relationship and the dysfunctionality of the companionate ideal. Finally, with a husband deceased and no children, the now widow was released from the depression of her married state. With the telling of her story to a female friend, she had resumed social intercourse and productive reflection. In publishing it, the woman entered the public arena. No longer numbed by indifference, she was free mentally and socially to engage the world.

The words *candour* and *indifference* recur throughout Bayard's essay. Sensibility marked the route between these two states of being. It was both the source of the couple's potential pleasure and the cause of their alienation.

By sensibility she meant feeling informed by rational reflection. When well balanced, sensibility facilitated openness and empathy between people; when overstrung, it could lead to its opposite, insensibility or indifference. Though both wife and husband had sunk into insensibility, their comportments were subtly gendered. The woman lacked candour; the man was indifferent.

The theme of male indifference was one Bayard had rehearsed with Smith over the last several years. She believed "the affections of your sex & ours are very different, before I knew this difference, I suffer'd from supposed indifference, but have now discover'd nature has not given to your hearts, such quick, such minute perceptions." The reason was that woman focused closely on everything that revolved around her heart, since "her line of life seldom distracts her attention." Employing men's mental faculties, the world occupied their egos, leaving their hearts underdeveloped organs to be tended by women. Men's professional occupations allowed them to compartmentalize their affections while women's narrow compass made them obsessively concerned with emotions (June 7, 1799; October 7, 1799; July 19, 1800).

Indifference was only part of the issue Bayard had with Smith, for what she increasingly desired was his approbation of her intellectual capacity. In May 1800, shortly before she exhibited her commonplace book to her friends, she lodged a plea with Smith for basing their marriage on intellectual companionship. Bayard was "mortified" that he seemed to forget that she was "a rational being, & have treated me as a mere girl." She asked that he would treat her "not only as the object of love, but the object of esteem, not as your mistress, but as your friend. The last is the character of which I am ambitious." She instructed him, "Forget that I am a woman; I wish you would remember only that I have a mind, which tho' now idle & contracted, nay, debased by ignorance, yet is capable of activity & expansion" (May 3, 1800). Over the past year, she had moved from accepting the notion of a woman's inferior rational faculties to embracing her full potential (October 7, 1799). Her rejection of the status quo echoed Wollstonecraft's and proved the conservative attacks on Wollstonecraft justified. The explosive combination of passion and intellect expressed by Bayard revealed the instability underlying a sensibility that liberated both. She let him know that

> I am every day less contented with the circumscribed & degraded situation to which our sex is condemned. As to the division of the duties of life, I am very well pleased; but allow us the power of discharging our share of these duties better than can now be done ... My restless & enquiring mind, will not keep in the beaten track, but is perpetually wandering into paths untrod before. There are moments when I feel an expansion of soul, which breaks the shackles by

which I am bound! I am for tearing away the dark veil of ignorance, which
conceals from me the light of knowledge. (May 3, 1800)

Vacillating between defiance and deference, in the end Bayard gave away the
game. She appealed to Smith, "Oh my friend will you not give life to my better
half; will you not feed a mind, hungering & thirsting after knowledge?"

Bayard admitted the gap between the companionate ideal and marital reality. The ideology served to leave men free outside the home, rendering them
less responsible within it, and to proscribe women's autonomous impulses,
redirecting them inward to heart and home (Jabour, *Marriage in the Early
Republic*, 1–7, 9–10, 22, 169–70). She confessed to him and to herself that
the "pictures of felicity" her imagination sketched were very "unlike those
exhibited, in real life!" Her idealistic vision knocked against the bedrock
of domesticity's constraints. In the structuring of her letter, as in her essay,
Bayard demonstrated the unequal relations between men and women that
she had set out to argue against. She posited a companionate marriage based
on intellect rather than affections, which she already recognized had put
women at a disadvantage. She ended by abdicating control to Smith, for
"it is you, yes my friend it is you who are to determine whether these fond
hopes be ever realized. You can make me what you please – make me then
your *friend*" (May 3, 1800). Try as she might, she failed to disentangle their
relationship from the gendered hierarchies of power that had led her to rely
on him. It was a concession of power that she would not live with easily.
The eruptive desires expressed in this letter were uncontainable.

Her second published piece in 1800 was a poem appearing in the *Monthly
Magazine* in November. Bayard penned "Lines By a Young Lady. Written at
the Falls of Passaick, July, 1800," on an outing with her New York friends.
In this poem she loosed her passionate yearnings for transcendence. She
equated nature's force with the force of her own desires. In the poetry's
measured verse she both released and controlled her emotional and intellectual strivings. In writing and publishing it, she transmuted her personal
longings into intellectual achievement. Commemorating the moment with
her friends, she celebrated the riotous variety of nature and their delight in
abandoning themselves to its vagaries. Their reflective mood responded to
the changing landscape. As their journey progressed toward the falls, the
drama of the scene and the passions evoked intensified. "The loud tumult
of the water's roar . . . yon foaming stream's impetuous tide" carried all before it, dashing "on the rocky shore, The oak, all shatter'd, once the forest's
pride." The bursting pressure of youth's (woman's) desires knocked down
age, male authority, and preeminence. Unstanchable, "exhaustless flood! no
interval is thine; . . . No winter's icy bands thy course confine." Ceaseless as

nature's course was, it was immutable while human life ebbed and eternal life beckoned.

> For ages shall these roaring waters glide,
> These rocks succeeding ages shall remain;
> While a few years shall stop the purple tide,
> That now with ardour swells the youthful vein.

> Yet rocks the ruthless hand of time shall feel;
> E'en Ocean's self, in years, shall roll away:
> Eternity on man has stampt the seal
> That gives the promise of eternal day. (399)

Writing her own ambitions on nature's crest, Bayard's passions found "Echo ... from her caves." But then she checked the flow. First, she delimited human desire within temporal bounds; then she dwarfed nature's might in the face of a greater power. Abruptly cutting the poem off, she recalled herself with a pious reminder that man's fate was sealed with the promise of eternity. "Lines ... at the Falls of Passaick" surged with the pleasures of participating in nature's scene and sharing youthful exaltation with others. The excitement of the moment and in the poem's creation was perhaps so exquisite that Bayard had to terminate both experiences by subsuming herself to a higher moral destiny.

She felt the tensions between self-realization and self-subordination. Her writings vibrated with countervalences of individual desires and collective obligations. When oppressed by the latter, she attempted to regulate her aspirations by submitting herself to duty, God's design, woman's destiny. When she felt she could not control her appetites, she took refuge in the conventions of social control. At the end of the eighteenth century, the ideology of companionate marriage sought to channel disruptive passions into societally constitutive roles. For the wife it substituted a tyranny of affections for a superimposed hierarchy of authority. The ideal left male governance vulnerable to the real possibility of female withdrawal of support (Teute, "Roman Matron on the Banks of Tiber Creek," 89–121; Barnes, *States of Sympathy*, 2–9, 74–8, 115–26).

By the time Bayard's poem appeared in print in November 1800, her days of self-expansion ostensibly had ended. She had been married to Smith for about a month. A year later they had their first child, Julia Harrison Smith. Bayard Smith had already discovered what she had intuitively known before her marriage. A month before her first child was born, she recorded in her commonplace book that "in the economical cares of my family, my thoughts & time became so entirely occupied, that I gave up all mental occupation & such was the influence of habit, that reading soon lost its attractions." She entered her loneliness and "lethargy" (October 9–13, 15, 17, 23, November 4, December 9, 1800; October 5, 1801, commonplace book).

In her diary entry of 1804, explicitly directed to her daughters, she began with a declaration of gratitude to God, yet her catalogue of life's vagaries revealed her apprehension of temporal contingency and belied any grounds for optimism. Bayard Smith went on to review the preceding year of her life and what emerged was not altogether a happy tale. Her accounting of 1803/4 was inflected with loneliness and depression. Certainly, the dangers and illness attendant on pregnancy and childbirth had a lot to do with her despair. But the sources of her unhappiness ran deeper than anxieties over ill-health. In her letters she revealed more about her relations with her husband than she confided in her diary, meant for her daughters. Her sense of isolation derived from the disappointments of married life.

Smith's absence over long stretches of time caused her many "melancholy hours" while she was at their farm. In the winter when Bayard Smith resided in the city with her husband, he was "always occupied"; when he was at home she found him "indifferent" from the press of business. The sense of female isolation experienced by Bayard Smith was not unique to her. What was significant was the unhappiness generated in married women in the post-Revolutionary period. The disaffection was grounded in the particular expectations and deflected opportunities of the period. Bayard Smith was notable for harnessing her ambitions to productive ends and articulating her discontents (May 8, 1803, June 19, 1803, to Smith; November 18, 1803, to Mary Ann Smith; October 26, 1804; May 25, 1806, diary; Jabour, *Marriage in the Early Republic*, 52–99). In her litany of life's vicissitudes, the telling phrase "the completion of our wishes, [so?] inadequate to our expectations" stands out. Her terminology in these passages recalls her "Evils of Reserve in Marriage." "Melancholy," "lethargy," "indifference," "disappointed" "expectations" captured the effects of affections diverted and unfulfilled. Finding the emotional and intellectual companionship less than she had wanted, she turned increasingly to the one person who could give her solace: herself. In her diaries she gave her intellect life. Voicing herself to her progeny, in front of them she argued over her fate, letting them know its costs. She structured her entries as debates, averring happiness as she fought off discontent. In the process, her pen gave flight to the words and ideas she loved, sending them out to her imagined audience. She gave wing to her intellect even as she pictured it caged.

In one long argument with herself in the fall of 1806, she rebelled against "insignificant" and "wearisome...domestic employments...With difficulty" could she "submit my mind to this kind of existence." If it were not for her "constitutional good humour & contentedness ... this variance between my duties & inclination [would] make me quite miserable." She claimed to have experienced an unusual "portion of placidity & cheerfulness" the preceding summer, except for "moments ... when my mind has refused to be chained to the monotony of family bussiness & has longed to soar in the regions of intellectual existence." Comparing woman's circumscribed sphere to a "horse chained to the mill," she envied "the unlimited sphere of man," who, like "the proud courser," leapt all barriers and had "no bounds opposed to the expansion & exercise of his powers." In those moments, she longed "to give *full* scope to that active & creative power that I feel within me, to break through the wires of the little cage that confines me, to expand my wings & rise far far beyond the mere vegetating life I now lead." She stopped: "*But I am a Woman.* And society says, 'Thus far & no farther shall'st thou come.'" She went on, debating woman's destiny back and forth, "to discharge my duties faithfully" or "to give full scope to the powers of mind." Finally, she gave it up. She had let her imagination soar; now she had to pull it back down to earth. With resignation, she began the process of submission that revealed the proscriptive, coercive basis to the ideologies of domesticity and companionate marriage. With one final reversal, she averted her eyes from worldly aspirations, for "alas to what end are all these thoughts." Having unburdened her soul to her children and herself, she recommitted her diary-keeping to "amuse, perhaps instruct me & you" (September 17, 1806, diary).

The anomalies produced in the cross-currents between individual autonomy and social bonds were no more starkly embodied than in enslaved African Americans. As forced servants and laborers, they provided the substructure for individuals' economic advancement and middle-class white families' support. Yet, the nation's political settlement deprived them of their rights to liberty and to binding affectional ties. Bayard Smith was acutely aware of this injustice at the heart of America. Although they did not own any enslaved African Americans in their first decade in Washington, the Smiths hired free and enslaved blacks as household servants and farm hands. Her days were enmeshed with their lives; her struggles entwined with the conflicts emanating from their dual status as their own persons and the property of others. The stories of these people punctuated her diaries and letters in her first years of married life. She recorded both her tussles with them over authority and her identity with them in resistance. In the covert stories of their lives were hidden discomfiting truths about white people who controlled their destinies.

In 1805 Bayard Smith published a children's story, *The Diversions of Sidney*. She addressed the book "To my youthful Readers," and she made them the subjects of her story. The *dramatis personae* were Bayard Smith, her husband, her sister Maria Bayard, daughter Julia, Matty, an eight-year-old enslaved girl whom the Smiths had hired to help about the house and to look after Julia, and the Fries children from a neighboring poor tenant farmer's family. A day in the life of Julia, who was at the time under five years old, structured the narrative. On first glance, the story presents an account of a happy family living a bucolic existence in the countryside. But signs of tension ripple the surface calm of the story, hinting at deeper disturbances beneath. Relations between black and white child, between mother and father, between parents and children are not what they seemed. The disjunctures, gaps, and silences contain a hidden story of centrifugal forces within the American family.

In the first episode, "Breakfast," Julia welcomes home her father, come from the city to breakfast with them. Julia and her mother surprise the father with a letter in verse, ostensibly from Julia to her father, entreating him to stay with them. By having the father read it aloud in the story, Bayard Smith had her husband publicly declaim her chastisement of him for abandoning the family. The poem reveals that Smith was not spending his leisure hours at home. To entice him back, Bayard Smith/Julia promises the mother's sexual offerings ("flowers" and kisses) and the children's good behavior. A disordered household, which perhaps had driven Smith away, would be made receptive and welcoming if the father would return. The wife and children would resume their obedient roles, ones they apparently had not been fulfilling. With the conclusion of these verses, the father disappears from the story.

The one who is playing her role well is Matty. Beyond being Julia's companion, Matty is her tutor and moral exemplar. The very fact of Matty's subservience underscores her moral superiority and intelligence. In the second chapter a dialogue between Matty and Julia demonstrates Matty's thoughtfulness and Julia's selfishness. Julia makes impertinent demands on another servant. In the exchange that follows, Matty reproves Julia for her bad manners and inconsiderateness. The black child expostulates concern for the servant and his horse, inculcating sympathetic identity with and good treatment of creatures who are forced to do whites' bidding. Throughout the book Matty exhibits a consideration for others' interests that highlighted Julia's peremptory demands. The mother never needs to reprimand the black child, as she does with Julia.

Within the frame of a happy family story, *Diversions of Sidney* contains a shadow narrative of broken family bonds and asocial behavior. Cloaked by her avowed intention of amusing and instructing her young readers, Bayard Smith's counter-propositions in the book were almost cruel. Samuel

Harrison Smith reads his own denunciation by his family. Matty is not just a paragon of virtue to Julia; she proves Julia's inferiority and Bayard Smith's disapproval of her own daughter. However good Matty is, the story stands as a reminder that she will always be in a subservient position to the white child. The most socialized and humane character in the book, Matty, is stripped of all family and personal ties. That Matty is the primary relation for Julia and the preferred child for Bayard Smith places in high relief the dissociation at work within the white family. Affections arise from natural affinities and cannot be relied on as a source of family cohesion or discipline.

The black enslaved child exemplifies individual potential and the restrictions placed upon fulfillment in the early republic. Her stance of moral authority and intellectual capacity throws into question the utility of family connections and support. White society casts her lot as depersonalized property, yet her personal accomplishments and sensibility abnegate that degrading classification. Her ambiguous status undercuts constituted lines of authority. In Bayard Smith's version of American society, whites look to blacks for moral precepts, and enslaved black Americans render whites' rule illegitimate.

In the period when Bayard Smith wrote and printed this children's book, she was in the midst of a prolonged crisis over Julia's development. Although confiding her anxiety about Julia's backwardness in letters to her sisters, Bayard Smith glossed over the fact of Julia's inarticulateness in both her diaries and in *Diversions of Sidney*. That Bayard Smith shaped a public version covering over her private dismay emphasized the discordant emotions she was experiencing in her family situation. In contrast, Matty outshone both the Smith girls in aptitude. As Bayard Smith trained her alongside Julia, the growing discrepancy became glaring. Matty became Bayard Smith's prize pupil. In her letters, she sometimes made invidious comparisons between her own daughters and Matty. She wrote to her sister in 1807 that "Maty has a mind & disposition that were it not for the misfortune of her birth, would make her a distinguished woman. How often when some trait of sensibility or genius, displays itself; do my eyes fill with tears as I look at her & from my heart I grieve that such a mind & heart is destined to servitude!" As if applying the lessons of her own life to Matty's, Bayard Smith observed that Matty had "such ambition to excell; such quickness of perception & such a lively imagination, that I fear calling those powers into exercise; even without reading she acquires knowledge too rapidly perhaps for her future happiness" (22 and 28 [?] 1807, to Maria Bayard).

Bayard Smith recognized the impact she had had on Matty. She "has caught many of my sentiments & feelings & has a refinement of taste that makes me tremble" for her fate in life. Nature's scenes and beauty "have for her, a pleasure, beyond what most children feel. She is excessively fond of poetry & commits it to memory with great facility, & a fine ear for musick. Poor Slave – And art thou doomed to bondage, to labour, to penury, with a heart & mind far more richly endowed than thy master's!" (April 1807, diary). Bayard Smith's rhetorical ending in her diary objectified Matty's status. As Bayard Smith scripted Matty's plight for her audience of posterity, she shifted the equation. From an equivalence of sensibility in which mistress and enslaved shared an identity of feelings and mental faculties, Bayard Smith elevated herself into an observer whose sympathy extended pity to the object of her regard. In adopting an almost elegiac tone, she placed a distance between Matty and herself, perhaps because of guilt at her dual role of nurturer and mistress (January 6, 1806, to Mary Ann Smith; *American Mother*, II, 33). She was all too aware of the contradictions of power. In both her letter and diary, she juxtaposed Matty's intellectual accomplishments with her inequivalent status.

No one knew better than Bayard Smith the frustrations of aspirations constrained by circumstances. Even as she inscribed the barriers of class and racial lines, she questioned their legitimacy, just as she resisted the boundaries enclosing families and confining women. In submitting to the duties of her station, she acknowledged them as constraints. She expected the same of enslaved blacks. In both cases, the act of submission eroded the structures of authority, rather than bolstering them. Early in her marriage, she had observed for herself "how incompatible, servile labour is with mental activity" (March 11, 1804, to Jane Bayard Kirkpatrick). She did not fail to apply the observation to those around her who were forced to labor, not only to Matty but to other enslaved blacks who worked for the Smiths.

In writing the stories of her servants Sukey and Jessy, along with Matty, into her diary, she projected their lives on to a screen for posterity – and herself – to view (May 25, 1806; July 4, [1806], diary). As she immersed herself in sympathetic feelings evoked by their plight, she also placed them at a distance (Stern, *Plight of Feeling*, 172–3). She objectified their sorrows in her historical record. While reflecting on the "dreadful scenes" precipitated by slavery's injustice, she participated in the system that produced them. Bayard Smith criticized "the distance at which most masters treat their slaves... They never become acquainted with the dispositions or characters of this unhappy race of beings." Unlike many slaveholders "who realy believe that their negroes are as devoid of understanding & affections as the brute creation & indeed esteem them in no other light than mere property," she knew "how different is this from reality." Bayard Smith's intimacy with her hired blacks made her feel their pain, but she was also a source of their pain. Like a voyeur, she experienced their sensations without suffering their circumstances. She identified with their desires and ambitions, but she exercised restraints on their autonomy that allowed her hers.

The complicated power relations between Bayard Smith and enslaved blacks reveal the limitations of sensibility. At the juncture of self-interest and fellow feeling, Bayard Smith suspended rational criticism and shifted to sympathy. Her feelings substituted for action; they lulled her into accepting the status quo both for herself and for them. Obscuring disparities in status and capacity between people, sympathy seemed to close the gap between self and others, but it also subordinated the other as an object of dependency, pity, or contempt. Although those in a dependent state could play upon emotions to serve their own ends, affections came into service for the subjection of others, most often females to the power of men and blacks to the needs of whites. Ensnared in her own family cares, Bayard Smith sympathized with the wrongs done to enslaved blacks, but her very sympathy could distance her from them. At times, it deflected her vision, shielding her from viewing her complicity in the system of subordination; but when confronted with the harsh terms of their condition, she did not avert her gaze from the unjust inequities between her and them.

In dismissing her black housekeeper, Sukey, for what Bayard Smith deemed intractable behavior, she nevertheless believed the servant to be "a most extraordinary woman, uniting the extreems of virtue & vice." Sukey's humane disposition and "most superiour powers of mind" greatly impressed Bayard Smith. She recognized that under different circumstances and with a good education Sukey's energy and ingeniousness would have led to exceptional accomplishments in whatever occupations she undertook. Bayard Smith's valediction for Sukey was "Her soul was not the soul of a slave" (c. July 4, [1806], diary). Bayard Smith saw herself reflected in Sukey. Her assessment of Sukey's potential and the limitations imposed upon it echoed her own feelings of constrained ambition.

As she had informed her fiancé on the eve of their marriage, she felt bound by "shackles" that her expanding soul would burst. To her sister, she confessed, "I have sometimes thought that my soul, when it was sent to seek its body here below, made some strange mistake, & that it was never design'd by its Creator, for the mansion it inhabits. Oh how hard at times, have I found it, to confine it within the narrow precincts, to which it is now circumscribed!" The record of her thoughts and sensations, "the history of my life," was so divergent from her life's external "circumstances & events" that the history "my biographer ... would write, would not be my history" (October 6 and 13, 1817, to Jane B. Kirkpatrick). This alienation from whom she appeared as opposed to whom she felt herself to be was the driving force behind her writing. Articulating her sense of herself let her see into others' inner qualities. In Sukey's and Matty's cases, their sensibilities resonated with her own.

In Bayard Smith's publications of the early 1820s, her American sensibility encompassed the possibility of social affiliations and intellectual capacity outside the bounds of middle-class white familial norms. She represented her disruptive critiques of social authority indirectly, through oppositional positions or from a moral posture. In her novel describing Washington's political life and women's role in it, *Winter in Washington, or Memoirs of the Seymour Family* (1824), the protofeminist Harriet Mortimer who articulated Bayard Smith's discontent with marital obligations was the antagonist, not the protagonist, proper wife and mother Mrs. Seymour. At the end of the novel, Bayard Smith blew up Mortimer in a steamboat accident. Her children's book *American Mother* (1823) contained the story "Old Betty," in which an old black woman's tale of profound racial alienation and hatred was resolved through Christian redemption (Teute, "In 'The Gloom of Evening,'" 48–58).

When she wrote her novel "Lucy" in the mid-1820s, she focused directly on the illegitimacy of patriarchal control and the intimate connections between blacks and whites. Her social realism communicated lower-class blacks' and whites' perspectives, unmediated. The lack of a middle-class moral frame offended her sponsors, who deemed the novel inappropriate for white female middle-class readers. "Lucy" never appeared in print. When Bayard Smith moved from sympathizing as an upper-class white woman with working-class blacks' and whites' aspirations to identifying their mutual interests in antagonism to race- and gender-based hierarchical authority, she eliminated the distance that objectified pity. She violated middle-class white sensibility and recorded an American sensibility that dared not speak its name, racial amalgamation (Teute, "'A Wild and Desolate Place'").

This censorship silenced black voices in Bayard Smith's subsequent publications and muffled her critical appraisal of American society. Wounded by the criticism and the novel's failure to get into print, she afterward wrote in more guarded tones on less controversial topics. Always in tension with itself, her sensibility shrank from its most expansive dimension. She did not abandon depicting family structures and a national political culture, but she refined her indirect modes for critiquing power relations in her subsequent publishing career. Knowing how to maintain family silences of her own, after the mid-1820s she kept silent about the darkest secret in the American family.

In her writings, as in her social life in Washington, Bayard Smith carried on a conversation constructing simultaneously the expansive potential of the American nation and her and other women's roles in it (Nina Baym,

American Women Writers). Because she apprehended the conflicting claims embodied in the American promise of freedom, embedded in all her works was a dialogue between social obligations and individual autonomy. Guided by a 1790s radical sensibility, Bayard Smith mapped a moral topography of the new republic. Rather than the endowment of explicit political privileges, the real power coordinates were the capacities of all individuals to exercise their reason and to experience fellow feeling. In spite of social inequalities, she recognized an equality in sensibility that legitimated for blacks and whites, women and men, the desire to achieve their own social and economic fulfillment. Her vision, like Lydia Maria Child's, encompassed a democratically heterogeneous society (Nelson, 104–9). Bayard Smith could imagine an inclusive America.

WORKS CITED

Barker-Benfield, G. J. *The Culture of Sensibility: Sex and Society in Eighteenth-Century Britain.* Chicago: University of Chicago Press, 1992.

Barnes, Elizabeth. *States of Sympathy: Seduction and Democracy in the American Novel.* New York: Columbia University Press, 1997.

Baym, Nina. *American Women Writers and the Work of History, 1790–1860.* New Brunswick: Rutgers University Press, 1995.

Brown, Chandos Michael. "Mary Wollstonecraft, or, the Female Illuminati: the Campaign Against Women and 'Modern Philosophy' in the Early Republic." *JER* 15 (1995): 389–424.

Cronin, James E., ed. *The Diary of Elihu Hubbard Smith (1771–1798).* Philadelphia: American Philosophical Society, 1973.

Fliegelman, Jay. *Prodigals and Pilgrims: the American Revolution Against Patriarchal Authority, 1750–1800.* Cambridge: Cambridge University Press, 1982.

Gould, Philip. *Covenant and Republic: Historical Romance and the Politics of Puritanism.* Cambridge and New York: Cambridge University Press, 1996.

Greenblatt, Stephen. *Renaissance Self-Fashioning: From More to Shakespeare.* Chicago: University of Chicago Press, 1980.

Jabour, Anya. *Marriage in the Early Republic: Elizabeth and William Wirt and the Companionate Ideal.* Baltimore: Johns Hopkins University Press, 1998.

Jones, Chris. *Radical Sensibility: Literature and Ideas in the 1790s.* London and New York: Routledge, 1993.

Kelley, Mary. "Designing a Past for the Present: Women Writing Women's History in Nineteenth-Century America." *Proceedings of the American Antiquarian Society* 105 (1995): 315–46.

"Reading Women/Women Reading: the Making of Learned Women in Antebellum America." *Journal of American History* 83 (1996): 401–24.

Lewis, Jan. "The Republican Wife: Virtue and Seduction in the Early Republic." *WMQ* 3.44 (1987): 689–721.

Lockridge, Kenneth A. *On the Sources of Patriarchal Rage: the Commonplace Books of William Byrd and Thomas Jefferson and the Gendering of Power in the Eighteenth Century.* New York: New York University Press, 1992.

Nelson, Dana D. *National Manhood: Capitalist Citizenship and the Imagined Fraternity of White Men*. Durham: Duke University Press, 1998.

Smith, Margaret Bayard. Papers. Library of Congress, Washington, DC.

American Mother; or, The Seymour Family. Part 1, *The Bees*, and part 2 [no half title]. 2 vols. in 1. Washington, DC: Davis and Force, 1823.

"By a Friend of Youth." *The Diversions of Sidney*. Washington, DC: n.p., 1805.

"The Evils of Reserve in Marriage," signed "N." *Monthly Magazine, and American Review* 2 (1800): 409–11.

"Lines By a Young Lady. Written at the Falls of Passaick, July, 1800," signed "M." *Monthly Magazine, and American Review* 3 (1800): 399.

Stern, Julia A. *The Plight of Feeling: Sympathy and Dissent in the Early American Novel*. Chicago: University of Chicago Press, 1997.

Teute, Fredrika J. "In 'The Gloom of Evening': Margaret Bayard Smith's View in Black and White of Early Washington Society." *Proceedings of the American Antiquarian Society* 106 (1996): 37–58.

"Roman Matron on the Banks of Tiber Creek: Margaret Bayard Smith and the Politicization of Spheres in the Nation's Capital." *A Republic for the Ages: the United States Capitol and the Political Culture of the Early Republic*. Ed. Donald R. Kennon. Charlottesville: University Press of Virginia, 1999. 89–121.

"'A Wild and Desolate Place': Life on the Margins in Early Washington." *Southern City, National Ambition: the Growth of Early Washington, 1800–1860*. Ed. Howard Gillette, Jr. Washington, DC: George Washington University Press, 1995. 47–68, 97–102.

Ziff, Larzer. *Writing in the New Nation: Prose, Print, and Politics in the Early United States*. New Haven: Yale University Press, 1991.

10

GAIL K. SMITH

The sentimental novel: the example of Harriet Beecher Stowe

When Rose Terry Cooke ended her 1884 biographical sketch of Harriet Beecher Stowe calling her "America's greatest woman," many readers might still have agreed with her.[1] Memories of *Uncle Tom's Cabin*, as well as the nearly forty other books and hundreds of articles Stowe produced during her long career, had not gone, though Stowe had largely stopped publishing after her last novel, *Poganuc People* (1878). Nor did those memories ever entirely die. Dramatic adaptations of *Uncle Tom's Cabin* appeared continuously on the American stage until at least the 1930s,[2] and the 1920s saw critics Constance Rourke and Vernon Parrington noting her importance in American literary history. From then on, Stowe has been gradually taking her place among the nineteenth-century authors who seem most worthy of study.

Particularly as the New Criticism gave way to reader-response criticism, feminist literary criticism, Marxist criticism, and cultural studies, Stowe became a natural choice for critics seeking interesting paradigms to study. *Uncle Tom's Cabin* (1852), probably the best-selling book of the century and certainly internationally famous, is a historical phenomenon impossible to ignore; its interpretation has ranged from protests against its racial stereotyping to admiration for its millennial evangelical feminism and its Balzacian scope. The New England novels, including *The Minister's Wooing* (1859), *The Pearl of Orr's Island* (1862), *Oldtown Folks* (1869) and *Poganuc People*, are taking their place in discussions of regionalism, feminist history, and the liberalization of Calvinist theology in which Stowe played so large a part. Her New York novels, *Pink and White Tyranny* (1871), *My Wife and I* (1871), and *We and Our Neighbors* (1875) are being studied as early exempla of the society novel of manners and morals that Edith Wharton and Henry James would soon perfect. Her most overtly feminist book, an exposé of Lord Byron's incest with his half-sister, *Lady Byron Vindicated* (1870), a sensation in its time, is beginning to claim the attention of scholars of nineteenth-century feminism. And her domestic essays remain fruitful sources for studies of national mores and the politics of gender.

As the first of the nineteenth-century American women whom we now call sentimental novelists to be recovered for serious and sustained scholarship in the last few decades, Stowe has played a vital role in the reevaluation of twentieth-century critical assumptions and practices that have for so long marginalized women writers, especially those of her century. The ability of her fiction and nonfiction to effect these critical revolutions comes in part from the way her work exhibits some of the methods and concerns associated with the traditional mid-nineteenth-century male canon codified in works like F. O. Matthiesson's *American Renaissance: Art and Expression in the Age of Emerson and Whitman* (1941, 1968). Her work repays study in the context of Hawthorne, Melville, and Whitman as much as it does in the context of Susan Warner, Elizabeth Stuart Phelps, and Sarah Orne Jewett.

Born into a famous family of evangelical reformers, and a well-informed lay theologian in her own right, Stowe occupies a distinct place in literary history. In particular, her constant interest in words and the Word marks a significant difference between her work and that of most other prominent women writers of her time. Other evangelical sentimental writers like Susan Warner and Maria Cummins share little of the concerns with language and its meaning, the Bible and its authority, that crop up so frequently in a work by Stowe. The same preoccupations make her work distinct from classic regionalist works like *The Country of the Pointed Firs*. Even other disgruntled Calvinist writers – Catharine Sedgwick, Elizabeth Stuart Phelps, Gail Hamilton, or Rose Terry Cooke – do not share Stowe's consistent fascination with the language of theology and the Bible.

Despite her reliance on a long-marginalized form, the sentimental novel, Stowe's work does not require readers to reject standards of "epistemological complexity," as Jane Tompkins has proposed.[3] Though critics continue to locate the nineteenth century's concern with reading, interpretation, and ambiguity primarily in Hawthorne's "A" or Melville's doubloon, Stowe was far more invested personally and professionally in the great hermeneutic debates of her day – particularly in the century's unprecedented upheavals in biblical criticism, on which many other interpretive struggles depended – than were writers like Hawthorne or Melville. Hermeneutic concerns fill Stowe's fiction and nonfiction, from her 1833 satire on "Modern Uses of Language" to her last novel. Repeatedly Stowe raises the kinds of textual questions that continue to engage theorists of literature, culture, and pedagogy: What does it mean to read as a woman or with the oppressed? Can a man read as a woman, or a European American as an African American? Can – or should – diverse readers achieve consensus? Do interpretive communities wholly construct textual meaning?

Critics like Sacvan Bercovitch and Jonathan Arac have highlighted the role of interpretive battles over the Constitution in works by Douglass, Melville, Hawthorne, and others. Yet as Stowe's work indicates, the century's anxieties about interpretation and epistemology were far more broadly diffused across gender and cultural lines than these studies have suggested, affecting such diverse areas as women's education, art criticism, Bible reading, and literary interpretation. Analyzing the hermeneutic cultural work performed in the fiction and nonfiction of Stowe allows us to examine a much wider representation of critical moments in nineteenth-century reading theory and practice. While this chapter can only highlight selected examples, its aim is to suggest the centrality of these issues in the work of a female author, their broad popular expansion from their highbrow origins, and their familiarity and relevance in our own current interpretive debates. Stowe's work within the sentimental novel tradition operates as a lens through which to view some of the critical issues in the politics of reading in the nineteenth century.

Linguistic ferment

Stowe began to publish during the heyday of American theorizing about sacred and secular words. Beginning in the 1820s and 1830s, intellectuals in the theological seminaries and universities and outside them were absorbing and applying the philological research of European scholars, especially the new German biblical criticism. Filtered through American intellectuals like George Bancroft, Edward Everett, Ralph Waldo Emerson, Moses Stuart, Andrews Norton, Joseph Buckminster, Horace Bushnell, Margaret Fuller, Elizabeth Peabody, and Theodore Parker, the so-called "higher criticism" used classical philological methods to question traditional ideas of biblical inspiration and authorship. European critics like J. G. Eichhorn, J. D. Michaelis, and J. G. von Herder had begun to call attention to the "Oriental" and mythic character of, for instance, Genesis and Revelation, which led to urgent questions about whether the Bible was really inspired, or simply to be read like any other ancient book. If parts of it were mythic, might the whole book be mythic? If Genesis is a myth, is the resurrection? If the Bible is a historically mediated document full of the detritus of its progress through millennia of human development, in what sense can the Bible be appealed to as a source of truth? Manuscript studies flourished in debates over the authorship and authenticity of individual canonical books. For instance, the traditional theory that Moses authored the Pentateuch was by the end of the century generally discredited. Many individual Old Testament books were shown to be spliced together from multiple traditionary sources. The Gospels were shown to date from decades after the life of Jesus, calling their eye-witness character into question. As a consequence, by the end of the century calls for "expurgating" the scriptures of inauthentic books or pernicious doctrine were becoming common, from Robert G. Ingersoll to Elizabeth Cady Stanton in *The Woman's Bible*. The wide impact, even today, of the higher criticism in religious and secular circles underscores Philip Gura's observation: "After the rise of the Higher Criticism, 'meaning' never again could be the same" (*Wisdom of Words*, 170).

In Stowe's time, the debates over the status of words and texts often mingled the sacred and the secular. Upheavals in biblical criticism were complemented by the popular media's frequent attention to linguistic subjects of all kinds. Even the miscellaneous new *Western Monthly Magazine* of raw 1830s Cincinnati often featured articles on sacred and secular language. Ideas abounded about signification, the origins of language, the "language" of nature, and the unity of all languages, with theories ranging from the sublime to what now seems the ridiculous.

Stowe's developing career as a writer coincided with these developments. Born a New Englander, Harriet Beecher moved West in 1832 with her entire family when her father, the Revd Lyman Beecher, took the post of president of Cincinnati's Lane Seminary, then an outpost of Calvinist orthodoxy. Nicole Tonkovich and Joan Hedrick have established the importance of this seedtime of Stowe's literary career, especially of the Semi-Colon Club, an informal literary society of displaced New Englanders for which Harriet Beecher wrote the kind of "parlor literature" popular at the time: sketches, satires, short stories, and poetry.[4] But her first published product from this literary apprenticeship, even before her prize story "Uncle Lot" (1834), was a satire on "Modern Uses of Language" published anonymously in the *Western Monthly* in 1833. The piece draws on the popularity of linguistic studies to lampoon the impenetrable language of some philosophers and theologians, and the utter vapidity of literary language in Jacksonian America. Though a light essay written primarily for entertainment, Harriet Beecher's first published piece nevertheless quietly and anonymously inaugurated her career as an interpreter of sacred and secular texts.

While Stowe was not educated as a biblical scholar or linguistic philosopher, she was a well-educated laywoman, familiar from her youth with the Bible; major works of Jonathan Edwards, Samuel Hopkins, and other Calvinist theologians; and various Calvinist theological controversies in detail. Her lifelong religious education began with her own very public family, whose crusading temperaments and disputatious intellects gave rise to the term "Beecherism." Simply being a Beecher meant that one absorbed a good deal of theological education; family discussions late into the night on serious doctrinal questions were commonplace, and the daughters were full participants. All six of Stowe's brothers followed their father Lyman Beecher – one of the nineteenth century's most famous preachers – into the ministry. Among them, Edward Beecher and Henry Ward Beecher in particular took leading roles in shaking the traditional foundations of American Calvinism. The scholarly Edward, in an effort to correlate original sin with future retribution, became notorious for positing the preexistence of souls. The eloquent Henry Ward became a giant of the American pulpit, making his Plymouth Church in Brooklyn both an antislavery stronghold and a center for the neo-Calvinist "liberal orthodoxy" he and his sister Harriet helped popularize. Unlike his revivalist father's more traditional Calvinism, with its emphasis upon the sinner's struggle toward true conviction of sin and a cataclysmic conversion experience of self-abasement before divine sovereignty, Henry Ward's theology exhibited "a confidence that religious truth could be perceived intuitively, an appeal to experience, a great stress upon the human consciousness and therefore upon religious education, and a highly Christocentric vision" (Caskey, *Chariot of Fire*, 229). Much like his sister's novels, Henry Ward Beecher's powerful sermons deemphasized dogma and divine wrath, wooing instead with the emotive power of the gracious love of Jesus.

Though barred from literal pulpits, most of the Beecher daughters nevertheless took evangelizing roles. The eldest, Catharine Beecher, became one of the century's most important educational and domestic reformers. Both alone and in her extensive networks, she raised the national consciousness in the cause of "female" education and influence, writing pioneering texts on domestic economy and the moral influence of the woman-led Christian home, and founding young women's secondary schools with curricula unusually rigorous and "masculine" for her time. The youngest Beecher daughter, Isabella Beecher Hooker, was an important player in the women's rights movements of the 1870s and 1880s, as well as a leading supporter of spiritualism.

Harriet Beecher, too, identified herself with the reforming preacher's role from the time of her earliest work experience, when she acted as spiritual counselor to her students at Catharine's Hartford Female Seminary beginning in 1827.[5] To her brother George she wrote in a prophetic letter around 1830, "Indeed it is as much my vocation to preach on paper as it is that of my brothers to preach viva voce."[6] In Cincinnati she married in 1836 the Revd Dr. Calvin E. Stowe, then Professor of Biblical Literature at Lane Seminary, and later at Andover Theological Seminary. Calvin Stowe was both a born scholar and a down-to-earth Yankee storyteller. He combined his gifts in reading voraciously in the new German biblical criticism, translating key texts into English, and bringing much of the new scholarship to the layperson's level in several popular books he wrote on the Bible. His wife gleaned a good deal from her "old Rabbi," as she called him, while herself reading daily in the Bible, biblical commentaries, and the religious press, and producing scores of reviews, editorials, and articles on religious questions.

Uncle Tom's Cabin and the slavery debates

Stowe's rhetorical and theological interests would stand her in good stead as the debates over slavery intensified, especially as the arguments on both sides turned to the Bible. By the mid-1830s the debate was at its hottest, reflecting the intense sectional differences leading up to the Civil War. On both sides, hundreds of tracts, books, and addresses mined the Bible for vindication while vilifying the opposing side for manipulating scripture. Drawing together her abolitionist sympathies and her interests in language, biblical interpretation, and preaching, Stowe began what was to be a long career in the sentimental novel, "a political enterprise, halfway between sermon and social theory, that both codifies and attempts to mold the values of its time" by its effect on the reader's heart (Tompkins, *Sensational Designs*, 126). In *Uncle Tom's Cabin*, Stowe plunges into the contested linguistics of slavery, highlighting questions of letter and spirit, literal and figurative, orality and literacy, sympathy and skepticism in ways that owe much to the higher criticism. Throughout the novel she plays with biblical language in order to bring her readers to participate in reading ambiguous texts for truth.

One way in which this happens is Stowe's play with the multivalency of particular words which had become battlegrounds in the biblical investigations of proslavery and abolitionist writers. *Uncle Tom's Cabin* and its sequel, *The Key to Uncle Tom's Cabin*, capitalize on the on-going disputes about the meaning of "buy," "sell," "own," "master," "servant" and other such economic terms in scriptural passages about servitude (e.g., did Abraham really "buy" as perpetual slaves the large human retinue that formed his household?). In *Uncle Tom's Cabin*'s interweaving rhetorics of accounting and reckoning, redeeming and buying, mastery and ownership, Stowe encourages us to read her words figuratively, for their heavenly sense – to perceive the spirit behind the letter. As she tells us when the check for a slave sale is sent up to "the Christian firm of B. & Co., New York," the reverse of the check should record the promise of recompense from "the great Paymaster, to whom they shall make up their account in a future day" (291).

Stowe also seeks to educate her reader through her novel's juxtapositions of biblical arguments on slavery. She never tries explicitly to resolve the contradictions she brings up. For instance, in a paradigmatic scene on the steamboat *La Belle Riviere*, two clergymen swap Bible passages on opposing sides of the slavery issue. One quotes a typical proslavery passage: "Cursed be Canaan, a servant of servants shall he be unto his brethren" (Genesis 9:25), Noah's curse on the progeny of his son Ham, who had disgraced his father when Noah lay naked in a drunken stupor (the passage became a rallying point for many who believed Africans to be descended from Ham). Stowe's other clergyman, however, promptly caps this citation with the New Testament's golden rule, "All things whatsoever ye would that men should do unto you, do ye even so unto them" (Matthew 7:12), a key text in the antislavery biblical arsenal (107–8). Simply by laying this juxtaposition before us, Stowe implies that we are to decide – whatever the letters of the Bible may be made to say – which man has the correct interpretation of the spirit of the Bible, in accord with the "sympathies of Christ."

The distinction between the spirit and the letter runs throughout *Uncle Tom's Cabin* as well. We see earthly life continually described as merely a shadow of, or code for, its heavenly reality. Stowe often presents the Bible itself as a set of earthly "hieroglyphics," "mystic imagery" which stands for God but can only be fully understood when read in faith by the liberated soul (226). The best readers of the Bible in the novel are those who remain uncorrupted by too much literary or theological education: Tom and Eva. Precisely because the Bible is written by "ignorant and unlearned men" (101), both Tom and Eva naturally read it with the kind of imaginative "sympathy" that the biblical critic J. G. von Herder argued was the one major requisite for reading the Bible aright.[7] Such artless reading is what the skeptical, educated Augustine St. Clare finds so difficult. In this most Protestant novel, no commentaries or learned notations are deemed necessary – just a simple, direct, unmediated encounter with the Word, reading the letters with your soul.

This method was also the way she hoped readers would read her novel. Stowe maintained that even her critics would come around if they simply "were permitted quietly & dispassionately to read" the novel.[8] Yet many readers publicly doubted its veracity as a picture of slavery "as it is." The proliferation of "misreadings" suggested that, in practice, some readers needed to be educated explicitly in how to read the novel. Like many a Protestant biblical scholar – including her own husband – Stowe surrendered and published a commentary on her sacred text: *The Key to Uncle Tom's Cabin* (1853).

The Key to Uncle Tom's Cabin

The title of the *Key* links it with numerous "keys" to the scriptures published before and after her novel. It suggests that *Uncle Tom's Cabin* is not immediately self-evident as a text – that it is a hieroglyphic Bible, not simply that readers who misread it needed to be educated to read it right. The very move to publish a *Key* signifies the dichotomy between faith in the reader (which implies a faith in an unambiguous text) and a fear of misreading. Nevertheless, it initially appears that Stowe translated her faith in the reader into the actual form of her commentary on *Uncle Tom's Cabin*. Placing key documents side by side throughout the *Key*, Stowe explains that she "has endeavoured to lay before the world, in the fullest manner all that can be objected to her work, that both sides may have an opportunity of impartial hearing" (129–30). She quotes frequently, for instance, from unfavorable reviews of her work and critical letters she has received from readers, then places next to them testimonies from slaveholders or escaped slaves, excerpts from slave law, and so forth, to prove them wrong. She juxtaposes southern claims of the kindly treament slaves receive with southern advertisements for runaways, who are frequently described as maimed in some way. Southern protestations about the security of the slave family are set beside newspaper advertisements of individual and single-sex slave sales.

The *Key*'s structure, then, implies Stowe's long-standing belief in the reader's ability to judge between two contradictory texts in order to strike out the truth. Nevertheless, she cannot, it turns out, trust to her readers to come to her own conclusions about conflicting texts. In the *Key*, she continually steps in to critique or extol individual documents while shepherding her reader through her arguments. Moreover, like the biblical debates it reproduces, the *Key*, despite Stowe's best intentions, inevitably highlights a contradiction in the text of scripture in its juxtapositions of Old and New Testament passages and of different readings of the same passage. Her attempts to educate the reader through juxtapositions ultimately backfire by suggesting the possibility of indeterminacy in the very Bible that was to resolve the conflict.

Dred; a Tale of the Great Dismal Swamp

Dred; a Tale of the Great Dismal Swamp (1856) is even more obviously conflicted in its treatment of slavery and the word. *Dred*'s focus – in and with its complex analysis of slavery – is on the meaning of literacy and the possibility of resolving interpretive conflict. Stowe attends in *Dred* to the literacy education of all her characters, and to readings of foundational American documents like the Declaration of Independence, the law, and the Bible. Moreover, characters' lives and happiness depend on how key texts are interpreted, and those interpretations are the subject of much thoughtful debate. With a variety of readers in the novel, interpretations proliferate.

Readings in *Dred* vary widely, depending on the gender, race, class, and creed of the reader. In *Dred*, the only way to approach truth and avoid a national Armageddon is to read with others who are unlike yourself. Ultimately, however, what was merely a specter raised in the *Key*, with its pro- and antislavery arguments taken from the same Bible, becomes a tangible threat in *Dred*: two or more people may honestly read the same words and come to irreconcilably opposed conclusions about their meaning. When the text in the scenario is important enough, violence is the result.

Dred took shape against the backdrop of several mission campaigns of the 1850s calling for "Bibles for Slaves." From *Uncle Tom's Cabin* onward, Stowe, too, helped keep the scandal of slave illiteracy before the public in the *Key*, her 1854 travel letters (*Sunny Memories of Foreign Lands*), and her 1855 *Geography*. Her disgust with the prevailing system of "oral religion instruction of the Negro" stemmed both from its prevention of literacy and from its censorship of the Bible to prevent slaves' knowledge of dangerous passages. But the character of Dred in Stowe's novel is built on the stories of literate slave revolutionaries Nat Turner and Denmark Vesey, who were in fact widely interpreted as cautionary tales against teaching slaves to read. It was their very literacy which spurred swift retribution in the form of antiliteracy laws in many southern states. In *Dred*, though the noblest characters argue strongly (like Eva) for teaching slaves to read, especially to read the Bible, Dred is the dominant figure of the black reader, and he is huge, Samson-like, a gigantic and fearful force for the white characters in the book, and evidently for Stowe herself as well. His Bible reading is as far removed from Uncle Tom's as one could imagine, based more on the Old Testament than the New, and finding in the Bible divine sanction for violence against white oppressors. His reading is what Stowe calls punningly a "portent of dread," a prophecy of imminent race war.

Dred's readings often come into conflict with those of other characters, black and white, male and female. And continually in *Dred*, cross-interpretations of authoritative political or religious texts happen either between black and white readers or between men and women. An especially striking demonstration of the impact of reading across racial lines occurs at the midpoint of the novel. At a southern camp meeting, Father Bonnie, a popular slaveholding divine, preaches a rousing revival sermon calling worshipers to the front to proclaim their conversion: "Brethren, we are seeing a day from the Lord! We've got a glorious time! . . . The Lord is coming among us!"

> But all of a sudden, every one was startled by a sound which seemed to come pealing down directly from the thick canopy of pines over the heads of the ministers.

"Woe unto you that desire the day of the Lord! To what end shall it be for *you*? The day of the Lord shall be darkness, and not light! . . . Let all the inhabitants of the land tremble! for the day of the Lord cometh!" (I, 319–20)

It is the sonorous voice of Dred, hidden among the trees, reinterpreting the white preacher's sermon about the "day of the Lord" with a completely different meaning – a day of wrath and mourning – taken from the prophet Joel. And in this *agon* of arguments, Dred significantly speaks from above and has the last word.

In other scenes Stowe similarly depicts the striking effects of reading a text across lines of race. The idealistic southern lawyer Edward Clayton, for instance, learns to loathe slave law by interpreting it through the eyes of a slave friend, Harry Gordon. Similarly, Dred's little swamp colony of fugitive slaves holds its own impassioned reading of the white-authored Declaration of Independence. And both the white heroine Nina Gordon and the illiterate old slave Tiff find the Bible comes alive as Nina reads daily aloud to him in his garden.

Readings which cross gender lines are nearly as important in *Dred*. The heroine, Nina Gordon, insists on her right to read Byron's *Don Juan* as much as any man. And as Dred and his male followers cry for an Old Testament-style vengeance after one of their number has been murdered, the slave woman Milly arrives to interpose an alternate biblical reading: "Vengeance is mine – I will repay, saith de Lord. Like he loved us when we was enemies, love yer enemies!" (II, 234).

Though most of Stowe's exempla in *Dred* stress the need for whites to read with the eyes of the slave, or men to read like women, Stowe complicates the picture by locating distortions even in the interpretations of the oppressed. Dred's Bible-reading, for instance, is certainly powerful, but it is also presented as distorted to some extent by his single-minded focus on wrath and revenge. Although Stowe's liberal white characters argue for freedom of the press and literacy education for the slave, the white hero, Clayton, stresses the need for "systematic education by which we shall acquire that influence over [the slaves'] minds which our superior cultivation will enable us to hold. Then, as fast as they become fitted to enjoy rights, we must grant them" (II, 314–15). The rebellious slaves' appropriation of the Declaration of Independence receives somewhat ambivalent support as well, with Clayton sympathizing but objecting to the complete fitness of the analogy. In effect the need for black readers to see through white readers' eyes seems greater than its counterpart. When Tiff rejects the idea of having another slave read to him, saying he "would rather have white teaching" (I, 33), Nina then selects the readings (the Gospels only, nothing from the books

Dred loves) and in fact carries out the same kind of selective "oral religious instruction of the Negro" that Stowe rails against elsewhere in the novel.

At the same time, Stowe points to problems which undercut her cross-reading model entirely: "There is no study in human nature more interesting than the aspects of the same subject seen in the points of view of different characters. One might almost imagine that there were no such thing as absolute truth, since a change of situation or temperament is capable of changing the whole force of an argument" (II, 213). The proliferation of cross-readings could therefore actually lead, not to "absolute truth," but to absolute uncertainty about the truth of a sacred text. This is precisely what begins to happen in the novel, especially in reference to the Bible.

Dred suggests that the varying interpretations of a text may finally not be entirely due to differences between readers. Stowe's explanations of the differences in interpretation raise the real possibility that the Bible itself may be, in each reading, a different book: that the text itself changes with the change of readers. As one proslavery character in *Dred* remarks, "That blessed book is a savor of life unto life when it's used right; but it's a savor of death unto death when ignorant people take hold of it" (I, 196). Harry declares to a lawyer friend, "I can assure you the Bible looks as different to a slave from what it does to a master, as everything else in the world does" (II, 203). Dred reads what Stowe calls "the Bible of his father" or "the Bible of Denmark Vesey," a way of phrasing that heightens the suggestion that each reader reads a different Bible – the Bible of whoever is reading it. In an intriguing scene, the Bible itself seems to fight on two sides. Father Bonnie, some time after his camp-meeting sermon, opens his Bible for a proslavery passage and inadvertently reads aloud, "Masters, give unto your servants that which is just and equal," before he recovers and reads instead, "Servants, obey your masters" (II, 193). In looking for a univocal Bible, he confronts a multivocal Bible instead.

The inviolability of truth suffers in *Dred*, then, because the many different readings of the Bible in the novel suggest not simply that readers differ, but that the biblical text contains difference. "The Bible of Denmark Vesey" is not the Bible of Tom or Eva. From *Uncle Tom's Cabin*, through the *Key*, to *Dred*, Stowe moves from a faith in the reader and the text, to a fear of misreading, to a fear of the unresolved contradictions in the sacred word. More than any other of Stowe's works, *Dred* presents the terrifying possibility that there can be no such thing as an authorized reading – because there is no such thing as "the text."[9] For a nation which posited its identity and unity on authoritative founding texts, this was a potentially devastating proposition. The novel, like the constitutional debates of the same time, suggests that interpretive contradiction may lead to national collapse.

The New England novels

From the apocalyptic *Dred* onward, however, race largely disappears from Stowe's fiction. Instead, gender and reading take key roles. In her New England novels of 1859–69, Stowe debates women's access to the sacred and secular word, both in private reading and in public schooling, and especially in coeducational schooling. In the culminating *Lady Byron Vindicated* (1870) and the 1869 article from which the book grew, Stowe takes up all the strands she had been weaving about sexual and literary double standards, the woman educated "like a man," and the pernicious effects of single-sex interpretation.

Typically, advice writers from the late eighteenth century onward offered cautionary tales about overreading – too many novels, too much study – featuring a disproportionate number of female examples. Horror stories abounded of seducers plying their potential victims with novels until they succumbed, of novel-obsessed mothers fatally neglecting their children, and of overeducated women unable to bear children. With the wrong reading so harmful to women's sexual purity and gender identity, advice writers generally insisted on limiting women's access to the word.

Stowe both asked a different question – "What effect does gender have on reading?" – and came up with a different answer. Familiar from childhood with the arguments for restricting access to fiction, Stowe shows a guilty yearning for fiction in several letters of her young womanhood.[10] By the 1850s she had read the scandalous novels of Eugene Sue and George Sand, and was reading Scott to her children.[11] In her fiction of the period, Stowe developed the argument not only that women need equal access to the word, but that men and women need to read and interpret the same texts together. Her fiction specifically counters the old horror stories about women reading, or reading like or with men. Where a quintessential scene of reading in *Dred* is a white reader and a black reader interpreting the same document (complicated by the "need" for white readers to temper and instruct the interpretations of black readers), the later fiction takes up a new idealized scene: the white male and female student, of the same middle or upper class, poring over a book together. The focus of national salvation through textual interpretation becomes the mutual reading of the sexes.

The Minister's Wooing features the heroine Mary Scudder's alter ego, Virginie de Frontignac, who has been educated in a French convent which forbade novel-reading. Educated in matters of the spirit but not of the body, Virginie knows nothing about her natural sexual feelings. As a result, she marries a man her family chooses but whom she does not love, leaving her wholly unprepared for the sexual allure of Aaron Burr. In a complete reversal of the normal novel/seduction horror story, Virginie is actually ripe for seduction because she has not read any novels. The loss Stowe laments is Virginie's knowledge of her own sexuality – just what advice writers sought to keep women readers from discovering through novels.

Oldtown Folks at first seems more vexed, as French novels in particular are critiqued for their license, and the talented and beautiful Emily Rossiter falls prey to her seducer, Ellery Davenport, after reading French novels (particularly Rousseau's *Nouvelle Héloïse*). However, Stowe takes pains to show that it is actually an inhuman strain of New England theology that is to blame for driving Emily away from home and into sexual immorality. And indeed, for Emily much of Rousseau's appeal – even the appeal of *La Nouvelle Héloïse* – is theological, perfectly suited to the quandaries into which Dr. Stern's preaching has thrust her. The novel most vehemently interdicted for American women thus becomes in Stowe's hands an alternate – and more humane – spiritual text for women.

As the nineteenth century progressed, the arguments over women's access to texts began to turn somewhat. Though worries about novels lingered in the evangelical press and more conservative educational institutions after the Civil War, concerns over women's access to the word turned more often to their unprecedented advances in intellectual attainments traditionally reserved for men. For example, Harvard trustee and former medical professor Dr. Edward Clarke argued at length and with the authority of his position in his famous *Sex in Education; or, A Fair Chance for the Girls* (1873) that young women who engaged in long periods of reading and study like that expected of college-bound young men risked becoming sterile, unsexed "agenes." Clarke's and similar claims continued to be cited for decades to link gynecological theories with women's education.

Even some women writers helped perpetuate this view. Augusta Jane Evans Wilson's best-selling romance *St. Elmo* (1866), for instance, featured an extremely learned heroine but sent a clear warning with her near-death from too much brain work. Stowe, however, showed intellectual women being fertile, maternal, even sexy. When her learned women suffer moral crises – Mrs. Marvyn in *The Minister's Wooing*, who studies optics and chemistry between household duties; Esther Avery, Emily Rossiter, and Miss Mehitable, in *Oldtown Folks* – it is from the sterility, not of their wombs, but of the male theologies they inherit. In fact, the only Stowe character injured by overstudy is a man, Horace Holyoke's father, in *Oldtown Folks*. Stowe's fictional portrayals of the relation of intellect to gender ally her therefore with her contemporaries who insisted on the lack of intrinsic relation between physical health and book-learning in women. Julia Ward Howe, for instance, argued that "Boys as well as girls break down under severe study, men as well as women, and at least as often."[12] Stowe's friend Elizabeth Stuart Phelps averred that if young female graduates become sick and debilitated, as Clarke claimed, it is because they have *"stopped* studying."[13] Stowe's intellectually gifted Tina Percival in *Oldtown Folks* illustrates the point. Her unhappy marriage to the rake Ellery Davenport happens in large part because of her postgraduate depression.

In one kind of female education, however, Stowe does acknowledge hazards to womankind. In *The Minister's Wooing, Agnes of Sorrento, The Pearl of Orr's Island*, and *Oldtown Folks* a young woman's male teacher falls in love with her with unfortunate consequences. (By *Oldtown Folks*, Stowe has Tina awaken passionate feelings in no fewer than three male teachers.) As the problem of the sexualized teacher–student relationship grows in Stowe's fiction, however, an alternate paradigm also enters its pages. In *Pearl* and especially *Oldtown Folks*, the model of young men and women being students together becomes clearly an ideal in contrast to the power-imbalanced relationship between older male teachers and younger female students. In *Pearl*, for instance, the otherwise largely irrelevant subplot of the passionate teacher–student relationship of Mr. Sewell and Dolores Mendoza serves as a foil to the more rational relationship between Moses and Mara that grows up under coeducation.

The Pearl of Orr's Island is an interesting stop along the way in the debates over gender and the word. Nineteenth-century arguments on coeducation were always intrinsically and explicitly linked with theories of male and female difference or likeness. The most successful arguments in the later nineteenth century – partly in response to the popularization of Darwinian concepts of the evolution of the sexes – were those that conceded that men and women were fundamentally different in body and mind, and for that very reason needed to be educated together. As *Pearl*'s heroine Mara Lincoln crosses over into male educational precincts by beginning the study of Latin with her foster-brother Moses Pennel, what had been a traditionally gendered balance of power between them begins to shift. Stowe makes clear the inequalities and injustices that remain in their relationship because of their genders. Moreover, while the novel takes a dim view of Moses's scornful masculinity, it only begins an ambivalent critique of Mara's Griselda-style womanhood. *Pearl* is consistent with the arguments of the time over coeducation and gender difference in the ways it mingles its meditations on both subjects and seems to be searching for a logically defensible position.

Oldtown Folks pays greater attention to the coeducational arguments and pushes further the coordinating thoughts about androgyny and the overlapping of gender characteristics. Tina and Harry Percival (brother and sister), Horace Holyoke (the narrator), and Esther Avery (daughter of the local clergyman) study together in Cloudland Academy under the gifted Jonathan Rossiter (modeled on Stowe's early teacher, John Pierce Brace, in the coeducational Litchfield Academy). Repeatedly the narrator of *Oldtown Folks* emphasizes the idyllic nature of their coeducation. Tina and Esther read Greek and Latin with Harry and Horace, and the novel offers much discussion of the mutual intellectual benefit of their reading together. When Harry and Horace begin at college, they lament for pages the absence of the young women and their insights in their reading.

Harry and Esther, Horace and Tina eventually marry, anticipating Julia Ward Howe's argument about solid marriages being formed through coeducation's rational companionship of the sexes. Stowe's rhetoric makes coeducation and marriage nearly indistinguishable, each sex fulfilling and complementing each other, forming what Horace calls a Platonic "MAN-WOMAN" (1305). Not only is each half of the two couples a complement for the other half, but each marriage avoids the traditional patriarchal model. Stowe even provides the self-consciously androgynous voice of Horace Holyoke to tell this story of coeducation and gender-crossing. *Oldtown Folks* embeds in its form the gender-swapping of its coeducational double-marriage plot.

Lady Byron Vindicated

But the most dramatic arguments Stowe made on the relation of sex to the word were her 1869 article and subsequent book on Lord and Lady Byron. By publishing "The True Story of Lady Byron's Life" in the *Atlantic Monthly*, and the expanded argument in book form, *Lady Byron Vindicated* (1870), Stowe enacted the ideas she was handling in her fiction. Her attempt as a female critic to reread and publicly interpret Byron's poems and life not only dealt her reputation a blow from which it never fully recovered, but also showed what became of her ideas of gender-crossing and cross-reading.

Since both Byrons were dead when Stowe wrote, everything in the case was now textual. Those texts, Stowe believed, demanded a literary *woman*'s interpretation. Throughout the article and the book, Stowe reinterprets every major document of both sides of the Byron question (what turned Lady Byron against Lord Byron, and why exactly did they separate?), selecting those sources she deems authentic and authoritative like a biblical scholar. Like Nina in *Dred*, Stowe publicly claimed her right to read all of Byron. In her book she seeks to establish that hitherto Byron's work, the Byrons' marriage, and the Byrons themselves have been read almost entirely by a male "band of initiated interpreters" (44) who have canonized Byron as a long-suffering genius with a vicious unwomanly wife.

Stowe also suggests the Byrons are a failed example of what could have been a coordinate marriage of two brilliant, beautiful people with a healthy mingling of gender characteristics: Byron had the potential to be a reformed, more womanly Moses Pennel; Lady Byron was already a stronger, more manly Mara Lincoln. But womanly only in his seductive powers on men and in his sensitive constitution, Byron as Stowe depicts him leads otherwise an exaggeratedly manly life of drinking, feasting, and womanizing. At the same time, Lady Byron as portrayed by Stowe is forced by the media into Mara's painful Griselda role of unrelieved womanly self-sacrifice and silent endurance, which paradoxically only encouraged the slanders on Lady Byron's womanly nature. Stowe thus attacks the English and American literary establishments as well as the gender stereotypes whose double standard she argues destroyed the Byrons and continues to warp Western marriage in general.

The Byron article and book, then, have many connections to Stowe's earlier and contemporaneous work. The defenses of Lady Byron are about sex and the word in all senses: they argue for a broader interpretive community of readers of both sexes, who can determine from texts the truth about a sexual triangle, and right an unjust double standard. But the subsequent virulent personal attacks on Stowe as unwomanly and unclean signaled that she had taken her understanding of gender's relationship to textual interpretation farther than much of her public was willing to accept.

Art as text in *The Minister's Wooing* and *Agnes of Sorrento*

At the same time, Stowe had been exploring in her novels of the 1860s another line of thinking about the nation's conflicts over texts. Compared to the thundering jeremiads of *Uncle Tom's Cabin* and *Dred*, the biblical rhetoric in the later fiction is much diminished. Stowe's characters and narrators speak of the sublime and universal imagery of the Bible, treating the scriptures as a work of art. The shift reflects changes both in Stowe's increasingly secularized audience and in her own increasingly higher-critical understanding of the Bible as literature at least partly mythic. It reflects, too, the growing influence of a new popular text in Stowe's America: high art.

As an increasing number of middle-class Americans (including Stowe herself, three times in the 1850s) traveled to Europe with their Baedekers, and lithographers pumped out cheap prints of European masterpieces, art, like the Bible in the Reformation, was suddenly available to the ordinary person. Having experienced a personal revolution herself as she first entered the Louvre in 1853, Stowe began to address the cultural debates that surrounded the new American access to art: could untutored "readers" of art be trusted to handle a hugely varied and enormously appealing new text? Stowe pushed these questions further, asking whether art, in place of a conflicted Bible of waning authority, might become that ideal text which could unite America's readers across lines of creed, race, and gender. Particularly after her encounters with hundreds of European Catholic images of the Virgin Mary, Stowe began in articles and novels to articulate the need for less specifically Catholic, more ecumenical representations (in word or image) of the Virgin, who would draw readers of every denomination to the divine.[14] Not surprisingly, she began to create in her fiction a series of Marys who mingle Catholic and Protestant, European and American readings of the divine presence in Woman.

In *The Minister's Wooing*, for instance, the quiet Puritan maiden Mary Scudder functions more as a sacred image of Mary than as a person. At her shrine characters come to confess their sins and to receive absolution and inspiration. As a work of sacred art, Mary acts as "priestess" and minister. But Mary at first has her drawbacks, and Virginie – her double and foil, as her name suggests – makes them clear. Their artistic correlatives highlight the contrast between them: Stowe compares Mary to "a sketch of Overbeck's" and Virginie to the voluptuous canvases of Rembrandt, Rubens, and Titian. The American Protestant Mary tends toward a passionless life as the wife of Dr. Hopkins, a marriage that Virginie notes would be rather "like taking the veil" (786). Virginie, the European Catholic, has the opposite problem: a newly awakened sexuality that almost leads her into adultery with Aaron Burr. Each woman ministers to the other; Mary's Puritan spirituality "cools" Virginie's unruly passion – sending Burr away to protect her – and Virginie's sexuality "warms" Mary's chastity – awakening her to her true passion for James Marvyn, not Dr. Hopkins. By ultimately becoming mothers, the Marys combine chaste purity with natural sexuality to become nondenominational representations of the divine in womanhood.

Agnes of Sorrento (1862) ponders more fully the literal and symbolic relations of womanhood, art, and the figure of Mary as it recounts the struggle to identify spiritual truth amid religious disarray. Through the recurrent motif of the palimpsest, we see the fifteenth-century Italy of the young heroine as a thin overlay upon the pagan, sensual culture of Roman antiquity, which survives in the antique works of art that continually emerge from Italian soil, and in the corruption and sensuality of the court of Pope Alexander in Rome. Stowe lambasts the church's interpretations of woman as either whore or virgin, and reclaims a place for sexuality in the artistic and religious ideal of sacred womanhood. Set in the time of Girolamo Savonarola's calls for a purified church and a purified art – especially the abandonment of the practice of painting prostitutes as the Virgin Mary – *Agnes of*

Sorrento is ultimately Stowe's attempt to reenact the Reformation, with art taking the place of the Bible entirely. If this is more than this rather garbled romance can bear, it does at least repay study and illuminate her other work.

Agnes is set up as an icon of the Virgin, through whom "Christ had been made manifest to the eye" (191). But although Agnes is drawn toward a celibate vocation, she has passionate potential beneath her chaste surface. She is herself a palimpsest, a Christian virgin as well as a throwback to the beauty of antique statuary, like the ancient marble nymph which the local nuns have baptized before placing in their garden. Through Agnes' uncle, Brother Antonio, the artist friar of Savonarola's San Marco monastery, Stowe links Agnes with Savonarola's (and Stowe's) project of Christianizing the fallen world of art by transforming the image of true womanhood from sexual object to spirit-filled wife and mother. If Agnes is to attain full womanhood, Stowe must chart a path for her between the celibacy and sensuality the novel equally condemns.

Agnes eventually becomes a pawn in the interpretive corruption that equally infects the art world and the church. Arriving in Rome on a pilgrimage, Agnes is kidnapped by a member of the pope's court for use as an artist's model – but a model of a nymph rather than a saint. The pope's servants thus misread Agnes, violating what Stowe considered the sacramental relation between the physical beauty of art and the divine purity it rightly signifies.[15] She is saved by the handsome cavalier Agostino, an admirer of Savonarola (and of Agnes) who, as a "poet and artist," knows what Agnes really signifies (100). Agnes's kidnapping also finally makes clear to her what the other characters have seen all along – that the Church of Rome is a false picture of the true church. Just as Agnes is forcibly separated from her true signification and treated as a mere body, the church of fifteenth-century Rome is unfortunately no longer the sign which stands for God on earth.

But meaning is righted at the book's end. Savonarola's death as a heretic includes his last words (corresponding to legend): "From the Church Militant you *may* divide me; but from the Church Triumphant, *no*, – *that* is above your power!" (373). To the end, like Uncle Tom, the martyr keeps the distinction between the corrupt sign and the true signified. Similarly, when Agnes renounces her celibate leanings to recognize her "vocation unto marriage" with Agostino, she rights interpretive wrongs. As priestess in the "holy and venerable" "sacrament" of marriage, Agnes draws the excommunicated Agostino to love the true church whose spiritual beauty she shadows forth. She acts, then, as art does, as an ecumenical text for God. Like the "symbolic forms, signs, and observances" of the Catholic Church, which Stowe sees as sacred texts for the illiterate Renaissance believer, Agnes becomes a sacred hieroglyph standing for the message of the Bible.

Woman in Sacred History and Poganuc People

Stowe's earlier, primary "sacred text," the Bible, is almost absent in *Agnes*. When she turns to her later project, *Woman in Sacred History* (1873), however, she combines her earlier biblicism with her later readings of the image of the divine woman. The result is a remarkable attempt to unite the churches, to unite the Old and New Testaments, and to unite the sacred text of the Bible with the once-condemned text of art. Along with her last novel, *Poganuc People* (1878), it attempts to bring together the principal interpretive issues she and much of the nation had wrestled with for forty years.

Particularly when contrasted with its near-contemporary, Elizabeth Cady Stanton's *Woman's Bible* (1895, 1898), *Woman in Sacred History*'s efforts to retrieve the Bible through its depiction of women are especially interesting. *The Woman's Bible* declares its intention to "revise" the scriptures (which it labels a human document), and consciously embraces the often disparate interpretive judgments of its multiple contributors in a self-described effort to unite denominations and genders around a revised Bible. In contrast, Stowe claims not to be "revising" the divine scriptures but simply depicting scripture's linear progression of prophetic and poetic mothers "under divine culture," leading up to the pair she calls "Mary and her son." Yet despite its claims to unity, Stowe's book is a highly contradictory text. Its insistently linear narrative (which requires a good deal of selectivity among biblical characters) is interleaved with surprisingly voluptuous chromolithographs of biblical women (and of secular women who are retitled with biblical names for the volume). Certainly the attempt to unite the biblical word and artistic images around an ecumenically appealing narrative based on the ideal of sacred womanhood is a logical outgrowth of *The Minister's Wooing* and *Agnes of Sorrento*. The often bare-breasted lithographs, however, threaten to disrupt both linearity and the sacred focus with their overt appeal to the sensual eye.[16]

In her effort to draw from the Bible a women's narrative around which Christians could unite, and to stabilize interpretation of the female body in religion and religious art, Stowe actually tacitly invites not a unified reading but highly different ways of reading through the opposed allurements of the book's visual and verbal texts. In *Poganuc People*, too, she celebrates the variety of denominational practices for their ability to meet the spiritual needs of diverse audiences, suggesting that such multiplicity of interpretation or practice no longer seemed to lead to Armageddon, as it had in *Dred*.

By the end of her career, then, Stowe seems to have reached a compromise between interpretive unity and contradiction, providing a model for her readers. Like her, they could select their own visual or verbal "sacred histories" from the texts in which they found the closest approximation to a personal truth.

With *Woman in Sacred History*, Stowe reaches the endpoint of a trajectory many nineteenth-century Americans experienced as they confronted problems in determining truth from an authoritative text. Stowe moves from the relative certainty of the old hermeneutic "rule of faith" to a nineteenth-century version of interpretive relativism. Finally, she arrives at an implicit – sometimes even explicit – celebration of textual disunity and interpretive variety. That final stage resembles what Paul Ricoeur in our own time has called a "second naïveté," in which one makes peace, from a postcritical perspective, with the older, mythic absolutes of one's original understanding of an authoritative text – in Ricoeur's and Stowe's case, the Bible.

At the same time, Stowe's development and career as a writer reveal significant historical trends as well. Beginning, like many women authors, with "parlor literature" and textbooks for schools, Stowe soon branched outward from the traditional female role of parlor entertainer and schoolteacher to become a novelist of considerable power – fueled at the outset by the great moral question of slavery, a reform movement which empowered many women writers. Moreover, *Uncle Tom's Cabin* opened the world market to an American writer as never before. Over her lengthy 45-year literary career, Stowe retained considerable market influence, even after the Byron fiasco. As America's then foremost "woman of letters," she served over the decades as mentor, friend, and promoter for a younger generation of women writers, including Elizabeth Stuart Phelps, Rose Terry Cooke, and Fanny Fern. As domestic novelist, she helped to codify the traditions tapped by Louisa May Alcott, Helen Hunt Jackson, and many others. As literary reformer, she inspired writers from Rebecca Harding Davis and Charlotte Perkins Gilman (Stowe's grandniece) to Upton Sinclair and beyond. With Jewett, Cooke, Mary Wilkins Freeman, Alice Cary, and others, Stowe helped create the genre of regionalist fiction and set its standards. If we consider the mutual admiration between her and Sarah Orne Jewett, who was inspired by *The Pearl of Orr's Island*, a line of literary descent stretches more or less directly from Stowe through Jewett to Jewett's admirer, Willa Cather. And from Harriet Jacobs' *Incidents in the Life of a Slave Girl* onward, African-American literary history has been profoundly affected both by Stowe's popularity and by her characterizations and plots. While it is of course impossible to quantify Stowe's influence, it seems certain that American literary history – and perhaps especially the place of women writers within that history – would have been markedly different without the popular resonance of her themes and the example of her unprecedented success.

NOTES

1. Cooke, "Harriet Beecher Stowe," 581–601.
2. Mary C. Henderson, *Theater in America*, 52.
3. Tompkins, *Sensational Designs*, 126.
4. Nicole Tonkovich, "Writing in Circles," 145–75; Joan D. Hedrick, *Stowe: A Life* 82–91.
5. For a full treatment see Joan D. Hedrick, "'Peaceable Fruits,'" 307–32.
6. Letter to George Beecher, February 20, [1830?]. Acquisitions, Stowe-Day Library, Hartford, Connecticut.
7. Calvin Stowe greatly admired Herder and often cited him in his work. Harriet Beecher Stowe not only uses some of Herder's key terms, but also carries his emphases into her understandings of literary reading. Her favorite literary critic was Charles-Augustin Sainte-Beuve, who like Herder consistently called for full sympathy with the personality and thoughts of the writer, in order to read the writer fairly.
8. Letter to Lord Morpeth, January 7, 1853. Clifton Waller Barrett Collection, Alderman Library, University of Virginia, Charlottesville.
9. For a modern correlative, see Stanley Fish, *Is There a Text in This Class?*
10. See Stowe, "Introduction," *Library of Famous Fiction*, vi; Letter to Edward Beecher, April 1828, in C. E. Stowe, *Life of Harriet Beecher Stowe*, 44; Letter to Georgiana May (*c.* 1832–3), in Charles E. Stowe and Lyman Beecher Stowe, *Harriet Beecher Stowe: the Story of Her Life*, 82–3.
11. Letter to Calvin E. Stowe, July 19, 1844 (Beecher-Stowe Collection, Schlesinger Library, Cambridge, MA); Letter to Henry Ward Beecher [mid-1870s], Letter to Henry Ward Beecher, n.d. [June? 1870], Letter to Eunice Beecher, [1850?] (all in Beecher Papers, Sterling Memorial Library, Yale University, New Haven, CT).
12. Howe, "Introduction," 9.
13. Phelps, "By Elizabeth Stuart Phelps," 134.
14. Like many writers of her time, Stowe held lifelong assumptions of a Christian America. As a result she did not seriously consider whether the Virgin would appeal beyond a Judaeo-Christian culture, and indeed seems in all her work to assume her readers' Christianity.
15. See on this point Stowe's *Sunny Memories of Foreign Lands*, 223, 232, and "The Old Oak of Andover – A Reverie," *Independent* 7 (1855): 33.
16. Stowe was not opposed to nudity in art if an artistic purpose beyond sensuality were evidenced, and in *Sunny Memories* she made clear her own comfort with one of the illustrations she eventually chose for *Woman in Sacred History*: Battoni's *Magdalen*. "[T]hough the neck and bosom are exposed, yet there is an angelic seriousness and gravity in the conception of the piece which would check an earthly thought" (II, 345). But in the same book she acknowledged stubborn individual interpretive differences: "Who can decide how much in a picture belongs to the idiosyncrasies and associations of the person who looks upon it ... [W]ho, therefore, shall establish any authoritative canon of taste? ...

Then, again, how much in painting or in poetry depends upon the frame of mind in which we see or hear!" (II, 40).

WORKS CITED

Caskey, Marie. *Chariot of Fire: Religion and the Beecher Family.* New Haven: Yale University Press, 1978.

Clarke, Edward H. *Sex in Education; or, A Fair Chance for the Girls.* Boston: James R. Osgood and Co., 1873.

Cooke, Rose Terry. "Harriet Beecher Stowe." *Our Famous Women.* Hartford, CT: A. D. Worthington and Co., 1884. 581–601.

Evans, Augusta Jane. *St. Elmo.* 1866. Tuscaloosa: University of Alabama Press, 1992.

Fish, Stanley. *Is There a Text in This Class? The Authority of Interpretive Communities.* Cambridge, MA: Harvard University Press, 1980.

Gura, Philip F. *The Wisdom of Words: Language, Theology, and Literature in the New England Renaissance.* Middletown, CT: Wesleyan University Press, 1981.

Hedrick, Joan D. *Harriet Beecher Stowe: a Life.* New York and Oxford: Oxford University Press, 1994.

" 'Peaceable Fruits': the Ministry of Harriet Beecher Stone." *American Quarterly* 40 (1998): 307–22.

Henderson, Mary C. *Theater in America.* New updated edition. New York: Abrams, 1996.

Howe, Julia Ward. "Introduction." *Sex and Education: a Reply to Dr. E. H. Clarke's "Sex in Education."* Ed. Julia Ward Howe. Boston: Roberts Bros., 1874. 5–11.

Kerber, Linda. " 'Nothing Useless or Absurd or Fantastical': the Education of Women in the Early Republic." *Educating Men and Women Together: Coeducation in a Changing World.* Ed. Carol Lasser. Urbana: University of Illinois Press, 1987. 37–48.

Phelps, Elizabeth Stuart. "By Elizabeth Stuart Phelps." *Sex and Education: a Reply to Dr. E. H. Clarke's "Sex in Education."* Ed. Julia Ward Howe. Boston: Roberts Bros., 1874. 5–11.

Stanton, Elizabeth Cady, *et al. The Woman's Bible.* New York: European Publishing Co., 1895, 1898.

Stowe, Charles Edward. *The Life of Harriet Beecher Stowe.* Boston: Houghton Mifflin, 1889.

Stowe, Charles E., and Lyman Beecher Stowe. *Harriet Beecher Stowe: the Story of Her Life.* Boston: Houghton Mifflin, 1911.

Stowe, Harriet Beecher. *Agnes of Sorrento.* Boston: Houghton Mifflin, 1896.

Dred; a Tale of the Great Dismal Swamp. 2 vols. New York: AMS Press, 1970.

First Geography for My Children. Boston, New York. 1855.

The Key to Uncle Tom's Cabin. 1854. New York: Arno, 1968.

Lady Byron Vindicated: a History of the Byron Controversy. 1870. New York: Haskell House, 1970.

The Pearl of Orr's Island. Boston: Houghton Mifflin, 1890.

Poganuc People: their Loves and Lives. New York. 1878.

Sunny Memories of Foreign Lands. 2 vols. Boston, New York. 1854.

Three Novels: Uncle Tom's Cabin, The Minister's Wooing, Oldtown Folks. Ed. Kathryn Kish Sklar. New York: Library of America, 1982.

Uncle Tom's Cabin. Ed. Elizabeth Ammons. Norton Critical Edition. New York: W. W. Norton, 1994.

Woman in Sacred History. New York: 1873.

"Introduction." *Library of Famous Fiction.* Ed. Harriet Beecher Stowe. New York: J. B. Ford and Co., 1873.

Letter to Eunice Beecher, [1850?]. Beecher Papers, Sterling Memorial Library, Yale University, New Haven, CT.

Letter to George Beecher, February 20 [1830?]. Acquisitions, Stowe-Day Library, Hartford, CT.

Letter to Henry Ward Beecher [mid 1870s]. Beecher Papers, Sterling Memorial Library, Yale University, New Haven, CT.

Letter to Henry Ward Beecher, n.d. [June? 1870]. Beecher Papers, Sterling Memorial Library, Yale University, New Haven, CT.

Letter to Calvin E. Stowe, July 19, 1844. Beecher-Stowe Collection, Schlesinger Library, Harvard University, Cambridge, MA.

"Modern Uses of Language." *Western Monthly Magazine* 1 (March 1833): 121–5.

"The Old Oak of Andover – a Reverie." *Independent* 7 (1855): 33.

"The True Story of Lady Byron's Life." *Atlantic Monthly* 24 (September 1869): 295–313.

Tompkins, Jane. *Sensational Designs: the Cultural Work of American Fiction, 1790–1860.* New York and Oxford : Oxford University Press, 1985.

Tonkovich, Nicole. "Writing in Circles: Harriet Beecher Stowe, the Semi-Colon Club, and the Construction of Women's Authorship." *Nineteenth-Century Women Learn to Write.* Ed. Catherine Hobbs. Charlottesville: University Press of Virginia, 1995. 145–75.

11

YOLANDA PIERCE

African-American women's spiritual narratives

Within African-American spiritual narratives, conversion most often happens during intense times of loss, grief, misery, pain, and despair, as both a psychological and physical reaction to conditions on earth. Hell is real and it exists on earth; conversion offers deliverance and salvation both for the spiritual body and the physical body. During times of the deepest despair, during the agonies of slavery, during "hell without fires," most African-American converts reveal that they have been transformed. The rhetoric of conversion relies not just on "otherworldly" experience: for the new believer, conversion offers hope that God can bring healing, comfort, and deliverance to everyday life. Theologian Orlando Costas explains why the conversion experience has special meaning for the "least" of a society:

> Conversion is, therefore, a passage from a dehumanized and dehumanizing existence to a humanized and humanizing life ... it is the passage from death and decay to life and freedom. In conversion, men and women are liberated from the enslavement of the past and given the freedom of the future; they are turned from the God of this age, who passes away, to the God who is always the future of every past. ("Conversion as a Complex Experience," 21)

Conversion offers the possibility of transforming a life that has been both dehumanizing and degrading into an existence that offers hope and salvation from the midst of despair, death, and slavery. In describing the power of African-American conversion narratives, literary critic William Hunter offers this view: "In the slave and ex-slave conversion tradition, the logical consistency in patterns of consciousness was temporarily disrupted, and the disruption created the possibility for apprehending new information that could radically alter the prior patterns of consciousness" ("'Do Not be Conformed Unto this World,'" 81). Conversion is the "disruption" in pattern in which new information – the reality of the equality of the Gospel – could then offer myriad possibilities of identity previously unknown to an African American. That one becomes a loved creation and not a loathed creature, that one is not the cursed son of Ham but the chosen son of God, makes conversion the most fundamental act of refusing the patterns and expectations of slave culture. This is the impact of the conversion experience, as presented in African-American spiritual narratives, a transformation so complete that what it offers is not only eternal life or the promise of rewards in heaven. Conversion offers a new allegiance, a new trust, a new life commitment, and a new journey for African Americans – in this present world.

A new thing

> Behold, I will do a new thing; now it shall spring forth; shall ye not know it? I will make a way in the wilderness and rivers in the desert. (Isaiah 43:19)

The beginning of the nineteenth century in America saw an unprecedented rise in the number of written "spiritual narratives," stories of men and women's religious conversion experiences – generally conversions to Protestant Christianity. According to literary critic Virginia Lierson Brereton, nineteenth-century spiritual narratives owed their greatest debts to seventeenth-century and eighteenth-century English Puritans, as, of course, American Puritans carried their English texts across the Atlantic Ocean (*From Sin to Salvation*, 7). Richard Baxter's *Call to the Unconverted* (1657), William Law's *Serious Call to a Devout and Holy Life* (1728) and Philip Doddridge's *On the Rise and Progress of Religion in the Soul* (1745) were popular models, widely read and carefully mimicked by early American writers. Perhaps Jonathan Edwards's *Faithful Narrative of the Surprising Work of God* (1738) is one of the first truly American spiritual narratives, composed and written on American soil and taking into account the complexities of the early American Christian Church. Edwards himself remarks, concerning written accounts of conversions, that "there is no one thing that I know of which God has made such a means of promoting His work among us, as the news of others' conversion" (381). Patricia Caldwell notes, in *The Puritan Conversion Narrative*, that the written spiritual narrative emerged as a result of the oral testimonies that were confessions "before the entire congregation of a genuine experience of conversion (not doctrinal knowledge or belief) ... required of all who would join the church" (45). These oral testimonies became the basis for the written and collected conversion stories of American Puritans. They were generally compiled into a collection for a certain congregation, edited to include remarks, prayers, or sermons by the minister. The movement from a simple confession of faith to a confession of conversion spoken within a church to a written and possibly published account of that same testimony had a great literary repercussion: it produced the first extended narratives written on American soil. By the beginning of the nine-teenth century, higher literacy rates, the fervor of the Great Awakenings,[1] and the rising popularity of evangelical denominations like the Methodists and the Baptists, all contributed to the growing popularity of written conver-sion accounts or spiritual narratives. Written accounts of conversion expe-riences were highly encouraged, particularly as the narratives yielded evan-gelizing and teaching tools. While conversion narratives helped to confirm and strengthen the convert's own faith, converts also pointed others to the same beliefs and experiences, for one of the primary purposes of the conver-sion story was to teach, edify, persuade, and exhort. By testifying about the great events in their lives, evangelicals hoped that the unconverted would be inspired to "go and do likewise." Religious narratives afford effective devices for Christian witness, since the stories "make concrete and familiar the abstraction of Christian theology ... the narrative fulfills a persuasive purpose, that of encouraging Christians to remember the wonder-working power of God" (Clements, "'I Once Was Lost,'" 109).

In the late 1730s and 1740s, the preaching of George Whitefield, the "Grand Itinerant" of the gospel whose fame stretched throughout the New England colonies, created an excitement for the gospel of Christianity un-like anything that had been previously seen. Preaching by other itinerants, camp meetings, revival meetings,[2] extensive missionary efforts by evangeli-cals – all marked what religion historian Daniel Shea calls "the most wide-spread and convulsive religious revival of its [America's] history" (*Spiritual Autobiography*, 223). However, the Second Great Awakening, led by evan-gelicals and itinerants from Methodist and Baptist churches, brought even greater religious fervor to nineteenth-century America. This movement cut across denominational lines; more and more people who did not live in New England, and who had not been born and reared within a close religious environment, were finally hearing the gospel. The itinerants of the Second Great Awakening made more of an effort to extend their evangelistic efforts throughout the entire eastern seaboard and not just within New England, where the First Great Awakening had been centered. This revival "cut across geographical boundaries from the southwestern frontier to the 'burned over districts' of Western New York so named because the fires of religious excite-ment swept it so often, to the eastern seaboard and New England" (Lindley, "*You Have Stept Out of Your Place*," 59).

It is no surprise, then, that the majority of American spiritual narratives were produced during this time of incredible religious fervor in the first half of the nineteenth century. The majority of the narratives "followed remark-ably uniform patterns. They typically opened with the convert's early life, went on to describe a period of increasing sense of sinfulness, climaxed with conversion proper, and concluded with an account of the fruits of the experience – usually zealous conduct of evangelical activity" (Brereton, *From Sin to Salvation*, 14). In his *Studies in Spiritual Autobiography*, Owen Watkins notes that the pattern narratives followed can be simply described as a sequence of "peace, disturbance and peace again ... the casting down and the raising up, the wounding and the making whole ... the conviction of sin and the coming to Christ" (37). The historical and literary circumstances that led to a growing number of white American spiritual narratives also influenced the production of a new genre by enslaved and formerly enslaved writers: the African-American spiritual narrative. The Great Awakenings "first stirred the religious imagination of the black Diaspora, and brought thousands of displaced African-Americans and their descendants into meaningful Christian communion for the first time" (Lincoln and Mamiya, *The Black Church in the African-American Experience*, 348). During this time of the Second Great Awakening, many African Americans and poorer white Americans (particularly women) previously denied access to religion, especially organized religion, began to have access to the Christian message. While those African Americans (slave and free) living in the North had experienced the First Great Awakening first hand, the Second Great Awakening finally penetrated the South, due to the immense missionary enterprises of the itinerants. Speaking of southern African Americans, theologians C. Eric Lincoln and Lawrence H. Mamiya claim: "many blacks became Christians as a result of the Second Great Awakening, which started in the frontier states of Tennessee and Kentucky and soared to the plantations of the south thorough the efforts of circuit riders and other clerical itinerants" (*Black Church*, 228). As this great religious fervor swept across America, more and more people wrote stories of their conversion experience.

The antebellum period saw an unprecedented number of evangelicals and itinerants traveling to plantations and farms in order to spread the gospel among the enslaved; and many of these men and women wrote letters home or kept diaries detailing their experiences. Many Methodist and Baptist churches became committed to a campaign of evangelizing the slaves, and some slaveholders (although not the majority) welcomed preachers and missionaries who would share the gospel with their slaves. As in the larger American tradition, the majority of spiritual narratives written by African Americans were composed during the first half of the nineteenth century.

The question we are left to ask is: Why? Why would African-American men and women want to share their unique and intimate experiences with their audience? For what reasons was the conversion experience – explicitly to Protestant Christianity – such a fundamental and life-altering experience to which they had to give voice? Why would African-American writers consciously employ the signs, symbols, and stories that comprise Christian dogma? Nineteenth-century Christianity was a contradictory faith for its African-American believers: its signs, symbols, words, and messages were used to enslave physically and mentally. Often the only "gospel" a slave would hear was the injunction for "slaves to obey their masters." When allowed to be "members" of white churches, enslaved African Americans did not have status as *full* members. They were forced to sit in the balcony or outside the church. They were often denied the ritual of Holy Communion and other religious sacraments. African Americans' churches were often expressly forbidden; when they did exist, they often did so in secret and at great personal risk to members. The issue of whether a slave was a human being, and thus could be saved, was still being debated. Did three-fifths of a person have a soul that was deserving of salvation? The few slaveholders who actively promoted and supported teaching "Christian" values to their slaves did so most often out of the hope that the message would make their slaves more docile and passive. Nineteenth-century Christianity for African Americans was the "slaveholding Christianity" described by Frederick Douglass in his autobiography: "corrupt, slaveholding, women-whipping, cradle-plundering, partial and hypocritical" (*Narrative of the Life of Douglass*, 153). Yet, despite all these facts, for many nineteenth-century African-American writers this hallmark experience of conversion to Christianity is the central theme in their autobiographical stories. Why and how were they able to transform a religion which Douglass calls "the climax of all misnomers, the boldest of all frauds, and the grossest of all libels" (153) into a system of belief that could sustain and nurture?

The actual structure of African American spiritual narratives provides part of the answer. Despite the similar literary and historical circumstances that produced the sister genres, African-American spiritual narratives are much longer, more autobiographical in tone, and focus more on extraordinary events and accounts of supernatural signs and wonders. These narratives, according to William Andrews, "tell a free story"; that is, they place the narrator and his or her personal transformation at the very heart of the narrative. Nineteenth-century African-American writers employed the form of the spiritual narrative in two ways: first, as the story of coming to religion, and second, as the opportunity for the "least of these" to give voice to stories, experiences, and histories. When otherwise silenced by the strictures of slavery and the reality of being African American in the nineteenth century, the spiritual narrative allows its narrator's voice to be heard. And these voices, which are otherwise silenced, access power through the spiritual narrative.

There are no simple patterns of "peace, disturbance, and peace again," the phrase which Owen Watkins uses as a description for the larger tradition of American spiritual narratives. Instead, conversion experiences within African-American texts resemble Paul's experience on the road to Damascus. The supernatural world, where God himself intervenes and alters the laws of the universe, collides with the physical world, resulting in signs and wonders, callings and responses. The pattern within African-American narratives is one of the supernatural colliding with the natural, transforming the physical and the mental. The conversion experience resulted in a transformation so complete that it facilitated a change of identity, even a change of name. Conversion offers a change in status for the new believer. He or she is no longer a slave and thus a sinner, but a saint, a believer, and a participant in the body of all Christian believers. For a people who had been denied the status of human being, conversion was proof that a particular person could be saved and redeemed: he or she was not merely a chattel, but an heir to the throne of God. At the heart of the African-American conversion narrative is the quest that the conversion represents: a quest for a new status; a quest for a new source of power; a quest for a new language and literacy; and the ultimate quest for freedom and salvation.

Zilpha Elaw's quest

And it shall come to pass in the last days, saith God, I will pour out my Spirit upon all flesh: and your sons and your daughters shall prophesy, and your young men shall see visions, and your old men shall dream dreams: And on my servants and on my handmaidens I will pour out in those last days of my Spirit; and they shall prophesy. (Acts 2:17–18)

What would the quest for conversion mean for nineteenth-century African-American women who employed the spiritual narrative form, given that their writing was in defiance of both institutionalized racism and patriarchy? For African-American women, their status was not only that of "chattel," but breeders and human incubators. Their sources of power were even more limited than their male counterparts' since they were decreed inferior by virtue of both race and gender. Their quests for literacy and language had to accommodate the notions of public and private spheres and restrictive ideals of roles for women. Their desire for earthly and heavenly salvation often took second place to the wishes of their brothers, husbands, sons, and fathers.

William Andrews's *Sisters of the Spirit* and the Schomburg's Library of Nineteenth-Century Black Women Writers *Spiritual Narratives* (ed. Gates) are two important anthologies of nineteenth-century African-American women who employed the spiritual narrative form. By the mid-nineteenth century, the majority of the African-American spiritual narratives were composed by women writers. And more are still being discovered and recovered. Nineteenth-century evangelist Zilpha Elaw provides us with important clues within her narrative as to the power of her conversion in allowing her not only to write the story of her life, but to preach the Christian message throughout slave and free states.

Zilpha Elaw's 1846 narrative, *Memoirs of the Life, Religious Experience, Ministerial Travels and Labours of Mrs. Zilpha Elaw, An American Female of Colour Together with Some Account of the Great Religious Revivals in America. Written by Herself*, documents her conversion, experience of sanctification, and the subsequent ramifications for an African-American woman living "a life of holiness." Elaw's meticulous account of her life and evangelistic travels offers us a window into the life of a black female evangelist, along with a glimpse of early nineteenth-century religious life for black women. Elaw uses the experiences of conversion and sanctification to address the appeal of Protestant Christianity to women; her evangelistic travels and preaching at camp meetings give us a powerful example of how black women negotiated the space between the private and the public spheres; and the "testimony" of her narrative directly confronts the restrictive ideals of nineteenth-century notions of "true womanhood" for black women.

Zilpha Elaw was a free black woman born in Pennsylvania to free "religious parents" (Methodists), who owned their own farm outside of Philadelphia. When Elaw was twelve, her mother died during the birth of her twenty-second child, of whom all but three died in infancy. Her father died soon afterward and Elaw was put into the care of Pierson and Rebecca Mitchel, a white Quaker couple, in whose household she became a servant. She notes that the transition to life with the Piersons was difficult since they were not as religious as her devout parents:

> In my father's house, family devotion was regularly attended to morning and evening; prayer was offered up, and praises of God were sung; but the persons with whom I now resided were Quakers, and their religious exercises, if they observed any, were performed in the secret silence of the mind; nor were religion and devotion referred to by them in my hearing. (54)

Elaw is careful to note the relative religious indifference in her new household, since these feelings of indifference prepare the scene for the first stage of her conversion: feelings of guilt and sin. Since her Quaker family was lax in its religious devotions, Elaw begins to give "way to the evil propensities of an unregenerate heart" and feels herself to be "so exceedingly sinful" (55). She recalls one sinful occasion in which she "even ventured to take the name of God in vain, in order to cater to the sinful tastes" of her companions (55). Her anxieties concerning her sins lead to the next stage of conversion, in which she feels distress about her spiritual welfare and begins to wonder about the possibility of freedom for her soul from the burdens of guilt and the weight of her sin. She recalls that she was "at times deeply affected with penitence, but could not rightly comprehend what it was" that ailed her, she being "ignorant of the great remedy disclosed by the plan of salvation afforded by the gospel" (55). Although the gospel has not been deliberately withheld from Elaw, she still remains ignorant of the plan of salvation, kept from it by the lack of religious sentiment on the part of her white Quaker family.

Elaw is prepared for the actual experience of conversion by "divine dreams" in which she has visions of the Angel Gabriel proclaiming to her that "time would be no longer ... Jehovah was about to judge the world and execute judgment on it" (55). After this dream, Elaw feels that "the intense horror" of her guilty mind was "such to defy description," and she begins to weep, feeling the "convictions of my sinfulness in the sight of God and incompetency to meet my Judge" (55). Although she shares her dream with her Quaker family, the mother informs her: "it was only a dream, that dreams have nothing ominous in them; and I ought not to give myself any more concern respecting it: but she failed in her attempt to tranquilize my mind" (55). And Elaw's Quaker mistress also fails in her attempt to recognize that for Elaw, the realm of dreams was perhaps her only realm of personal identity and freedom. This Quaker family completely controlled their servants' actions. It was only in the quiet solitude of night that Elaw was not at the family's disposal. Kimberly Rae Connor's *Conversions and Visions in the Writings of African-American Women*, Joanne M. Braxton's *Black Women Writing Autobiography*, and Jean McMahon Humez's *Gifts of Power*, three works exploring black women's spiritual narratives, all point out the inherent importance of the dream realm for black women (and for black men such as Nat Turner, the visionary slave who led a rebellion and was guided by vivid spiritual experience). Black women's "personal power" was often expressed in "dreams, premonitions and visions," according to Braxton (49). These dreams and visions provided symbolic and prophetic guidance, phenomena that were interpreted as purposed intervention by the divine in one's daily life.

Elaw's conversion begins shortly after her attendance at a Methodist camp meeting. While milking a cow in a stall, she has a manifestation of the presence of God, so clear that "even the beast of the stall turned her head and bowed herself upon the ground" (57). Her vision was of a "tall figure ... with long hair, which parted in the front and came down on his shoulders; he wore a long white robe down to the feet; and as he stopped with open arms and smiled upon me, he disappeared" (56). Elaw says that she might have been persuaded that she had imagined the whole scenario had it not been that the "beast of the stall gave forth her evidence to the reality of the heavenly appearance" (57). It was "after this wonderful manifestation" which Elaw records that "the peace of God which passeth understanding was communicated to my heart," and she went on "rejoicing in the blooming prospect of a better inheritance with the saints in light" (57):

> The love of God now shed abroad in my heart by the Holy Spirit, and my soul transported with heavenly peace and joy in God, all the former hardships which pertained to my circumstances and situation vanished; the work and duties which had previously been hard and irksome were now become easy and pleasant; and the evil propensities of my disposition and temper were subdued beneath the softening and refining pressure of divine grace upon my heart ... in the year 1808. (57)

The hardships and duties Elaw faced were not only spiritual trials, but also the loss of both parents, separation from her only two remaining siblings, and the constant harshness of field work on an early nineteenth-century farm. While she is born free, to free parents, her way in the material world is still difficult. After her conversion, her Quaker mistress who frequently used to charge her with "pertness and insolent behavior" began to charge her with "sullenness and mopishness," and this accusation often led Elaw to prayer and mourning for the loss of her "dear mother" (59). Conversion provided Elaw with strategies for negotiating the trauma and alienation of everyday life.

Not until the year 1817, while attending a camp meeting, does Elaw experience the power of sanctification.[3] Known as the "second blessing," because its occurrence was thought to be the second experience of God's grace after the initial conversion experience, sanctification was a step beyond the initial conversion experience in which the sinner was simply forgiven from all sin and promised salvation. Sanctification was the start of a process whereby believers were being continually indwelled by Christ, continually being purified in a process whereby their lives, souls and bodies were set apart for a special purpose:

> It was at one of these meetings that God was pleased to separate my soul unto Himself, to sanctify me as a vessel designed for honour, made meet for the master's use. Whether I was in the body, or whether I was out of the body, on that auspicious day, I cannot say; but this I do know, that at the conclusion of a most powerful sermon ... I became so overpowered with the presence of God, that I sank down upon the ground, and laid there for a considerable time; and while I was thus prostrate on the earth, my spirit seemed to ascend ... I distinctly heard a voice speak unto me, which said, "Now thou art sanctified; and I will show thee what thou must do"... and I clearly saw by the light of

the Holy Ghost, that my heart and soul were rendered completely spotless –
as clean as a sheet of white paper, and I felt as pure as if I had never sinned in
all my life. (67)

Elaw's sanctification experience, in which she is set apart for God, represents her belief that, both literally and spiritually, she had been made the
habitation for the spirit of God. Even before death, in which the soul was
traditionally thought to "ascend" and to separate from the body to be one
with God, the sanctified person claims that her soul has already been specifically chosen as God's vessel for work here on this earth. Sanctification is not
an "otherworldly" belief of justice in the afterlife, but a very present help
for those in the current world.

William Andrews suggests in *Sisters of the Spirit* that sanctification means
being in total harmony with the will of God; it is "being perfectly pure in
intention and action insofar as his or her acts are determined by individual intention" and, for this reason, the "sanctified Christian enjoys the inner peace
that comes of being convinced that, having been liberated from sin, one is
now completely identified with God in thought, word and deed" (14). Sanctification, according to Andrews, freed eighteenth-century and nineteenth-
century African Americans to trust the promptings of their innermost selves,
"because of their conviction that what came from within was of the Holy
Spirit, not corrupt ego" (15). So in a time in which to be black was to be
a slave, Elaw is able to state confidently that she is the equal to any white
man or woman; according to her, the "Almighty accounts not the black races
of man either in the order of nature or spiritual capacity as inferior to the
white" (85). When women were not allowed to speak in the church, a "poor
coloured woman" began to exhort sinners "as it were involuntarily, or from
an internal prompting" (82).

Sanctification allowed Elaw to believe that she had been "called," specifically chosen as an evangelist of Christ, in an age when evangelistic travel
was even difficult and dangerous for white men. She hears a voice that tells
her: "Now thou knowest the will of God concerning thee; thou must preach
the gospel; and thou must travel far and wide" (82). This voice leads Elaw
to believe that she was chosen in "commission for the work of the ministry,"
which she received "not from mortal man, but from the voice of an invisible and heavenly personage sent from God" (82). And the assurance of this
"commission" causes Elaw to travel as an evangelist throughout the Middle
Atlantic and Northeastern states, including Vermont, Maryland, Virginia,
and finally on to London, England, where she writes her narrative and ends
her evangelical career. Her confidence in the power of the Holy Spirit gave
her the strength to travel to slaveholding states despite the very real danger

of being arrested or kidnapped or sold. In describing the power of sanctification for white nineteenth-century female evangelists like Phoebe Palmer and Sarah Lankford, historian Nancy Hardesty states that, after this transforming experience, "many women felt compelled to let go of their resistance to public speaking. Whether or not God asked that initially, it was clear that all must testify to the experience to retain it. So speak out they must" (*Women Called to Witness*, 64). Elaw not only speaks out, she also writes. Her narrative is a witness, a testimony to the ultimate triumph of a life in which she experiences God's power.

Through sanctification, men and women believed that they had recovered their true, pristine identity in Christ; what humankind was like before the Fall.[4] However, most female adherents to sanctification still felt obliged to cite some Bible verse, some precedent to authorize their convention-shattering views or behaviors. They did not feel that they were unaccountable to any law, but through sanctification, they had an intuitive sense of God's will and calling in their lives. Elaw initially disbelieves that she had been called of God to preach, saying she "could not believe that any such line of duty was enjoined" upon her (75). But her confidence in the reality of her own experience with the divine created an assurance in her own abilities to be this "chosen vessel":

> I enjoyed so intimate and heavenly an intercourse with God, that I was assured He had sent an angel to instruct me in such of His holy mysteries as were otherwise beyond my comprehension. Such communications were most gratifying and delightful to me ... I had sufficiency from God for the proclamation of His gospel. *Not that we are sufficient of ourselves to think any thing as of ourselves, but our sufficiency is of God.* 2 Corinthians 3:5. (76–7)

The courage and the liberty to speak, preach, evangelize, and witness in word and in letter are at the heart of the sanctification experience. While Elaw claims she is not sufficient in herself, that she alone has no power, sanctification has allowed her to lay claim to spiritual and material blessings. Not only has she received salvation for her soul, she also has received divine revelation to spread the gospel and to decipher mysteries which were otherwise beyond her comprehension:

> How often have I said, "Lord! send by whom thou wilt send, only send not by me; for thou knowest that I am ignorant: how can I be a mouth for God! – a poor, coloured female; and thou knowest we have many things to endure which others do not." But the answer was "What is that to thee? follow thou me." (91)

The sin of slavery was as much of a threat to Elaw as was the slavery of sin. In the antebellum South it was customary to jail and auction off any free black who could not prove his or her free status through certificates registered and issued by the courts of the state. Some states, including Virginia, prohibited any slave or free black from conducting religious meetings. While Elaw was on an evangelistic trip in a small town in Virginia, a crowd gathered outside the house where she was staying and holding services. Elaw strongly felt "the prospect of an immediate arrest and consignment by sale to some slave owner" (91). She recalls:

> I removed from my seat to a retired part of the room, where, becoming more collected, I inquired within myself, "from whence cometh all this fear?" My faith then rallied and my confidence in the Lord returned, and I said, "get thee behind me Satan, for my Jesus hath made me free." My fears instantly forsook me, and I vacated my retired corner, and came forth before all the people again, and the presence and power of the Lord became greatly manifested in the assembly during the remainder of the service. (91)

Elaw's sanctification is a gift of presence and power. In a situation in which she legally or physically has no authority, her anxieties forsake her and she is able to present herself, without fear or shame. Phoebe Palmer (1807–74), evangelist, camp-meeting leader, and author of three books, declares in her *Way of Holiness* (1843): "holiness is a gift of power, and, when understandingly received by either old or young disciples, nerves for holy achievement" (Hardesty, *Women Called to Witness*, 66). This personal power should be understood to mean "power with God" and "power through God," both at the core of spiritual narratives for African-American women.

One obvious aspect of the appeal of sanctifying power for women, particularly black women, is that sanctification and a life of holiness is the work of the Holy Spirit – the only member of the Trinity not specifically associated with the male gender as white men were usually the mental and physical representations of God. God is the father; Christ walked the earth as a man and as the Son. The Holy Spirit is actually a spirit, without shape, form or gender. As the Holy Spirit of the first-century New Testament Church was given to all the disciples of Christ, both male and female, so did female believers of sanctification feel as if this second blessing was for them: that it was the Holy Spirit who mandated that the daughters prophesy, along with the sons. Elaw writes in response to those who tried to deny the validity of women preaching:

> It is true, that in the ordinary course of church arrangement and order, the Apostle Paul laid it down as a rule, that females should not speak in the church, nor be suffered to teach; but the Scriptures make it evident that this rule was not intended to limit the extraordinary directions of the Holy Ghost, in reference

to female Evangelists, or oracular sisters, nor to be rigidly observed in peculiar circumstances. (124)

Again, Elaw makes it clear that the Holy Spirit takes precedence even over the written word and over the instructions of Christianity's greatest apostle, Paul. Elaw cites the biblical example of Phoebe being a deaconess, employed by the Church to manage affairs, and of the Apostle John writing his second epistle to a Christian woman who was a mother of the early Christian Church. And while the argument against women preaching often noted that these women were simply assistants to the men and had no real authority in the Church, Elaw's rebuttal is that at least in the early Church the "brethren ... extensively possessed the gift of utterance, and were therefore in no need of female speakers" (124). It is obvious to Elaw that there was a great need of female speakers since the men no longer possessed the true and holy "gift of utterance" from God. Braxton states that these female believers in sanctification "formed their self-authorizing and proto-feminist concepts on their directed experience of the Holy Spirit," whose divine source they explicitly saw was "no respecter of either gender or the hierarchies of temporal based religions" (*Black Women Writing Autobiography*, 56). As Braxton argues, these women were able to go "against the external limitations imposed on them by their respective denominations and in their personal secular lives" (56). Elaw's evangelism was self-supported; she preached under no license or denominational sanction or financial support. She herself chose her missions and journeys solely in consultation with her inner spiritual promptings.

Conversion narratives by African-American women, including Elaw's, indicate that the experience of sanctification had begun to surpass even the initial conversion experience as the most important transforming experience in a female believer's life. In her study of white women's nineteenth-century conversion narratives, Brereton found that conversion was seen as "too easy," too "inexpensively obtained" and less than emotionally satisfying, for one could undergo conversion and still revert to sin. Sanctification as the path to holiness – obtaining perfection and a sin-free life – was a much harder road to travel. It was not the instantaneous gift of grace bestowed upon a believer at the moment of salvation, but the day-to-day denial of sin and of flesh. Phoebe Palmer says that one had to "consecrate all upon the altar of sacrifice to God, with the resolve to enter into the bonds of an everlasting covenant to be wholly the Lord's for time and eternity, and then acting in conformity with this decision, actually laying all upon the altar" (Hardesty, *Women Called to Witness*, 57). Even when Elaw has doubts about her sanctification, fearing that she "ought not to make so bold a profession of an entire sanctification and holiness of spirit, lest I should be unable at all times to maintain it," she ultimately finds comfort in believing that "He which hath called you is holy, so be ye holy in all manner" (68). Sanctification is no longer a choice, but an obligation of the true believer, who has sincerely separated herself from unbelievers.

Literary critic Jean McMahon Humez indicates that "holiness had a particularly strong appeal for black women ... that the joyful sense of complete security, of attaining to sanctification in life, should be of great psychological value for a woman who had to deal daily with white racism" ("My Spirit Eye," 5). Amanda Berry Smith, a well-known African American evangelist of the last half of the nineteenth century and author of her own conversion narrative, *Autobiography: the Story of the Lord's Dealings with Mrs. Amanda Smith, the Colored Evangelist,* sums up the psychological value of sanctification when she says, "I think some people would understand the quintessence of sanctifying grace if they could be black for about twenty four hours" (Humez, "My Spirit Eye," 5). It was her contention that it would take the literal indwelling of God within an African-American woman to provide her with the inner peace and external fortitude to negotiate a racist and sexist world.

Thus, sanctification very early on becomes almost exclusively the realm of women. Ladies' auxiliary groups, women's missionary societies, and female prayer bands were formed as women gathered together to promote and strengthen each other's beliefs in this second blessing. Among teachers of the sanctification doctrine, women preachers and evangelists may well have been in the majority, although they were not officially ordained. African-American women, out of a need for emotional and material, as well as spiritual, support formed numerous predominantly female praying and singing bands. Sanctification was so strongly embraced by women that it became a threat to male leadership; these "sanctified" women were religious leaders, even though denied official leadership through male-controlled religious groups.

Elaw likens herself to the New Testament character of Phoebe, one of "the matrons of the apostolic societies" (67). Her initial calling was the "family or household ministry," which she describes as a "particular duty, a special calling, which I received from the Lord to discharge for the space of five years" (71). And even beyond the spiritual guidance that Elaw is providing for other women and their families, she concerns herself with the needs of African-American children and their education:

> I then opened a school, and the Lord blessed the effort, and increased the number of my pupils, so that I soon had a nice little school; many of the Society of Friends came and visited it, and assisted me with books and other necessaries for it. They were also much pleased with the improvement of the children ... and it was gratifying to many of them to see a female of colour

teaching the coloured children, whom the white people refused to admit into their seminaries and who had been suffered formerly to run about the streets for want of a teacher. (85)

Sanctification provided Zilpha Elaw with the boldness to challenge the tradition of male leadership; to become an independent evangelist apart from the sanction of any established church; to form a female "household" ministry; to travel and preach in slave states, despite laws prohibiting it; and to educate black children, despite its prohibition. Unlike many other African-American spiritual narratives, Elaw's does not document her own "coming to literacy." Born free, her narrative seems to indicate that she had been taught to read and write as a child. Yet, the quest of literacy remains a central feature of her conversion story, especially as she teaches others to read, aware that literacy is often the key to freedom – both freedom from ignorance and sometimes physical as well as psychological freedom from slavery.

The resistance to women's embracing of sanctification doctrine seemed greatest among the families, friends, and husbands of the sanctified believers. Since their mortal bodies had been crucified and they were now handmaidens of the Lord, they could not be controlled, either spiritually or physically. Elaw's husband, in fact, provided the main opposition to her ministry. She recounts that in 1810, she "surrendered" herself in marriage to Joseph Elaw, who although a respectable young man was not a Christian, "that is a sincere and devoted disciple of Christ, though nominally bearing his name" (61). Since Joseph Elaw was a Christian in name only, Zilpha Elaw has some doubts as to whether their union was even valid, and thus her responsibility to consider him as the "head" of their marriage and household was undermined: "By the Jewish law, the marriage of a Jew with a woman of a prohibited nation, was not accounted marriage, but fornication, and it is a very serious impropriety also under the Christian dispensation" (62).

Joseph Elaw used every means to induce his wife to "renounce her religion" and stop her attendance at church. She recalls that he was "passionately fond of music and dancing, and determined to introduce me to such merriments of the world, and hoping thereby to accomplish his object: but that God whom I served night and day, preserved me in the hour of temptation and shielded me from harm" (63). After her sanctification experience, Elaw's husband becomes even more averse to her religious activities: "tidings came to his ears, and were tauntingly disclosed" by someone who revealed that Elaw was a preacher, that she had been preaching "for two months" before her "husband knew any thing about it; for he never went to a place of worship" (83).

It appeared to him so strange and singular a thing, that I should become a public speaker; and he advised me to decline the work altogether, and proceed no further. I was very sorry to see him so much grieved about it; but my heavenly Father had informed me that he had a great work for me to do; I could not therefore descend down to the counsel of flesh and blood, but adhered faithfully to my commission. (84)

On several occasions, Elaw cites Galatians 3:28: "There is neither Jew nor Greek, there is neither bond nor free, there is neither male nor female; for ye are all one in Christ." In response to objections from her husband and various male religious authorities, Elaw succinctly says: "Oh! that men would outgrow their nursery prejudices and learn that God hath made of one blood all the nations that dwell upon the face on the earth" (86).

Zilpha Elaw, considered a "weaker vessel" because of her sex, and of "poorer stock" because of her race, confounds the mighty of her time through her preaching, traveling, and writing. She spreads the gospel – the good news not just of Christianity, but the message of sanctification, particularly for its female believers. Elaw's language is a new, female language. It is not the male language preserved by the scriptures – an ancient language which does not suffice to communicate the realities of women's lives. Elaw speaks in a new tongue and she writes in a new language. She is communicating the news of her own self-actualization through her conversion and sanctification. Sanctification is a message whose promise of fulfillment is not located in some future time and in some future place; a believer can immediately receive the indwelling of the Holy Spirit and be freed to live a holy life. Elaw embraces this as the answer to her struggle to see justice and right prevail within her lifetime: to see the acceptance of the authority and power of God, even as voiced from a black female body.

A new quest

In the beginning was the Word . . . and the Word was God. (John 1:1)

The spiritual narratives of black women living in the nineteenth century give powerful insights into issues of race, gender, and religion. Zilpha Elaw's narrative demonstrates how she was able to use her preaching and traveling to transgress notions of the domestic sphere and a woman's "rightful place." Her narrative provides us with concrete examples of how she was able to use biblical rhetoric to challenge both racism and sexism. The story of her life is a testimony to one way in which nineteenth-century black women could have a powerful voice. A look into other spiritual narratives by nineteenth-century black women, including Amanda Berry Smith, Jarena Lee, and Rebecca Jackson, reveals that all of these woman also include their "calls" to preach in their narratives. They insist upon their right to be able to speak before mixed crowds in public settings; they insist that the pulpit is an appropriate place for women.

Zilpha Elaw eloquently expresses what the sense of freedom found in conversion and sanctification means for the African American believer, particularly the female believer. She finds within Christianity that her sins are forgiven; she has access to salvation and eternal life; and most importantly, in her present world, she is a handmaiden of God. God promised to pour out his spirit on all flesh, including black flesh and female flesh. Elaw's conversion allows her to cast aside patriarchal ideals and language about women's roles in the Church. She writes of "sanctification" and "holiness," new ways to communicate the news of women's liberation. Where the words of the Bible have been used as weapons of superiority and oppression, used to debase, among others, African Americans and female believers, Elaw dares to step outside these racist and sexist constructs of language and behavior, and recreate God in her own image – a God that would allow a woman to leave her family and husband and pursue an independent career as a messenger of the gospel. Elaw's newly fashioned God is one that gives women authority to preach the gospel to both men and women, black and white, in the wilderness of the camp meetings or from the pulpit of the grandest cathedrals.

NOTES

1. The Great Awakenings were a time of intense religious fervor in America. The First Great Awakening began in the middle of the eighteenth century and the Second Great Awakening lasted from approximately 1795 until 1830. These Awakenings mirrored the Wesleyan revivals that were taking place in England at the same time. Extensive proselytizing efforts by preachers, missionaries, and evangelists attempted to spread the gospel throughout all parts of early America.

2. Revival meetings were usually a series of indoor church services featuring a well-known evangelist. The sole purpose of these meetings was to create new Christian converts and to call sinners into repentance. Camp meetings were prolonged outdoor revivals, sometimes lasting several weeks. Families, often accompanied by their slaves, would set up camp in a rural area and attend a series of open-air services. Camp meetings were well known for their religious "frenzy," and the services would last several hours, sometimes into the following morning.

3. Sanctification was also known as the "holiness" experience. Modern-day African-American Holiness churches (Pentecostal) can trace a direct link between their church doctrines and the doctrine of sanctification as it was experienced by a nineteenth-century woman like Zilpha Elaw.

4. What was truly revolutionary about sanctification, and blasphemous to those who disputed the claim, was the belief that sanctification not only cleansed you from all sin, but also created a pure sin-free nature within you; you could therefore live the rest of your life in a sin-free state if you had been truly sanctified.

WORKS CITED

Andrews, William. *To Tell a Free Story: the First Century of Afro-American Autobiography, 1760–1865.* Urbana: University of Illinois Press, 1986.

Andrews, William, ed. *Sisters of the Spirit: Three Black Women's Autobiographies of the Nineteenth Century.* Bloomington: Indiana University Press, 1986.

Braxton, Joanne M. *Black Women Writing Autobiography: a Tradition Within a Tradition.* Philadelphia: Temple University Press, 1989.

Brereton, Virginia Lierson. *From Sin to Salvation: Stories of Women's Conversions.* Bloomington: Indiana University Press, 1991.

Caldwell, Patricia. *The Puritan Conversion Narrative: the Beginnings of American Expression.* Cambridge: Cambridge University Press, 1983.

Clements, William. "'I Once Was Lost': Oral Narratives of Born-Again Christians." *International Folklore Review* 2 (1982): 105–11.

Connor, Kimberly Rae. *Conversions and Visions in the Writings of African-American Women.* Knoxville: University of Tennessee Press, 1994.

Costas, Orlando. "Conversion as a Complex Experience." *Gospel in Context* 1 (July 1978): 14–39.

Douglass, Frederick. *Narrative of the Life of Frederick Douglass, an American Slave.* 1845. Ed. Houston A. Baker, Jr. Harmondsworth: Penguin.

Edwards, Jonathan. "Personal Narrative." *The Norton Anthology of American Literature.* 4th edn. Vol. I. New York: W. W. Norton, 1994.

Elaw, Zilpha. "Memoirs of the Life, Religious Experience, Ministerial Travels and Labours of Mrs. Zilpha Elaw." *Sisters of the Spirit.* Ed. Andrews.

Gates, Henry Louis, Jr., ed. *Spiritual Narratives: the Schomburg Library of Nineteenth-Century Black Women Writers.* New York and Oxford: Oxford University Press, 1988.

Hardesty, Nancy. *Women Called to Witness: Evangelical Feminism in the Nineteenth Century.* Nashville: Abington Press, 1984.

Humez, Jean McMahon. *Gifts of Power: the Writings of Rebecca Jackson, Black Missionary, Shaker Eldress.* Andover: University of Massachusetts Press, 1981.

"My Spirit Eye: Some Functions of Spiritual and Missionary Experiences in the Lives of Five Black Women Preachers, 1810–1880." *Women and the Structure of Society: Selected Research from the Fifth Berkshire Conference on the History of Women.* Ed. Barbara J. Harris and JoAnn K. McNamara. Durham: Duke University Press, 1984.

Hunter, William. "'Do Not be Conformed Unto this World': an Analysis of Religious Expression in the Nineteenth-Century African-American Spiritual Narrative." *Nineteenth-Century Studies* 8 (1994): 75–88.

Lincoln, C. Eric, and Lawrence H. Mamiya. *The Black Church in the African-American Experience.* Durham: Duke University Press, 1990.

Lindley, Susan Hill. *"You Have Stept Out of Your Place": a History of Women and Religion in America.* Louisville: Westminster John Knox Press, 1996.

Shea, Daniel, Jr. *Spiritual Autobiography in Early America.* Princeton: Princeton University Press, 1968.

Watkins, Owen. *The Puritan Experience: Studies in Spiritual Autobiography.* New York: Schocken Books, 1972.

12

LISA A. LONG

The postbellum reform writings of Rebecca Harding Davis and Elizabeth Stuart Phelps

In 1867, young, fledgling author Elizabeth Stuart Phelps wrote a tribute to the work of her equally young contemporary, Rebecca Harding Davis. Davis's work, Phelps exclaimed, "made you feel as if she knew all about you, and were sorry for you, and as if she thought nobody was too poor, or too uneducated or too worn-out with washing days, and all the things that do not sound a bit grand in books, to be written about" ("At Bay," 780). As this chapter will suggest, both writers expressed reformist sentiments by writing passionately of the pressing social ills of their times. However, Phelps and Davis also developed a literary form devoted, as Phelps noted of Davis's work, to "knowing all about us" and the internal struggles that, she claims presciently, "do not sound a bit grand in books." Though Phelps and Davis acknowledged their thematic and philosophical kinship, few students of American women writers have explored the sophisticated nature of the reform literature that the two friends developed simultaneously during the next five decades. Their work, and the critical responses it has elicited, has much to teach us: about the limits of generic classifications and the perils of literary history; about the continuing need for critical work that elucidates the many American women writers who remain if not "lost," at least hidden; and about the utility of creating new connections between an author and her various texts, as well as between an author and her fellow writers. We must look not only to Phelps's and Davis's adult fiction, but also to their essays, autobiographies, and juvenile texts to discover the fullness of their thought. While individually they have failed to compel significant critical attention, the intertextual conversation the two carried on reveals a more complicated notion of reform fiction than is allowed under current understandings of the genre.

Phelps's and Davis's mutual admiration apparently nourished both their personal relationship and professional achievements. While neither Davis nor Phelps scholars know of any correspondence between the two that has survived, Sharon M. Harris's archival detective work reveals that each gave the other's writing serious consideration. In addition to a number of public expressions of affection and admiration such as that offered in "At Bay," Harris cites letters from Davis to the two young writers' mutual friend, Annie Fields, which offer evidence of their relationship. Davis wrote to Fields in 1866, asking if she knew "a Miss Phelps of Andover?" Though Davis continued that she liked Phelps "thoroughly – and some things she has written – too," Harris maintains that Davis found Phelps's "hyperbolic language" and "overt sentimentalism" distasteful (Harris, *Rebecca*, 118). Yet Davis also counted Phelps among the best of her contemporary realists – a seeming contradiction that is significant to my argument. In her article, "Women in Literature," Davis singles out Phelps as a powerful practitioner of "genre pictures of individual characters in our national drama" (402–4). Phelps again articulated her debt to Davis in a piece published after Davis's death, which claims Phelps's "personal indebtedness" to Davis's "Life in the Iron Mills" for forcing upon her the "claims of toil and suffering upon ease" in a powerful manner (quoted in Harris, *Rebecca*, 307). In a letter dated February 12, 1906[?], Davis claims to know Mrs. Phelps-Ward "so well" that she feels as if she should know Phelps's father-in-law, indicating that the intimacy between the two writers extended the length of their long careers and lives (quoted in Harris, *Rebecca*, 339).

Perhaps the two writers marveled at the similar trajectories taken by their careers: Davis received critical acclaim for her first published story, "Life in the Iron Mills" (1861), while Phelps achieved phenomenal commercial success with her first novel of the Civil War, *The Gates Ajar* (1868). Their reformist sensibilities were born during the "feminine fifties" and were subsequently shaped by the debates of the Civil War era; thus, throughout their sustained and prolific post-Civil War careers, both authors remained attuned to regional, racial, gender, and labor conflicts in their writing. Yet Davis was more sensitive to racial issues than Phelps, whose work consistently negotiated issues of class. Davis's residence in slaveholding Alabama and Virginia during her youth may account for this difference; Phelps remained comfortably ensconced in New England throughout her life, yet her summers spent working in the Gloucester tenements shaped her social thought. Davis enjoyed a relatively happy marriage and the birth of three children, while Phelps married late in life, choosing a much younger man with whom she had a difficult relationship. Yet the texts of both authors are filled with women who are challenged by combining married life and ambitious careers, suggesting that they lived the struggles about which they wrote.

Critical responses to reform: problems of type and time

The resonance in their thinking extends to subsequent critical treatments of their work. Despite the fact that both women were well-respected and visible forces in the late nineteenth-century literary scene – published and reviewed in the best journals of their times – they are not typically considered "major figures" of American literature. Davis published over 500 texts during her five-decade career, ranging from adult novels and stories to children's fiction, travelogues, editorials, and essays. Phelps produced a similarly impressive number and variety of texts during her own half-century career. A handful of fine single-authored studies acknowledge the importance of these bodies of work, treating the entire œuvres of each. Yet Davis and Phelps are more likely to appear as footnotes in larger treatments of nineteenth-century literature. In part, the wholesale dismissal of the vast majority of each writer's œuvre derives precisely from the fact that each is reclaimed primarily as an early proponent of social reform fiction. Davis's "Life in the Iron Mills" and Phelps's *The Silent Partner* (1871) (along with Harriet Beecher Stowe's *Uncle Tom's Cabin* [1852]) are cited as the fundamental texts of social re-form literature, and, in Davis's and Phelps's cases, as anomalies in their long careers. David Reynolds's dismissal of Davis's body of work is typical of the exceptionalism argument marshaled against Davis's and Phelps's liter-ary productions. He writes sweepingly of mid-century women writers, "we see that each approached a highly fertile moment of artistic autonomy but then withdrew from final, complete commitment to literary art ... Davis, after her triumphant portrait of class- and gender-related degradation in 'Life in the Iron Mills,' suffered a nervous collapse and then was forced by her family's poverty to write profitable domestic fiction for magazines" (*Beneath the American Renaissance*, 419). Indictments of Phelps, too, cite her chronic ill health as tempering her literary success. Thus while "Life in the Iron Mills" and *The Silent Partner* are praised for their passion and social commitment, subsequent social reform fictions are often panned on aesthetic grounds, accused of excessive didacticism, religiosity, and/or sentimentality. Ann Douglas offers a blanket criticism of Phelps as a woman and an author, describing her as "seldom likeable, always a sentimental writer, [and] often a sloppy one" (*Feminization of American Culture*, 223). Henry James be-gan the literary assessment that would hound Davis's post-"Life in the Iron Mills" fiction, skewering her novel, *Dallas Galbraith* (1868), for "instruct-ing us, purifying us, stirring up our pity," rather than remaining objectively interested in aesthetics (review, 331).

Selected fictions were initially reclaimed within the context of a femi-nist tradition, one that some readers assume eschewed interests and debates besides the "personal" concerns of the women writers and their ostensibly emotional female readership. For example, in Tillie Olsen's influential afterword to the 1972 reprint of "Life in the Iron Mills," Olsen forged a sympathetic bond – a "hunger to know" – between the seemingly oppressive life Davis suffered during her twenties, the poverty-stricken workers whose lives she imaginatively entered, and the lives of twentieth-century women like Olsen. Works perceived as more religious or didactic have suffered in comparison to the few texts which apparently prefigure the dilemmas facing "modern" women. It is no coincidence that Phelps's *The Story of Avis* (1877) is her most popular novel today, for recent critics have embraced it as an "expression of feminist social activism" (Kessler, introduction, xiv). This text follows the conventions of the *Künstlerroman* (artist's novel), for it charts the development and maturation of a painter. Phelps uses this familiar form to critique the painful sacrifices required of wives and mothers who have artistic aspirations, demonstrating that she was, as the Feminist Press's cover material phrases it, "ahead of her own time." Yet Phelps's *The Gates Ajar* – one of the most important and best-selling novels of the nineteenth century – is often dismissed as a religious tract or melodramatic escapism. Some of the most influential efforts by feminist critics to carve out a powerful space for nineteenth-century American women writers have largely bypassed Davis and Phelps altogether. Jane Tompkins focuses on antebellum authors and the "cultural work" accomplished when "sentimental" writers of that era tapped into familiar tropes to elicit emotional responses and sympathy from their readers. Periodization bears on Phelps's and Davis's marginality in this scholarship. Nina Baym's work on women novelists stretches just past the antebellum era to 1870; however, she, too, ignores Davis and leaves Phelps dangling at the end of her study as representative of the "next generation" of American women writers, who were "less socially progressive and optimistic" – and, then, less attractive to contemporary students of nineteenth-century American women writers – than their literary mothers (*Woman's Fiction*, 246, 298).

I contend that critics have sought a particular kind of feminism in the work of these women writers – a cultural feminism that privileges "women's ways" of knowing and doing, champions activism, and ultimately promotes female community as human salvation. In part, so much of Davis's and Phelps's work has apparently foundered because it denies the possibility of community and frames its gender analysis in broader, more theoretical terms. In making this claim I do not deny Phelps's and Davis's crucial place as early critics of American patriarchy, nor do I seek to erase gender as a primary category of analysis. It is just such claims that have kept Phelps, Davis, and a host of other American women writers at the margins of literary history.

Rather than revaluing women's culture or fitting so-called feminine genres to their own ends as antebellum writers such as Harriet Beecher Stowe and Lydia Maria Child had done so compellingly, Phelps and Davis work to dismantle gender identity – indeed, go so far as probing our identity as human beings. They destabilize the seemingly sure category of gender, showing that the "natural" behaviors ascribed to men and women are not natural at all. Gender emerges as one of a number of nebulous terms used by nineteenth-century Americans to construct their identities.

The relatively fixed generic parameters of discussions of nineteenth-century literature also have been instrumental in marginalizing Davis's and Phelps's work. Primarily, it is women authors who began writing during the Civil War, came of age in the immediate post-Civil War period of national Reconstruction, and aged in the subsequent era of conspicuous consumption labeled the "Gilded Age," who are typically assigned places either at the tail end of sentimentality or as early precursors of realism. At best, their works are labeled fruitful transitional experiments in genre; at worst, awkward hybrids of two established forms. As a result, many recent reclamations of nineteenth-century women's literature are often premised on revaluing and redefining sentimental elements – not questioning whether or not mid-nineteenth-century women writers all wrote sentimentally. The complementary strategy has been to place women writers in more "respectable" generic terrain. Realism, the literary form that gained ascendancy after the Civil War, was understood by male literary critics of the time as the antithesis of the sentimentality and romance that reigned before the war, for it sought to imitate "real" life. Realism's supposed objectivity was opposed to the subjective emotionalism of sentimental fiction and the fantasies of literary romances. As such, the realist label was thought to lend fiction a seriousness and validity that it could not otherwise claim. Nancy Glazener argues that Henry James attacked Davis's work so vehemently (labeling it "lachrymose sentimentalism") precisely because he suspected that "she might have been taken for a realist" even though she did not, in James's view, observe realist-professional emotional proprieties (review, 127, 3). Subsequent critics more favorably disposed towards Davis's work, such as Harris and Jean Pfaelzer, have argued for her place as a seminal realist (Harris, *Rebecca*, 2; Pfaelzer, *Parlor Radical*, 6). Phelps's work evokes even more confusion; she is labeled religious and sentimental as often as she is assigned a place in the realist tradition. Tompkins, Douglas, and most Phelps critics bring Phelps into the fold of sentimental writers, with incipient utopianism identified as a strain of her larger sentimentalism by critics such as Kessler. Interestingly, her social reform fiction – typified by *The Silent Partner* – is often pulled into the realist camp, while works not overtly engaged in depicting the world of filthy lucre are labeled sentimental, seemingly by default. Phelps's and Davis's critics often have made persuasive cases for reading their respective authors into generic traditions from which they have traditionally been barred. But I believe that Phelps and Davis remain peripheral figures in part because they still do not fit; the terms which continue to dictate critical discussions of nineteenth-century American literature do not account fully for their style and thinking.

Perhaps their most heinous literary transgression is that Phelps and Davis were born at the wrong time. Too young to be part of the literary and political innovations of the "feminine fifties," and by the 1880s and 1890s too staid to be audacious New Women, these authors and their works often fall through the cracks of literary periodization and feminist history. The 1860s – the decade during which they began publishing – has been figuratively consumed by the Civil War in literary scholarship. Contemporary critics of Civil War literature still contend with Daniel Aaron's and Edmund Wilson's dire but influential pronouncements on the disappointingly "unwritten" nature of Civil War experience and the corrupted partisanship of the Civil War literature which does exist. The story goes that the country's preoccupation with the bloody conflict distracted all writers from their craft, resulting in compromised texts that in no way capture the trauma and grandeur of the era. Despite recent critical efforts to resuscitate Civil War literature, the supposed literary aridity of this period serves as a convenient delineator between pre- and post-Civil War America, labels that we still use to organize study of nineteenth-century history and literature. The "transitional" fiction of writers like Phelps and Davis is the bridge which American literary historians traverse, moving smoothly from the banks of Hawthorne's romance and Stowe's sentiment to the shores of Howells's and James's realism, Norris's naturalism, and Twain's regionalism. Thus the bulk of Davis's and Phelps's early work remains obscure, bearing the weight of this historical march. Their innovative texts have created no crises and drawn little attention, but rather have offered neat solutions to the problems of literary history. Their post-Civil War efforts are also affected by what we might call Phelps's and Davis's literary illegitimacy; their generic line of origin is swallowed up in the morass of the Civil War era, and thus their subsequent writing remains orphaned, as well.

Reimagining reform

In order to reimagine reform we must first, as Phelps and Davis do, unimagine it, for the label of "reform fiction" has been a way of bracketing nineteenth-century American women writers from the mainstream of American literature. Reform has been employed as a monolithic category, tying together women writers separated not only by region, race, and class, but also by generations: Fanny Fern, Lydia Maria Child, Harriet Beecher Stowe; Louisa May Alcott, Davis, Phelps; Charlotte Perkins Gilman, Pauline Hopkins, Frances Ellen Watkins Harper. Those who have been particularly susceptible to the label are writers who were outspoken and successful professionals in their own days; who refused to remain disengaged from social/political debates; who wrote in a variety of forms – verse, prose, journalism. The reach of these writers has been read as compromising their aesthetic achievements. In the cases of Phelps and Davis, the reform label has encouraged readers to focus upon a set of characteristics that lead us away from more pressing and complicated issues. This is not to say that their so-called social reform fictions do not have the features that scholars traditionally attribute to that genre. Both draw on "real life" events, dramatizing the evils that befall those in need of reform and the salvation available to victims and reformers alike; they address readers directly or have explicitly didactic passages; and they appeal to readers through sentimental tropes, such as the death of a beloved character. Yet their works are not overtly or primarily pragmatic or motivational documents meant to touch their readers and inspire action.

I argue that in Davis's and Phelps's work, reform is reimagined, not only as nurturing empathy and soliciting aid from one's readers, but also as a hermeneutic task. Questions of what forms and informs us are intimately linked to nineteenth-century notions of reform, and dictate the genre that these writers developed – one that has remained largely invisible to contemporary readers. Rather than offering guides to a better future, Phelps's and Davis's texts seem to express ineffable grief, a sense of surreality, and impotence. They end inevitably with deaths, departures, disappointments, and ask questions more often than offer answers – about the possibility of personal intimacy, about our ability to impact our worlds, about how we exist in the world and where we go after our bodies fail us. As Phelps writes in her autobiography, "one thinks wistfully of that fair, misty world which is all one's own, yet on the outside of which one stands so humbly and gently" (*Chapters from a Life*, 2). Phelps's and Davis's fictions are efforts to articulate and plumb those two inexorably separated worlds: the one that is "all one's own" – which holds the promise of authenticity, coherent identity, and of origin – and the other that is the disassociated waiting place one inhabits. Their texts are audience-oriented primarily in that they encourage self-examination of the fragmented, alienated self; social action is a fortuitous by-product of such psychological labors.

Nowhere does reform fiction announce its difference from sentimental and realist fictions more explicitly than in its tone. These texts are characterized by an alienation and distance – ironically, a lack of passionate emotion and connection – that acknowledges the impossibility of Davis's famous plea that we "come right down with [her] into the thickest of the fog and mud and foul effluvia" ("Life in the Iron Mills," 13). Hers is not a conventionally warm welcome, but one that invites readers to roam a stifling yet vacuous, almost existential geography of body and mind. The world of "Life in the Iron Mills" is enveloped in smoke and fog, sodden with rain and alcohol, and consumed by the Dantesque fires of the mill. I argue that this brand of reform fiction does not seem to compel a corporeal response from its readers – the involuntary tears that we conventionally associate with a sentimental response. Rather, Davis's and Phelps's work engenders an almost schizophrenic response – one of detached concern evoked by suffering viewed from an intractable distance. Their heroes and heroines serve as models for their readers, for they do not weep and wail; though moved to action by the plights of others, Davis's and Phelps's characters fold in on themselves rather than opening up to embrace the world. Davis's *Margret Howth* (1861) is a case in point. Early in the novel the anonymous narrator describes Margret as desire-less and self-possessed: "She had not the usual fancy of her sex for dramatizing her soul in writing, her dress, her face, – kept it locked up instead, intact; that her words and looks, like her writing, were most simple, mere absorbents by which she drew what was needed of the outer world to her, not flaunting helps to fling herself, or the tragedy or comedy that lay within, before careless passers-by" (8). Inured to even her own suffering, each morning Margret thinks "she might as well get up and live the rest of her life out; – what else did she have to do?," facing each new day with "still, waiting eyes that told nothing" (58, 12). The novel ends happily for mill-worker Margret: good fortune brings her a husband and wealth, and she conventionally witnesses the redemptive death of another character. Still, she remains emotionally frozen and detached from her community: "She has no prophetic insight, cares for none, I am afraid," the narrator informs us (265).

Phelps's Perley Kelso and Sip Garth, too, are not ultimately nurturing, maternal figures. Reform is not a communal project in *The Silent Partner*, but an individual journey. Admittedly, heiress Perley, moved by the plight of local mill workers and her own sense of superfluousness, joins forces with poverty-stricken Sip. But at the end of the novel Perley and Sip part ways: "I left her to her work, and I keep my own" Perley tells her society friend, Fly, from whom she also feels an "impassable" distance (293, 302). Sip, too, turns in on herself at the end, speaking to her dead sister, who she claims is merely "out of sight," more often than to living people (291). Offered a marriage proposal and told that "other folks" marry and have children, Sip claims, "I seem to think that I'm not other folks. Things come to me someways that other folks don't understand or care for" (288). Though we are told that their class differences are the unbridgeable gap between the two women, the ending narrative emphasizes the profound singularity of each. Even the quote with which I opened this chapter, in which Phelps voices her appreciation for Davis's work, does not claim that texts are able to make palpable connections between author and reader. Phelps writes that Davis's work makes her feel "*as if* she knew all about you" (emphasis added). Her qualifier emphasizes that reform literature offered gentle fictions for readers willing to suspend daily realities, while insisting upon each woman's ultimate impenetrability.

Other scholars have noted that the "concept of a unified self" – that is, the absence of feelings of fragmentation, alienation, or surrealism – is an "untenable ideal" according to some mid-nineteenth-century women writers (Pfaelzer, *Parlor Radical*, 7). Yet traditional theories of social reform offer community as the antidote to this troubling sense of detachment and impotence. For example, the stated goal of the Boston Women's Educational and Industrial Union (WEIU) was to "break down barriers which for so long had interposed themselves between women," for they could then "begin to understand one another through these needs of the body, the heart, and the mind" (quoted in Spencer-Wood, "Feminist Historical Archaeology," 411–12). Davis and Phelps dramatize the ways that women *cannot* know each other. As Phelps writes of her life in Reconstruction America, "a phantom among phantoms I was borne along. Incredulous of the facts and dubious of my own identity, I whirled through readjustments of scene, of society, of purposes, of hopes, and now, at last of ambitions" (*Chapters from a Life*, 110). The social milieu is less important to Phelps than the "whirling," unsettled consciousnesses that mediate reality in her fictions. In her 1871 editorial, "Unhappy Girls," she exhorts her readers to "train" young women "from infancy to 'be' something" (1). Though Phelps meant that parents should offer their girls a profession, this passage can also be read as insisting on the difficulty of coming to terms with how one exists in the world – the philosophical problems of just "being." Clearly, social reform through communal activism is doomed to failure if one's fellows are as ethereal as phantoms, and one's own sense of self so tenuous.

The difficulty of "being" in post-Civil War America is reflected in Davis's and Phelps's unsettled aesthetics, too, for they self-reflexively explore the instability of text itself. The titles of their respective autobiographies hint at the limits of language to tell the whole story. In the introduction to her autobiography, *Bits of Gossip*, Davis eschews her personal history, writing that she has not offered "the story of [her] own life," but rather has "collect[ed] these scattered remembrances of my own generation." In her *Chapters from a Life*, Phelps explains how she was encouraged to explain what had "form[ed] and sustain[ed]" her literary career, admitting, "A stranger to my chart, I, doubtful, put about, and make the untried coast" (2). In stringing together "bits" of "gossip" (secondhand tales) and chapters from "a" life (Phelps does not claim it as her own, as "my" life), Davis and Phelps emphasize the inadequacy of narrative to represent lives from which they remain estranged, the "untried coasts" of their identities and memories. Personal history eludes Davis and she must collect "scattered remembrances" of her distant youth and friends; in doing so, she acknowledges the constructed nature of memory and history and implies that identity fails as a mechanism for holding together her texts. In their fictions, too, Davis and Phelps painstakingly chart the failure of identification, of image, of narrative to give form, and hence resonance, to what must remain unformed and, then, unreformable. I do not make the anachronistic claim that Phelps and Davis are postmodern writers. They consistently turn to religious faith to recuperate their traumas (no matter how facile and half-hearted that move might seem to this reader). But they do resist closure, stasis, and definition. Indeed, in questioning the nature of reality and the possibility of a stable identity, Phelps and Davis make the possibility of reform, itself, the subject of their works: how can one re-form what refuses to form, or what is constantly in the slippery process of re-forming itself?

Nineteenth-century social reform movements

Reform was a constant by-word throughout the nineteenth century. Both the 1830s and 1840s and the last twenty years of the nineteenth century are dubbed the Age of Reform by historians. If one chooses to view the purge of the Civil War and the Reconstruction era's subsequent reformulation of national culture as eras of reform as well, one could describe the nineteenth century as consumed by notions of reform. Despite the apparently radical possibilities of such a century, Phillip Brian Harper points out in his review of postbellum reform fiction that the appellation "reform" signaled gradual change of existing structures, rather than a revolutionary "transformation" of institutions. Thus reform movements and fictions often worked as much to preserve the status quo as to change it (Harper, "Fiction and Reform II," 226). As Phelps wrote in her autobiography, "I may not always believe all I was taught, but what I was taught has helped me to what I believe" (*Chapters from a Life*, 69). Both women championed numerous social causes: Phelps believed in higher education and enfranchisement for women, dress reform, the abandonment of vivisection, and homeopathy. She writes in her autobiography of how she devoted three years of her life to temperance activism at her beloved summer home in Gloucester. Phelps's description of her work there reads like a scene out of one of her social reform novels. Hearing that a poor mother of twelve has lost her husband in a barroom brawl, Phelps offers her comfort: "nothing and nobody quieted the woman; and so I went up, saying no words at all, and took her in my arms" (*Chapters from a Life*, 204–5). Conventionally, the touch of a middle-class woman soothes the more savage spirit of the destitute one. Subsequently Phelps preached at a local bar and lectured at the Reform Club. Most interesting is the effect her reform work has upon Phelps; rather than emphasizing the transformation within her community, Phelps observes, "It has never given me another hour when I felt that I had found the chief privilege of existence, as I felt when I forgot myself and pleaded with Heaven for those miserable men" (*Chapters from a Life*, 210). Again, an unbridgeable gap between Phelps's developing sense of self and the "miserable" people who enable her personal reformation undermines the communal effect of her efforts.

Davis shared Phelps's abolitionist and enfranchisement sentiments, and she also extended her sympathies to the plight of incarcerated Americans. While Phelps transcribed into fiction the real world effects of her reform work, Davis's reform writing had real world effects: *Put Out of the Way* (1870), a novella dramatizing the mistreatment of the mentally ill, led to the revision of the Pennsylvania laws. Rebecca and her husband, Clarke, wrote a number of pieces during the early 1870s that exposed the corruption of American asylums and the insufficiency of the laws meant to protect the mentally ill. Though it was Rebecca's dramatization of the tragedy that publicized these issues most powerfully, the governor of Pennsylvania appointed Clarke to a commission established to revise the state laws (Harris, *Rebecca*, 154–60). Though the range of reform activities available to Davis was limited both by gender proscriptions and by her own inclinations, her authorial activism continued throughout her life. An 1899 US Congressional Report incorporated Davis's "The Curse of Education," which argues that education should become part of prison reform.

According to historian Lori D. Ginzberg, the antebellum reform ethos prevalent during Davis's and Phelps's youths had relied on moral persuasion to affect transformations; such assumptions about reform emphasize its evangelical, fanatical – or to use late nineteenth-century terms, "hysterical" – tendencies. Phelps and Davis clearly denigrated reform in that incarnation. Both were critical of transcendental faith in the universal perfectibility of all human beings, and they disassociated themselves both from organized reform and the potentially radical implications of reformist beliefs. In *Bits of Gossip*, Davis vehemently scourges abolitionists in particular, and reformers in general, for their pathological behaviors. In the chapter "A Peculiar People," she notes that abolitionists "were generally regarded as madmen running about with a blazing torch to destroy their neighbors' homes. But their frenzy was usually recognized as an unselfish madness" (36, 163). And Phelps notes that despite her best efforts, often unfashionable causes would "burst the reformer out of [her] evangelical husk" (*Chapters from a Life*, 6). Her analogy suggests that though reform concerns lay dormant in each of us, they are always in some sense unripe and forced to maturity too soon.

Yet their fictions did not embrace the more disciplined reform that followed. Professional post-Civil War reformers apparently abandoned antebellum ardor, steeped in the "scientific management" methods developed by the United States Sanitary Commission during the Civil War. Thus they increasingly approached reform as a business, using organizations and governmental agencies to enforce appropriate behaviors from American citizens. As Ginzberg writes, "fervent faith in the possibilities of human change" was replaced by a "passion . . . for controlling human inadequacies" (*Women and the Work of Benevolence*, 211). The psychological work entailed in Phelps's and Davis's reform fiction became increasingly disconnected from the institutionalized business of social reform. Professional reform connoted firmness and discipline, while reform fiction favored fluidity. In writing of the future of "Women in Literature," Davis hopes that new women of "broad and accurate thought" will not be content to "expend their force in . . . charitable work." She encourages them to "leave something more permanent behind them than reports of Sanitary or Archeological clubs, and . . . paint as they only can do, for the next generation, the inner life and history of their times" ("Women in Literature," 404). Phelps's most successful reformer, Perley Kelso, claims "I am not a reformer . . . I am only a feeler," affirming Phelps's and Davis's receptivity to the depths of the inner life (*Silent Partner*, 241). Not as optimistic about the possibility for human change as their antebellum ancestors, nor as pessimistic about individual willpower as their Gilded era contemporaries, Phelps and Davis seem content merely to follow and record the vagaries of a living mind.

Thus the "social" half of the genre label is something of a misnomer for Phelps and Davis. The work that explicitly critiques a corrupt and unfair capitalist system has largely been acknowledged as social reform; but so much more of their work becomes visible under this fine-tuned definition. Not to overstate the significance of semantics, I would like to make a distinction between the prefixes *re* and *trans* in the context of *form*. Trans- implies a horizontal or vertical movement from one state to another, a sort of linear progress. Re- denotes a circularity in its logic; reform is a perpetual return. Rather than progressing horizontally, then, Phelps's and Davis's reform fictions as I understand them are more static in narrative, developing vertically through layers of bodily, social, and spiritual apprehensions of the world. The narrator of Phelps's *The Story of Avis* invokes the author as a "soul-geologist," someone who can fathom the soul's "topography" (4). It follows that Phelps reverts to the language of metallurgy to give form to her human subjects. Piqued by the question "What was it about her?" – what constitutes protagonist Avis's charm – Avis's best friend can only conclude that she is "without alloy, loadstone" (3, 5). But Avis resists categorization; an artist committed to "color divorced from form," she, as Phelps's mouthpiece, seeks essence undisciplined by structure or shape (7). In large part, both Phelps and Davis are engaged in finding out what their characters are "made of," of mapping the internal unseen.

Spectacular bodies and the impossibility of reform

Phelps and Davis provided resonant visual iconography of these issues for their readers, bodily traumas or cataclysmic events that stood in for the reformation they wished to express. *The Silent Partner*'s Perley Kelso, for example, "never do[es] anything that is not worth watching" (11). She is one of those "indexical persons" whose every move is spectacular. Within the context of the novel, such characters are conventionally enlisted in efforts to attract attention to extratextual reforms. For example, the symbolic crucifixion of Phelps's deaf and mute mill worker, Catty, on some unloosed logs, "occupie[s] the eyes of a thousand people"(277). The very public death of this disabled character prompts the two female protagonists to reject marriage and take on lives as social reformers. Throughout their fiction, Phelps and Davis – often through an anonymous narrator – invite their audience to gaze at horrifying sights, but always through some sort of barrier: the famous second-story window in "Life in the Iron Mills" (11); the prismatic mirrors of an unknown heaven in *The Gates Ajar* (80); the carriage window "frame" in *The Silent Partner* (19). In each case, readers take the position of voyeurs persuaded to peek at trauma through the protective shield of fiction. The aestheticizing distance from the site of trauma – what Mark Seltzer terms the composition of the "still life" (*Bodies and Machines*, 124–5) – keeps narrator and reader at bay. After all, we do not really see trauma when we read about it, but only imagine it – the view is tempered by our own desires and life experiences. Many scholars agree that a sociological belief in the possibility of objective observations of individuals and cultures, rather than a moral identification with the subjects of study, marks the realist turn in social reform circles. Yet Phelps knew full well that professional disinterestedness was impossible. "The literary artist will make over the world... portray[ing] what he knows, and little else" (*Chapters from a Life*, 235). It is not the pose of objective sociologist that keeps narrator and reader apart from the subjects of Phelps's and Davis's work, but a sensitivity to the subjective nature of human experience and thought.

It is a commonplace that reform fiction breached the apparent gulf between the private and public spheres for women by illustrating that individual action can affect social reforms. Yet the deaths of key characters such as Davis's Hugh Wolfe and Phelps's Aunt Winifred, and other characters' inability to trans-form or catapult themselves across the seemingly uncrossable chasms of race, class, gender, and disease insist that projects of self-reformation are often self-destructive, if not fatal. The most famous reform icon is Davis's korl woman, the spectacular symbol of "soul-starvation" in "Life in the Iron Mills." Hugh Wolfe's art is explicitly an act of reform, as he molds the raw garbage left over from the mill into a powerful work of art. Often overlooked, however, is Wolfe's final act of re-formation – the knife strokes that carve wounds in his own flesh and which cause his death. Able to shape the materials around him into fantastic, commanding shapes, Wolfe is unable to manufacture an appropriate self. Physical reformation is a dismal failure and poor substitute for the spiritual and political transformation he desires. Phelps, too, charts the intransigence of flesh. *The Gates Ajar*'s Aunt Winifred, who has proffered an alternative theology throughout the novel, cannot cure her own cancerous breast: "She walked feebly towards the window, where a faint, gray light struggled in, and opened the bosom of her dress" (230). Her wordless disclosure is an evangelical act, both speaking the cost of her unorthodoxy and working as a reforming agent on her listener. Yet her efforts are transitory and symbolically immolate her. Both Karen Sánchez-Eppler and Rosemarie Garland Thompson argue that some bodies "decline to be re-formed," thwarting notions of self-determination and self-improvement; at the same time, they insist upon the centrality of the body in American concepts of citizenship and personhood (Sánchez-Eppler, *Touching Liberty*, 1; Thompson, "Benevolent Materialism," 577). Phelps and Davis use human corporeality's resistance to reform as a way of expressing the impracticability of all reforms.

Phelps's and Davis's juvenile fictions are just as earnestly engaged in dramatizing the tensions at the heart of their adult reform texts. These novels may seem even better suited to the task, since we view adolescence as the time when we are explicitly and intensely initiated into the rites of reform.

Significant, then, is that Davis's and Phelps's youngsters grapple with the impossibility of forming appropriate adult identities. As Phelps's 1867 juvenile "Sunday School" novel, *Gypsy Breynton*, opens, Gypsy's older brother has found his twelve-year-old sister's bedroom in shambles. In order to tease Gypsy about her messiness, he uses the flotsam and jetsam left by the frenetic activities of his sister to fashion a representation of her:

> He put a chair in the middle of the room, tied a broom to it (he found it in the corner with a little heap of dust behind it, as Gypsy had left it when her mother sent her up to sweep the room that morning), and dressed it up in the three dresses, the cloaks and the cape, one above another, the chair serving as crinoline. Upon the top of the broom-handle he tied the torn apron, stuffed out with the rubber-boots, and pinned on slips of the geography leaves for features; Massachusetts and Vermont giving the graceful effect of one pink eye and one yellow eye, Australia making a very blue nose, and Japan a small green mouth. The hatchet and the riding-whip served as arms, and the whole figure was surmounted by the Sunday hat that had the dust on its feather. From under the hem of the lowest dress, peeped the toes of all the pairs of shoes and rubbers. (*Gypsy Breynton*, 16–17)

Cobbled together from the objects that clutter her room and which, this early scene reveals, she refuses to – indeed is incapable of putting in – order, Gypsy is domestic and public, national and international, feminine and masculine, human and monstrous, fleshed-out and disembodied. Eventually, the *faux* Gypsy is dismantled and its components subjected to "system." Yet Gypsy still struggles to unknot the "natural kink" in her nature, to discover the "bolt left out of her" – in short, to manufacture ladylike forms of behavior and sentiment which, she proclaims, "isn't in me" (37, 63). Clearly renegade, Gypsy has the most potential to dramatize reform for Phelps's readers. However, in this passage, Gypsy is not defined by what she is or makes, but rather by what she isn't and doesn't: unmended dresses and hats, an unswept room, unstudied geography books. Despite paying lip service to the ideology of the self-made woman, Phelps here makes the unmade woman the focus of her reform fiction.

In her most successful juvenile novel, *Kent Hampden* (1892), Davis, too, turns the self-made man inside out. The novel's action centers upon fifteen-year-old Kent's heroic efforts to discover the true thief of money believed to be stolen by his charismatic but imprudent father, Ralph. But the real crime and motivating tension of the novel is that Ralph "Spr[ang up in his community] like a mushroom in the night! No roots!" (4). Ralph's lack of origins and his stubborn unwillingness to betray any hint of his boyhood make him suspect on more than one level. As one friend counsels him, "No one really believes you took the money, but there is an unfortunate mystery. You have kept your early life a secret" (56). Even Hampden's wife, Sarah, knows nothing of her husband's youth. While he sleeps she manufactures enabling reform fictions about his past: "she lay with strained, burning eyes, her brain full of stories which she remembered of the many good men who had been tempted to crime in their youth and – had fallen" (16). Though the discovery of such a background would surely have been disappointing, it also would have served as a comfort to Sarah, offering a familiar cultural script about self-made men and the possibility for reform.

The explanation offered at the novel's final trial scene surpasses Sarah's modest expectations: Ralph had altruistically hidden his identity so that his unfortunate, crippled cousin could collect a family fortune. Yet the central question posed of Ralph at the dramatic trial scene – "Who and what are you?" – overshadows the answered mystery. At the end as at the beginning Ralph is "a man whom nobody knows," an unformed and, thus, unreformable man (134, 13). The real climax occurs not at the trial scene, but during the novel's denouement when Kent recognizes the fictional nature of origins and the impossibility, then, of reform. Denied his family history, Kent's thoughts turn awkwardly to God the Father on the last page of this otherwise secular novel (a move that Phelps also makes to affect Gypsy's ultimate transformation in her novel). "He felt for the first time in his life that God was a Something alive and near him," the narrator tells us (151). Davis searches still for a palpable "Something" – whether cause, community, self, or God – with which to prop up her characters.

Searching for form

The effort to locate and articulate that ineffable "Something" compels reform fiction. The verse which serves as an epigraph to Phelps's *The Story of Avis* – "And all I saw was on the sunny ground, / The flying shadow of an unseen bird"(3) – immediately draws the reader's attention to the presence of invisible worlds. Davis entitled her successful collection of short stories *Silhouettes of American Life*, emphasizing the sketchy, incomplete nature of modern existence. Ultimately, these shadows, ghosts, and imprints constitute Phelps's and Davis's reformist impulses. They cannot capture "origins" in any sense of the word, but only momentary traces and glimpses of a sustained, authentic self. Like the modernist writers who came after them, reform writers were compelled by explorations of subjectivity, a recognition of the inherently fragmented nature of human existence, and the insufficiency of traditional belief systems. Davis and Phelps were loathe to abandon their tenuous hold on "reality" and on timeliness, while American modernists such as

T. S. Eliot, Djuna Barnes, H. D., Gertrude Stein, and William Faulkner often slipped out from under the weight of such mundane restrictions. Certainly, Davis and Phelps rarely revealed the ironic detachment these writers cultivated. Yet these modern inheritors of reform, like Davis and Phelps, spend much of their time charting their characters' desperate searches for coherent selves, for unified form, even as they insist upon the fictional nature of reform. Debating the orthodox idea that we do not retain our individuality in heaven, one of the characters in Phelps's *The Gates Ajar* laments:

> We should be like a man walking down a room lined with mirrors, who sees himself reflected in all sizes, colors, shades, at all angles and in all proportions, according to the capacity of the mirror, till he seems no longer to belong to himself, but to be cut up into ellipses and octagons and prisms. How soon would he grow frantic in such companionship, and beg for a corner where he might hide and hush himself in the dark? (80)

Her protagonists are displaced and fragmented; their bodies are felt and seen in such distorted ways that they become unrecognizable. Traditional heaven holds no promise of individual coherence here, and thus must be reworked in the novel.

Davis's treatment of this subject is more personalized and, in some sense, more poignant. In her short story "Anne" (1889), the widowed protagonist awakes from a dream about her youthful but doomed romance, determining to "run away" from the comfortable reality of her adult children, her aging body, and her conservative life choices. Gazing at her fifty-year-old face in the mirror, "something within her cried out, 'I am here – Anne! I am beautiful and young!' " – signaling a belief in some essential self that persists despite the passage of time ("Anne," 330). Yet what she sees in the mirror is not authentic, but merely a reflection. On her short-lived trip, Anne's train is wrecked, she gets rheumatism, and meets her long-lost love only to discover that he is debauched. She is carried home and put to bed by her solicitous family. Though the lesson of the story is that Anne should be thankful for the life she's made for herself, the last lines of the story hint at a deeper meaning. In the midst of her happy homecoming, "Mrs. Palmer will say to herself, 'Poor Anne!' as of somebody whom she once knew that is dead. Is she dead? She feebly wonders; and if she is dead here, will she ever be again?" ("Anne," 339). Davis expresses doubts about the existence of an essential self. She even suggests that Anne may have died in the wreck and has entered an uncanny afterlife. Davis clearly wrestled with herself about the viability of such a world. She vented her spleen at the transcendentalists in *Bits of Gossip*, claiming "their views gave you the same sense of unreality . . . [and] left you with a vague, uneasy sense that something was lacking, some back-bone of fact. Their theories were like beautiful bubbles blown from a child's pipe, floating overhead, with queer reflections on them of the sky and earth and human beings, all in a glow of fairy color and all a little distorted" (36). Yet she praised Hawthorne for his "second sight," which "naturalized" him "into the world of ghosts [where he] could interpret for us their speech" (59). Her own ambivalence about the existence of invisible realms surfaces here. Apparently, Emerson's vision was corrupted by distortion – childishly optimistic reflections of an absent "fact." Yet Hawthorne trafficked in shadows, too, however "authentic" they may have seemed to Davis.

Phelps's *The Gates Ajar* confronts these issues head on, struggling with the way that traditional notions of heaven negotiate the conundrum of earthly and spiritual lives grounded in a sense of corporeality. Initially, Phelps's protagonist is horrified by a sermon, delivered after the death of her beloved brother, that offers only "glittering generalities, cold commonplaces, vagueness, unreality, a God and a future at which [she] sat and shivered" (73). Later, she is comforted by her aunt's insistence that heaven is a perfectly re-formed version of earth where bodies, homes, and relationships are reconstituted in idealized forms. By the end of the novel, Phelps's characters are either dead or happy in the belief that their loved ones wait for them at their heavenly homestead. "It will be like going around a corner, don't you see?," dying Winifred assures her grief-stricken niece, "You will know that I am there all the while, though hidden, and that if you call me I shall hear" (235). Dead relatives are omnipresent ghosts, ethereal and very human all at once. Yet Phelps cannot resolve the theoretical problem the novel takes on. In an odd move, she insists that heaven has become the "reality," the "substance," while life on earth is the "shadow," "the dream" (194). Ultimately life will be the most "life-like" in heaven; postbellum America is a surreal shadow of its lofty ideal. Ironically, the promise of the afterlife quells the need for reform on earth, or at least suggests its insufficiencies when compared to the profound and true transformation to come in the afterlife.

Reform fiction is characterized in some sense by the unsustainability of its subject matter. Questions, equivocations, and seeming inconsistencies in both theme and form have traditionally made these novels difficult for students and scholars to understand. Davis and Phelps seem aware of the challenges their texts – indeed all texts – pose. Davis writes of her childhood reveries while staring in her home fires:

> on this base [of coal] was a gray lettering that incessantly formed itself into words and then crumbled away. You knew that the words, if you could read them, would tell you the secret of your life, and you would watch them late

into the night, until you fell asleep and woke to watch again. But the words always crumbled away before you could read them. (*Bits of Gossip*, 9)

Here Davis imagines the ash and smoke as a text that constantly forms and reforms itself such that the reader is able to glimpse only momentary impressions of the complete text and, then, complete knowledge. It is the shadowy, transitory nature of these moments that makes Phelps's and Davis's texts so frustrating for many readers. This passage suggests the inadequacy of narrative as well. Words "crumble" – they are unequal to the task of holding the place for Phelps's and Davis's "stories of to-day," which Davis always urged her editors to publish as expeditiously as possible. The unremitting pace of these authors' publications at times, and the sustained nature of their work, speak not only of economic exigency, but also of the need to enact a theory of authorship and readership. Since moments of composition (as both writer and reader) are transitory, repetition and replacement are required of author and reader alike. Phelps and Davis were clearly pessimistic about the possibility of sustaining form through narrative; their attitudes toward their autobiographies show that they had little faith in the staying power of written history. Though language often eluded them, the ritual of writing and reading seems to have held value for both authors. I think that it is in these texts' larger indeterminacies, their dramas of becoming and unbecoming, that their meanings reside.

The future of reform fiction

In his now familiar treatment of American literary realism, Eric Sundquist acknowledges that the literature produced between the Civil War and the first decades of the twentieth century resists convenient generic classification, and that one could see this period as merely laying the groundwork for fully realized twentieth-century realism (*American Realism*, 5). I suggest finally that the traditional parameters of this argument have limited our critical approaches to many writers; "category crises" are not rarified occurrences for nineteenth-century American women writers (Pryse, "Sex, Class, and 'Category Crisis,'" 525). Phelps's and Davis's contemporaries such as Louisa May Alcott, Harriet Prescott Spofford, Elizabeth Stoddard, Frances Ellen Watkins Harper, and Constance Fenimore Woolson – to name but a few – are still marginalized, disparaged for their seemingly sentimental moments while barred from a realistic tradition that continues to focus on tragic and heroic characters, inventors, soldiers, and entrepreneurs. I contend that these women, too, write reform fiction. But I would argue that male writers such as John William De Forest, Albion Tourgée, and Dr. S. Weir Mitchell have fallen prey to this generic shuffle as well. De Forest scholarship in particular is dictated by "genre wars," as one critic puts it (Fick, "Genre Wars," 474). One camp argues that "De Forest's work represents an important transition from romantic to realistic writing," while those who read his generic fusion less charitably note "the mixture of sentiment and comedy with the brutal struggle for survival breaks down the aura of realism achieved by De Forest" at other points (Antoni, "Miss Ravenel's Conversion," 58; Solomon, "The Novelist as Soldier," 83). These male writers are not completely invested in verisimilitude, nor do they retreat into fanciful or imaginative worlds. Like the women writers, they attempt to give voice to the unvoiced – not only the marginalized characters who conventionally populate social reform fiction, but the psychological crises that informed life in post-Civil War America.

Ironically, "soul-geology" does not make compelling reading to contemporary audiences. For example, *The Gates Ajar*, one of the most popular novels of the nineteenth century, has just been reprinted. Indeed, the majority of Phelps's and Davis's texts have never been reprinted, and as a result have been unable to find new audiences. Elsewhere, I have argued that this sort of work is protomodern, so that, for example, Phelps's *The Gates Ajar* should not only be read in conjunction with contemporaneous sentimental and consolation fictions, but also with late century, modern works: "Comparing Mary's rebellion with Henry Fleming's psychological permutations, Winifred's heaven with [Ambrose] Bierce's spectral landscapes, reveals *The Gates Ajar*'s shadows and depths, and its resonance with the fiction of the modern period" ("'The Corporeity of Heaven,'" 801–2). I now believe that such strategies do not encourage us to fully value this literature for what it is, but, rather, to frame it in terms of what it isn't quite. Phelps's autobiographical anecdote about becoming reacquainted with one of her early works is instructive here. She analogizes, "the half-effaced negative came back to form under the chemical of some new perception" (*Chapters from a Life*, 91). Her reference to watching the story re-form may seem ironic in light of the way that I have argued these writers dispute the possibility of reformation. Yet she also insists upon the unreality of even the most accurate and lifelike mode of representation available to her. After all, her observation that the story has come "back to form" implies that it had been unable to sustain form while unperceived. Still, her perception that "new chemicals" – substitute new methods, new times, new readers – can make visible what has remained obscured, is compelling. Viewed through the lenses of sentimentality, romance, realism, or modernism, these works will always be found lacking. Attempting to follow reform fictions' own shifting terms may lead to us to surprising new insights.

WORKS CONSULTED

Aaron, Daniel. *The Unwritten War: American Writers and the Civil War*. New York and Oxford: Oxford University Press, 1973.

Antoni, Robert. "Miss Ravenel's Conversion: a Neglected American Novel." *Southern Quarterly* 24.3 (1986): 58–63.

Baym, Nina. *Woman's Fiction: a Guide to Novels by and about Women in America, 1820–1870*. Ithaca: Cornell University Press, 1978.

Davis, Rebecca Harding. *Bits of Gossip*. Boston: Houghton Mifflin, 1904.

Kent Hampden. 1892. New York: Charles Scribner's Sons, 1914.

Margret Howth: a Story of To-Day. Ed. Jean Fagan Yellin. 1861. New York: Feminist Press, 1990.

"Anne." *A Rebecca Harding Davis Reader*. Ed. Jean Pfaelzer. Pittsburgh: University of Pittsburgh Press, 1995. 329–42.

"Life in the Iron Mills." *Life in the Iron Mills and Other Stories*. Ed. Tillie Olsen. New York: Feminist Press, 1985. 11–65.

"Women in Literature." *A Rebecca Harding Davis Reader*. Ed. Jean Pfaelzer. Pittsburgh: University of Pittsburgh Press, 1995. 402–4.

Diffley, Kathleen. *Where My Heart is Turning Ever: Civil War Stories and Constitutional Reform, 1861–1876*. Athens: University of Georgia Press, 1992.

Douglas, Ann. *The Feminization of American Culture*. New York: Doubleday, 1977.

Fetterley, Judith. "Checkmate: Elizabeth Stuart Phelps's *The Silent Partner*." *Legacy* 3 (1986): 17–29.

Fick, Thomas. "Genre Wars and the Rhetoric of Manhood in *Miss Ravenel's Conversion from Secession to Loyalty*." *Nineteenth-Century Literature* 46.4 (March 1992): 473–94.

Ginzberg, Lori D. *Women and the Work of Benevolence*. New Haven: Yale University Press, 1990.

Glazener, Nancy. *Reading for Realism: the History of a US Literary Institution, 1850–1910*. Durham: Duke University Press, 1997.

Harper, Phillip Brian. "Fiction and Reform II." *The Columbia History of the American Novel*. Ed. Emory Elliot. New York: Columbia University Press, 1991. 216–39.

Harris, Sharon M. *Rebecca Harding Davis and American Realism*. Philadelphia: University of Pennsylvania Press, 1991.

"Literary Politics and the Political Novel." *Redefining the Political Novel: American Women Writers, 1797–1901*. Ed. Sharon M. Harris. Knoxville: University of Tennessee Press, 1995. vii–xxiii.

James, Henry. Review of *Dallas Galbraith* by Rebecca Harding Davis. *Nation* (October 1868): 331.

Kelly, Lori Duin. *The Life and Works of Elizabeth Stuart Phelps, Victorian Feminist Writer*. Troy, NY: Whitson, 1983.

Kessler, Carol Farley. *Elizabeth Stuart Phelps*. Boston: Twayne, 1982.

Introduction. *The Story of Avis*. By Elizabeth Stuart Phelps. New Brunswick: Rutgers University Press, 1992. xiii–xxxii.

Lang, Amy Schrager. "Class and the Strategies of Sympathy." *The Culture of Sentiment: Race, Gender and Sentimentality in Nineteenth-Century America*. Ed. Shirley Samuels. New York and Oxford: Oxford University Press, 1992. 128–42.

Long, Lisa A. "'The Corporeity of Heaven': Rehabilitating the Civil War Body in

The Gates Ajar." *American Literature* (December 1997): 781–812.

Olsen, Tillie. Biographical interpretation. *Life in the Iron Mills and Other Stories.* New York: Feminist Press, 1985. 67–174.

Parker, Alison M. *Purifying America: Women, Cultural Reform, and Pro-Censorship Activism, 1873–1933.* Urbana: University of Illinois Press, 1997.

Pfaelzer, Jean. *Parlor Radical: Rebecca Harding Davis and the Origins of American Social Realism.* Pittsburgh: University of Pittsburgh Press, 1996.

Phelps, Elizabeth Stuart. *Chapters from a Life.* Boston: Houghton Mifflin, 1896.

The Gates Ajar. 1868. Boston: Houghton Mifflin, 1893.

Gypsy Breynton. 1867. New York: Dodd, Mead, and Co., 1876.

The Silent Partner. 1871. Ridgewood, NJ: Gregg Press, 1967.

The Story of Avis. 1877. Ed. Carol Farley Kessler. New Brunswick: Rutgers University Press, 1992.

Three Spiritualist Novels: The Gates Ajar, Beyond the Gates, The Gates Between. Ed. Nina Baym. Champaign, IL: University of Illinois Press, 2000.

"At Bay." *Harper's New Monthly.* May 1867.

"Unhappy Girls." *The Independent.* July 27, 1871: 1.

Pryse, Marjorie. "Sex, Class, and 'Category Crisis': Reading Jewett's Transitivity." *American Literature* 70.3 (September 1998): 517–49.

Reynolds, David. *Beneath the American Renaissance: the Subversive Imagination in the Age of Emerson and Melville.* Cambridge, MA: Harvard University Press, 1988.

Rigsby, Mary. "'So Like Women!': Louisa May Alcott's *Work* and the Ideology of Relations." *Redefining the Political Novel: American Women Writers, 1797–1901.* Ed. Sharon M. Harris. Knoxville: University of Tennessee Press, 1995. 109–27.

Rose, Jane Atteridge. *Rebecca Harding Davis.* New York: Twayne, 1993.

Samuels, Shirley. Introduction. *The Culture of Sentiment: Race, Gender, and Sentimentality in Nineteenth-Century America.* New York and Oxford: Oxford University Press, 1992. 3–8.

Sánchez-Eppler, Karen. *Touching Liberty: Abolition, Feminism, and the Politics of the Body.* Berkeley: University of California Press, 1993.

Seltzer, Mark. *Bodies and Machines.* New York: Routledge, 1992.

Solomon, Eric. "The Novelist as Soldier: Cooke and De Forest." *American Literary Realism* 19.3 (1987): 80–8.

Spencer-Wood, Suzanne M. "Feminist Historical Archaeology and the Transformation of American Culture by Domestic Reform Movements, 1840–1925." *Historical Archaeology and the Study of American Culture.* Ed. Lu Ann De Cunzo and Bernard L. Herman. Knoxville: University of Tennessee Press, 1996. 397–446.

Sundquist, Eric. Introduction. *American Realism: New Essays.* Baltimore: Johns Hopkins University Press, 1982. 3–24.

Thompson, Rosemarie Garland. "Benevolent Maternalism and Physically Disabled Figures: Dilemmas of Female Embodiment in Stowe, Davis, and Phelps." *American Literature* 68.3 (September 1996): 555–86.

Tompkins, Jane. *Sensational Designs: the Cultural Work of American Fiction, 1790–1860.* New York and Oxford: Oxford University Press, 1985.

Wilson, Edmund. *Patriotic Gore: Studies in the Literature of the American Civil War.* New York: Farrar, Straus, and Giroux, 1962.

13

SANDRA A. ZAGARELL

"Strenuous Artistry": Elizabeth Stoddard's *The Morgesons*

Eyeing her sister Cassandra, Veronica Morgeson asks for Georges de Buffon's multivolume encyclopedia, proclaiming, "I want to classify Cass."[1] Veronica's indication of how difficult it may be to categorize even one person points to the preoccupation many characters in Elizabeth Stoddard's *The Morgesons* (1862) have with explanatory labels. This preoccupation is understandable, for the world in which these characters live is so fluid and bewildering that what the novel's protagonist, Cassandra Morgeson, calls "comprehension of self" and "comprehension of life" (9) is never fully available to even the most observant of them. Much of the power of *The Morgesons*, I will suggest, lies in its complication of assumptions about "life" and "self" which prevailed in the 1860s. Its characters – and its readers – are challenged to recognize that neither life nor self is actually commensurate with existing concepts and that making sense of both entails ceaseless intellectual and emotional work, work which reliance on conventional classification impedes.

These challenges distinguish *The Morgesons* from most contemporary American novels, including the popular domestic fiction of the era such as Susan Warner's best-selling novel *The Wide, Wide World* (1850). Women like Warner and Harriet Beecher Stowe embraced both Christian doctrine and the ideology of domesticity. Viewing their fiction as a combination of didacticism and entertainment, they told readers what to think and feel, soliciting readers' identification with their narratives by featuring accessible characters and familiar situations. Stoddard, however, viewed her novels as "art." She saw them in aesthetic and philosophical terms. She was determined to inscribe "truth" in them without explanation and with little direct appeal to emotion, leaving to readers the work of ascertaining just what "truths" her art suggested. Her artistic credo, a passage which she came across in Goethe's *Truth and Poetry* a few years after writing *The Morgesons*, suggests how far removed her concept of art was from a concept of literature which accommodated an explicit injunction like Stowe's, in *Uncle Tom's Cabin* (1850), that readers "Feel right" (that is, in a manner becoming a Christian) about slavery. The passage from Goethe reads: "The highest problem of every art is, by means of appearances, to produce the illusion of a loftier reality. That is, however a false effort which, in giving reality to the appearance, goes so far as to leave in it nothing but the common everyday actual."[2]

Art, this statement implies, should not explain, let alone enjoin. The artist should render ordinary life in ways which suggest that it has philosophical significance but do not specify what that significance might be, leaving each reader to determine what questions are raised and how to engage them. For Stoddard herself, these questions involved the very anchors of domestic fiction and prevailing systems of classification such as that of de Buffon's encyclopedia: religious and philosophical certainty. For, in contrast to most American women writers at mid-century, Elizabeth Stoddard was a professed religious nonbeliever, and what she termed her secularism was inseparable from her concept of art. Rendering the "common everyday actual" in ways which speak to the desire for belief but reveal the absence of grounds for faith, *The Morgesons* subtly and consistently assails the disposition of many of its first readers to believe in a "loftier reality." In a passage which seems to evoke Christianity, for example, the teenage Cassandra experiences the stirrings of religion as she watches her Aunt Mercy preparing the sacrament for a revival at church, "mix[ing] loaves [of bread] in a peculiar shape, and launch[ing] them into the oven." Tasting the bread, Cassandra finds it without "solemnizing powers," and when she later sees her aunt perform the reverse transubstantiation of "boil[ing] the remnants with milk for a pudding" after the revival is over, "the sacred ideality of the ceremony I had seen at church was destroyed for me" (45).

The passage from Goethe also speaks to Stoddard's view of literary art as something carefully crafted. Whereas, as Nina Baym has shown, most contemporary women writers viewed themselves as professionals, not as artists, and wrote with financial success in mind, Stoddard saw herself as a professional *and* an artist. Although she turned out formulaic short fiction for desperately needed cash, she took great pains with the form and style of what she thought of as her art – her two later novels, *Two Men* (1865) and *Temple House* (1867), as well as *The Morgesons*, risking failure in the marketplace by her experimentation.[3] Her novels' demanding character and their oddness in comparison with most mid-nineteenth-century American literature, in other words, represent deliberate artistic choices. (Stoddard's careful revisions of them at various points in her life and the contrast they present to her short stories, which were quite conventional, bear witness to the fact that she was making such choices.) Thus what commentators have almost always treated as stylistic peculiarities – a sort of garnish – are actually essential aspects of her strenuous artistry: understatement, ellipsis, and other formal elements which command readers' attention – extended dialogues without exposition; offbeat pacing and rhythm; unexpected shifts in tone and focus; a compelling but oblique form of characterization; an emphasis on individual scenes which frustrates the ready comprehension of the narrative by concentrating on plot.

Many modern commentators' responses to *The Morgesons*, including my own earlier ones, have in effect bespoken our inclination to preserve ways of reading nineteenth-century American literature with which we are comfortable rather than allowing *The Morgesons* to unsettle those ways. Sidelining its oddness even as we have acknowledged it, we have tried to shoehorn the novel into categories which we habitually apply to American fiction of the era: domestic, or "woman's," fiction, various kinds of gothic, the "literature of misery," the *Bildungsroman* (a novel which tracks its protagonist from youth to maturity, charting his or her development or decline).[4] Yet our employment of familiar labels is not so much off the mark as a very limited response to Stoddard's artistry, for it does respond to her cosmopolitan immersion in a wide range of contemporary literary strains, British and European as well as American. To anyone conversant with contemporaneous literature, *The Morgesons is* likely to seem familiar, even if it also seems strange. Its emphasis on the on-going mutability of life and the demands it makes of readers ally it with Emersonian transcendentalism. It resembles domestic fiction in its focus on the domestic realm and on the life of a female protagonist. Like *The Scarlet Letter*, it calls attention to the gothic provincialism of elements of New England culture. Like writing by a number of British and French women authors whom Stoddard admired – Charlotte and Emily Brontë, George Sand – it accentuates its protagonist's sexuality.

But part of the strenuousness of *The Morgesons'* artistry lies in the particular way it evokes or alludes to these strains of literature, which is to exert pressure on their key premises. In contrast to domestic fiction, it presents domestic life as lacking inherent meaning. Portraying "self" as a matter of ongoing, open-ended process, it repudiates as schematic the notion of a life trajectory of progress (or decline) which the *Bildungsroman* takes for granted. Its insistence on Cassandra Morgeson's sexuality disclaims the sexual innocence attributed to American heroines and sidesteps the diverse concepts of moral order embraced by Charlotte and Emily Brontë. Moreover, Stoddard's skepticism and pessimism distinguish *The Morgesons* from most other contemporary philosophic American writing, including Emerson's, because of the novel's refusal of any transcendental vision. Indeed, its focus on the flow of daily life and on sexuality, along with its denial of a "loftier reality" and its insistence that readers make meaning, not receive it, are forward-looking, aligning it with modernism. But even this match is partial. Unlike, say, *To The Lighthouse* or *Ulysses*, *The Morgesons* is a fiercely earnest book. Its distinctively Victorian standpoint is that even if there is no "loftier reality," life must be pursued with the same kind of intensity as if there were, and with a grim determination which owes a good deal to the latter-day Calvinism of Stoddard's native New England.

The discussion which follows explores the challenges which *The Morgesons'* representations of life and self presented its nineteenth-century readers and continue to present to readers today. My premise is that current readers' understanding of *The Morgesons'* artistry requires what might be called historicized textual interpretation: close attention to the novel's specific textual elements – philosophic, stylistic, generic, structural – combined with attention to historical and cultural context, especially fiction by contemporary American women, which Stoddard frequently reviewed in the 1850s and against which she partly measured her achievement of artistry. Historicized textual interpretation allows us to get at the sometimes subtle, sometimes less than subtle ways in which *The Morgesons* departs from domestic fiction and female *Bildungsroman* and where it overlaps with them. This approach also permits acknowledgment of the novel's connections with transcendentalism and its anticipation of modernism, at the same time granting due weight to its many idiosyncrasies, such as the description of the reuse of the sacrament for pudding. Finally, it allows us to take the measure of the particular ways in which the unique and the familiar blend and clash in this highly original book.

"Life"

The Morgesons teems with descriptions of domestic life: of dishes and food; of dresses, handkerchiefs, and shoes; of the furnishing of rooms and the layout of houses. Many of its numerous small scenes center on how people act and what they say in ordinary domestic situations, especially during meals. The prominence of daily domestic life aligns the novel with domestic fiction. But whereas true domesticity as portrayed by *The Wide, Wide World* and its fictional kin rests on Christianity, harmony, order, and maternal sustenance, the very nature of domestic life in *The Morgesons* precludes these. In Stoddard's novel, the clutter of domestic life denotes, not a correctable disorganization, but a fundamental and unchangeable flux. No housewifely program – "a place for everything and everything in its place," the motto of Lydia Sigourney's 1858 novel *Lucy Howard's Journal*, for instance – can bring meaningful order to it.

The details of the first mealtime scene in *The Morgesons*, an extensive recounting of a tea Mary Morgeson gives for the women of her parish, capture the novel's insistence on the cluttered randomness of domestic life. The scene unfolds as the first-person narrator Cassandra, here about eleven, experiences it, without the expression of the values of domestic order or Christianity in which narrators of domestic novels often engage.

> The table was laid in the long keeping-room adjoining the kitchen, covered with a striped cloth of crimson and blue, smooth as satin to the touch. Temperance [the "help"] had turned the plates upside-down around the table, and placed in a straight line through the middle a row of edibles ... With the sugar-tongs I slyly nipped lumps of sugar for my private eating, and surveyed my features in the distorting mirror of the pot-bellied silver teapot, ordinarily laid up in flannel. When the company had arrived, Temperance advised me to go in the parlor ...
>
> [I] stood behind mother's chair, slightly abashed for the moment in the presence of the party – some eight or ten ladies, dressed in black levantine, or cinnamon-colored silks, who were seated in rocking-chairs, all the rocking-chairs in the house having been carried to the parlor for the occasion ... They were larger, more rotund, and older than mother, whose appearance struck me by contrast. Perhaps it was the first time I observed her dress; her face I must have studied before, for I knew all her moods by it. (16–17)

Cassandra's survey of Mary Morgeson follows, adhering to the viewpoint of the child; then the voice of the adult Cassandra reflects that "I never understood [my mother]" (17). The text shifts to Veronica's command of Cassandra's attention by imitating a guest' then to the guests' conversation, then to Cassandra's returning focus on her sister. My difficulty in ending – or condensing – this quotation while capturing the feel of the text reflects the fluidity and absence of tendentiousness of *The Morgesons*. In *Lucy Howard's Journal* or *The Wide, Wide World*, domestic details usually serve a purpose and make a point; characteristic yet relatively brief passages can be lifted out fairly readily. If this (quite characteristic) scene from *The Morgesons* has a point, it is that succession and flow, not meaning, are endemic to domestic life. As the scene moves from detail to detail, no composite picture or synthesis emerges. From the first sentences' identification of the color and feel of the tablecloth to particulars about the normal and the company disposition of the teapot and the unusual assembling of the Morgeson rocking chairs to Veronica's amusing imitation of Mrs. Dexter, the scene takes in the look or feel of one object, statement, act, or person, then another, then another. Each merits Cassandra's attention, not because of its significance, but because it is there. Moreover, whereas in domestic fiction omniscient narrators typically provide a stable perceptual and moral center, Cassandra's very focus is ephemeral; she cannot even examine her puzzling, compelling mother for long. Likewise, each segment of the larger scene ends not by concluding, but by giving way to the next. Throughout *The Morgesons*, similarly, moments of fixity are usually fortuitous and always momentary; each dissolves into a succeeding moment. The succession of vignettes often creates a rapid tempo, as it does here, but not a pattern of either progress or purpose.

This emphasis on the fluidity, randomness, and the essential "thingness" of ordinary life is one way in which Stoddard's novel resembles work by some of her contemporaries now regarded as protomodernist (most of whom worked in forms other than the novel): Emerson, Whitman, Melville, Dickinson. Her conception of flux as the predominating principle of existence makes her almost Emersonian, although her religious–philosophical skepticism makes her more akin to Dickinson and Melville. And for Stoddard, as for Emerson, Melville, Dickinson, and for many modernists, humanity cannot abandon the effort to create order and meaning, however dubious the status of religious truth may be. Brief though Cassandra's attempt to comprehend her mother at the tea party is, it reflects the need for meaning. So, too, does the articulation of principles to live by in which many of the novel's characters engage, although the disastrous consequences of their often-mechanical application of conventions attest to the incommensurability of fixed codes with life's actual fluidity. (When Cassandra, having been invited by Charles Morgeson to spend a year at his Rosville home, asks her mother what she should "Do," Mary Morgeson can only respond "in a mechanical voice," "Read the Bible and sew more" (64). Cassandra goes to Rosville; there she and Charles have an unconsummated affair.)

But Stoddard's skepticism actually exceeds that of many of her protomodernist contemporaries. Not only does she present the order her characters impose as residing in the human need for order; she shows this need to be without any extrahuman validation. Unlike Emerson in "Nature," she affirms no inherent connection between humans and the natural world; in contrast to Emerson's "Self-Reliance," *The Morgesons* envisions no epiphanic moments which may change how one's descendents see the world. On the few occasions when *The Morgesons* seems to invoke a spiritual or transcendental realm, such as the description of the baking of the sacramental wafer, the novel is almost brutal in its repudiation of that realm. Yet *The Morgesons* is as exacting of readers as the more optimistic "Self-Reliance," for in spite of her nihilism, Stoddard emphasizes the necessity of human valor and fortitude. These, she shows, involve the confrontation of life's essential uncertainty, but also the continuing creation of provisional meaning.

Just as unusual is Stoddard's focus on domestic life in representing this outlook. For many of the male thinkers of her day, domesticity was trivial.

In "Self-Reliance," Emerson, regarded as America's chief philosopher, identified domestic pursuits as a distraction from reality, not reality itself. When Thoreau undertook his experiment at Walden Pond so as to slough off the inconsequential life of Concord, the domestic was so negligible that it did not even figure in his decision. Yet even though *The Morgesons* equates "life" with what was culturally designated as the domestic – primarily homes and their surroundings – and concentrates on everyday events, household minutiae, family relations, and "self" as it emerges within these, the novel does not code domesticity as female or cast it as a refuge from the world, or even use the discourse of domesticity in evoking it, as domestic fiction did. The domestic realm is "home," not in the sense of being secure, knowable, morally grounded and sustaining, but simply because it is the world, at least the world that counts. It is actually daily life: the term *quotidian* suggests the particularity, randomness, and gritty commonplaceness of domesticity as *The Morgesons* portrays it. Business, the only other arena *The Morgesons* envisions to any extent, merely offers an escape from the existential demands of the quotidian. Cassandra sardonically applies religious language to the men who participate in business to suggest that business functions as an evasion: they "appear" "as if pursuing something beyond Gain, which should narcotize or stimulate them to forget that man's life was a vain going to and fro" (142). Stoddard points forward to Woolf in her representation of the domestic as the quotidian, and thus the primary medium for advancing the apprehension of the "truth" that that life is irreducibly particular and utterly ordinary, and, as well, exacting, precarious, and inescapable except by death.

Close examination of a Morgeson family meal casts into high relief what is particular, what cultural commonplace, in *The Morgesons'* representation of the quotidian. In its frequent portrayal of family meals the novel shares ground with domestic literature, where such meals were not just a prominent feature but an icon of the ideology of domesticity as a whole. Innumerable works of domestic fiction, including Sarah Josepha Hale's novel *Northwood*, published as that ideology was coalescing in 1828, Sigourney's *Lucy Howard's Journal*, much of Stowe's fiction, as well as cookbooks, magazines, and books on decorum, celebrated family meals flourishing under benevolent maternal direction. Often these meals exemplified not only the harmony and emotional–spiritual–physical sustenance of the domestic sphere, but the very foundation of the nation's values and well-being. In *The Morgesons*, too, family meals are metonymic. At Grandfather Warren's and at the Somers home, they betoken emotionally barren family lives. They also form the bedrock of the life of Cassandra's family, and the comparatively pleasant atmosphere of Morgeson meals indexes the quality of Morgeson family life. One such meal, dinner on the day Cassandra returns home from her year's exile at her grandfather's, is portrayed in particularly positive terms, and it therefore provides a useful basis for comparing *The Morgesons'* representation of domesticity with the celebrations typical of domestic fiction.

The scene is suffused with Cassandra's new appreciation of her family. After she and her mother obey the summons to the dining room, and

> we began our meal, Veronica came in from the kitchen, with a plate of toasted crackers. She set the plate down, and gravely shook hands with me, saying she had concluded to live entirely on toast, but supposed I would eat all sorts of feed, as usual ... [Cassandra examines Veronica closely and sympathetically] ... The plenty around me, the ease and independence, gave me a delightful sense of comfort. The dishes were odd, some of china, some of delf [*sic*], and were continually moved out of their places, for we helped ourselves ... Temperance ... was much too engaged in conversation to fulfill her duties [as a waiter]. I looked round the room; nothing had been added to it, except red damask curtains, which were out of keeping with the old chintz covers. It was a delightful room, however; the blue sea glimmered between the curtains, and, turning my eye toward it, my heart gave the leap which I had looked for ... clapping my hands, [I] said I was glad to come home. (51)

Like many meals in domestic fiction, this one characterizes a family. All the Morgesons (with the exception of Cassandra's father, who is off conducting business) clearly appreciate gathering around the table. People interact; conversation flows. Cassandra herself experiences a sense of "comfort" at the food's bounty and her family's presence. But the Morgesons' dinner has peculiarities which will come into even sharper focus in the discussion below of more conventionally presented family meals in *Uncle Tom's Cabin* and *The Wide, Wide World*. It is not emblematic of "domesticity" writ large, nor is it unambiguously positive. The "ease and independence" of Morgeson dinners reflect the autonomy of each individual, not the coherence of the family unit. Diners straggle in; people help themselves rather than being served and they eat different things; even class distinctions, though not abandoned, are blurred. Whereas mothers are usually in charge of family meals, Mary Morgeson is merely one of many people at the table, and no one is in control. And while harmonious order is often idealized in contemporary depictions of family dinners, what Cassandra relishes is the accommodation of family members' peculiarities, especially Veronica's, and the miscellaneous nature of the dining room, with its mixture of crockery and china and its out-of-place curtains. Moreover, her pleasure in the family supper is in part merely circumstantial. She is finally free from the silent, regimented dinners at Grandfather Warren's, which began with his lengthy and inaudible prayers (the Morgesons appear never to pray at meals) and in which he distributed second helpings wordlessly, by "touching the spoon in the pudding or knife on the pie" (31).

In fact, the pleasure which suffuses this scene is brief and specific to the situation: the Morgeson supper delights Cassandra because its fluidity seems liberating after the constraints of her grandfather's. The meal can also be seen as a mechanical activity which brings the family into brief and pleasant but not terribly meaningful proximity, and this view of it soon takes precedence, as the agreeable fluidity abruptly turns discordant. Veronica comments on her mother's earlier chiding of her for intemperateness, to which Mrs. Morgeson responds, "Verry, you drive me wild. Must I say that I was wrong? Say so to my own child?" (52). Soon the dinner seems merely a partial lull in the stormy flow of daily life, as the narrative resumes its recording of the rapid succession of words, acts, events, and emotions which form the continuous unfolding of the quotidian. In the short paragraph following the exchange between Veronica and her mother, Verry irritably turns her head to the wall, the lamps are lit, Verry's mood improves, a neighbor enters the dining room, and Mrs. Morgeson sends Arthur off to be undressed and put to bed. Then Cassandra's emotions, too, modulate. She becomes pensive when her father makes, after his return home, remarks on the desirability of parent–child "confidentiality," which the Morgesons lack. The chapter concludes with her acknowledgment of the ephemeral nature of even her own thoughtfulness: "in the morning I found that I had not thought of [this] at all" (54).

The radical character of even *The Morgesons'* most positive depictions of the quotidian is even more apparent when this scene is compared to depictions of family meals in conventional domestic fiction. Stowe and Warner, the very popular authors from whose fiction I take my examples, were enthusiastic participants in the discourse of domesticity. Stowe was a major articulator of domestic ideology; Warner contributed to the domestic novel's suffusion of the *Bildungsroman* with that discourse. The breakfast scene at the home of Rachel Halliday in *Uncle Tom's Cabin* and the first meal depicted in *The Wide, Wide World* evince the ways in which these works' didactic purposes inform them both stylistically and thematically.

As Jane Tompkins has shown, the Halliday breakfast functions as a skillfully wrought exemplum (*Sensational Designs*, 141–3; see also Brown, *Domestic Individualism*, 13–34). It models the Christian, cooperative, woman-headed domestic order which Stowe, like her sister Catharine Beecher, proffered as the utopic alternative to what they saw as the (masculine-based) Godless individualism and ruthless desire for economic and material gain which were marring the nation. Every aspect of the breakfast scene contributes to its ideological appeal. Stowe celebrates the family as a unit of cooperative domestic labor. Everyone except the father, who is shaving, unites to prepare the meal under mother Rachel's benevolent supervision; there are no servants. So strong is Stowe's accentuation of the harmony of the food's preparation that she affectionately mocks – and reinforces – her own glorification of cooperation: "There was such an atmosphere of mutual confidence and good fellowship everywhere ... the chicken and ham had a cheerful and joyous fizzle in the pan, as if they rather enjoyed being cooked than otherwise " (169–70). Reflecting the continuousness of the production and consumption of food in Stowe's idealized domestic economy, breakfast is eaten in the kitchen. Under Rachel's officiation, the meal has such a sacred, communion-like character that Tompkins terms it "a redeemed last supper." Stowe emphasizes the "motherliness and full-heartedness in the way [Rachel] passed a plate of cakes or poured a cup of coffee, [which] seemed to put a spirit into the food and drink she offered" (170).

The narrative not only showcases the ideal family meal; it also models Stowe's claim that Christian domesticity will save the nation. The meal so entirely embodies the Christianity which unites the Halliday family in belief, practice, and purpose that it has an immediate redeeming effect. Sitting "on equal terms" at a white man's table for the first time, the escaped slave George Harris perceives that the Hallidays constituted "a home, – *home* – a word that George had never yet known a meaning for" (170; author's italics) and experiences the conversion to Christianity which transforms him from a potential insurrectionist against slavery to what is for Stowe an ideal African-American leader: devout and pacific.

The Wide, Wide World offers a somewhat different contrast to the Morgeson dinner. Unlike Stowe's work, Warner's novel focuses intently on "self": it is centered in one character, Ellen Montgomery. Meals are important to Ellen, and the novel highlights them. Some nurture her spiritually and emotionally as well as physically; some, especially those prepared by her mean-spirited aunt, Miss Fortune, merely provide food.

Like Stowe's novels, *The Wide, Wide World* celebrates certain meals as emblematic of domesticity itself. The novel's first meal, a tea shared by Ellen and her mother, involves the food's preparation as well as its consumption. Mrs. Montgomery watches her young daughter prepare the evening tea some days after her husband has announced his decision to take her abroad for her health, leaving Ellen behind.

[T]he curtains were down, the lamp lit, the little room looked cosey [sic] and comfortable ... Mrs. Montgomery knew that such occasions were numbered ... and she felt each one to be very precious. She now lay on her couch, with her face partially shaded, and ... watched [Ellen], with thoughts and feelings not to be spoken, as the little figure went back and forward between the table and the fire; and the light, shining full upon her busy face, showed that Ellen's whole soul was in her beloved duty. Tears would fall as she looked, and were not wiped away; but when Ellen ... brought with a satisfied face the little tray of tea and toast to her mother, there was no longer any sign of them; Mrs. Montgomery arose with her usual kind smile, to show her gratitude by honoring as far as possible what Ellen had provided. (23–4)

Ellen and her mother then eat and talk; the scene closes with Mrs. Montgomery promising Ellen her own Bible.

Coherence is the operative concept here. The scene is organized around two explicit moral axes, good (Mrs. Montgomery and Ellen and their "cosey" religious–domestic world) and bad (the absent Captain Montgomery, with his devotion to business and his antidomestic rootlessness). Pivoting on unity of action and closely following a clear temporal pattern, it traces Ellen's preparation of tea, then, briefly, the meal's consumption. The details are tendentious. They inscribe the themes of the novel as a whole: the ideal nature of the mother–daughter bond; the central role that bond plays in creating domestic order – itself the core of home and family – because of the mother's absolute and generous love for her daughter and the daughter's lovingness and potential for self-disciplined domestic competence; the spiritual sustenance of Christian faith; the father's power over the family and his indifference to its well-being. Almost every element contributes to these ends – adjectives ("little," "busy," "beloved," "kind"), the play of light and shadow, the detail of Mrs. Montgomery's tears, no longer visible when she goes to the table, Ellen's absorption in her task, the framing declaration that "Mrs. Montgomery knew ... such occasions were numbered ... and ... felt each one to be very precious," the long, repetitive sentences which play to readers' emotions. Visually, stylistically, morally, cognitively, emotionally the scene idealizes the domestic life presided over by mothers and passed on to their daughters and, soliciting readers' identification, appeals to them to idealize domesticity too.

The portrayal of domesticity in *The Wide, Wide World* and *Uncle Tom's Cabin* is founded on the ideology of separate spheres which pervaded white American bourgeois culture: the assumption that life was divided into domestic/female and public/male realms. Stowe's and Warner's affirmations of domesticity's moral and religious superiority and its ethos of human connection rest on domesticity's presumed separation from public life and freedom from contamination by it. Elizabeth Stoddard stands apart from almost all of her published white female contemporaries in not mobilizing this ideology. She did not characterize the domestic as being separate and distinct from the public sphere, and she was relatively indifferent to the claims many of her contemporaries made in the name of the home or woman's sphere. To be sure, in some ways she did reproduce this ideology. *The Morgesons* does not take on material designated as public or "masculine," such as politics or the question of procuring income (though it does dwell on the "improper" subject of the erotic, and Stoddard's subsequent novels feature male protagonists). Indeed, *The Morgesons*, and most of Stoddard's other fiction, concentrates intensely on places, processes, activities, and subjects which were culturally designated as domestic/feminine. But in depicting these as quotidian, not domestic, *The Morgesons* presents what would have conventionally been construed as "domestic" simply as "life": the demanding circumstances within which everyone, male and female, must live. Characters have gender; they are shown to be culturally assigned certain expectations and, too often, to allow themselves to be guided by gendered norms. But "life" is not gendered: it *is*. In a culture in which gender constituted a major explanatory discourse, in which not just "spheres" or people but virtually everything – character traits, habits of mind, appearances, decorum, activities – were routinely categorized as male or female, masculine or feminine, gentlemanly or ladylike, Stoddard's relative indifference to the ethos of separate spheres and to the extensive gender coding which complemented it is remarkable. Even if one considered her apparent presumption that domesticity was not germane to her art an illusion, her ability to write about home and family without invoking domestic ideology and the discourse of separate spheres was connected with her artistry in ways which deserve our close attention.

Moreover, even though, in literal terms, the imaginable world of *The Morgesons* is more closely aligned with home than is the imaginable world of Stowe or Warner, or many other writers of domestic fiction, home is less restricted for Stoddard because it is continuous with the social milieu, not distinct from it. Home and the world are one, to borrow a phrase from Nina Baym, not in keeping with domestic fiction's objective of reforming the world, but because the quotidian is partly constituted by forces which were conventionally regarded as public, or at least public in origin, such as religious desiccation, increasing ethnic chauvinism, increased immigration, class elitism, and the vicissitudes of sea commerce and related industries. In *The Morgesons*, even alcoholism and social hypocrisy, which domestic fiction typically construed as socially engendered problems to which domesticity's values and practices offered solutions, are simply part of life. Ben Somers's alcoholism, for example, is less a detachable subject than one among many matters. As part of a welter of phenomena, it may surface in the context of, say, conversations about literature or the consumption of food: it is rarely a discrete, detachable subject. Moreover, "alcohol" itself is not evil, as it often is in contemporary women's writing. Ben's death results from excessive drinking, not from alcohol *per se*, and alcoholic beverages are also presented as ordinary refreshment; Cassandra herself sometimes drinks them.

Likewise, while *The Morgesons'* concentration on what may seem conventional domesticity actually transforms domesticity, the novel's occasional depictions of what would conventionally have qualified as the "public sphere" disregard the public–private divide by indicating that life "outside" the home is continuous with life "within." Consider the brief scene after Cassandra has shifted from railroad to coach as she returns to Surrey from Belem.

> I was the only lady "aboard," as one of the passengers intelligently remarked when we started. They were desirable companions, for they were gruff to each other and silent to me ... When I took a sip from my flask, two men looked surprised, and spat vehemently out of the windows. I offered it to them. They refused it, saying they had had what was needful at the Depot Station, conducted on the strictest temperance principles.
>
> "Those principles are cruel, provided travelers ever have colic, or an aversion to Depot tea and coffee," I said.
>
> There was silence for the space of fifteen minutes, then one of them turned and said: "You have a good head, marm."
>
> "Too good?"
>
> "Forgetful, may be."
>
> I bowed, not wishing to prolong the conversation.
>
> "Your circulation is too rapid," he continued.
>
> The man on the seat with him now turned round, and examining me, informed me that electricity would be first-rate for me ...
>
> I was forgotten in the discussion which followed. (204)

As an unaccompanied woman traveling with men she does not know, Cassandra is situated in the kind of circumstance many other women writers depicted as alien and hazardous. In *The Morgesons*, though, such circumstances are not substantively more perilous than Somers family life or more unpredictable than a Morgeson family dinner, and Cassandra, though discomfited, handles matters with the same skill she has just deployed at the Somers' home. There Mrs. Somers was given to hostile outbursts; here the men object, unpleasantly enough, but with less drama, to Cassandra's drinking of wine mixed with water. Cassandra controls both situations with resourcefulness and hypercorrect deportment, and in both the friction dissipates. Moreover, "life" on the road resembles life at home in the multitude of issues which may crop up. Among the most obvious subjects that circulate through the stagecoach scene are the class and gender heterogeneity which travel entails; the refreshing properties of alcohol, to which women as well as men have legitimate recourse, and the restrictions which temperance imposes on individuals' choices; phrenology's tenets and possible fraudulence (e.g. in the reference to Cassandra's "good head"); the potential medicinal or disciplinary powers of electricity. Unlike most domestic fiction, *The Morgesons* does not thematize or even accentuate these topics. They appear as part of the normal flow of life. To discern them, readers must use the same kind of inductive skills required for capable reading of scenes depicting the Morgeson or Somers families at the dining table. If Cassandra's stagecoach ride is harrowing, it is harrowing in an unremarkable way – as one in an on-going series of edgy situations. Life is not divided into places of refuge and places of peril. All circumstances are multifaceted and unstable; scrutiny, resilience, and grit are necessary everywhere.

"Self"

Fictional representations of "self" take the form of character. As Nina Baym and others have shown, readers around mid-century not only concentrated on characters and on the plots which charted their fates, but relied on characters' familiarity and comprehensibility so as to make sense of fiction (*Novels, Readers*, 82–107). Thus readers expected characters to conform to common notions of psychology, religion, morality, and, for women characters especially, of gender. (Reviewers, as Baym has shown, routinely assessed characterizations of women in terms of their supposed conformity to real life, definitions of which included prevailing concepts of femininity.) *The Morgesons* confounds both the creation of character and the idea that "self" should be unified which these conventions affirmed. Although most of its characters resemble familiar types, even minor characters depart from or exceed the types they reference. Many characters are fraught with contradiction and act unpredictably; many manifest traits out of sync with their apparent temperament. In thus being discouraged from presuming character as classifiable or fixed, contemporaneous readers were in effect also being deprived of a cornerstone of religious or philosophic certainty, since the self, taken as a relatively coherent entity, functioned as an epistemological, ontological, and spiritual foundation for both Protestantism and Romanticism. Comprehension of "self," like that of "life," is provisional in *The Morgesons*; the novel's unusually fluid characters demand readers' on-going scrutiny and frequent reassessment.

Even minor characters who clearly refer to types familiar in the literature of the period exhibit incongruous traits. The Morgesons' pious neighbor Mr. Park, for example, apparently conforms to the image of the narrow-minded, sanctimonious churchgoer evident in numerous contemporary portrayals of New England. But he is prurient in a way not suggested by other contemporary literature: Veronica reports to Cassandra that he "likes mother" and "watches her so when she holds [i.e., nurses?] Arthur!" (42, 43). Similarly, Gorgon-like Bellevue Pickersgill Somers resembles the kind of controlling matron who appears in short fiction in *Godey's Lady's Book* or in *Pride and Prejudice*. But she, too, is atypically sexual – she has just given birth to her sixth child – and her earmark aggression is inconsistent. When she detects the attraction between Cassandra and Desmond, something unidentified – decorum? failure of will? – prevents her from "being as angry [at Cassandra] as she wished" (194).

Major characters defy more fully readers' tendency to process fictional characters by viewing them through the prism of prevailing types. Mary Morgeson is religious and, in her way, domestic, but far too distant and mysterious to conform to the images of Christian motherhood that circulated widely in Stoddard's America. Just as radically, contemporary readers would have expected established paradigms explaining alcoholism as either a disease or a sin to account for Ben Somers' addiction,[5] but *The Morgesons* is inconclusive about the cause of Ben's problem and it does not clarify why his more dissolute brother Desmond stops drinking, while he does not. Moreover, the characterization of Ben as deeply conventional, fearful, self-righteous, yet also honorable, warm, and bountiful exceeds the codified category of "the alcoholic." Most strikingly, Veronica Morgeson, to whom the novel returns repeatedly, eludes classification almost completely. Veronica is brilliant, creative, masochistic, narcissistic, keenly perceptive, acutely self-protective. Threatened by the fluidity of life and by her own predilection for anger, she makes an aestheticized refuge of her own room. While alluding to the ideology of separate spheres, her chosen confinement does so in a parodic form which suggests the limitations of that ideology. The inapplicability to Veronica of that or any established paradigm is underscored when Cassandra, acknowledging that her sister was "educated by sickness; her mind fed and grew on pain," offsets her own long, complicated, and inconclusive description of Verry with their father's conventional and extraordinarily inadequate pronouncement that "[h]ome ... was [Veronica's] sphere" (59, 60).

Readers' inclination to comprehend character by mobilizing extant explanations is challenged most extensively by the blend of the singular with the familiar which constitutes the characterization of Cassandra. Cassandra partly resembles prominent characters or character-types: the rebellious but gifted childlike Jane Eyre or Gerty of Maria Cummins's 1854 best-selling *The Lamplighter*; the New England individualist; the belle interested mainly in men. But standard American heroines generally had nothing of the "belle" about them, and Cassandra's characterization far exceeds any blend of extant types. "Self" in Cassandra's case is commensurate with "life" as *The Morgesons* construes it: dynamic and changeable, composed of many elements, not all of them fully aligned with one another, somewhat discontinuous but not merely chaotic.

The very structure of Cassandra's story inscribes the concept of self as process. Like *Jane Eyre, The Wide, Wide World, The Lamplighter,* and other female *Bildungsromane, The Morgesons* tracks its heroine from childhood to maturity; so clearly does it resemble *Jane Eyre* in presenting discrete stages of Cassandra's life, situated in distinct places, that many commentators have read it as a narrative of unambiguous character development, or as a reverse *Bildungsroman* charting Cassandra's decline (see Weir, "*The Morgesons*"; Zagarell, "Repossession of a Heritage"; Alaimo, "Stoddard's *The Morgesons*"). (Interestingly, as if to compensate for the novel's many gaps, many commentators, myself included, have used the rhetorical strategy of renarrating Cassandra's life as a progressive story.) Yet *The Morgesons* actually disturbs the conventions of female *Bildungsroman* that it references. Rather than following a straight line, as does *Jane Eyre,* it is recursive, tracing Cassandra's repeated departures from and returns to home.[6]

Another other major factor complicates the task of reading Cassandra: Stoddard's use of a first-person narrator. First-person female redactors of their own lives were not unknown in British novels (Jane Eyre; Lucy Snowe; Esther Summerson), but they were rare in novels by contemporary American women.[7] Cassandra-as-narrator is especially unusual because of her variable dependability. As narrator of her own earlier life, she makes frequent pronouncements about herself. Some are accurate, some miss the mark or are qualified by what she depicts. Moreover, *The Morgesons* also often deploys retrospective verisimilitude without the overlay of narratorial comment. That is, it gives readers seemingly direct access to the earlier Cassandra's perceptions, emotions, thoughts, and/or states of mind as she experienced them and to extended dialogues between her and other characters as they occurred, without exposition and often without narratorial identification of who says what.

The partial presence, partial suppression of Cassandra's voice as narrator, coupled with apparently veracious and unmediated renderings of her interior life, actions, and conversations exert pressure on readers' deductive and interpretive powers which differs from the appeal to readers to identify, sympathize, and/or judge leveled by much of the era's fiction. Readers of *The Morgesons* are called upon to attend continuously to the dense tissue of described gesture and word, of articulated perception, emotion, thought, and impulse, of narratorial reticence, judgment, and misjudgment, and of silence which converge under the name "Cassandra Morgeson." We must come to terms with Cassandra, not as a unitary character who unfolds and develops in keeping with a discernible pattern, but as a multifarious, sometimes contradictory self-in-process. Reading "Cassandra" in this way differs sharply from the effort to classify to which Veronica sardonically alludes in the quotation with which this chapter begins: readers must, rather, continually keep pace with the permutations, continuities, and discontinuities of this self. If such a reading process was seldom solicited by other contemporary fiction, and almost never for women characters, it has become familiar to readers of Joyce, Proust, Woolf, and other modernists.

Any effort to delineate Cassandra as self-in-process thoroughly would entail discussing every nuance of that self as *The Morgesons* inscribes it. Consideration of several discrete junctures in Cassandra's life will serve to suggest the demands made by so complicated a characterization and so changeable a character. The three distinct points in Cassandra's life I have selected – first, Cassandra as a relatively unconscious child, second, as she initially encounters sex and her own sexuality and third, when she resolves to embrace life fully just after her mother has died – indicate the range of techniques used to represent her and the shifting demands her representation makes on readers.

Like many *Bildungsromane*, *The Morgesons* features the protagonist as a young child, but unlike *Jane Eyre* or *The Wide, Wide World*, Stoddard's novel solicits multiple and tentative interpretations of the child. The empathy to which most *Bildungsromane* appealed is tempered by the distance of Cassandra as narrator. The adult Cassandra voices considerable skepticism about herself as child. She often takes her youthful shallowness to task, disapproving of the unchecked pursuit of "amusement" which her family's latitude allowed her and chastising herself for lacking an inner life, as in a reference to "my shapeless mind" and a judgment that "I was moved and governed by my sensations" (14). Retrospective verisimilitude, however, disrupts this judging narrator, complicates judgment as a mode of comprehension, and reveals a more complex child than the adult Cassandra acknowledges – but it does not fully invalidate the assessments she makes as an adult. At numerous points the narrative unfolds either by means of extended dialogues, especially between Cassandra and Veronica, or by representations of the child Cassandra's thoughts, feelings, and activities which are unaccompanied by narratorial comment. The longest dialogue between Cassandra and Veronica, which occurs at the tea party, indicates a sensitive child, though one who is undeniably impulsive and rough-edged (see Buell and Zagarell, *The Morgesons and Other Writings*, xvi–xvii). More interiorized passages, such as the one involving Cassandra's perceptions before and during the tea party that was discussed earlier, reveal a mixture of inclinations and capabilities: curiosity about "life" and intermittent attentiveness to it alongside susceptibility to abrupt shifts in mood and attention, all accompanied by a nearly complete absence of self-awareness.

Passages without narratorial judgment also present a young girl with an unmistakable inner life which she is without the means to comprehend. Overhearing a conversation between her mother and Mr. Park about whether she is yet capable of understanding "the law of transgression," Cassandra initially relishes the realization that she can feign childish innocence and continue to do as she likes. But when Mr. Park begins a hymn about human depravity, she is ambushed by a sense of guilt, which she also experiences as total – she suddenly feels "lonesome" – and then by a sense of sin – "the life within me" seemed "a black cave" (21). The narrator's silence about the causes of Cassandra's emotions, what they signify, or their relationship to each other contributes to the scene's immediacy and intensity. It presses readers not only to make sense of the rapid sequence of feelings and the child's incapacity to understand herself or predict how she will feel, but also to recognize that the adult Cassandra's tendency to underestimate her childhood self is linked to a strikingly unmaternal indifference to children.

The representation of Cassandra's first engagement with sexuality – the period of her extended residence in Charles Morgeson's home in Rosville – relies heavily on retrospective verisimilitude and engages in little *ex post facto* explanation, prodding contemporary readers to suspend the moral norms which informed most literature's treatment of sex as they worked to comprehend the increasing intensity with which Cassandra explores sex and the concomitant changes she undergoes. What readers are thus spurred to understand is not simply a woman's encounter with "sex," but her pursuit of her own desire – something which sets Cassandra apart from the heroines of American domestic fiction. (Even the contemporary British heroines for whom sex entails desire – Jane Eyre, Maggie Tulliver – experience desire within an intensely moral framework.) *The Morgesons'* unorthodox use of the first-person narrator insists on the primacy of Cassandra's experience of sex, side-stepping the prefixed meanings of prevailing moral discourse. Cassandra is shown to feel herself a sexual subject with intensely embodied desire and to have little sense of herself as immoral, and none of victimhood. She articulates a strong bodily experience of Charles's gaze (it projects "a light which filled my veins with a torrent of fire"; 86); she expresses a powerful sense of physical connection to him ("the chain between us"; 115). Unmediated by overt narratorial comment, her acts and statements affirm her acceptance of her own sexual agency: she tells Alice Morgeson that she and Charles "influence" each other, not that he influences her (85); she participates forcefully in the charged dialogues which occur between herself and Charles.

Sustained dialogue – resonant exchanges between Cassandra and her friend Helen, Cassandra and Alice, Cassandra and Ben, and Cassandra and Charles – stresses the aspects of self precipitated by Cassandra's pursuit of the erotic and presses readers to comprehend these aspects as they process the exchanges. One such dialogue occurs between Cassandra and Helen just after Charles has told Cassandra that he loves her and Cassandra, biting her mouth so sharply that it bleeds, orders him "Never [to] say those frightful words again. Never, never" (109). Walking into a room filled with people, she encounters Helen. Helen notices her turmoil and asks what has happened.

> "You shall never know; never – never – never."
> "Cassandra, that man is a devil."
> "I like devils."
> "The same blood rages in both of you."
> "It is mulled wine, – thick and stupid."
> "Nonsense."
> "Will there be tea, at supper?"
> "You shall have some."
> "Ask Ben to order it."
> "Heaven forgive us all, Cassandra!"
> "Remember the tea." (110)

The density of this dialogue focuses readers on what is not said as well as on what is, on who says what, on how statements are phrased, on sequence, on what each speaker intends, and how each may understand what is said. Cassandra adheres to decorum in not telling Helen what has occurred, but she also maneuvers conventions about reticence ("You shall never know") to imply what she will not state. Despite her distress, she also plays with propriety by deliberately shifting planes of discourse both times she refers to the ladylike beverage of tea. She expresses, further, her acceptance of her desire as well as her concern about it: both attitudes inflect her declaration about devils, a term prominent throughout the Rosville section, which connotes the thrill and the danger of Charles's sexual magnetism. Her repetitions of the word "never" and the allusion to mulled wine (which Charles has just spilled on her dress) emerge as forms of self-communication. Although Helen, not knowing the referents, cannot understand them, readers are in a position to recognize that Cassandra is reaffirming to herself her sense of connection to Charles, despite having just commanded him never again to tell her he loves her.

Like many other Rosville dialogues, then, this exchange exhibits the ability which Cassandra's exploration of sexuality gives her to express feelings and attitudes unthinkable for most contemporary heroines. Just as striking, however, is what she does not express and apparently does not understand: what her feelings about Charles actually are. She uses the word "bond" but not the word "love," and is conspicuously unable to conceive of the erotic as something distinct from romantic love, even though it is clear that she does not actually like Charles and has little in common with him aside from their "bond." While such matters were not addressed directly in most contemporary discourse, certainly not in domestic fiction, *The Morgesons* makes the absence felt as a lack. It also plays out the consequences of this lack. Unable and unwilling to think clearly about the liaison, Cassandra is deadlocked, neither leaving Rosville nor consummating the relationship. Although the carriage accident which kills Charles ends her standstill, Cassandra must nevertheless grapple with what she has not understood, for her desire does not cease – she tells Alice that "I hunger now for the kiss [Charles] never gave me" (123). In conversations with each of her parents and between herself and her new consciousness (characterized as a "Specter"), she gradually confronts the integrity of her own sexuality without romanticizing either it or Charles. Readers are invited to link her later sense of connection to Desmond to this very conscious sexual self-acceptance – it is she who initially gazes at Desmond, she who initially "wishe[s] him to please me" (199) – and, later, to recognize that self-acceptance as the source of her ability to identify her "love" for him as a "matter of soul and sense, blood and brain" (226).

The portrayal of Cassandra's transcendental epiphany by the shore shortly after her mother's death places demands of a different sort on readers. The several pages over which this scene plays out are so deeply immersed in the immediacy of Cassandra's experience that they seem designed to prompt readers' identification with her romantic self-encounter and to endorse her sense of self-fulfillment unambiguously. Cassandra's initial alienation from herself, recorded in her distanced self-observation of "the shadow of my face" in the water, is followed by an almost formal portrayal of her self-affirmation. As the eddying sea, which she has always regarded as a mirror of her own vitality, gradually inspires her to a renewed sense of selfhood, she again observes her shadow, then becomes attuned to her emotions, her own "slow, internal oscillation, which increased till I felt in a strange tumult." Putting her "hand in the pool and [troubling] its surface" leads to an intensified sense of her own depths; the agitated waters evoke what she externalizes as a "flying Spirit" which calls "Hail, Cassandra, Hail"; she then embraces natural fluctuation – the rising wind, darkening sky, and swirling sea – in symbolic acceptance of her own spiritual–emotional changeabilty. In an intensely sensuous act, she lets the sea wet her feet, and her own physical and psychic boundaries dissolve: "[The sea] gave tongue as its lips touched my feet, roaring in the caves, falling on the level beaches with a mad, boundless joy" (214). Her reawakened "senses" cry, "Have then at life!... *We* will possess its long silence, rifle its waiting beauty ... its madness – *we* will have all – *all*" (214–15; first two italics mine). The dramatic self-reference as "we" captures the depth of her sense of self-integration.

Powerful though this peak of romantic coherence is, though, it is stunningly ephemeral. Its brevity is registered by the abrupt replacement of interior narrative and soliloquy with distant self-observation and dialogue, and by the terse description of Cassandra's activities when she returns home and acknowledges the disorder which has devastated the Morgeson household since her mother's death. Despite having just determined to "have at life," she instantly takes over the running of the home, overriding her aunt's protest that "you will give *yourself* up" and disowning the turbulent water with which she has identified ("Confound the spray; it is flying against the windows") (215; author's italics). In piecing together what Cassandra undergoes and why, readers are confronted with a character whose submission to necessity gainsays the romantically absolute imperatives of self she has just embraced. Yet they cannot take Cassandra's self-suppression as complete either: it is marked by the persistence of her imagination, emotional intensity, and sexuality.

The Morgesons affirms the continuation of change even beyond the boundaries of the novel's end. Its final section brings the narrative into the present of Cassandra-as-narrator ("these last words I write in the summer time at our house in Surrey ... in my old chamber"; 252). She surveys the mix of circumstances which make up her life in the present moment: Veronica's catatonia and the deformity of Veronica's child, Ben's death, but also her own fulfilling marriage to Desmond. Ending without concluding, *The Morgesons* redirects Cassandra and Desmond, and the novel's readers, to the unceasing exigencies of life and of self. Questioning the viability of spiritual comfort, Desmond's cry of religious despair, "God is the ruler ... Otherwise let this mad world crush us now" (253), points to life and self, with their many adversities and occasional pleasures, as the sole domain available to the novel's characters, and by extension to its readers.

While we may admire the fierce integrity with which *The Morgesons* pursues Stoddard's concepts of truth and of art, of life and of self, the novel is in some respects quite narrow in comparison with much fiction by nineteenth-century American women. Whereas women who participated in the discourse of domesticity helped form the culture of the burgeoning middle classes, Stoddard is plainly elitist, valuing status, wealth, and leisure. In contrast to many women writers who embraced the values of domesticity – and some of her male contemporaries – she exhibits virtually no sense of the commonweal: the individual is her primary interest. And *The Morgesons* is almost narcissistically apolitical. It engages in no coherent social critique. Although it does emphasize the tyranny of some male characters, especially Grandfather Warren, it does not rebuke patriarchy as do *The Wide, Wide World* or *Uncle Tom's Cabin*. Even though it was written in 1861, one would never know that slavery had long been practiced in much of the United States or that the country was on the verge of a civil war.

If historicized textual interpretation makes apparent this mix of attitudes and discourses and *The Morgesons'* originality, it should prompt our caution about how we use the models we have thus far developed for understanding the writing of nineteenth-century American women. Calling attention to the nuances of one text which does not conform to our current expectations about women's writing, historicized textual interpretation can also help us reconsider whether the work of nineteenth-century American women writers as a whole was actually as coherent as the paradigms we have crafted would suggest. Testing the extent to which individual works by Warner, Sigourney, Cummins, and even Hale, one of the major architects of the discourse of domesticity, participated in that discourse, exploring other elements also at play in their writing, historicized textual interpretation can aid us in addressing "nineteenth-century American women's writing" as a question or a set of questions, rather than taking it for granted as cultural terrain about which we already pretty much know what we need to. This will not only challenge us to incorporate the writing of women into our understanding of American literature in more complex ways; it will urge us to take the measure of that literature's variety, contradictions, and continuities more fully.

NOTES

1. Georges Louis Leclerc de Buffon, *Histoire naturelle, générale et particulière*, 40 vols. (1749–1804). My thanks to Joanne Dobson, Philip Gould, Franziska Kirchner, Wendy Kozol, and especially Katherine Bailey Linehan and Paula Richman for their astute readings of drafts of this chapter.

2. Quoted in Buell and Zagarell, *The Morgesons and Other Writings*, 357. The passage is from Johann Wolfgang von Goethe, *The Auto-Biography of Goethe. Truth and Poetry*, trans. and ed. Parke Godwin (New York: Wiley and Putnam, 1846–7), Part III, book XI, 35.

3. In the Introduction to the second edition of *Woman's Fiction*, Baym reflects that she had used the concept of "literary artist" somewhat anachronistically in the first edition (1978) and suggests that the term "genius" is more historically apt. Even so, Stoddard's heavy concentration on the craft of her novels breaks the mold. It should be noted that despite her choice to write idiosyncratic and demanding novels, Stoddard was embittered at their commercial failure (the first two did, however, receive respectful reviews).

4. For the first, see Zagarell, "The Repossession of a Heritage," Harris, *Nineteenth-Century American Women's Novels*, and Alaimo, "Stoddard's *The Morgesons*"; for the second, see Buell and Zagarell, *The Morgesons and Other Writings* especially xviii–xix, Zagarell, "Repossession of a Heritage," and Buell, *New England Literary Culture*; for the third, see Reynolds, *Beneath the American Renaissance*; for the last, see especially Weir, "*The Morgesons*," Alaimo, "Stoddard's *The Morgesons*," and Zagarell, "Repossession of a Heritage." Henwood ("First-Person Storytelling") discusses the novel somewhat differently, in terms of realism and romance.

5. See, for example, Reynolds, *Beneath the American Renaissance*, 65–71, and Nicholas O. Warner, "Temperance, Morality, and Medicine in the Fiction of Harriet Beecher Stowe," in Reynolds and Rosenthal, *The Serpent in the Cup*. Warner explains that the disease and the sin models often fused.

6. The narrative follows her from her family's home in Surrey to Barmouth to Surrey to Rosville to Surrey to Belem back to Surrey; at the end she also refers to a stay in "Europe" and another return to Surrey. *Jane Eyre*, by contrast, inscribes Jane's progress through the successive locations of Gateshead, Lowood, Thornfield, Moor's End, and Feardean.

7. Exceptions include *Lucy Howard's Journal*, some short fiction including Harriet Prescott Spofford's "The Amber Gods," some of Stoddard's own short stories, and stories by Alice Cary.

WORKS CITED

Alaimo, Stacy. "Elizabeth Stoddard's *The Morgesons*: a Feminist Dialogics of Bildung and Descent." *Legacy* 8.1 (1991): 29–38.

Baym, Nina. *Novels, Readers, and Reviewers. Responses to Fiction in Antebellum America*. Ithaca: Cornell University Press, 1984.

Woman's Fiction. A Guide to Novels by and about Women in America, 1820–1870. 2nd edn. Urbana: University of Illinois Press, 1993.

Brown, Gillian. *Domestic Individualism. Imagining Self in Nineteenth-Century America*. Berkeley: University of California Press, 1990.

Buell, Lawrence. *New England Literary Culture From Revolution Through Renaissance*. Cambridge: Cambridge University Press, 1986.

Buell, Lawrence, and Sandra A. Zagarell, eds. *The Morgesons and Other Writings, Published and Unpublished, by Elizabeth Stoddard*. Philadelphia: University of Pennsylvania Press, 1984.

Harris, Susan K. *Nineteenth-Century American Women's Novels: Interpretive Strategies*. Cambridge: Cambridge University Press, 1990.

Henwood, Dawn. "First-Person Storytelling in Elizabeth Stoddard's *Morgesons*." *ESQ: a Journal of the American Renaissance* 41.1 (1995): 41–63.

Reynolds, David S. *Beneath the American Renaissance. The Subversive Imagination in the Age of Emerson and Melville*. Cambridge, MA: Harvard University Press, 1989.

Reynolds, David S., and Debra J. Rosenthal, eds. *The Serpent in the Cup. Temperance in American Literature*. Amherst: University of Massachusetts Press, 1997.

Stoddard, Elizabeth Drew Barstow. *The Morgesons and Other Writing, Collected and Uncollected, by Elizabeth Stoddard.* Ed. Lawrence Buell and Sandra A. Zagarell. Philadelphia: University of Pennsylvania Press, 1984.

Stowe, Harriet Beecher. *Uncle Tom's Cabin.* In *Three Novels.* Ed. Kathryn Kish Sklar. New York: Literary Classics of the United States, 1982.

Tompkins, Jane. *Sensational Designs: the Cultural Work of American Fiction 1790–1860.* New York and Oxford: Oxford University Press, 1985.

Warner, Susan. *The Wide, Wide World.* Ed. with afterword by Jane Tompkins. New York: Feminist Press, 1987.

Weir, Sybil. "*The Morgesons*: a Neglected Feminist *Bildungsroman.*" *New England Quarterly* 49 (1976): 427–39.

Zagarell, Sandra A. "The Repossession of a Heritage: Elizabeth Stoddard's *The Morgesons.*" *Studies in American Fiction* 13 (1985): 45–56.

14

FARAH JASMINE GRIFFIN

Minnie's Sacrifice: Frances Ellen Watkins Harper's narrative of citizenship

Born to free parents in Maryland in 1825, Frances Ellen Watkins Harper was one of the most well-known women of her day. During her life she was a poet, activist, novelist, and orator. After teaching at Union Seminary in Ohio (later named Wilberforce University), Harper was unable to return to home because Maryland prohibited the entrance of free blacks. Instead, in 1853 she went to Philadelphia – the black cultural and political capital of the nineteenth century. There, she lived in an underground railroad station, a home where fugitive slaves were hidden and where she listened to the tales of runaways. These tales, coupled with her exile from the state of her birth, influenced her decision to become an abolitionist. Because of her education and self-presentation, she became a major orator, giving speeches and reading her poems around the country. During this period, she published her first collection of poetry, *Poems on Miscellaneous Subjects* (1854).

Throughout her career, Harper published essays, short stories, and serial novels in black publications such as the *Christian Recorder* and the *Weekly Anglo-African*. From 1865 to 1875 – the period roughly coinciding with Reconstruction (the period following the Civil War) – she traveled extensively throughout the South, lecturing to black and white audiences. She also lived with the freedmen and recorded her observations in a series of letters published in black and abolitionist newspapers. According to Harper scholar, Frances Smith Foster: "Harper had a particular gift for combining social issues, Afro-Protestant theology and literary innovations" (*Written by Herself*). Following Reconstruction, she continued to write and was one of the founders of the burgeoning Black Women's Club movement. Harper died on February 20, 1911.

Two of Harper's novels, *Minnie's Sacrifice* (1869) and *Iola Leroy* (1892), reflect her experiences in the Reconstruction South. *Minnie's Sacrifice* is the story of Minnie and Louis LeCroix, two mulattos who are raised to believe they are white until early adulthood, and who, like Iola Leroy, choose to cast their lots with the newly freed slaves of the South. They dedicate themselves to the moral, economic, and political uplift of the freedmen. The marriage of these two educated, fair-skinned mulattos assures their role as part of a leadership elite who will help to guide the emerging black nation made up of newly freed slaves and an educated, propertied, mixed-race middle class. *Iola Leroy*, Harper's most well-known work, though set in the Reconstruction South, expresses the concerns of the 1890s, a period known as the nadir of African-American history.

The plot of *Iola Leroy* is similar to that of *Minnie's Sacrifice*, but it focuses more on an individual character, the mulatto Iola Leroy. As with Minnie and Louis, Iola believed herself to be white until the death of her white father. Sold into slavery, Iola witnesses at firsthand the horrors of the institution. Following its abolition, she joins a community of educated free blacks, comprising professionals and intellectuals and including her new husband. The novel is longer and wider-ranging than *Minnie's Sacrifice*. Harper uses it as an opportunity to explore issues as diverse as women's suffrage, black civil rights, and temperance. Furthermore, she articulates a theory of black intellectuals which greatly resembles and precedes W. E. B. DuBois's Talented Tenth – the educated elite who would provide leadership for the black masses.

Though very similar, the two novels are products of their times. During Reconstruction (1865–77) African Americans made major advances following the end of slavery. The period saw the establishment of refugee centers, hospitals, and schools for free blacks and poor whites. In 1867 Congress passed the Reconstruction Act and established the Freedman's Bureau to protect black lives and rights. By 1868 over 4,000 schools were founded including Morehouse, Fisk, Hampton, Howard, and Atlanta. The period also witnessed the passage of three major constitutional amendments: the 13th Amendment, outlawing slavery; the 14th Amendment, making the freed persons citizens; and the 15th Amendment, granting black men the right to vote. During the decade following the Civil War, the newly enfranchised blacks helped to elect a black governor of Louisiana, sent sixteen black congressmen to Washington, DC and changed the complexion of state legislatures throughout the South.

The end of Reconstruction is marked by the withdrawal of Federal Troops from the South in 1877. At this time the Democrats returned to power and the Ku Klux Klan, founded in 1866, stepped up its campaign of racial harassment and terrorism. The 1890s witnessed major setbacks for black Americans. In 1895 Frederick Douglass died and Booker T. Washington delivered his accommodationist Atlanta Exposition Address. The Atlanta Exposition gave Washington the opportunity to address southern white leaders about the South's race problem. In 1896 the Supreme Court decision in *Plessy* v. *Ferguson* made Jim Crow – the doctrine of so-called "Separate but

Equal" – the law of the land. Finally, during this period the number of lynchings increased dramatically. Over 90 per cent of these were the result of white mob violence on black men.

While Harper had published poems prior to the Civil War, it was during Reconstruction that she began to publish longer fiction. An early black feminist, Harper focused much of her attention on the women of the South, and they would emerge as the most significant characters in her creative writing as well. Although black women were not granted many of the privileges of citizenship, including the right to vote, Harper saw them as central to the development of a New South. Minnie of *Minnie's Sacrifice*, Iola of the novel *Iola Leroy* and Aunt Chloe of *Sketches of Southern Life* are feminists and express their anger and protest over the fact that black women are not enfranchised at the same time as black men.

Harper's Reconstruction writings differ from those that follow. In her important study of post-Reconstruction writings by black women, *Domestic Allegories of Political Desire: the Black Heroine's Text at the Turn of the Century*, Claudia Tate argues that following the failure of Reconstruction, black women's "novels of 'genteel domestic feminism' ... reflect the viewpoint widely held among turn-of-the-century African Americans that the acquisition of their full citizenship would result as much or more from demonstrating their adoption of the 'genteel standard of Victorian sexual conduct' as from protesting racial injustice" (4). According to Tate, these novels allowed black Americans to define themselves politically during a time when hard-won civil rights gains were under assault (4). This was certainly the context in which *Iola Leroy* was published.

The writings of Reconstruction differ from *Iola Leroy* in several important ways. Among these, the most significant is Harper's articulation of her notion of black citizenship. These works – letters, three volumes of poetry, and the serialized novel, *Minnie's Sacrifice* – suggest that during Reconstruction, Harper moved from the integrationist vision of her abolitionist days and toward an emergent black nationalism.

In the context of the time, black nationalism would have been a radical political stance that differed from much of the abolitionist movement in its consistent challenge of the fundamental tenets of white supremacy as well as calling for the eradication of slavery. Elizabeth J. West writes: "Although its meaning has not remained unchanged, black nationalism in its broadest sense means the collective effort of blacks to secure social, political, and economic group interest" ("Black Nationalism," 76). Martin R. Delaney, Alexander Crummell, and Henry Highland Garnet are widely recognized as the major proponents of black nationalism in the nineteenth century. I have never seen Harper listed among them. In its insistence on black landownership, what

I am referring to as black nationalism preceded the social vision of Booker T. Washington. However, its proponents never advocated a capitulation to white supremacy as did Washington.

Harper's Reconstruction writings all directly engage the issues that consumed the nation during this critical period of American history. These texts offer a direct commentary on urgent political debates. Furthermore, as critics like Hazel Carby, Claudia Tate, Carla Peterson, and Frances Foster have argued about *Iola Leroy*, all of Harper's Reconstruction writings served a pedagogical function. They were written and published as Harper's contribution to the public debate about black citizenship, and they sought to teach, inform, and shape the opinions of her black audiences. They were also written during a time when Harper became aware of the increasing class divisions within the black community that emerged following emancipation. Finally, Harper's Reconstruction writings were also more experimental and more democratic than novels or slave narratives in their content but especially in their form and reach. As objects, books assume a certain kind of audience: a literate one with the leisure time to read. Because Harper's Reconstruction writings included open letters from the road and the text from her speeches, both of which were published in newspapers, she reached a broader audience than she would have had she only published books. In addition, she read her poems aloud at public gatherings and audiences eagerly awaited her recitation of them.

Minnie's Sacrifice was published in installments in the black publication the *Christian Recorder*, a publication of the AME Church. As such, it is meant to be read in quick snatches of time, to be read aloud. Finally, *Minnie's Sacrifice* is of special significance in the African-American literary tradition in that it is one of the very first novels by an African-American to portray black women as victims of lynching as well as rape. Frances Foster's discovery of this novel significantly alters our reading of the early African-American literary tradition.

I want to suggest that Harper's articulation of a more radical notion of black citizenship is more explicit during this period than later, because Reconstruction provided more room for a greater range of discussion and debate about black participation in American social, civic, and economic life. This was certainly not the case during the 1890s – a period that witnessed the systematic dismantling of the minimal progress made during Reconstruction. By radical notion of black citizenship, I mean Harper's insistence that in order for the newly freed blacks to participate fully as citizens of the American democracy, they not only needed the franchise, but also should: (1) be granted access to quality education; (2) benefit from the redistribution of land; and (3) be granted protection from racial violence. In fact, for Harper, these three things were even more important than the franchise, for she believed that without the acquisition of education, land, and protection, the freedmen would be incapable of exercising their right to vote in an informed and responsible manner. Melba Joyce Boyd, Harper's biographer, notes that Harper's vision for the freedmen included a program of "Literacy, Land, and Liberation."

Harper's growing black nationalism is most evident in her advocating of cross-class alliances between blacks and free people of color, rather than a coalition between poor whites and the freed people. She addressed her writings to free blacks and free people of color in an effort to convince them of their shared fate with the former slaves. However, unlike President Johnson, who warned poor whites against aligning themselves with former slaves because the freedmen were their competitors, Harper questioned the viability of such an alliance because she recognized poor whites' investment in whiteness. This investment allowed them to support racist agendas that were not in their best interest.

In a letter dated July 26, 1867, which was later published as "Affairs in South Carolina" in the *National Anti-Slavery Standard* (August 1867), Harper writes:

> Freedom comes to the colored man with new hopes, advantages and opportunities. He stands on the threshold of a new era, with the tides of new dispensation coursing through his veins; but this poor "cracker class," what is there for them? They were the dregs of society before the war, and their status is unchanged. I have seen them in my travels, and I do not remember ever to have noticed a face among a certain class of them that seemed lighted up with any ambition, hope or lofty aspirations. The victims and partisans of slavery, they have stood by and seen their brother outraged and wronged; have consented to the crime and have received the curse into their souls ... I think the former ruling class in the South have proved that they are not fit to be trusted with the welfare of the whites nor the liberty of the blacks. (Harper, *A Brighter Coming Day*, 124)

In this letter, Harper understands the plight of poor whites to be that of a people who have been exploited by an elite class but whose capitulation to that elite contributes to their own oppression. She identifies white supremacy as the ideology which facilitates this capitulation. Over a century later this would become the central argument of Edmund Morgan's classic *American Slavery, American Freedom*. In contrast, Johnson misinformed poor whites that black enfranchisement would lead to an "alliance of blacks and planters" and as such would restore the prewar slavocracy of which, in his view, poor whites were true victims.

By 1865, Johnson's policies and the newly elected representatives drawn from the prewar slave-owning class created an atmosphere that led one visitor to the south to note that "Murder is considered one of (southern whites) inalienable state rights." In Texas alone, while 500 white men were indicted for the murder of blacks between 1865 and 1866, not one was convicted (Foner, *Short History of Reconstruction*, 95). Harper documents state-sanctioned terrorism against the freedmen in her letters. Later, this becomes central to her Reconstruction fiction as well. Such acts of violence are not as explicit in *Iola Leroy*.

In a letter from Eufaula, Alabama dated December 9, 1870 and published in William Still's *The Underground Railroad*, Harper notes: "a number of cases have occurred of murders, for which the punishment has been very lax, or not at all, and it may be will never be." She recounts the murder of a black man who had married a white woman, and the beating of a black woman by a group of white men who forced themselves into her cabin. These acts of violence against the freedmen as well as other acts of political and economic disenfranchisement are central to Harper's creative writing.

Harper published three volumes of Reconstruction poetry, *Moses: a Story of the Nile* (1869), *Poems* (1871), and *Sketches of Southern Life* (1872). The last of these, *Sketches of Southern Life* draws most extensively on her experiences in the South and it begins to map out the terrain of Harper's political vision for the newly emancipated blacks. It is also pioneering in its introduction of the persona Aunt Chloe, who is of the newly emancipated folk but who is not pushed to the margins of the poem's narrative as such characters are in the novel *Iola Leroy*. While the protagonist of *Iola Leroy* is a member of an educated mulatto elite who cast their lot with the poor freedmen, Aunt Chloe is a former slave who speaks in dialect. However unlike the folk characters of the *Iola Leroy*, Aunt Chloe learns to read, is articulate, literate, political, and comes to own property.

Carla Peterson notes that the Aunt Chloe poems are significant in that they "are no longer grounded in sentimental culture." According to Peterson, these poems posit a notion of home that is no longer "the sentimental site" of those victimized by the slave system. Instead, it is a "political locus in which the socially active and empowered work collectively to implement black political Reconstruction" (*"Doers of the Word,"* 212). This theme of the home as a site of activism and empowerment becomes one of Harper's major concerns throughout Reconstruction. Furthermore, Aunt Chloe is one of the first nonelite black characters in black writing. She is juxtaposed against the stereotypes of loyal, loving black "aunts" of southern lore. The Aunt Chloe poems present Harper's vision for the newly freed blacks, especially for the women, in whom she held such faith.

Louis LeCroix, of *Minnie's Sacrifice*, articulates Harper's political opinions and vision. Throughout the narrative, Louis's perspective on the possibilities for black participation in American democracy shifts significantly. At first, upon arrival in the South, Louis notes:

> We are going to open a school, and devote our lives to the up building of the future race. I intend entering into some plan to facilitate the freedmen in obtaining homes of their own. I want to see this newly enfranchised race adding its quota to the civilization of the land ... We demand no social equality, no supremacy of power. All we ask is that the American people will take their Christless, Godless prejudices out of the way, and give us a chance to grow, an opportunity to accept life, not merely as a matter of ease and indulgence, but of struggle, conquest, and achievement.

In asking not for social equality, but for access to literacy, the removal of social and political barriers, and the chance for the freedmen to prove themselves, Louis prefigures Booker T. Washington. Furthermore, his notion of black citizenship is even less radical than that of the early proponents of Reconstruction Radicalism. Eric Foner notes that "Reconstruction Radicalism was first and foremost a civic ideology, grounded in a definition of American citizenship. On the economic issues of the day no distinctive or unified Radical position existed." The Radicals advocated equal opportunity regardless of race (Foner, *Short History of Reconstruction*, 106–7). Like Louis, the Radicals felt that the national government had to guarantee "equal political standing and equal opportunity in a free-labor economy" (108). Neither the Radical Republicans nor the earlier Louis call for federal protection of southern blacks or for the redistribution of land. Note the "us" and "them" sensibility of this passage. There is the "we" of the mulatto class who help the "freedmen." And the "we" of the leadership class and the freedmen who are not included under the rubric of "the American people."

As the narrative develops and as Louis becomes more aware of the constant threats of violence under which southern blacks live, he becomes an advocate not only of black suffrage, but of black self-defense as well. Speaking to the freedmen, he says, "Defend your firesides if they are invaded, live as peaceably as you can, spare no pains to educate your children, be saving and industrious, try to get land under your feet and homes over your heads" (86). In their insistence on black self-defence, Ida B. Wells and Malcolm X echo Louis's words. Wells admonished black readers and audiences to take up arms in self-defense against the terrorism of lynch mobs. Malcolm X criticized the turn-the-other-cheek doctrine of Martin Luther King and encouraged black Americans to defend themselves against racists and bigots. Through Louis, Harper articulates her theme of Literacy, Land, and

Liberation as well as a critique of a federal government that refuses to protect its very own citizens.

Louis also blames the federal government for providing an atmosphere that would allow for the emergence of the Ku Klux Klan in 1866: "If Johnson was clasping hands with rebels and traitors was there no power in Congress to give, at least, security to life? Must they wait till murder was organized into an institution, and life and property were at the mercy of the mob? And, if so, would not such a government be a farce, and such a civilization a failure?" (86). In calling into question the federal government's ability and willingness to protect the freedmen, Louis might be commenting on Johnson's veto of the Civil Rights Bill of 1866. The bill sought to assert "national power to protect blacks' civil rights." It was a radical act which "defined all persons born in the United States (except Indians) as national citizens and spelled out rights they were to enjoy equally without regard to race – making contracts, bringing lawsuits and enjoying the benefit of 'all laws and proceedings for the security of person and property.' No state law or custom could deprive any citizen these rights" (Foner, *Short History of Reconstruction*, 110).

As radical as the bill was, it did not create a federal force to protect the rights of citizens. This was left to the states. The federal courts were expected to enforce the bill. The primary focus of the bill was on eradicating discriminatory state laws and not on protecting the freedmen from violence. Johnson claimed that guaranteeing blacks full citizenship would discriminate against white people. In spite of the flood of reports coming in from the Freedman's Bureau documenting numerous acts of violence against blacks who sought to exercise their rights, Johnson asserted: "the distinction of race and color is by the bill made to operate in favor of the colored against the white race" (Foner, *Short History of Reconstruction*, 112–13). In an effort to counter Johnson's veto, the Republicans introduced the 14th Amendment, which declared all persons born or naturalized in the US national and state citizens with all the rights and privileges thereof.

Louis grows more and more convinced of the need for Radical Reconstruction as he confronts and tries to counter the continuing violence and violation of citizens' rights in the south. Although blacks remained committed to the Republican Party, Harper, through Louis, was critical of the party. "My faith is very strong in political parties," he says. However the narrator notes: "Yet there were times when his words seemed to him almost like bitter mockery. Here was outrage upon outrage committed upon these people, and to tell them to hope and wait for better times but seemed like speaking hollow words" (86). Furthermore, Louis, like Harper, differs from even the most radical Republicans in that he knows that political rights mean little without economic independence for the freedmen. Eventually, Harper joined the freedmen in their plea for redistribution of land. For most freed-men, landownership was an integral part of their definition of freedom. In calling for land for the freedmen, Harper and Louis depart from southern mixed-race landowners.

One consequence of Louis' outspokenness is the danger it brings to him-self and his family. The violence that Harper reports in her letters provides her with material that drives her narrative as well in that she incorporates specific instances of violence into the novel. For instance, in a letter from Darlington, South Carolina dated May 13, 1867, Harper relays the true story of a lynching of a young black woman:

> About two years ago, a girl was hung for making a childish and indiscreet speech. Victory was perched on our banners. Our army had been through, and this poor, ill-fated girl, almost a child in years, about seventeen years of age rejoicing over the event, and said that she was going to marry a Yankee and set up housekeeping. She was reported as having made an incendiary speech and arrested, cruelly scourged, and then brutally hung. Poor child! she had been a faithful servant – her master tried to save her, but the tide of fury swept away his efforts. (Harper, *A Brighter Coming Day*, 123)

Harper's letter refers to the murder of a young black woman, Amy Spain, who was lynched in Darlington in 1865. She is reported to have shouted "Bless the Lord the Yankees have come." The story of her lynching appeared in *Harper's Weekly*, September, 30, 1865 (E. Forbes 47). This episode also finds its way on to the pages of *Minnie's Sacrifice*. A recently freed slave woman tells Louis:

> Well, you see it was jist dis way. My darter Amy was a mighty nice chile, and Massa could truss her wid any ting. So when de Linkum Sogers had gone through dis place, Massa got her to move some of his tings over to another place. Now when Amy seed de sojers had cum'd through she was might glad, and she said in a kine of childish way, 'I'se so glad, I'm gwine to marry a Linkum soger, and set up house-keeping for myself.' I don't spect she wer in arnest 'bout marrying de sojer, but she did want her freedom. Well, no body couldn't blame her for dat, for freedom's a mighty good thing ... Well, when she said dat, dat miserable old Heston — Well, he had my poor girl tookened up, and poor chile, she was beat shameful, and den dey had her up before der sogers and had her tried for saying 'cendiary words, and den dey had my poor girl hung'd. (87–88)

Harper's audiences would have been used to stories of black women's experiences of sexual harassment and abuse. Writers such as Douglass and Harriet Jacobs had provided scintillating suggestions of the sexual exploita-tion of white women. However, these audiences probably were not as used to the black women being the object of lynching and other forms of murder. *Minnie's Sacrifice* adds black female martyrs to the pantheon of murdered black men that fill black political and literary history. Furthermore, the story of the young girl's death is recounted at the funeral of the novel's heroine, Minnie. That the story of the lynched girl is narrated at the funeral of the more privileged lady links the two women and suggests that despite differences of class and color, their fates are inextricably bound. Unfortunately, the installment that narrates the circumstances of Minnie's death has not been found; however, earlier chapters suggest that her death might have resulted from the political work in which she and her husband are engaged.

Finally, while Harper relays the historical account of this story in her own voice and language in her letter, in the novel she allows the young woman's mother to tell the story in dialect. Harper gives voice to the less educated freedwoman and in so doing allows her to draw the link between her own child and the fair, lovely, educated Minnie. The mother and her daughter come from the class of blacks most vulnerable to white southern violence, and Harper reminds her reader of this by focusing on the violence done to the child and not that done to Minnie or one of her class. As such, she seems to be saying to her reader, "you must have sympathy for all victims of such violence, not simply those with whom you identify."

The concluding installment of the series is Harper's direct address to her readers about the pedagogical and political intent of the story. It reads like the traditional "Dear Reader" of abolitionist literature, except the intended reader is not from a northern middle-class white audience, but from a northern middle-class black one. "May I not modestly ask that the lesson of Minnie shall have its place among the educational ideas for the advancement of our race?" (90). Harper's plea is to the newly educated black elite: "It is braver to suffer with one's own branch of the human race ... for the sake of helping them, than to attempt to creep out of all identity with them in their feebleness, for the sake of mere personal advantages" (91).

Some might argue that this plea is a classic example of the doctrines of racial uplift – doctrines that recent scholars identify as elitist. Racial uplift was the name given to the belief that the black elite could "uplift" the masses of poor black people by being moral exemplars and acting as spokespersons for and representatives of "the race." I read Harper's plea as a call to those who might have greater access to opportunity because of the brief but significant gains of Reconstruction. Harper warns them not to abandon those blacks who are incapable of taking advantage of such opportunities because of continued violence and other forms of opposition from the southern states. By aligning Minnie's death with that of Amy, Harper is also telling her readers that their fates are aligned with those of the most oppressed freedmen. In fact their position was indeed quite tenuous. The black upper class was quite small and their economic security was always in jeopardy. In spite of this, Carla Peterson notes, "The post-bellum period witnessed the slow emergence of a new class structure and sensibility that separated the mass of common laborers from a growing black professional and business class. This class was not always able to comprehend the labor issues facing black workers and felt at times that the political and social interests of the two groups no longer necessarily coincided" (*"Doers of the Word,"* 198). Harper's plea was not only to this growing black professional and business class of the South, but also to black northerners whom she feared would lessen their vigilance once the cause of abolition was won.

In closing, the final call of the novella is a call for action as well as a warning to her readers not to be fooled by the appearance of progress. The novella serves as a warning about the very tenuous nature of black citizenship and the necessity of remaining vigilant against the forces that would seek to deny it. Finally, it also illustrates Harper's belief in the power of fiction to engage political issues and to shape public opinion. By ending her narrative with the death of the major character and not with a scene of familial bliss or racial progress, Harper asserts that in the midst of great progress and social change the status of black people remains precarious. By the time Harper again turned to fictionalize her Reconstruction experiences in 1892, those hard-won elements of black citizenship were already being dismantled. A consideration of her Reconstruction writings sheds new light on her better-known later efforts and suggests the way that the political climate influences the form and content of creative efforts.

WORKS CITED

Berlant, Lauren. "The Queen of America Goes to Washington City: Harriet Jacobs, Frances Harper, Anita Hill." *American Literature* 65.3 (September 1993): 549–74.

Boyd, Melba Joyce. *Discarded Legacy: Politics and Poetics in the Life of Frances E. W. Harper.* Detroit: Wayne State University Press, 1994.

Carby, Hazel. *Reconstructing Womanhood: the Emergence of the Black Woman Novelist.* New York and Oxford: Oxford University Press, 1987.

Foner, Eric. *A Short History of Reconstruction.* New York: Harper and Row, 1990.

Forbes, Ella. *African-American Women during the Civil War.* New York: Garland, 1998.

Foster, Frances Smith. *Written by Herself: Literary Production by African American Women, 1746–1892.* Bloomington: Indiana University Press, 1993.

Foster, Frances Smith, ed. *A Brighter Coming Day: a Frances Ellen Watkins Harper Reader.* New York: Feminist Press, 1990.

Griffin, Farah Jasmine. "Frances Harper in the Reconstruction South." *SAGE: a Scholarly Journal on Black Women* (1988): 45–47.

Harper, Frances Ellen Watkins. *Minnie's Sacrifice, Sowing and Reaping, Trial and Triumph*. Ed. Frances Foster. Boston: Beacon Press, 1994.

Peterson, Carla. *"Doers of the Word": African-American Speakers and Writers in the North (1830–1880)*. New York and Oxford: Oxford University Press, 1995.

Tate, Claudia. *Domestic Allegories of Political Desire: the Black Heroine's Text at the Turn of the Century*. New York and Oxford: Oxford University Press, 1993.

West, Elizabeth J. "Black Nationalism." *Oxford Companion to African American Literature*. New York and Oxford: Oxford University Press, 1996.

MARY KELLEY

Conclusion

Anyone who is not familiar with the scholarship of the decades following World War Two will find it difficult to imagine that there once was a time when the categories "woman" and "women" were entirely absent from the literature. Until literary critics and cultural historians challenged the canonical and theoretical premises of Cold War America, the only writing that mattered trafficked in the male quest for authenticity. Women and their writing were either ignored or, if acknowledged at all, consigned to the "other." Of course, that "other" was the "feminine," which literary critic Fred Lewis Pattee damned as "fatuous, fevered, furious, fertile, feeling, florid, furbelowed, fighting, and funny." Pattee's dismissal in his landmark *The Feminine Fifties* did more than display a predilection for alliteration. In the decades following its publication in 1940, many a scholar took pleasure in delivering similar judgments, albeit without the alliteration. Nina Baym made short work of Pattee and company, exposing their biases in the now classic "Melodramas of Beset Manhood," which she published in 1981. In showing "How Theories of American Fiction Exclude Women Authors," Baym participated in a critical project already years in the making. Since the publication of Baym's essay, interrogation by Judith Fetterley's "resisting readers" has proceeded apace. Scholars now bring to women's writing a host of critical premises and languages that locate "woman" and "women" where "man" and "men" have always been – at the center of historical and literary discourse. Contributors to the *Cambridge Companion to Nineteenth-Century American Women's Writing* build upon these premises and languages. And they do more, not only continuing the process of recovery and revision but also intervening with insights that startle, provoke, tantalize, and illuminate. Perhaps most strikingly, they interrogate the process in which we are currently engaged, asking us to enlarge upon and to complicate still further our more recent readings of women writers.

Some contributors explode traditional generic classifications and literary periodizations that still attend the study of nineteenth-century American literature. In her chapter on Elizabeth Stoddard, Sandra Zagarell asks us to move beyond the labels with which we have marked women writers, regardless of their self-identification. Instead of classifying Stoddard's novels as "domestic," as "gothic," or as partaking in "*Bildungsroman,*" Zagarell uses the yardstick by which Stoddard measured herself – as an "artist" who distinguished herself from contemporaries engaged in "cultural work" designed to achieve a moral and spiritual transformation of America. We see Stoddard anew in Zagarell's reading of *The Morgesons*. There is the fluidity, the randomness, the emphasis on the quotidian that anticipates modernism. There is the refusal to deploy an ideology of domesticity that celebrated a hermetically sealed and morally superior home. There is the many dimensional self-in-process embodied in the character of Cassandra Morgeson. In all this, Stoddard engaged in a "strenuous artistry" that confounds expectations about a woman writing in nineteenth-century America. Like other writers who are the subjects of this volume's "Case Studies," Stoddard cannot be comprehended by older models that relegate women to the "other." But neither can she be subsumed by the more recent paradigms we have invented. Instead, and perhaps the most tellingly, writers such as Stoddard lead us, in Zagarell's words, to reflect on the "models we have crafted and, more generally, on how we use models altogether."

In an illuminating chapter on Rebecca Harding Davis and Elizabeth Stuart Phelps, Lisa Long exposes the limits of other classifications and periodizations that have distorted the meanings and strategies pursued by women writers. Challenging the placement of Davis and Phelps at either the concluding moments of sentimentalism or the early stages of realism, Long interrogates their fiction on its own terms. Like Zagarell's Elizabeth Stoddard, the Phelps and the Davis of Long's chapter resist scripts that literary critics and cultural historians have written for them. The embodiment of Marjorie Pryse's "category crises," they invite the complications that Long's reading provides. They remind us, as she concludes, to value writing "for what it is, rather than always framing it in terms of what it isn't quite."

Lisa Long also "reimagines reform" in the fiction of Davis and Phelps as designed not only to generate the moral identification with society's victims that we have long associated with reform literature, but also to prompt meditations on deeply alienated characters who are unable to act on behalf of the oppressed. The subject of Farah Jasmine Griffin's chapter, Frances Ellen Watkins Harper, makes more radical the meaning we have attached to reform itself. In the decade of Reconstruction that followed the Civil War, Harper engaged in the most radical of reforms – the mapping of a fundamental transformation in the meaning of black citizenship. In letters published in newspapers, in three volumes of poetry, and in *Minnie's Sacrifice*, a novel serialized in the AME Church's *Christian Recorder*, Harper called not only for enfranchisement but also for "Literacy, Land, and Liberation," as her biographer Melba Joyce Boyd characterized Harper's expansive definition of citizenship, a definition that included protection from racially motivated violence. Griffin recovers an equally fundamental transformation in the strategy that Harper advocated as she turned away from integration and came to support in its stead a separatist black nationalism. Like the historical moment in which she articulated these reforms, the Harper of *Minnie's Sacrifice* is more radical than at any other time in her long career. The hopes with which Harper filled the pages of *Minnie's Sacrifice* met a violent death in the racial harassment, terror, and lynching of the post-Reconstruction years. Much less explicit in its claims for African Americans, *Iola Leroy*, the novel which she published in 1892, acknowledges the passing of a historical moment in which Harper's call for black empowerment might have been implemented.

Susan Griffin's chapter takes a different but equally radical turn in defining reform. Readers in the twenty-first century may look upon nineteenth-century America's demonizing of Roman Catholics as a deformation. However, no small number of militant Protestants who insisted they were building God's kingdom staked a claim for themselves as their century's quintessential reformers. Griffin's strikingly original reading of Protestant polemics introduces us to the multiple uses anti-Catholicism served for these "defenders," including the lambasting of liberal and evangelical Protestants deemed insufficiently militant in doing battle with Rome.

The contributors who revisit canonical genres remind us that we are long past the nearly exclusive focus on fiction. In the last two decades, literary critics have recovered women poets and, as Elizabeth Petrino notes, have claimed for them the linguistic complexity and stylistic eloquence long accorded to their male counterparts. Petrino's chapter revises two long-standing commonplaces in criticism, whatever the genre. Sentimentalism, once thought to be a female's sole literary strategy, is shown to be only one of many stylistic approaches taken by women writers who engaged imagism, traditionalism, modernism, and symbolism. A gender divide, which had been based on the presumption that males did not deal in sentimentalism, is also dismantled by Petrino. We can now include with Alice Cary, Frances Osgood, and Lydia Sigourney, all of whom shared in the language of sentimentalism, male poets such as Philip Freneau.

In addition to revisiting canonical genres, contributors bring to the fore a host of long-neglected genres, including the African-American spiritual narratives that are the subject of Yolanda Pierce's chapter. In her reading of conversion's liberating potential for enslaved African Americans, Pierce shows that the experience of conversion made possible the ultimate refusal of the master's designation of a slave as chattel. No longer the slaveholder's cursed son of Ham, African Americans could embrace the identity of a chosen people, beginning a journey toward literacy and language, freedom and salvation. Conversion narratives, which in the words of William Andrews "tell a free story," were also gender inflected, as Pierce demonstrates. Locating sanctification at the center of many of their narratives, women invoked the requirement that the converted walk in the way of the Lord to liberate them from strictures against public speaking. Women such as evangelist Zilpha Elaw, whom Pierce takes as her primary example, were then free to "tell a free story" that exhorted against sexism as well as racism.

And, as Stephanie Smith's path-breaking chapter shows, we have begun to look at texts that speak in forms other than the word. In concert with Smith, we read the "clothes-talk" that called into question gendered attributes supposedly ordained by God and nature. Donning trousers, as Amelia Jenks Bloomer did in 1851, declared the feminine and the masculine to be social constructions subject to the same radical revision that was signified by the wearing of "Bloomers." In performing an alternative construction of gender relations, "panting" in public spoke to the claim that women have the same freedoms as men, including the freedom to participate in social and cultural domains that had been reserved for men.

In this Companion we see scholars remaking the language of gender in chapters that focus upon the continually shifting meanings of feminine and masculine. In the dazzling "Women at War," Shirley Samuels considers the connection between the emotional violence of domestic fiction and the physical violence of Civil War battlefields. Carroll Smith-Rosenberg's now classic "The Female World of Love and Ritual," which claimed deeply loving and loyal bonds between women, vanishes before portrayals of resentful mothers who commit stunning acts of betrayal against their daughters. Conversely, armed conflict and devastating loss of life erode strictly enforced sexual demarcations, leaving heroines free to come together in passionately loving relations. In Samuels's revisionary reading, we see the direction in which literary critics are moving. However, as is indicated in a couple of the chapters in the Companion, traces still remain of Barbara Welter's "Cult of True Womanhood." The persistence of "True Womanhood," which, as literary critic June Howard has noted, "continues to be cited long after more dynamic accounts have prevailed among historians," is puzzling ("What is Sentimentality?," 73). In the three decades since Welter's influential paradigm appeared, we have learned that domestic ideology's impact, which was once presumed to have been uniform and transparent, was instead as diverse and complicated as the lives of those for whom it had been designed – antebellum women, white and black. Although Welter's article provided the impetus for these interpretations, little if any "piety, purity, submissiveness, and domesticity" is still intact today. It now appears that the ideology did not have the constraining impact on the behavior of white women that scholars initially presumed. Instead of limiting impulses of self-determination, white women revised its tenets to serve expansive purposes. Its impact on black women was more complicated. Either enslaved or subjected to discrimination, they encountered a set of prescriptions that whites exploited for racist ends. Nonetheless, writers, including Nancy Prince, Harriet Wilson, and Harriet Jacobs, managed to rerepresent "True Womanhood" and to use its tenets to forward their projects of emancipation.

In remaking the language of gender, contributors also engage the debates about key terms that have defined nineteenth-century women's writing as "other." No term has been more contested than the cluster of words that are used to mark all matters sentimental – as Gail Smith suggests in her study of Harriet Beecher Stowe. And no term has been used more frequently in literary criticism devoted to nineteenth-century women's writing. Indeed, as Joanne Dobson has remarked, the term itself "is perhaps the most overworked, imprecise, misapplied, emotionally loaded, inadequately understood term in American literary classification" ("Reclaiming Sentimental Literature," 169). In a recent essay devoted to exploring the question "What is Sentimentality?," June Howard observed that scholars, instead of taking the category as an object of study, have tended either to celebrate or to condemn, to insist upon either subversion of or complicity with dominant ideology, to be, in short, either for or against the sentimental, whatever the context in which it is articulated. Contributions in this volume show that we have begun to move beyond debating the merits of eighteenth-century sympathy and sensibility and its nineteenth-century formulation, sentiment and sentimentality. With the deliberate rationality that bespeaks a debt to the Enlightenment project, contributors are shifting critical consideration to the cultural life of the emotions, elaborating on the many uses made of and meanings attributed to the suprarational in eighteenth- and nineteenth-century America.

In attending to the context in which Americans made their meanings of the suprarational, cultural historian Fredrika J. Teute exemplifies the most recent scholarship. Using as her point of departure the claim of Elizabeth Barnes and Julia Sterne that sentiment served as one of the early republic's foundational discourses, Teute highlights the intersection between the conserving social cohesion and the liberating individual potential manifest in this discourse. Nowhere were the resulting ideological tensions more apparent than in Margaret Bayard Smith, the subject of Teute's chapter. Teute places in sharp relief the contradictory impact of a sensibility that propelled Bayard Smith's resistance to the constraints of domesticity, while encouraging her to practice wifely deference. That same sensibility led her to identify with African Americans' claims to freedom, while allowing her to treat them with condescension. Oscillating between the countervalences of individual desire and collective obligation, Bayard Smith illustrated the tensions that contributors made the subject of *The Culture of Sentiment*, the landmark collection edited by Shirley Samuels. In chapters that ranged across the nineteenth century, contributors to Samuels's collection looked at sentimentality as a cultural practice, which if generally designed to generate empathy, was nonetheless a far more complicated phenomenon than we had previously thought.

The same process of recovery and revision that has transformed the reading of women's writing has taken place in the historical and literary scholarship on the writers themselves. Alternately conceived either as a "republican wife" or as a "republican mother," post-Revolutionary women all too frequently were represented as disembodied entities hovering above the past. Writers already vulnerable to these stock portrayals also suffered at the hands of cultural historians and literary critics who trafficked in ideologically freighted stereotypes, as Dana Nelson's impressive survey shows. In *All The Happy Endings: a Study of the Domestic Novel in America*, Helen Waite Papashvily delighted in the paper tigers she found lurking in the pages of this fiction. The authors were deeply angry women who "waged their own devious, subtle, undeclared war against men – their manual of arms, their handbook of strategy was the sentimental domestic novel" (24). Ann Douglas took an opposite tack in *The Feminization of American Culture*. The perpetrators of literary sentimentality had filled their novels with "the timid exploits of innumerable pale and pious heroines," characters who were more akin to paper dolls than paper tigers (3). So far as Douglas was concerned, the impact of these authors on American culture was as disabling as the fiction was banal. In "feminizing" the intellectually rigorous, the imaginatively precise, and, above all, the tough-minded Calvinism that Douglas found compelling, these women had betrayed their heritage. The judgment she delivered was severe: in Calvinism's stead, the authors had crafted a culture that "seemed bent on establishing a perpetual Mother's Day" (6).

Instead of cardboard figures, readers of this Companion will discover writing women deeply engaged in the literary culture of a newly independent America. The subjects of Rosemarie Zagarri's chapter, these were the women who were educated in the early republic's female academies and seminaries, who apprenticed in the newly available history, biography, travel literature, and fiction, who took to print, and who, as Zagarri declares, "could change the world with their words." As indeed they did. The successors to the members of British America's elite who had established institutions of sociability in towns and cities throughout the colonies, these women were deeply involved in the post-Revolutionary world of salons, literary clubs, tea tables, and assemblies. Designed as discursive institutions, these were sites at which elite women engaged in polite conversation, in the performance of *belles-lettres*, and, most notably, in the making of public opinion. Simultaneously, these women claimed for themselves a place in the world of print. Publishing in the rapidly expanding number of newspapers and periodicals, they traversed the boundaries between reading and writing and moved into print as the authors of essays, historical sketches, poetry, and short fiction. Later generations built upon the precedents established by these women, as can be readily seen in virtually all of the chapters in this volume.

Complicating the representation of nineteenth-century women writers did not necessarily mean that literary critics and cultural historians negotiated a second and equally important transition – constructing a truly multidimensional profile of these writers. Instead, a profile that still obtains in some literary and historical discourse continued to hold sway until little more than a decade ago. Supposedly, the woman who wrote was white, she was elite, she was a New Englander. With some frequency, she was, as is readily apparent in the presence of Catharine Maria Sedgwick, Harriet Beecher Stowe, and Sarah Orne Jewett, all of whom sustained long and successful careers. But the woman who wrote also came from a much more diverse population. She was one of the "immigrants" whose narratives are the subject of Priscilla Wald's chapter. Negotiating cultural differences, taking on particular gender roles, she mirrored the ambivalence of peoples marginalized by race, ethnicity, and class as they struggled to become "American." She might be one of the "immigrants" we would most likely anticipate – the Irish Catholic Mary Anne Sadlier, who cautioned her readers about the threat posed by assimilation, or the Russian Jewish Anzia Yezierska, who spoke for daughters caught between cultures old and new. But in Wald's expansive definition of "immigrant," she might be the African-American Harriet Jacobs, the Jewish American Emma Lazarus, or the Native American Zitkala-Sa. In perhaps her most striking contribution, Wald reminds us that definitions of an "immigrant" and her "narrative" are based less on the writer's origin than on her experience – of ethnic and racial marginalization, of assimilation as its forces pressed upon her, and of survival of a self that was constantly evolving, as in the captivity narratives that Kathryn Zabelle Derounian-Stodola discusses. However they designed their narratives, these "immigrants" were their own heroines if only because they spoke to the silences of those who were not able to tell their own stories. Wald concludes her chapter with one such heroine – the silenced Typhoid Mary, who provides a telling reminder of the demonization accomplished by anti-Catholic crusaders.

In the last two decades, literary critics and cultural historians have redrawn the map of nineteenth-century American literature. Before then, scholars and their students read only Emily Dickinson – herself a relatively recent rediscovery. Judith Fetterley, a signal force in this project of recovery and revision, had begun research on nineteenth-century women writers as early as 1980. But, as she recognized, before critical conversation about women's writing could take place, the texts themselves had to be made available for readers. In 1985, Fetterley published *Provisions: a Reader from Nineteenth-Century American Women*. The next year, Rutgers University Press under the editorial leadership of Leslie Mitchner began the American Women Writers Series. Edited by Fetterley, Joanne Dobson, and Elaine Showalter, the series reissued Lydia Maria Child's *Hobomok* in 1986. Child's novel was followed by seventeen more volumes in the next six years, each of which appeared with a critical introduction and selected bibliography. Catharine Maria Sedgwick, Alice Cary, Maria Cummins, Rose Terry Cooke, Fanny Fern, E. D. E. N. Southworth along with others entered the world of print after an absence of nearly a century. Simultaneously, Martha Ackmann, Karen Dandurand, and Dobson, all of whom were then pursuing Ph.D.s at the University of Massachusetts at Amherst, founded *Legacy: a Journal of American Women Writers*, the ground-breaking journal that began the recovery of the writers themselves. The recovery and revision initiated in these projects will now be sustained by the recently established Society for the Study of American Women Writers. *The Cambridge Companion to Nineteenth-Century American Women's Writing* bears the mark of all these enterprises. Most obviously, contributors build upon the scholarship of the last twenty years. They also mirror the mutual commitment and intellectual generosity that distinguished these earlier projects. And perhaps most important, they bring readers who have been working in relative isolation into rich and diverse collaborations.

WORKS CITED

Dobson, Joanne. "Reclaiming Sentimental Literature." *American Literature* 69.2 (June 1997): 263–88.

Douglas, Ann. *The Feminization of American Culture*. New York: Knopf, 1977.

Howard, June. "What Is Sentimentality?" *American Literary History* 11.1 (spring 1999): 63–81.

Papashvily, Helen Waite. *All the Happy Endings: A Study of the Domestic Novel in America, the Women Who Wrote It, the Women Who Read It, in the Nineteenth Century*. New York: Harper, 1956.

INDEX

Index

Index

Davis, Rebecca Harding, 8, 12, 240, 262–81, 321; "Life in the Iron Mills", 8, 263, 265, 269, 275; "Women in Literature", 263, 273; *Dallas Galbraith*, 264; *Margret Howth*, 269; *Bits of Gossip*, 271, 273, 278, 279–80; *Put out of the Way*, 272; "The Curse of Education", 272; *Kent Hampden*, 276; *Silhouettes of American Life*, 277; "Anne", 278

Davis, Varina Jefferson, 187
De Burton, Maria Amparo Ruiz, 187
De Forest, John William, 280–81
Dearborn, Mary, 166
Decker, Karl, 193
Declaration of Independence, 230
"The Declaration of the Rights of Women", 76
Dehgewanus (Mary Jemison), 106–10, 119; *A Narrative of the Life of Mrs. Mary Jemison*, 106–11, 119
Delaney, Lucy, 106, 116–20
Delany, Martin, 310
Derounian-Stodola, Kathryn Zabelle, 131, 324
Dhu, Helen (Charles Edwards Lester), 167–68
Dickinson, Emily, 3, 11, 43, 122, 124–25, 135, 137–39, 157, 327
Dietrich, Marlene, 92
Dobson, Joanne, 9, 126–27, 131, 324, 327
Doddridge, Philip, 245
domestic fiction, 145, 264, 286–87, 303
domesticity/domestic ideology, 2, 5, 7, 38–62, 149, 155, 156, 159, 161, 168, 169, 172, 210, 213, 221, 225, 259, 284, 287, 289–96
Donovan, Josephine, 50
Dougherty, Norma Jeane (Marilyn Monroe), 72, 93
Douglas, Ann, 1, 4, 49–52, 157, 161, 264, 325
Douglass, Frederick, 85, 154, 248, 309, 316
Dreiser, Theodore, 96
dress reform, 73, 75, 76, 79, 81, 87–89, 94–95
DuBois, Ellen, 40, 46
DuCille, Ann, 5, 55
Dunlap, William, 204
Dustan, Hannah, 108

Eaton, Edith Maud (Sui Sin Far), 193; "Leaves from the Mental Portfolio of an Eurasian", 193–96

Eddy, Mary Baker, 157
education, 10, 20, 22, 24, 124, 127, 162, 163–64, 179
Edwards, Jonathan, 245
Eichhorn, J. G., 223
Elaw, Joseph, 258
Elaw, Zilpha, 12, 249–60, 323
Eliot, T. S., 139, 278
Elizabeth, Charlotte (Elizabeth Tonna), 170
Ellet, Elizabeth, 7–8
Ellul, Jacques, 107
emancipation, 89, 95
Emerson, Ralph Waldo, 127, 223, 286, 289
Enlightenment, 21, 62, 178–79, 184
environmentalism, 127
Everett, Edward, 223
Ewing, Elizabeth, 89, 93

Faulkner, William, 278
Faust, Drew, 155
Federalists/Federalist Party, 27–28
Female Sanitary Commissions, 148
feminism, 45, 47, 50, 56, 72–73, 84, 86, 90, 92, 96, 98, 99, 105, 111, 157, 172, 197, 221, 310
Fern, Fanny (Sarah Willis Payson Parton), 9, 84, 240, 268, 327
Fetterley, Judith, 1, 50, 320, 327
Fiedler, Leslie, 44
Fields, Annie Adams, 124, 137, 263
Finch, Annie, 128
First World War, 72, 92
Fischer, Gayle V., 70, 73, 93, 97, 98
Fitzgerald, F. Scott, 91
Fliegelman, Jay, 9, 58, 207
Flugel, J. C., 86
Forten, Charlotte L. (Grimké), 69, 83
Foster, Frances Smith, 308, 311
Foucault, Michel, 55
Fox-Genovese, Elizabeth, 47
Franchot, Jenny, 158, 160, 169, 172
Frank, Waldo, 176, 198
Franklin, Wayne, 75
Fraser, Nancy, 7, 58
Freedman's Bureau, 315
Freeman, Mary Wilkins, 240
Freibert, Lucy, 1
Freneau, Philip, 11, 127–30
Freud, Sigmund, 79
Friedan, Betty, 38–39, 84
frontier romance, 53
Fugitive Slave Law, 116
Fuller, Margaret, 6, 8, 130–31

Index